Regions in Transition

The Northern Great Plains and the Pacific Northwest in the Great Depression

Rolland Dewing

UNIVERSITY PRESS OF AMERICA,® INC.
Lanham • Boulder • New York • Toronto • Oxford

University Press of America,® Inc.
4501 Forbes Boulevard
Suite 200
Lanham, Maryland 20706
UPA Acquisitions Department (301) 459-3366

PO Box 317
Oxford
OX2 9RU, UK

Printed in the United States of America
British Library Cataloging in Publication Information Available

Library of Congress Control Number: 2006929379
ISBN-13: 978-0-7618-3544-8 (paperback : alk. paper)
ISBN-10: 0-7618-3544-X (paperback : alk. paper)

The paper used in this publication meets the minimum requirements of American National Standard for Information Sciences—Permanence of Paper for Printed Library Materials,

Contents

Preface v

Acknowledgments ix

1 Introduction 1

2 The Unpredictable Northern Great Plains 6

3 Dust, Grasshoppers, Thistles and Radical Protest 22

4 The New Deal Responds 40

5 The Pacific Northwest: An Underdeveloped Favorite 57

6 Washington: The Evergreen State 73

7 Oregon: The Land of Promise 96

8 Idaho: The Gem State 114

9 Baked Out, Blown Out and Broke 127

10 Adapting in Eden 159

11 Prosperity Returns 185

Bibliography 209

Index 239

Preface

No sound basis exists for believing history is inevitable, predictable or subject to universal laws. Although identifiable similarities and threads frequently exist, every historic event differs fundamentally from every other. Even if it were possible for a historian to write a definitive interpretation of an event, the problem of how to think about the event would not be solved. If everything seems clear it is often because of oversimplification, misunderstanding, and lack of emphasis. As the years distill history's broad flow, the nuances of major events tend to be overlooked in favor of what appears to be the most noteworthy, creating a monolithic interpretation. A defining example is the profound impact of the Great Depression upon the Northern Great Plains and the Pacific Northwest and the close relationship between the two regions.

Passing time tends to smooth the rough edges of the Great Depression that arguably packed more clout than any other event that happened to America between the Civil War and the atom bomb. Hardly any type of human activity was untouched. Fewer and fewer who experienced its worst remain and they tend to ignore the adverse times of the 1930s, perhaps because of a sense of guilt for their predicament, preferring to recall more favorable and successful experiences. Those born after the 1930s, who as a group have enjoyed consistent affluence, are inclined to place more emphasis on World War II and the many momentous events that followed. Having never experienced the Great Depression firsthand, they tend to underestimate the profound impact of the worldwide economic catastrophe of the 1930s.

"Dust Bowl" has become one of the most identifiable icons of the 1930s and not unjustly so. Overshadowing all other droughts on record in the United States, scientific evidence indicates it was the most extreme natural event in

350 years. It concentrated on the arid Great Plains, but at one time or the other affected most of the country, not only ruining lives but also causing thousands of deaths. Two areas—the Northern Plains and the Southern Plains suffered the most. Now historians and journalists increasingly have confined the Dust Bowl to only the Southern Plains. The plight of the equally distressed Northern Great Plains has faded to the extent that it is rarely mentioned in textbooks, periodicals, and general studies of the era.

This oversight stems largely because Dust Bowl migrants tend to be associated with the flight from the Southern Plains to California forever immortalized in John Steinbeck's 1939 Pulitzer Prize winning novel, *The Grapes of Wrath.* Steinbeck's impact on Great Depression thought has been compared to that created by Harriett Beecher Stowe's anti slavery work, *Uncle Tom's Cabin.* With around sixteen million copies in print *The Grapes of Wrath* is one of the best selling novels ever. The 1940 movie of the same title also is considered one of the all-time best. Perhaps this helps explain why the Southern Great Plainsconsistently are identified by survey history textbooks and most other references as the only Dust Bowl in spite ample proof that the Northern Great Plains were devastated at least as much or even more. California, by far the chosen destination of most southern migrants, and many others as well, moreover, receives almost all the attention while the migration to the Pacific Northwest mostly is ignored.

Much of the motivation to pursue this work stemmed from first hand experience as one of the many North Dakotans who joined the 1930s migration to the Pacific Northwest. Spending most of my life in Nebraska and Washington State built a firm foundation of understanding the two regions. Most close relatives, many who can recall the 1930s, moreover, reside in North Dakota, Montana, Idaho, Washington, Oregon and California. They provided vital information and significant contacts with others. Publication of several articles concerning the Great Depression and the Dust Bowl Experience cemented the conviction that a unique opportunity to make a needed historical contribution should not be ignored. Although family history played an important role and provided a matchless frame of reference, a more inclusive approach was set from the start.

This effort is designed to provide an original in depth contribution to the existing extensive Great Depression scholarship. It stresses the influence of geography, politics, economics and demography on the two contrasting regions, striking a balance between the traditional top-down method and a bottom-up approach. The work suggests a firm foundation for Pacific Northwest expansion was in place before World War II, facilitating the enormous wartime growth. Although acknowledging man's excessive exploitation of natural resources, the

Dust Bowl disaster and its consequences are balanced by the significance of what nature did to man as well as what man did to nature.

A broad portrait demanded exploration of as many available resources as possible and an understanding of the dynamics of the two regions. As the research and writing evolved it became clear that the migration pattern needed placement within the contrasting transitions of the then under populated Pacific Northwest and the overpopulated Northern Great Plains.

Before you create anything new, you need to understand what is already there. Fortunately, an almost inexhaustible amount of information from a wide variety of sources emerged. Personal interviews, on-site visits, local histories, books, periodicals, government documents, theses, dissertations, newspapers, and films all provided vital information. The inter-net was especially useful for corroborating factual data and updating the many events and personalities included. Study of the Great Depression also is enhanced by the New Deal emphasis on regional planning, documentary studies, and detailed record keeping. Of all academic resources the University of Washington libraries, deserve special mention. It would have been an impossible task to access much of the specialized material had it not been concentrated there.

Some geographic qualifications are in order given the scope of the topic. The arid western portions of the two Dakotas and Nebraska were the research focus for the Northern Great Plains with the understanding that eastern Wyoming and eastern Montana also belong to that region. Washington, Oregon and Idaho constitute the Pacific Northwest in this study, although western Montana, northern California and even Alaska could also fit. Because much of the activity concentrated there, North Dakota and Washington receive considerable attention. Having read the obituaries in the *Seattle Times* almost daily since 2001, it is impressive that sometimes one edition has two or three entries who were born in North Dakota. Although not as numerous, South Dakota, Nebraska, Wyoming, Montana and Idaho also are well represented.

Acknowledgements

All academic scholarship rests on a foundation built by many and gratitude is extended to all. Most will be identified in the bibliography, footnotes and acknowledgments, but many librarians, journalists, historical society workers, and others unfortunately will not. Chadron State College allowed me to pursue this writing and research as a part of my phased retirement. The Chadron State Research Fund also supported three other pertinent projects and two research trips to the Dakotas. College and university library staffs that were especially helpful included University of Washington, Chadron State College, Dickinson State University, and Central Washington University. Public library staffs at Seattle, Renton, Aberdeen, Ellensburg and Cle Elum in Washington; Chadron, Nebraska; Rapid City, South Dakota; Williston and Crosby in North Dakota, and Modesto, California, assisted ably. Libraries and exhibits at the state historical societies of Washington, Oregon, Nebraska and Minnesota helped immensely. The Renton Public Library was especially helpful during the final stages of research. Vital information also was gleaned from trips to the Museum of Flight (Seattle); the Seattle Museum of History and Industry; the Bremerton Naval Museum; the Aberdeen (WA) Museum of History; the Columbia River Maritime Museum at Astoria, Oregon; Mount Rushmore National Monument; the Senator George Norris State Historic Site at McCook, Nebraska; and the Arbor Lodge State Historical Park at Nebraska City. The staffs of the Bethany Lutheran Home of Williston, North Dakota, and the Good Samaritan Center at Crosby, North Dakota, also were most accommodating.

The following provided much appreciated assistance, insights and information. Some contacts were fleeting while others have been lifetime. They include: John Andrist, Steve Andrist, Ross Armstrong, Cormell Barth, Pearl

Stompro Berget, Sam Bloom Kristi Bohl, Richard Brauhn, Mary Dalebout Brown, Tom Buecker, Vern Chicoine, Wally Crites, Bridget (Dewing) and Richard Cromwell, Cornelia Dalebout Cross, Tom Cummings, Rollin Curd, Selmar Dahl, Carl Dalebout, Cornelius Dalebout, Karel Dalebout, David Danbom, Genie DeVine, Francis and May Dewing, Jake and Elsie Dewing, Jim Dewing, Lloyd and Mary Dewing, Ralph and Helen Dewing, Jenny Dalebout Dillon, Dorothy Earl, Tom Ellis, Gerald and Grace (Koppelslone) Farren, Lillian Husa Feist, Les Ferguson, Sophia Filleau, Selmer Gafkien, Glenda Gamby, Ann Gibson, Milton Grantham, Wilma Carroll Groeschell, Frances Ellis Hanson, Bill Harris, Walter Hovde, Lois Phillips Hudson, Don Huls, Lennie Husa, Nurmi Husa, Chet Johnston, Deb Kantrud, Doug Kyes, Gary Largo, Jim Larson, Bill Lentz, Bill Lindeken, Vern Lineback, Richard Loosbrock, Ronald MacDonald, Con Marshall, Lorraine McConaghy, Mace McGinley, Mark Miller, Phil Miller, Richard Miller, Gary Murrell, Jeri Neuharth, Virlyn Norgard, Chester Oas, Lloyd Olson, Cornelia Dewing Peabody, Carl Peterson, Barbara Pozner, William Pratt, Sam Rankin, Carlos Schwantes, Bruce Schwartz, Allen Shepherd, Susan Shilling, Mike Siebol, Palmer Skaar, Jim Soester, Fran Spencer, Arthur Streumpler, Russell Veeder, Myron and Gerdis Watterud, Norma Husa Winkler, Beth Witters,Sally Zahn and Lee Zurchen. Cousin Larry Dalebout and his wife Alcine and Cousin Geraldine Moun deserve special thanks for making my second research trip to North Dakota so profitable.

Michael Merrill is deserving of gratitude and appreciation. His computer expertise proved indispensable and his numerous suggestions and keen editorial abilities also helped avoid a number of pitfalls. My wife, Deloris also edited every page and demonstrated enduring patience with a spouse who could be difficult during long hours of research, composition and editing. The author assumes full responsibility for any errors that may remain.

An impressive number of journal and periodical articles, books, newspapers and primary sources laid the foundation for this effort. They were immensely useful in providing background information, suggesting fruitful paths of inquiry and helping avoid incorrect interpretations about a broad, highly complex subject.

Chapter One

Introduction

From colonial times westward movement has played a key role in the United States' evolution. Citizens and immigrants were lured there by the potential to build a better life developing the vast natural resources of the hinterland. Wars, dating all the way from the pre-independent French and Indian War, frequently precipitated change. For the Pacific Northwest and the Northern Great Plains the Civil War and World War I were crucial to their expansion. Both regions benefited dramatically by the Civil War's Homestead Act, which made "free" land available and cleared the way for coast-to-coast railroad expansion.

Many who moved to the upper Midwest in the late nineteenth and early twentieth centuries elected to pursue opportunities on the West Coast, joining the large segment of Upper Midwesterners who already had migrated there. World War I created a booming demand for the agricultural products of the Great Plains and the Pacific Northwest, especially wheat from both regions and timber from the Pacific Northwest. The already established Puget Sound ship building industry also prospered, and timber baron William Boeing won a government contract to build naval airplanes, hiring shipbuilders whose skills carried over to airplane manufacture. In 1920 the Pacific Northwest states of Washington, Oregon and Idaho held only a small edge in total population over the Northern Plains states of North Dakota, South Dakota, and Nebraska. Perhaps surprising in retrospect, Nebraska's 1,296,000 population was a close second to Washington's 1,357,000 and almost 60 percent more than Oregon's 783,389.

Unfortunately the predominantly agricultural Northern Plains did not reflect the general prosperity of the Roaring Twenties. The weather was generally poor and grain prices dropped precipitously from the heavily inflated wartime prices as the world supply again exceeded demand. The change to mechanization was costly, too. Increased capital investment and efficiency mandated larger individual acreage, driving land prices up. Low grain prices, poor crops and rising costs forced a continuing movement of farmers out of the Great Plains. Additionally, large numbers who stayed were forced to become tenants because of lack of capital. Despite the steady migrant outflow, the Great Plains entered the Depression era with far more population than needed to accommodate the new technologically oriented system of grain production. Young people who hoped ultimately to own their own farm comprised much of this surplus.

When the world wide economy collapsed in 1929, almost everyone was affected, but none more than Great Plains residents. Northern Plains farmers not only saw farm prices plummet, but experienced severe drought almost every year in the 1930s, highlighted by the 1936 disaster caused by the driest, hottest weather ever recorded in the region. Although departure had been constant, 1936 created a torrent of migrants who mostly chose the Pacific Northwest, where many had contacts among friends or relatives who had moved there previously. Drained by years of crop failure and record low farm prices most were almost flat broke and had no job awaiting them. Typically, although certainly not always as the popular stereotype implies, they carried only a few personal possessions with an old automobile pulling a home made trailer. In the 1930s about 300,000 left Nebraska and the Dakotas, mostly for the Pacific Northwest. This substantial transition proved immensely significant for both regions, signifying continuing growth for one and a steady decline for the other.

Several factors besides Steinbeck's celebrated *Grapes of Wrath* account for the lack of attention paid the Northern Plains exodus to the Pacific Northwest. Except for a few much smaller areas like the Yakima Valley, agriculture was not centralized like the Central Valley of California with its demand for a large labor pool. Most other areas had little demand for large concentrations of agricultural laborers. The dominant timber industry, more stable and with much better wages, offered by far the most significant labor demand in the Pacific Northwest.

Migrants from the Northern Plains assimilated into their new environment with comparative ease. Even though they faced considerable hostility and derision, migrants from the Northern Plains had educational and socio-economic levels about equal with those of the host areas. This contrasted with the pronounced differences between native Californians and the considerable number of incoming sharecroppers and laborers from the Southwest. Many established Pacific Northwest residents, too, were either born in the Upper Midwest or had roots there, which eased the way for newcomers from that region. Although many of the northern migrants remained in agriculture, at least at first, about half of them had never farmed, and few turned to it. The Northern migration peaked in 1936, moreover, several years later than the apex of the flow to California. By then the Pacific Northwest was beginning to pull out of the Great Depression and opportunities in mills, factories and extractive industries such as logging, fishing, and mining were appearing. Because the resident workforce was aging and declining in numbers, the benefits of the infusion of young, ambitious workers helped ease resistance, especially from would-be employers.

Whereas the Depression struck the Pacific Northwest a little slower than some regions, it struck with devastating effect when it fully arrived. The severe pullback in construction ravaged the all-important timber industry, dropping the demand for lumber so much that production fell more than half by 1932. Many unemployed loggers left their small farms for regional urban areas or for California, selling or abandoning their homes and acreage. Much of the land that could not be sold became tax delinquent and reverted back to government control as was true for much of the timber land depleted by logging companies. Although many migrants had to wait for well-paying, steady employment, by 1936 the West Coast was well on its way to recovery. Northern Great Plains migrants quickly established a reputation as reliable, efficient workers, allowing them to readily meld into the work force when given the opportunity.

Before the New Deal's policy of direct federal economic intervention, immediate assistance for the unemployed and the destitute was limited to private charities and state and local agencies, unable or unwilling to provide even basic support. Desperate conditions made drought devastated Northern Great Plains farmers and unemployed Pacific Northwest timber workers receptive to radical protest. Early in the 1930s Soviet Union Communists viewed the virtual collapse of capitalism as the opening they needed to promote international Communism by radical revolution through unemployed labor organizations and radical farm groups. Communists were especially active in the Dakotas and in Washington State. Their activity, although perhaps far overrated, provides and interesting phase to the politics of the era. Those Americans, seemingly abandoned by the free enterprise system, appreciated Communist assistance, but very few approved the Party's radical doctrine. Established governmental agencies, newspapers, businessmen, and farmers were bitterly opposed. But Communist radicalism no doubt pushed President Franklin Roosevelt to promote passage of his liberal New Deal programs, heavily favoring farmers and laborers. Communists, who thought the capitalist system could only grow worse, lost ground rapidly after the New Deal stole their thunder by pouring money into depressed agricultural regions, supporting organized labor, and launching a host of direct relief programs.

Roosevelt, who had visited the Pacific Northwest several times before his election, was convinced that the still much under populated region had great potential to serve as a safety valve for the Dust Bowl migrants. FDR enjoyed a most favorable position to institute change because the federal government still owned well over half of the area. He had also observed the severe problem created by lack of electrical power generation during World War I and wanted to avoid it in case of another conflict, which he accurately anticipated. Boulder (now Hoover) Dam, begun in Herbert Hoover's administration, was well underway and appeared to be a great success. It not only employed thousands of workers and created demand for construction materials, but its hydroelectric power, flood control, and irrigation promised to transform the American Southwest.

Granted almost unlimited spending authority by Congress, and encouraged by the rise of Democratic Party leadership in Washington and Oregon, Roosevelt determined to exploit the prodigious hydroelectric potential of the Columbia River. Roosevelt first pushed through funding for Bonneville Dam, then maneuvered funding for Grand Coulee Dam, at the time the largest concrete structure in the world and a symbol of the New Deal for many. FDR shrewdly stressed the irrigation potential of Grand Coulee, suggesting the new land would provide a haven for many Dust Bowl farmers. Based on past experience this eventuality was dubious at best, but World War II stalled the irrigation aspect and emphasized the need for electricity. The enormous hydroelectric production of the Columbia River dams helped transform the Pacific Northwest into a major World War II manufacturing center.

The prevailing belief that increasing the farming capacity of all three Pacific Northwest States was the solution for handling their numerous Dust Bowl migrants proved to be a miscalculation. Northern Idaho and western Oregon and Washington had adequate rainfall and lots of inexpensive cutover land that seemed capable of being converting into thousands of new farms. Eking out an adequate living by farming cutover land, however, proved impossible for most migrants who followed the pattern of many of their predecessors by working mainly in the timber industry and living on small unproductive "stump ranches."

Most migrants, having survived grim hardship and deprivation before their move, adjusted to their relocation with impressive patience and resilience. As was true of the states they left, Pacific Northwest states fought for reduction of state expenses and balanced budgets. All willingly pursued New Deal programs but offered little state financial support for those in need. Even though Democrat governors prevailed in both regions throughout the 1930s, they reflected a conservatism that appealed to their constituencies. The more colorful included "Cowboy" Ben Ross, Idaho; retired general Charles Martin, Oregon; and Tom Berry, South Dakota. North Dakota's Nonpartisan League governor "Wild" Bill Langer was unique, but also was no supporter of the New Deal. None spent any more state tax money than was absolutely necessary and none strongly supported the New Deal, especially in liberal social change that encouraged labor unions and minority rights. Fortunately, the two regions had several outstanding members of the United States Congress who effectively used their influence to help gain relief for the dispossessed. Among the better known were Senator George Norris, Nebraska; Senator Peter Norbeck, South Dakota; Senator William Borah, Idaho; and Senator Charles McNary, Oregon.

World War II finally ended the Great Depression. Dramatic expansion of war related industries such as aircraft, ships, and timber products created an insatiable demand for labor. The war transformed the Pacific Northwest from a heavy dependence upon eastern industry and capital to an industrialized economic leader. Although the impact of World War II looms large and easily is documented by economic statistics, the Pacific Northwest's economic preparation prior to the war contained more of an evolutionary quality than many have recognized. Much of the essential infrastructure: a strong educational system, a core of capable executives and workers, Grand Coulee and Bonneville Dams, the logging industry, Boeing Aircraft, shipyards, a sound transportation system, and much more was in place. While World War II set the stage for a continuing, massive expansion for the Pacific Northwest, arid rural areas of the Northern Great Plains after brief wartime prosperity suffered the opposite fate, declining continually with no end in sight. On the other hand, urban centers in the region, spurred in large part by world class coal, oil, and natural gas production, have shown considerable growth.

Chapter Two

The Unpredictable Northern Great Plains

Defined by precipitation levels the Great Plains extend from northern Canada to southern Texas and from the Rocky Mountains about four hundred miles eastward, sloping to the Central Lowland at the rate of ten feet a mile. As elevation drops precipitation increases to over eighteen inches annually at the about 98th meridian, originally creating the short grass and high grass prairie. This study defines the Northern Great Plains in the United States as the western Dakotas, western Nebraska and eastern Montana and Wyoming. Characterized by hot, windy summers and cold winters, the weather is noted for its unpredictability. Sometimes moisture arrives too early or too late and about once a decade a serious drought occurs. Severe blizzards and hailstorms can endanger man, beast and crops. A scorching gale in late June or early July can demolish a promising crop in less than a week as can hordes of grasshoppers. Even when nature smiles, low prices for meat and grain can be ruinous. With an agricultural economy based upon marginal moisture levels combined with other natural hazards, the area evolved dependent upon more urban areas.[1]

Before the Civil War the Great Plains, described as the "Great American Desert," remained relatively vacant. Harsh conditions, plus effective Indian resistance discouraged would-be settlers who guided their covered wagons across them to the more promising land of California and Oregon. Nebraska, the first Northern Plains territory to achieve statehood, entered the union in 1867. In comparison, California was admitted in 1850, Oregon in 1859.

When southern slave states seceded in 1861, ending the controversy over extension of slavery into new territories, the Homestead Act of 1862 promptly followed. It promised 160 acres of federal land free (except for $18.00 filing fee) to all citizens over twenty-one willing to resettle. To "prove up" homesteaders were required to live on their land five years and establish a house and other improvements. After two neighbors or friends vouched for the improvements and filing fees were paid, the settler received a certificate of ownership in the name of the current President. It proved an effective means for the government to dispose of huge tracts of undeveloped land and provided a true opportunity for many ambitious pioneers. Following post Civil War railroad expansion, the first wave of homesteaders settled on the Great Plains in the 1870s and 1880s. By 1889, all of the territories in the Northern Great Plains had achieved statehood. Six hundred thousand farmers obtained title to about eighty million acres by 1900.[2] Much of this acreage enjoyed enough fertility and moisture to provide a decent livelihood. As the more desirable land was taken, homesteaders gambled on the more arid land still available to the west. More than one hundred ninety million acres was homesteaded in the twentieth century. Much of it was semi-arid and marginal but many accepted the popular theory that "rainfall followed the plow." They were disillusioned when severe drought returned in the mid-1880s.

Long before the disastrous Dust Bowl of the 1930s, the hard realities of the Great Plains had taken their toll on aspiring settlers. The record of the drier parts of the Great Plains was largely one of settlement and abandonment before 1930. Although some still awaited the railroad and did not bloom until the early twentieth century, many Great Plains counties boasted more population in 1890 than at the start of the Great Depression. By 1920, the ten Great Plains states, with the exception of Texas, were exporting population.[3]

Many who left believed the government and the railroads had deceived them. Encouraged by generous grants of land and money from both state and federal governments, rapidly expanding railroads needed traffic and aggressively promoted settlement, advertising heavily throughout the United States and Europe. The Northern Pacific established a Bureau of Immigration in London with several other branches in Europe. Jay Cooke, the Northern Pacific financier, painted the region is such glowing terms that journalists began calling the territory adjacent to the railroad "Jay Cooke's Banana Belt."

Western railroads opened booths in eastern cities and inundated the United States with promotional literature. While railroad propagandists gilded the lily unmercifully prospective settlers also were lured by severely discounted transportation rates. One writer suggested the only illness which even remotely touched the residents of Montana was the pangs of over-eating, resulting from excessive indulgence of the hearty appetite attendant upon the invigorating atmosphere. He added, "The very babies seem to know that it is their duty to keep well at all times."[4] Cooperative deals were arranged with steamship lines to provide immigrants with low fares. Those en route to settle upon lands purchased from the Northern Pacific were granted free transportation for themselves and their families.

Settlers intending to buy or homestead government land were given reduced rates.[5]

James J. Hill arguably promoted settlement of the Great Plains and the Pacific Northwest more than any other. A shrewd, self-made Canadian who wrested a fortune in coal, freight, and merchandising in St. Paul, Minnesota, Hill completed his Great Northern line from Duluth to Seattle in 1893. Unlike his rival the Northern Pacific, Hill insisted on the best workmanship and materials for his railroad and received no public land for the effort. It took seven years to finish the line from Minot, Dakota Territory, to Seattle. Through his colonization bureau, based in Chicago, Hill sent agents to Europe, especially Great Britain, Sweden and Norway. Generous benefits were offered to those willing to settle along his line. They were charged ten dollars for travel as much as half way across the country. Entire families rented freight cars, called immigrant cars, for a little more. Lumber shipped on the Great Northern was sold to settlers at just above cost. Farmers were encouraged to follow the most effective agricultural practices by experts traveling in exhibition trains. An advocate of agricultural diversity, Hill also imported purebred cattle from Europe and gave them to selected farmers along his route.[6] His attempts to encourage farmers to avoid the uncertainties of over reliance on wheat were largely ineffective. Of course, all of the newly formed Northern Plains states promoted their agricultural potential with unashamed exaggeration.

Norwegians, faced with unfavorable social and economic conditions coupled with harsh military requirements, especially accepted the promise of prosperity. The Great Northwest was a natural choice for them and although northwest North Dakota attracted an impressive concentration, they dispersed along the entire line from Minnesota to Washington. Norwegians represented the highest percentage of foreign born in the 1930 and 1940 censuses in Minnesota, North Dakota, South Dakota, and Washington. Besides a tremendous work ethic, Norwegians brought much to their new country. Illiteracy was almost unknown among them. A 1736 law required all persons to be confirmed and the state Lutheran church mandated candidates for confirmation to be familiar with Luther's Catechism, the hymnbook, and the Bible. Norway established public schools in 1739. Norwegians also had an inclination for politics, having enjoyed considerable democratic participation after nobility was abolished on May 17, 1814—the Norwegian Fourth of July.[7]

Even though they predominated in many communities, hospitable Norwegians melded easily with other groups and willingly settled in heterogeneous environments. The northwest corner of North Dakota has been described as a "Norwegian Sea with islands of other groups."[8] Towns in the area featured a diverse population, but industrious, independent Norwegians dominated in rural areas, where they tended to stay.[9] About one-third of North Dakotans have Norwegian ancestry; Minnesota and South Dakota have about one-fifth; Montana has about one eighth. Their influence upon the cultural fabric in areas they settled has proven profoundly significant, including a marked preference for the Lutheran church and liberal politics.[10]

German-Russians, Germans by blood and heritage lured to Russia as a defensive wall, equaled the Norwegian influence in North Dakota. Russia had granted generous land grants and allowed the Germans to keep their national character, but the German's success and growing influence led the czarist government to repudiate favoritism toward them. When Russia withdrew military exemption in 1876 many decided to leave. Most migrated to South Central North Dakota by way of Kansas and South Dakota. Hard working and acquisitive like the Norwegians, but not as gregarious or as education oriented, many succeeded as wheat and cattle ranchers. German-Russians settled in either all Catholic or all Protestant communities—mainly Catholic. German-Russians and Norwegians both leaned toward socialist economic policies, creating a liberal political base for North Dakota's extraordinarily liberal legislation in the 1920s and 1930s. Both groups, however, strongly favored the Republican Party. Bandleader Lawrence Welk, born on a farm near Strasburg, is perhaps the best-known descendant of German-Russian ancestry.[11] Welk's homespun, believable Dakota style helped account for his astounding popularity after World War II.[12]

While the migration of settlers from Europe to the Great Plains receives justifiable recognition, the role of Yankee migration to the area seems under appreciated. As is true throughout the West, Yankee influence in all aspects of development was indispensable. They pushed into the Great Lakes area fairly late, but spread rapidly after the completion of the Erie Canal in 1820. By 1840, they had moved north from Ohio and Illinois and were in southern Wisconsin and Iowa, pushing into Minnesota in the 1850s and 1860s. Of the 450,000 people in Minnesota in 1876 about 29,000 were Yankees.[13] Their children were the original settlers of the eastern Dakotas in the 1870s. Although the Yankee influence remained strong, Wyoming and Western Nebraska attracted a number of southern cattlemen after the Civil War, promoting more of a Missouri-Texas influence than their northern neighbors. These roots helped account for the strong presence of the Ku Klux Klan in Western Nebraska in the 1920s.[14]

Yankees, lacking in a meat-animal tradition, favored cash crop farming. They were leaders in developing the huge bonanza wheat operations of the Northern Plains, which were the dominating factor in the agricultural development of North Dakota in the 1870s. Their success helped convince would-be settlers that wheat ranching on the Great Plains could be profitable. Most of the bonanza ranches, however, were in the moister Red River Valley, not on the arid Great Plains. Common throughout the West, Yankee influence was ubiquitous on the Northern Great Plains where they tended to dominate urban areas and small towns. They created an atmosphere where education was emphasized, local institutions were supported strongly, and the act of belonging was important. Yankees also transplanted their love for baseball to the Upper Midwest and Great Plains.[15]

Lured by still available homesteads or inexpensive land more than 250,000 entered North Dakota during the Second Dakota Boom, 1898–1915.[16] Settlers followed the rapidly expanding railroads to the western Great Plains. Described as Hill's "competitive nemesis," the Milwaukee, St. Paul, and Sault Ste. Marie or "Soo" line extended through northern North Dakota in the 1890s, reaching Minot in the northwest corner in 1902. From Minot the Soo crossed the Canadian border at Portal to link with its parent, the Canadian Pacific, providing serious competition for the Great Northern for long haul as well as short haul traffic. Another Soo route was built from near Portal to Whitehall, Montana, to compete for the grain trade.[17] Hill responded by building a Great Plains system of north-south feeder lines in 1905.

Railroad expansion in Nebraska, South Dakota and Wyoming benefited from competition between the Chicago-Northwestern and Burlington Northern. The former had pushed from Valentine, Nebraska, to Chadron, Nebraska, in 1885 and intended to make Chadron the end of the line for at least two years. When the Burlington unexpectedly pushed out of Broken Bow, Nebraska, in 1885 with the intention of controlling the Black Hills market, CNW countered by pressing on to Rapid City, South Dakota, by July 4, 1886. A westward branch reached Casper, Wyoming, in June 1888.[18] No transcontinental railroads traversed South Dakota because of the newly established Sioux Indian reservations.

Drawn by the opportunity to acquire land at bargain basement prices and the assurance of transportation for its products, settlers flocked to the Great Plains at a record breaking pace. The Dakotas, Montana, and Washington became states in 1889. Wyoming, nicknamed the Equality State because of its provisions for women's rights, was hurried into the Union in 1890 along with Idaho. John Wesley Powell, Director of the United States Geological Survey from 1881–1894 and recognized as the leading scientific authority on the Great Plains, was invited to address the North Dakota Constitutional Convention in 1889. Powell warned that while the Red River Valley usually had adequate rainfall, the middle portion of North Dakota would have a series of abundant crops followed by disaster, forcing thousands of people to leave. Powell pointed out the more arid western area was even more unpredictable and proposed irrigation from rivers as a solution.[19]

It did not take long for pioneers who moved west of the 98th parallel to learn that their new environment imposed the higher risk Powell had predicted. The general rule for grain production on the Northern Great Plains is that fifteen inches of rain is adequate providing most of it falls in late spring. Forty to 50 percent of the time it falls below that mark.[20] The area was plagued by drought, grasshoppers and hail from 1886 to 1895 Many settlers abandoned the plains and either moved west or returned to their origins in eastern neighboring states. Discontented farmers who stayed organized politically in a radical Populist Party that commanded such high levels of support in the wheat states that they dominated state legislatures in Kansas and Nebraska. After unsuccessfully running a third party candidate for President in 1892, most Populists fused with the Democrats in 1896. Their candidate, Nebraska's William Jennings Bryan proposed free coinage of silver, government control of railroads, a federal income tax, and direct election of United States Senators. These "radical" proposals electrified opposition from the business community whose members poured money into Republican William McKinley's successful campaign. Many of the discontented departed the Great Plains, either back to the more humid east or on to the Mountain West and the Pacific Coast. Numerous Great Plains counties never again have achieved the population level of 1890.[21]

Late blooming because of lack of transportation, the western Dakotas and eastern Montana attracted half a million new settlers during the first fifteen years of the twentieth century. Twenty percent were foreign born.[22] Wheat prices had greatly improved and much of the land still could be homesteaded or purchased for a few dollars an acre. In contrast good land in Iowa sold for $135 and up.[23] Few young people or immigrants possessed enough capital for a start in the more desirable areas and were encouraged by railroads and government officials who promoted the canard "rainfall follows the plow."

Hardy Webster Campbell became the leading guru of dry land farming. Born in Vermont, Campbell homesteaded three quarters of a section in Brown County, South Dakota Territory, in 1879. There he developed the practice of "scientific soil culture" for effective cultivation of dry lands. His practice involved deep fall plowing, then using his invention to pack the subsoil while loosening the topsoil. The idea was to preserve moisture deep in the soil. For the same purpose Campbell also touted summer fallow, the policy of keeping strips plowed for an entire year. Campbell's *Soil Cultural Manual* went through four editions. He also founded the Western Agricultural Improvement Society in 1905 and began a popular Dry Farming Congress in Denver in 1907.

Western railroads employed Campbell to encourage settlement of their arid lands. First, he ran five demonstration farms across North Dakota; then he worked for Burlington near Holdrege, Nebraska, and finally in the 1920s promoted farming in Eastern Montana for Northern Pacific. When his teachings imploded in the dry 1920s and 1930s Campbell was considered a charlatan. A more honest appraisal might portray him as a true believer promoting a failed concept.[24]

In North Dakota the population of the western counties more than quadrupled from 1900–1910. The western counties of South Dakota, which contained more unproductive gumbo soil and the Black Hills, increased 200 percent.[25] Fueled by increased prices for farm products, improvements in farming, a speculative psychology and large amounts of easy credit, the area boomed. Between 1900 and 1910 land prices increased 231 percent in Nebraska, 377 percent in South Dakota and 321 percent in North Dakota.

Although other grains such as flax, barley, corn and oats were grown, hard red spring wheat covered the vast majority of acreage because chances of producing a saleable crop from it were better. Spring wheat, grown in the Dakotas, Minnesota and Montana, is described as the "aristocrat" of wheat for baking bread because of its high protein content, usually 13–16 percent, and its strong gluten characteristic, an elastic quality that helps retain the shape of baked goods. Wheat also adapts better to machine methods and thus can be planted and harvested on more land more efficiently. A yield of twenty bushels to the acre was considered adequate. Wheat prices ranged from sixty-five to eighty-five cents a bushel during the period to 1915 then soared to over two dollars during World War I. Record prices and favorable weather allowed wheat farmers to enjoy unprecedented prosperity. Only three years, 1904, 1910 and 1913, had annual precipitation below fifteen inches and 1904 and 1913 were only slightly below that mark. Drought in Hardin County in Northwest South Dakota was so severe from 1910–11, though, that it almost was abandoned. Marked differences in soil and climate determined that western Nebraska and western South Dakota raised a much larger percentage of corn and hay and were more oriented to cattle and sheep raising. Alfalfa hay and alfalfa seed played a major role in these two areas.[26]

As settlers poured into the area, towns providing goods and services sprang up. Invariably they were located along railroad lines and their water towers and grain elevators were visible for miles on the open prairie. Although usually basic, much more infrastructure—schools, stores, newspapers, theaters, churches, and the like, was established than the economy proved able to support.[27] A local government pattern designed to serve a relatively dense population developed. During the boom days bond issues floated easily and the progressive political policies of the states to the east, Minnesota, Iowa, and Illinois—where most of the settlers originated, prevailed.[28] Town dwellers as a rule were heavily Yankee Republicans while rural areas heavily populated by Norwegians and Russian-Germans in the more arid west provided a stronghold for more leftist politics, especially in hard times.[29] Citizens of the Dakotas and Montana expected government to be honest and efficient and fight for the public good, while citizens of Nebraska and Wyoming, with more residents from the upland south, used more political patronage and spoils of office. Jobs and morality were valued more.[30]

Differences between the Dakotas impressed John Gunther so much that he asserted (perhaps too strongly) in his popular post World War II *Inside USA,* "Nothing is more remarkable in the United States than the difference between the Dakotas."[31] Gunther called North Dakota probably the most radical state in the union and described South Dakota as one of the most conservative. He attributed the difference to North Dakota's dependence on wheat, her two transcontinental railroads and South Dakota's none, and North Dakota's somewhat colonial relationship with Minnesota, whose banks, grain companies and railroad interests dominated them economically.[32] North Dakotans, determined to protect their agrarian economic interests, became embroiled in Populist politics. A popular pun claimed North Dakota's principal crops were wheat and politics.[33]

North Dakota farmers' hostility toward the greed of large institutions that milked the fruits of their labor combined with a large population of liberal Scandinavians and Germans to nurture an active Socialist Party. Centered in Minot, Williston, and Fargo. Socialists published their own newspaper, held regular meetings and met for an annual state convention until World War I. Radical Socialist proposals included a state run bank and a state run flour mill and grain elevator.[34] North Dakota became the only state to own these two institutions which were achieved by the Nonpartisan League (NPL), the organization of farmers that evolved in 1915 and essentially ended the Socialist Party.

In 1915, A. C. "Always Cash" Townley, a former Socialist Party organizer and a failed flax farmer from Beach, North Dakota, founded the NPL as an agriculturally oriented organization. Born near Browns Valley, Minnesota, Townley joined his brother to farm near Beach. After a large farming venture in Colorado failed, he returned to Beach where he became known as the "flax king of the Northwest." In 1912, crop failure and depressed prices forced him into bankruptcy. Townley smartly designed the NPL to support candidates based on their political positions rather than party affiliation. Because North Dakota had an open primary NPL candidates could capitalize on overwhelming rural support to defeat the official Republican slate, which had ordinarily dominated in North Dakota.

Although limited in formal education, Townley became an astute master orator and organizer. He described the independent farmer as "in" about as far as he could get and "dependent" on everything in sight. Perhaps Townley's most famous quote was, "If you put a lawyer, a banker, and an industrialist in a barrel and roll it down hill, there'll always be a son-of-a-bitch at the top."[35] His virulent opposition to World War I sped his political decline. In 1921, Townley served ninety days in a Minnesota jail on the dubious charge of "conspiracy to discourage enlistment." In the 1950s, Townley completely reversed his politics and became a red baiting Anti-Communist.

Although NPL candidates officially ran as independents, they were mostly liberal Republicans. The farther west in North Dakota, the more the NFL was favored. NPL candidate Lynn J. Frazier, a Republican farmer from Steele County whose parents had moved to Minnesota from Maine, was elected governor in 1916. By 1918, the NPL gained full control of North Dakota government and North Dakota became a center of progressive reform.[36] *Northern Lights* (1979), an award winning documentary, portrayed the attempt to organize the NPL in Divide County. During Frazier's term (1916–1921) North Dakota established the state owned Bank of North Dakota and a state mill and grain elevator.[37] An Industrial Commission consisting of the governor, the attorney general and the commissioner of agriculture and labor was established to oversee operations of the state-owned industries, as was a constitutional amendment allowing a recall vote of public officials.

Frazier's good friend William Lemke ran his campaign. Lemke captained the University of North Dakota football team on which Frazier played. Lemke, whose Prussian father originally immigrated to Minnesota, moved to Towner County, North Dakota, at age five. There the family farm prospered and his father served in the state legislature. Lemke earned a law degree from Yale in 1905. Clean living and high minded Lemke delighted in rough and tumble debate. Westbrook Pegler, the noted conservative columnist of the 1930s and 1940s, described Lemke as "a skinny little guy with a puckering squint of a smile and a casting director would type him as a hick . . . [but] he went to Yale . . . and . . . is positively not a yokel."

Many conservative North Dakotans, mostly old-stock Republican townspeople, angered by the NPL's socialist stance, supported the Independent Voters Association (IVA), the NPL's bitter foe. Ironically, Frazier, after being elected three times was recalled in 1921when North Dakota's economy declined sharply. He became the first state official in the country's history to suffer that fate. New governor Ragnvold Anderson Nestos, a Norwegian immigrant, supported state owned industries even though he was backed by the IVA. Voters quickly forgave Frazier as evidenced by his quick election to the United States Senate, where he served from 1923 to 1940. The Nonpartisan League maintained its strong presence in North Dakota politics until it merged with the Democratic Party in 1956.[38]

Regrettably, after the war the boom ended quickly as grain prices dropped and dry weather returned. It soon became apparent that the population base could not support adequately the number of schools, churches, newspapers, businesses, and other infrastructure. The 160 acres permitted by the Homestead Act were just not enough for Great Plains agriculture. Many homes were little more than shacks with limited space and privacy. Most had no tended yard and few had electricity or running water. Adequate infrastructure was not well established and what existed was difficult to maintain.[39] Only a minimal percentage of farms on the Northern Great Plains were lit by electricity by 1930. North Dakota had only 7.9 percent, South Dakota 14.5 percent and Nebraska 16.5 percent.[40] Given a taste of the harsh climate combined with primitive, isolated living conditions a many settlers quickly moved on, allowing more opportunity for farmers who stayed. In order to succeed those who stayed immediately began consolidating holdings through purchase and lease. Many homesteaders, moreover, had no intention of staying from the start. A study of twelve townships in western North Dakota classified nearly one-half of the 669 farm operators who had moved out by 1925 as having come chiefly for speculative purposes. Most of the speculators were native-born Americans whereas those born in foreign countries tended to establish permanent farms. No more than one-fourth of the native-born had had any farming experience before filing on their homesteads. Most of them left more quickly than the ones with farming experience intending to stay.[41] A full 40 percent of western North Dakota farm operators present in 1919 had moved by 1926.[42]

Abundant crops and record high prices generated by the war in Europe, however, appeared to validate the promotional promises of Great Plain's agricultural prosperity in 1916. Eastern Montana, which averaged only 8.2 inches of rainfall a year over a sixty-eight year period, averaged twenty-five bushels of wheat an acre in 1916. Throughout the region confident farmers bought more machinery, built more buildings and welcomed more children, unaware that two disastrous decades loomed ahead.

High prices from 1917 to 1920 offset poor crops, but prices collapsed rapidly after that. The severe winter of 1916–17 killed 75 percent of the wheat crop in Nebraska followed by a poor year in 1918. Drought in western North Dakota shaved one-third from the average yield in 1917 followed by a poor year in 1918 and the worst crop on record to that point in 1919. Western South Dakota experienced poor crops in both 1919 and 1920.[43] Drought in eastern Montana, began in 1917, climaxed by a mere 2.4 bushels an acre in 1919. Wheat prices in Minneapolis dropped from $2.96 a bushel in July 1920 to $.92 in December 1921, adding to the disaster.[44] Between 1919 and 1925, 20,000 mortgages were foreclosed and an estimated 11,000 farms were vacated. An estimated 60,000 people left Montana during the 1920s. Over half of the state's commercial banks failed.[45] James J. Hill became the villain for disillusioned Montanans. Many opined, "Twixt Hill and Hell, there's just one letter: Were Hill in Hell, we'd feel much better."[46] Constant severe drought in eastern Montana from 1929–1931 created further economic disaster.

Although Montana suffered more in the 1920s, other Great Plains States were not far behind. While wheat prices remained low, farmers drove land prices higher to accommodate the higher overhead of increased mechanization that demanded more acreage to be efficient. Not unlike investors in the soaring stock market, most farmers expanded their holdings through bank loans, assuming the land would continue its steady accretion. With inexpensive land no longer available, many young would-be farmers were forced to seek other options, frequently requiring a move to another state. Purchase of tractors, trucks and other expensive machinery to replace horses added to the debt burden but greatly reduced the need for hired labor. The demise of the horse also made more grain available for market, further depressing prices.

Demand for grain failed to match the increased production for several reasons. Grain production in Europe returned to normal after the war. Consumption of cereals declined nearly one hundred pounds per capita between 1909 and 1930. Mechanization freed land formerly devoted to horses to produce more grain for the market. Restrictive immigration laws and lower birthrates slowed population growth. High tariff barriers of the 1920s restricted international trade, which accounted for about one-third of the United States' grain market. Plains states politicians, isolationists generally, supported high tariffs thinking they would protect their constituents from foreign competition. It did to a degree, but foreign buyers turned to other markets such as Canada, Australia, and Argentina, clamping retaliatory tariffs on United States' farm products.[47] Congressional attempts to involve the federal government in agricultural marketing, such as the McNary-Haugen Farm Relief bill of 1927, were vetoed by conservative Republican Presidents Coolidge and Hoover. Pressured by the need for credit for expansion, bank regulations were loose. By 1920, North Dakota had 898 banks, more per person than any other state, and the other Plains states were not far behind. By 1922, the loans of state banks averaged 120 percent of deposits with some national banks at more than twice that rate. During this period 60 percent was the accepted norm. By 1923, ninety-three cash-strapped banks toppled because of the farm depression which saw the per capita personal income in North Dakota drop to $375 in 1929, almost half the national average of $703. The toll continued at a steady pace until the bank crisis peaked in the early thirties. By then 575 of the 898 banks had closed at a loss of an estimated $50,000,000 to depositors.[48] Neighboring states reflected a banking crisis similar to North Dakota's.

When the United States' economy crashed in October 1929, the overpopulated Northern Great Plains states were set for a disaster fueled by settlers' blind faith in nature's generosity and a continuing increase in land values. Instead, the region suffered the double blow of collapsed prices and record shattering drought. Between 1929 and 1941 there were only two normal wheat crops. It was the driest period in the region's history featuring almost complete crop failures in 1934 and 1936. Land prices in Divide County, North Dakota, dropped from an estimated $32 an acre in 1920 to $10 an acre in 1940. As late as 1935, acreage in Divide County was estimated at $21 an acre. Other wheat producing counties in the region experienced the same decline. Wheat acreage in Dawes County, Nebraska, for example, dropped from $29 an acre in 1920 to $9 in 1940.[49]

As the economy spiraled downward, prices for agricultural commodities collapsed. In 1930, a bushel of wheat, in terms of gold, sold for the lowest price in four hundred years in the international market. By 1933, United States' wheat fell from a 1931 record low forty-five cents a bushel to twenty-seven cents a bushel; corn dropped to thirteen cents; cattle, hog, and sheep prices also plummeted. Some farmers chose to burn their corn for heat, finding it more economical than coal. John Larsen, who farmed for some fifty years near Chadron, Nebraska, reported that in 1932 he sold five steers averaging 661 pounds for a total of $95.02. That same day, he sold thirty-two feeder pigs weighing eighty pounds each for $64.08. Neighbor Milton Grantham said, "I can remember the times when I helped my dad put in a wheat crop, and we didn't even raise enough wheat to get the seed back." After three straight crop failures the Grantham farm was lost.[50]

Northern Great Plains residents now faced an unprecedented economic disaster. Prices on their products dropped to impossibly low levels, and the worst and longest drought ever recorded devastated the region. Tax delinquencies brought about a vicious circle of higher tax rates on a diminishing tax base. Most impacted was the northwest corner of North Dakota, which had over 45 percent real estate taxes delinquent in 1932–33.[51] Many simply abandoned their property and moved out. Schools and other public services suffered as well as private institutions such as churches, fraternal organizations and service clubs.[52] The traditional progression from hired hand to farm owner was destroyed, creating thousands more tenant farmers with little or no income. Desirable free land to the West, moreover, no longer existed. The common alternative of moving from farm to factory, used by so many in Western Europe and the Northeastern United States, was not available on the Plains because of lack of manufacturing and urban growth. Most destitute Northern-Plains citizens were forced to tough it out on the farm or meet the crisis by moving west by the hundreds of thousands abandoning relatives and in many cases decades of commitment of labor and capital.

Those who play down the significance of the 1930s exodus from the Northern Plains argue that it was an inevitable process merely accelerated by unusually harsh economic and natural circumstances. Modern technology had ended the already precarious chances of succeeding at dry land farming on small acreage. The departure process begun in the late nineteenth century, stalled temporarily before and during World War I then continued in the 1920s, was bound to go on. That the migration of the 1930s differed little in numbers than that of the twenties enhances the conservative argument that the Dust Bowl migration accounts over emphasized a small minority and overlooked the larger picture.[53] Not fully taken into account, however, is the absolute devastation on the arid western plains combined with the dramatic collapse in farm prices that prohibited a planned, adequately supported departure. Previous droughts and economic depressions had lasted two or three years. Those of the 1930s prevailed for a decade, featuring unheard of heat and drought conditions, especially in 1936. Many fled in haste with only a few personal belongings and an automobile to their name. They were not selfish land speculators trapped by their own greed. Others simply could not afford to leave and were forced to accept whatever assistance available to survive where they were.[54]

NOTES

1. James H. Madison, ed. *Heartland: Comparative Histories of the Midwestern States* (Bloomington, IN: Indiana University Press, 1998), passim.

2. Richard Pence, "The Homestead Act of 1862," http://www.Users.rcn.Com/deeds/ Homestead. Htm—6k. (accessed February 28, 2005)

3. Conrad Taeuber and Carl Taylor *The People of the Drought States* (Washington, DC: WPA Research Bulletin, Series 5, Number 2, 1937).

4. James B. Hedges, "The Colonization Work of the Northern Pacific Railroad," *Mississippi Valley Historical Review* 13 (December 1926): 311–42; Carlos Schwantes. *Going Places: Transportation Redefines the Twentieth-Century West.* (Bloomington: Indiana University Press, 2003), 78–80; Ronald Ridgley, "The Railroads and Rural Development in the Dakotas" *North Dakota History* 36 (Spring 1969): 163–87.

5. Hedges, "Colonization Work," 320. Cattle ranchers and sheep ranchers strongly disliked homesteaders. They frequently referred to them as "honyockers," a corruption of a German expression meaning "chicken chasers."

6. Ralph W. Hidy, et al., *The Great Northern Railway: A History* (Boston: Harvard Business School Press, 1988), passim.

7. Elwyn B. Robinson, *History of North Dakota* (Lincoln: University of Nebraska Press, 1966), 282–84.

8. William C. Sherman, *Prairie Mosaic: An Ethnic Atlas of Rural North Dakota* (Fargo, ND: North Dakota Institute for Regional Studies, 1983).

9. WPA Writer's Program, *North Dakota: A Guide to the Northern Prairie State* (New York: Oxford University Press, 1950), 85.

10. Robert P. Wilkins and Wynona H. Wilkins, *North Dakota: A History* (New York: W. W. Norton, 1977), 51–52, 61–66; Carrie Young, *Nothing To Do But Stay* (New York: Delta, 1993), passim. This is an excellent personal account of Norwegian family life on a Williston area wheat farm from homesteading in 1905 to World War II.

11. Wilkins, *North Dakota History*, 69–74; Gordon L. Iseminger, "The McIntosh County German-Russians: The First Fifty Years," *North Dakota History* 51 (Summer 1984): 4–23.

12. *Newsweek,* "It Was a Wunnerful Life: Heartland Hero Lawrence Welk: 1903–1992," (June 1, 1992): 76.

13. Stewart H. Holbrook, *The Yankee Exodus: An Account of Migration from New England* (New York: Macmillan, 1950), 170; Jon C. Hudson, "Who Was the 'Forest Man?': Sources of Migration to the Great Plains," *Great Plains Quarterly* 6 (Spring 1986): 69–83. The entire issue is devoted to the Dust Bowl.

14. Michael W. Schuyler, "The Ku Klux Klan Nebraska, 1920–1930," *Nebraska History* 66 (Fall 1985): 234–56; Author's experience—Alliance, Crawford, Chadron and Long Pine are examples of strong 1920s KKK support.

15. John C, Hudson, *Plains Country Towns* (Minneapolis: University of Minnesota Press, 1985), 128–29; Gary *Lucht*, "Scobey's Touring Pros: Wheat, Baseball, and Illicit Booze," *Montana* 20, (Summer 1970): 88–93.

16. Wilkins, *North Dakota History*, 55.

17. Hidy, *Great Northern*, 111–14.

18. Rolland Dewing, "From Hell on Wheels to That Splendid Little War," in *Chadron* [NE] *Centennial History*, ed. Rolland Dewing (Freeman, SD: Pine Hill Press, 1985), 21.

19. Frank E. Vyzralek, "The Commons*:* The *Life* Cycles of the Great Plains Has Inspired Good and Bad Ideas Over the Decades," *North Dakota Horizons* (Winter 1991): 4–9.

20. Mary Hargreaves, *Dry Farming the Northern Great Plains, 1900–1925* (Cambridge: Harvard University Press, 1957), 13.

21. Francis Moul, "The Biggest Partner: The Federal Government and Sioux County, Nebraska," *Nebraska History* 80, (Winter 1999): 150–65; Dewing, *Chadron Centennial History,* 175; "Population change by county, 2000–04," *USA Today*, 15 April 2005, 7A.

22. Walter Nugent, *Into the West: The Story of Its People,* (New York: Knopf, 1999), 138; Percy Wallaston, *Homesteading: A Montana Family Album* (New York: The Lyons Press, 1997), passim.

23. Hargreaves, *Dry Land Farming*, 13.

24. James C. Malin, *The Grasslands of North America: Prolegomena to Its History.* (Lawrence, KS: Private Printing, 1947), 227–42; Tom Isern. "Plains Folk: A Misguided TrueBeliever,"http://www.ext.nodak.edu/extnews/newsrelease/1999/010799/18plains,htm. (accessed February 14, 2005)

25. Howard W. Ottoson, et al., *Land and People in the Northern Plains Transition Area* (Lincoln: University of Nebraska Press, 1966), 49.

26. Paula M. Nelson, *The Prairie Winnows Its Own: The West River Country of South Dakota in the Years of the Great Depression* (Iowa City: University of Iowa Press, 1996), 19; Dewing, *Chadron*, 66.

27. Carey McWilliams, *Ill Fares the Land: Migrants and Migratory Labor in the United States* (New York: Barnes and Noble, 1941), 66–67.

28. Great Plains Committee, *The Future of the Great Plains,* House Document 144, 75th Congress. (Washington, DC: United States Government Printing Office, 1937), 5.

29. *WPA Guide to North Dakota*, 4.

30. Madison, *Heartland*, 6.

31. John Gunther, *Inside U.S.A.* (New York: Harper, 1947), 237.

32. Ibid., 237.

33. Sophisticated discussions of politics, wheat, and baseball impressed the author when he first returned to North Dakota in 1947.

34. Henry R. Mortinson, "Comes the Revolution. . . .!: A Personal Memoir," *North Dakota History* 16 (Winter 1969): 40–109,

35. Wilkins, *North Dakota History*, 139.

36. Michael Anderegg, "The Fiction Film as Artifact: History, Image, and Meaning in 'Northern Lights'," *North Dakota History* 57 (Summer 1990): 14–23. North Dakota farmers' antipathy toward Socialism is highlighted.

37. Edward Blackorby, *Prairie Rebel: The Public Life of William Lemke* (Lincoln: University of Nebraska Press, 1964), 11.

38. *Journal of the West* 41 (Fall 2002) Special Issue, "Depression Politics in the West."

39. Hargreaves, *Dry Land Farming,* 502: WPA Guide to North Dakota 76–77; Paula M. Nelson, "Traveling the Hope Highway: An Intellectual History of the West River Country of South Dakota," in *The Centennial West: Essays on the Northern Tier States,* ed. William L. Lang (Seattle: University of Washington Press, 1991), 244–64.

40. Great Plains Committee, 52: Gladys Leffler Gist and James Marten ed., *Chasing Rainbows: A Recollection of the Great Plains, 1921–1925* (Ames, IA: Iowa State University Press, 1993), 87.

41. E. Wilson, H. C. Hoffsommer, and A. H. Benton, *Rural Changes in Western North Dakota.*" Bulletin Number 214. (Fargo: North Dakota State Agricultural College, 1926).

42. McWilliams, *Ill Fares*, 67.

43. Ottoson, *Land and People*, 53.

44. D. Jerome Tweton, and Daniel F. Rylance. *The Years of Despair: North Dakota in the Years of Depression* (Grand Forks: University of North Dakota Press, 1973), 3.

45. Michael P. Malone, Richard B. Rader, and William L. Lang, *Montana: A History of Two Centuries* (Seattle: University of Washington Press, 1991), 282–84.

46. Ibid.

47. Arthur R. Mangus, *Changing Aspects of Rural Relief* (Washington, DC: United States Government Printing Office, 1938), 6.

48. Tweton and Rylance, *Years of Despair*, 10–14.

49. Thomas Pressly and William Scofield, *Farm Real Estate Values in the United States by Counties, 1850–1959* (Seattle: University of Washington Press, 1965), 67.

50. Dewing, *Chadron*, 112.

51. Great Plains Committee, 61.

52. Nelson, *The Prairie,* 125–26.

53. Gordon M. Bakken, *Surviving the North Dakota Depression* (Pasedena: Wood and Jones, 1992).

54. Discussions with family members, especially during the March 2000 North Dakota visit.

Chapter Three

Dust, Grasshoppers, Thistles and Radical Protest

When asked to share their remembrances of the 1930s Northern Plains, those who lived there almost unanimously respond, "dust, grasshoppers, and thistles," usually in that order. Dust blew everywhere. Most of the land in the grain producing area virtually is rock free and light in texture, not stable in windy, dry conditions. Grain farmers accepted the conventional wisdom that the way to conserve moisture and ensure crops was deep plowing and summer-fallow. The latter, sometimes referred to as strip farming, left alternating fields cultivated, but without crops on alternate years. This process, designed to improve crop potential, provided a layer of dry soil to conserve subsoil moisture. Unfortunately, the Great Plains has the highest wind velocity in the world, averaging 10–12 miles per hour with a much higher potential, frequently reached in the dry 1930s.[1] Severe dust storms had occurred on the plains every decade since settlement, but none approached the magnitude of the 1930s.[2] Of the approximately four hundred million acres of tillable land in the entire Great Plains area it was estimated that about half were severely damaged and 10 percent were thought destroyed forever.[3]

Although the drought-induced dust storms ravaged the Northern Plains as much or more than those in the Southwest, most maps in recent publications do not even include the Northern Plains as part of the Dust Bowl. They usually only discuss the flight from the Southern Plains to California. For example, almost all college level history texts follow this pattern. Noted western historian Howard Lamar identified three Dust Bowl areas, two in the United States and one in Canada. Lamar indicated the one on the Southern Plains received more publicity, but was no more severe than that in the Northern Plains, especially in parts of North and South Dakota and Eastern Montana.[4] All government publications and local Northern Plains' histories that deal with the subject confirm Lamar.[5]

Dust provided a common denominator of the Northern Plains in the 1930s. "Uff da" muttered Norwegian Palmer Skaare When asked about the dust, Skaare indicated it was everywhere. "People hung blankets over windows, but it did little good," said Skaare, who lived near Williston. "They were dusty," said neighbor Selmer Gafkjen when asked to characterize the 1930s.[6] At times the dust was so thick that streetlights came on at noon. Cattle and sheep died from inhaling too much dust. Motor vehicles choked to a stop. Dust piled up so high on fences that they were no longer effective. It was claimed that people also died of "dust pneumonia" although medical experts denied its existence. When this writer was born April 11, 1934, in the middle of a North Dakota dust storm, Mother's attempt to clear away the dust before the midwife arrived failed completely.

Grasshoppers, which had accompanied drought conditions in the past, scourged the entire Great Plains in devastating waves during the hot, dry 1930s. From 1931 to 1939, with only a brief respite in 1934, the invasive insects prowled the plains.[7] They were everywhere, but the western Dakotas and northwestern Nebraska endured the heaviest concentrations. A 1933 grasshopper distribution map indicated that almost one-third of North Dakota endured "very heavy infestation" and another one-third "heavy infestation." The droughts of 1934 and 1936 brought more, heavily infesting almost all of North Dakota. At Killdeer, swarms completely darkened the sky; four-inch piles lay on the streets.[8] Crawford, Nebraska, resident Virlyn Norgard remembered slowing down for highway curves because the grasshoppers were so thick his vehicle might skid on them.[9]

Almost all green plant life in the path of the hoppers was devoured and stories of what else they consumed abound. They ate clothes off clotheslines. They ate softwood and even ate corks out of water jugs. "There were years when the grass never even got green. Those grasshoppers would eat it as fast as it would come up. One time I had a little tree that I had started and I thought I would be smart and put a little tub over it and they wouldn't bother it. They got in there and stripped it from the bottom up," said Dorothy Earl of Chadron, Nebraska.[10] Local governments spent heavily to control the infestation but it had little effect. A concoction of arsenic and molasses was designed to stop them and heavily deployed. In Cavalier County, North Dakota, 2,000 tons were spread in 1933. Nearby Walsh County spread 680 tons in 1935.[11] Not only did it fail to stop the hoppers, livestock and poultry often were victimized because the arsenic tended to filter into the water supply. Poultry that ate the poisoned grasshoppers often suffered the same fate as the hoppers. Noted journalist Ernie Pyle reported from Rapid City, July 30, 1936, "The Grasshopper opens and closes every conversation. He holds second place only to the drought itself . . . This is the third and worst year of the cycle."[12]

Resourceful farmers were forced to turn to a weed—the Canadian and Russian thistle, to feed famished animals. Both were brought in from Europe by immigrants and are noted for their incredible hardiness and tenacity. The Canadian thistle features a single, erect stem that grows up to five feet tall. Russian thistle, commonly called tumbleweed, grows as a round many stemmed plant that breaks off at maturity, spreading seed everywhere it tumbles. Its ubiquity made it the most utilized of the two. South Dakota governor Tom Berry remarked, "There's two crops out there that never fail—Russian thistles and kids." Many of the more thrifty and energetic farmers cut the thistles while they were still green and put them up for hay. Although thistles had the protein value of alfalfa, it adversely affected animals' digestive systems. "You didn't want to stand behind a cow that had been eating thistles," said Sam Bloom of Crosby, North Dakota.[13] Occasionally housewives also canned small thistles for greens.

Failure of crops, hay, and pasture forced the government to purchase starving cattle under the Livestock Purchase Program of the Agricultural Adjustment Act. Northwest North Dakota, southeastern Montana and north central South Dakota had the highest percentage of cattle purchased through 1934.[14] Veterinarians examined affected animals and those cattle deemed too weak to survive were destroyed. Chadron attorney Wally Crites remembered, "While I was working at Oral, South Dakota, at the gravel pit, I saw them drive in a herd of four hundred of the scrawniest, thinnest, most beat up cattle you ever saw. They just shot them all and dumped them in a big pit and poured gasoline on them and set them on fire."[15] In South Dakota the government purchased a total of 915,039 head, representing 42 percent of the states estimated cattle population. Many were processed at canneries set up for use by relief agencies. The federal government also purchased about 150,000 South Dakota sheep during the same period.[16] In Nebraska, the government bought 470,000 cattle and 438,000 hogs. Canneries were established to can meat for distribution to the needy. Government officials were not allowed to give the meat of condemned animals away, but many times they would look the other way as locals picked over the better carcasses. Of the 8.3 million cattle purchased by the government between June 4, 1934 and January 31, 1935, more than 20 percent were from the Dakotas.[17] In McIntosh County, North Dakota, one of the most active areas, 1,042 farmers sold 22,757 cattle for more than $300,000.[18] The government's policy of destroying livestock and crops to better equate the supply and demand balance did not set well with critics who were appalled that at the same time people were going hungry.

In spite of some conservative denial, severe hunger existed. Frank Miller, a student at Chadron Normal in 1933, said there were days when he did not have anything to eat. Miller remembers several co-eds fainted in class because they had gone without food. "There wasn't any money," he said. Chadron charged no tuition and had National Youth Administration (NYA) students handle most of the janitorial work at twenty-five cents an hour. In 1934, the NYA supported stipends to students chosen to assist professors. Miller's first teaching position at Pedro, South Dakota, paid fifty dollars a month in warrants that took him thirteen years to collect. Miller said they had pancakes for breakfast, bread and gravy for dinner and the same for supper.[19]

Some rural Plains residents relied on income from fur trapping and hunting wild game for food to scrape by. A common practice was to shoot wild rabbits and hang them in an unheated area during the winter months, making them available as needed. Rabbit skins sold for about ten cents apiece. Les Ferguson, who lived near Hot Springs, South Dakota, caught 150 to 200 skunks a year that averaged about one dollar a fur; about the same number of muskrats at fifty cents a fur; plus mink, beaver, bobcat, coyote and badger. By Depression standards prices for mink and beaver were attractive. Mink averaged twelve dollars a pelt and beaver averaged five dollars. "We paid our taxes and some insurance policies with fur money," said Ferguson.[20]

That the economic crash of 1929 would end soon and recovery would follow quite efficiently as held true in most other downturns evolved into only wishful thinking. Year by year conditions worsened. Crops, drought retarded in 1929 and 1930, faced disaster in 1931. Farmers were forced to cut Russian thistles for hay in both 1930 and 1931.[21] By May 1931, grasshoppers appeared throughout the northern region. They were followed by hot, dry weather marking the beginning of "bare-earth" farming. Mohall, North, Dakota, had received no rain for the year at mid-June.[22] Noonan, where rainfall had been less than ten inches five times in the previous fifty years, accrued only 7.8 inches in 1931.[23] Rapid City, South Dakota, accustomed to a mean of 17.34 inches received only 9.31. The woeful conditions for growing anything did not let up. A Meade County, South Dakota, farm wife wrote in 1933 that it was the fourth straight summer that she had to buy vegetables instead of raising them.[24]

Grasshoppers and summer heat waves drove farmers, who prided themselves on their independence, to seek relief. By July 1931, Senator Gerald Nye and Congressman Richard Sinclair visited western North Dakota to assess the need. A week later the Williston American Legion complained, nonetheless, that drought relief was "wholly inadequate."[25] Assistance from the federal government was limited because President Herbert Hoover believed that the federal government should only assist significant economic institutions and they in turn would maintain economic stability—the well-known "trickle down" theory. Independent agencies such as churches, service clubs, and the Red Cross should cooperate with local government to provide direct assistance to individual citizens during economic downturns. Private relief organizations, however, were not geared for the massive relief effort required, and state and local governments were almost as inadequate. The Red Cross, especially, tried to step into the breech, but accomplished little because of lack of funds. With an estimated annual income of two million dollars plus interest income of one million, it proved a straw in the wind.[26] Hoover asked the Red Cross to take charge of relief in 1931 and offered $25 million in federal aid, which was refused because the Red Cross believed unemployment was not an "Act of God."[27] By May 1932, the North Dakota Red Cross, inundated with demands on its limited resources, closed its offices there. Bloom, a former member of the North Dakota legislature, remembered the Red Cross as a "hopeless outfit" in his state in the 1930s.[28] Rural areas began to meet the need for unemployment relief only when federal funds became available. Between July 1933 and June 1935, South Dakota claimed to lead all states in regard to percentage of total population on relief.[29]

By early July 1932, drought and grasshoppers had take such a toll on the spring wheat crop that the *Williston Herald* reported "a below average yield is sure for the '32 crop." Farmers with wheat to sell were forced to accept record low prices of thirty-nine cents a bushel. By August, farmers in the Williston area were organizing to declare a strike. A reported five hundred farmers signed the strike agreement under the auspices of the North Dakota Farm Holiday Association (NDFHA). Its main purpose was to create public opinion against foreclosure at a time when poor prices for farm commodities had rendered the farmers unable to pay their interest, their taxes, or any other debts, and when farmers all over the state were on relief.

Minnesota born Populist Usher Burdick, a Williston lawyer and rancher, headed the NDFHA. A massive man who had played end for the University of Minnesota Golden Gophers, Burdick would serve ten terms in the United States House of Representatives from 1935–1958. Burdick was listed as a Republican but voted for the Democrats almost as often as against. Burdick's son Quentin became a Democrat and represented North Dakota in the United States Senate for thirty- two years (1960–1992). The NDFHA lead a marketing strike from September 20,1932, until November 17, 1932. The election of NPL-backed William Langer as governor working with a more liberal legislature and Democrat Franklin Roosevelt, who had promised farmers a New Deal, and delivered, ended the need for the NDFHA.[30]

Rapidly escalating unrest prompted the *Chicago Tribune* to send reporter Arthur Henning to investigate. He confirmed that western North Dakota was in as state of political ferment, which prompted a biting attack by the conservative *Tribune.* In an early September 1932 editorial "A Year's Living for a Month's Work" the *Tribune* blamed Dakotans for much of their difficulty.

"They are blaming everyone and everything except themselves, an omission which is startling in view of their responsibility for much of the trouble in which they now find themselves." The *Tribune* suggested North Dakotans were overly reliant on wheat instead of diversifying with other crops and more livestock. "A state which regards laziness as a virtue and political quackery as statesmanship is now considering an experiment in thievery," the *Tribune* concluded.[31]

Hard-working North Dakotans were outraged by the *Tribune's* canard. Newspaper editorials throughout the state charged the *Tribune* with slander. Angry farmers sent a flood of letters to the editor detailing the amount of work involved in maintaining a successful wheat farm. The *Noonan Miner* surmised the *Tribune* opposed direct government assistance, so camouflaged it with the laziness charge, refusing to recognize the roots of the problem.[32]

The Hoover administration finally offered loans for feed and seed, but the terms were demanding. The government wanted payment within a year and farmers had to pay back at least twenty-five percent before using the crop for other purposes. Hoover's main relief agency, the Reconstruction Finance Corporation, increasingly granted loans to local governments for work relief projects. These loans evolved into a thinly disguised form of direct relief.[33]

Hard times triggered an outbreak of suicides, murders, robberies, and protest. Apparently propelled by the stress of failure, the suicide rate significantly increased on the Great Plains as it did throughout the nation.[34] The 1931 national suicide rate of 20,160 was the highest since 1912. Great Plains' newspapers reported numerous suicides from 1932–1936 with 1932 the apparent leader. The 1932 list for South Dakota included a Notre Dame graduate, 34, found dead at his ranch near Deadwood; and a murder-suicide in Rapid City. North Dakota instances included a Williston resident, two area farmers and a Sioux County farmer who hung himself in his barn. A Grafton man unsuccessfully twice tried to hang himself in one day. In 1934, a Noonan area farmer blew himself up with dynamite. In September George Keup, Columbus mayor and former vice president of the closed Farmers State Bank, was shot to death in his office by a farmer disgruntled over a past mortgage foreclosure.[35]

Ordinarily law-abiding, now desperate farmers violently picketed and demonstrated through their radical Farm Holiday Association. Highways were blocked and commodities, especially milk, were destroyed. Neighboring farmers united to limit bids when bank foreclosures forced auctions of failed farm's livestock and equipment. These "penny auctions" became common in the Midwest. In October 1932, Theresa Von Bonn, a widow with several children, who farmed near Elgin, Nebraska, was foreclosed. No one was allowed to bid over five cents for her property. The net proceeds of $5.35

were returned to the widow. The Victor Nielson farm near Westby, North Dakota, yielded $2.44 for six horses, twenty-three cattle, and a line of machinery in September 1933.[36] Many sheriffs sympathized and went hunting or fishing or engaged in other activities to avoid the auctions.

Eugene Lux remembers attending what he called a "Sears and Roebuck" auction at Grand Island with his activist father Harry. Eugene said, "Everybody would ring the general ring on the telephone to alert the neighbors." The youthful Lux was most impressed by tables heaped with summer sausage and homemade potato salad.[37] Harry Lux, state coordinator of the Farm Holiday Association, was arrested and jailed for his role in a penny auction near Wilbur, Nebraska. Eugene remembers visiting the Lincoln jail and was impressed by the casual treatment accorded his father that was perhaps generated by the event's extensive publicity.

Across the nation a number of glamorized desperadoes such as Bonnie Parker and Clyde Barrow, Charles "Pretty Boy" Floyd, John Dillinger, Kate "Ma" Barker and sons, and George "Machine Gun" Kelly emerged. All were either captured or killed in the early 1930s.[38] Highlighted by the celebrated Lindbergh abduction, one person was kidnapped every twenty-four hours and armed guards protected many homes of the wealthy. The penchant for lawlessness, perhaps spurred by much publicized examples, reached the Northern Plains as well. Banks at Whitewood and Flandreau in South Dakota were robbed in September 1932. In November five men robbed the Beresford bank. In response South Dakota organized a force of about two thousand "Minute Men" to "suppress banditry and other illegal acts."[39] North Dakota announced similar plans.

Divide County in Northwestern North Dakota was selected by officials as typical of an area which had suffered unfavorable crop years since 1929 and where an exceptionally large proportion of farmers was receiving public assistance in 1934. A total of 544 feed and seed loans had been made for every 100 farms in the county by late 1934, creating individual indebtedness of $542 for every farmer. Each farm in Divide County added $265 more in 1934. Gross receipts per farm in 1934 for each farm in Divide County averaged less that $800 and that included the unprecedented liquidation of livestock. During the period 1928–34 more than 85 percent of the land in Divide County was delinquent at some time.[40] North Dakota led the nation in delinquent loans.[41] Decades and even generations of hard work resulted in abysmal failure and a flurry of bankruptcies. The average per capita income in North Dakota fell to $185, less than half the national average. In 1934, eighty-six of every thousand farms in North Dakota suffered foreclosure.[42] By spring 1934, one in every three North Dakotans received FERA funds and throughout the year the state had a higher percentage of its population on relief than any other state.[43] Increasingly, taxes and mortgages went unpaid.

Contrary to their public perception as cold-blooded oppressors, bankers strove to help their farm clients stay afloat in large part because demise of the farm economy also spelled disaster for banks. Journalist Eric Severeid discussed his banker father's concern in Velva, North Dakota, as his bank finally went broke and the family moved to Minneapolis. Warren Christopher, a future Secretary of State, spent his early childhood (1925–1939) in Scranton, North Dakota, where his father headed the local bank. Christopher recalled, "Behind the scenes, Dad fiercely resisted foreclosing on any of the bank's farm mortgages, but he could only do so much." Christopher frequently rode along with his father to deliver the bad news. "The human scenes I witnessed in the flat, dry North Dakota plains while at my father's side may account more than anything else for the tilt of my social and political concerns in the direction of the unfortunate," said the future Secretary of State. Christopher praised his mother for generously giving food to the many hoboes who knocked at her door and her refusal to accept work in exchange.[44] Because of his father's failing health the Christophers moved to Hollywood, California, in 1939.

Preliminary to the 1932 election North Dakota farmers attempted to stop the marketing of wheat in Western North Dakota. The Nonpartisan League, Farmer's Union, and Farm Holiday Association coalesced in the effort. L. C. Miller, publisher of the *Bowbells Tribune,* supported the strike and was attacked as Communist by Leo Eugene Mahoney in his competing *Columbus Reporter.* Mahoney wrote the FHA originally chose leaders he deemed "staunch and able" but the organization had become too radical.[45] Picketing and strike actions in Burke County did not last long and never involved the majority of FHA members.[46]

In retrospect the Communist threat seems too magnified because it never got far. But it created great concern in the 1920s and 1930s as witnessed by the fervent government and media opposition it engendered. Legal in the United States until after World War II the Communist movement had developed a strong base among the intellectual and laboring class in large urban areas like New York, Detroit, Cleveland, Seattle and San Francisco. Membership in the United States, estimated at only 18,000 in the 1920s, ballooned to around 60,000 in the 1930s, however, that still constituted only a minute fraction of the total population. Communist visibility and influence far outweighed their popularity at the ballot box, mainly because they received scant voter support from the ordinary farmer and laborer.[47]

By 1928, Stalinist Communists had decided they had reached the "third period," meaning capitalism had destabilized. Stalin, in order to undercut the more moderate Trotsky, ordered Communist parties throughout the world to adopt ultra-revolutionary tactics. As early as 1930, Communist Party USA

(CPUSA) judged "agrarian petty bourgeoisie" (small farmers) would be discontented enough to accept Communism. Before the New Deal there was no national old-age pension system, no federal unemployment compensation, no aid to dependent children, no national minimum wage, and more.

The cornerstone of the Party's agrarian strategy was the plausible assumption that the farm crisis was permanent and would worsen.[48] Communists focused on organizing discontented farmers by supporting militant protest organizations and attempting to recruit party members. Much CPUSA activity focused on the distressed Upper Midwest, especially liberal, Scandinavian western North Dakota. Because they offered a protest vehicle and hopes for some economic relief, they attracted some support. Mostly ideologically and politically conservative, Dakotans rejected CPUSA doctrine promoting overthrow of the government, however. Communist support faded when the various favorable New Deal programs stole their thunder.[49] None of the Communist candidates in North Dakota attracted significant voter support.

Among the usually conservative established citizens of the area deep hostility toward Communism was almost universal. A man who had formerly lived in Russia moved to Burke County and described Russia as "the hellhole of the Universe." After the 1932 election the editor of the *Noonan Miner* wrote, "We just wish that the 62 half-witted 'Shot-Gun' Socialists in Burke County, commonly known as communists, had the desire, patience and ability to sit down for about 30 minutes and listen to this strictly unbiased first hand information coming directly from Russia."[50] Roosevelt's New Deal allotment programs soon stilled any momentum the Communists may have had. Even UFL leaders who vigorously opposed the new programs signed up for them.[51]

Ella Reeves Bloor, "Mother Bloor," headed the CPUSA effort to organize the Upper Midwest. Born into privilege during the American Civil War at Staten Island, New York, Bloor was raised in New Jersey as a friend and neighbor of poet Walt Whitman. Married at nineteen, Bloor became active in reform movements supporting prohibition and women's rights. She joined the Socialist Party of America in 1902 and became a trade union organizer and also did investigative reporting in the Chicago meat packing plants for leading social protest author Upton Sinclair. Her work was instrumental in the publication of Sinclair's influential muckraking novel, *The Jungle*. Bloor joined the Communist Party in 1919 and moved to the Soviet Union for a while with fellow American Earl Browder, returning to the United States as a CPUSA leader.[52] Although in her late sixties by the 1930s, Bloor frequently was called the "dowager fertility goddess" for her frolicsome ways.

Bloor's son, Harold Ware, provided agricultural expertise for the organization. After earning a degree in agriculture from Penn State Ware worked as a harvest hand in the Dakotas and the Great Plains. When famine struck Russia in 1922, Ware recruited nine young North Dakota farmers to help. He also took twenty carloads of modern American farm machinery, a supply of Canadian rye seed, two passenger cars, tents and other equipment. His work on four different state farms earned a commendation from Lenin in *Pravda.* In 1931, Ware returned to Washington, D.C., with $25,000 United States dollars to promote Communism in American agriculture.[53] He penetrated the non-Communist Farmers' Holiday Association, but, although FHA leaders gladly accepted Communist assistance, they remained unwilling to adopt its radical political ideology.

In 1925, Ware had volunteered as a dollar a year consultant for the Department of Agriculture in the Coolidge administration and maintained that status until 1932. There he furnished statistics on Soviet farm experiments. Wholesome, reassuring, and dedicated, Ware organized an underground Communist group in the Agricultural Adjustment Administration in 1933 known as the Ware group.[54] Members included Lee Pressman, Alger Hiss, Nathan Witt, and John Abt.[55] Whittaker Chambers, who later gained fame as an anti-Communist was associated closely, but was not a member of the Ware group.[56] Wealthy, Harvard educated Lem Harris worked at one of Ware's Soviet state farms and became a life-long convert to Communism, serving as an effective front man for organizational activities in the United States.[57] Ware's penchant for speeding proved fatal when he crashed his car into a coal truck in Pennsylvania in August 1935.

After devastating drought struck western North Dakota in 1930, Communists launched a vigorous campaign. Headquartered at Minot, Bloor and her associates concentrated on socialist-oriented wheat farming Scandinavians in Northwest North Dakota. In mid-September, while campaigning for the Communist ticket at Bowbells, the Burke County seat, Bloor said, "There is no independent working class; slaves is what you are." Atypically, local newspaper editor L. C. Miller thought she made a good impression.[58]

Bloor and her associates stayed active in 1931. Diverse activities included organizational meetings, making speeches, sponsoring dances and even presiding over funerals. L. C. Miller reported Mother Bloor held several meetings at the Sons of Norway hall at Columbus in May. Communist sponsored dances for young people were quite popular. "We went to the dances for fun, but had no interest in the Communist line," said Sam Bloom. Palmer Skaare, who lived near Williston in the 1930s, remembered Mother Bloor and Communist organizational efforts, but indicated they "never developed anything" in his area.[59] Bloor and her Communist associate, George Maki, made several trips to Frederick, South Dakota, during the fall of 1931 where they promoted a successful drought relief caravan led by UFL leaders. Trucks hauled coal from a mine near Van Hook, North Dakota, to the Frederick area, which in turn sent wheat to North Dakota. The effort gained favorable publicity for the protestors, but little direct support from the more livestock oriented South Dakotans.[60] Prescient observers considered cattleman and Radical a contradiction in terms.

Capitalism faltered at its lowest ebb in 1932 with massive unemployment and a general feeling of economic paralysis, the country appeared ready to consider a drastic political change. Communists launched a determined effort to elect their candidates on the drought stricken Great Plains that included a third party run by Bloor for United States Senator for North Dakota. Great Plains' communities usually viewed Communists with open hostility, as was the case around the nation. When Bloor spoke at Watford City in late September, hostile pickets set up at the edge of town.[61] In June 1932, the mayor of Flaxton refused to allow a Communist Youth Group use of public buildings and also denied a permit to speak. They came anyway and went to private vacant lots where they were charged by national guardsmen and ordered to leave. L. C. Miller complained bitterly about Flaxton's violation of constitutional rights, concluding, "To the city of Flaxton we say: By thy deeds thou shalt be known."[62]

Involved in an acrimonious battle with Mahoney to retain the all-important designation as the official Burke county newspaper, Miller wrote a long column indicating he was not a Communist, but he was a supporter of the United States Constitution.[63] When his paper lost official status in November, Miller blamed the "city vote" of Columbus for the defeat. By January 1937, Miller left Bowbells, indicating he needed more income.[64]

Communist candidates, unable to gain popular support, suffered the same fate at the ballot box as Miller. The Kjorstad family of neighboring Williams county was among the most active in Communist politics. John Kjorstad was the unsuccessful Communist candidate for sheriff in 1932. His daughter, Effie, ran for Congress in 1934 and state senate in 1936 but received only a handful of votes.[65] In Wyoming, Communist Party members ran for governor, congress, and secretary of state in 1932 and averaged only between 150 and 170 votes. In 1936, only 91 Wyoming voters supported Earl Browder, the Communist candidate for president.[66]

Mother Bloor, Browder's close friend, was slowed by her arrest and conviction for fomenting a riot in Loup City, Nebraska, in 1934. Nebraska farmers had voiced their dissatisfaction in 1932 by organizing Committees of Action throughout the state, but strong opposition from business and religious leaders stymied them after an estimated three to four thousand demonstrated for legislative relief at Lincoln in February 1933.[67] In June 1934, Loup City's Sherman County had just been designated as one of the worst drought areas in the region. Bloor moved to nearby Grand Island to coordinate a demonstration against unfair labor practices at a chicken packing plant, Loup City's largest employer. Harry Lux, helped organize the protest.[68]

The confrontation developed when a twenty-year old woman took a job at the packing plant, apparently to incite dissatisfaction among the workers over low wages and harsh working conditions. According to Lux's son Eugene, who was with his father at Loup City, the dispute involved management's insistence that chickens that died in their crates while awaiting slaughter had to be picked at the same pay rate. Because the feathers had set they were much more difficult to pick.[69] Wednesday morning a group of men went to the plant and demanded admission but were turned away by law enforcement officers. The next day a much larger group, many of whom were outsiders, gathered in the county courtyard making inflammatory speeches and demanding an audience with packing plant management. A committee of twenty-five was allowed to confer with the plant manager. Not satisfied with the meeting the protestors started a vicious, ten-minute riot using large cakes of soap in long socks as their chief weapon. Authorities quickly suppressed the violence and jailed the leaders. "Red blooded citizens in Sherman County displayed their loyalty to the Stars and Stripes last Thursday when they drove Red invaders who came here looking for trouble, out of Loup City," said the local newspaper editor.[70]

Bloor and several of her associates, including several African Americans from Grand Island, were arrested for rioting. She received the maximum sentence of a $100.00 fine and ninety days in jail. When the Loup City defendants appealed, District Judge Bruno Hostetler upheld the conviction. Hostetler had received a telegram signed "Communist Party of Bismarck" demanding dismissal of all charges. His reply carried nation wide, said, "Your cowardly and unsigned threatening telegram received. You don't dare sign your names. I will not be deterred from the right performance of my duty as judge by all the reds from Russia to Hell."[71]

Recognizing their now severely limited potential on the Great Plains, many among the "radical" element decided to move to seek opportunities on the more liberal West Coast. Harry Lux, a Trotskyite, quit the Communist Party in 1935 in disagreement over radical Stalinist doctrine. A plasterer by trade, but broke and unemployed, Lux obtained a $25 loan and left Nebraska alone for Seattle with only his tool bag. There he worked as a plasterer and took an active role in Socialist Workers Party. The family joined him in 1942. After World War II Eugene Lux joined his father in the construction business and was elected to the state legislature in 1973, serving thirteen years in the House of Representatives.[72] The King County Democratic Party honored Lux with a Lifetime Achievement Award in 2005. Nominators described Lux as a living legend, a role model and a true liberal Democrat.

Historian William Pratt, a leading authority on radicalism on the Northern Great Plains, said, "Numerous other radicals were among the North Dakota 'Okies' who ended up on the West Coast." Pratt also found that many Communists moved west from the Frederick, South Dakota, area.[73] Most went to Washington. Burke County UFL leader James Pearson moved there in late 1934. Ivar and Sophia Husa of Belden moved to Washington in 1936, but were motivated more by the failure of their wheat farm than by political concerns. They were liberal Finns who had first immigrated to Minnesota, then homesteaded in North Dakota where they met. The Husas were associated with the UFL and Mother Bloor had presided over their grandmother's funeral in 1931. In Washington they continued their liberal, though hardly radical, orientation.[74]

Charles "Red Flag" Taylor, long time editor of the neighboring Plentywood, Montana, *Producers News*, also fled to Washington. Taylor, also a Trotskyite, was purged from the Communist Party in 1935 when an estimated one-third of the Party members dropped out or were dismissed because of the Stalin-versus-Trotsky issue.[75] Taylor, a big fellow and a good speaker, was descended from old American stock. His grandfather was an abolitionist and follower of Horace Greeley. His father was active in the Farmer's Alliance in Minnesota. Taylor was born in Wisconsin in 1884 and grew up with a family of twelve in a log cabin in central Minnesota. While gaining experience as a newspaper editor, Taylor studied law by correspondence and won election as a county judge, but left for Wyoming for six years because of tuberculosis. In 1918, Taylor joined the Nonpartisan League which sent him to Plentywood to launch the *Producers News*.[76]

Plentywood, a county-seat town of about one thousand, located next to Divide County, North Dakota, had been settled by a large percentage of Danes and Norwegians and tended to nonconformity from its beginning. Spring wheat provided a good economic base until six straight years of bad crops after 1915 encouraged rural discontent. In the 1920s, Plentywood became widely known as the only American community actually governed by practicing "Reds." With Communist support the *Producers News* openly supported and promoted bolshevism.[77]

Between 1922 and 1928, the Communist Party controlled the major offices in Sheridan County. Plentywood's Farmer-Labor temple served as Communist Party headquarters, locally and regionally. Communist summer camp meetings were held in the area with a strong direction towards recruiting youths. Lillian Husa Feist recalls hearing Taylor at Plentywood and was impressed with the powerful performance.[78] Communist candidates dominated the 1932 Sheridan county election with 575 voting the straight Communist ticket. Following Roosevelt's election the Party declined rapidly after that high water mark.[79]

Established community leaders, never supportive, mounted vigorous opposition to Communists. Both the schools and the strong Lutheran and Catholic churches increased an anti Communist drive.[80] Tension mounted when early in 1933 Young Communists raided the Red Cross Office and seized a supply of winter clothing. Although charismatic, Taylor's happy go lucky ways and almost complete lack of business sense began to catch up with him. With his newspaper faltering and opposition mounting, Taylor had reached the brink of disaster but held on. He attributed rural support for his temporary survival. "They probably would have mobbed me, but they were afraid of the country. We had a lot of young, pretty husky guys that would do things out there. They were rough," said Taylor.[81]

Apparently upset with Stalinist Communism, Taylor left the Party in June 1935, perhaps not voluntarily. The new leaders established a paramilitary young Communist training center in the Farmer-Labor Temple that failed to flourish. On September 12, 1936, Taylor's house burned. Shortly after that Mother Bloor deposed Taylor as editor of the *Producers News*. By March 1937, the *Producers News* collapsed completely.[82] Taylor moved to Seattle where he avoided active participation in radical politics and worked as a proofreader for the *Seattle Post Intelligencer* until his retirement in 1962. Feist knew Taylor in Seattle, too, and thought his memory and his energy level had declined severely.

Although 1936 provided the most trying economic disaster in the history of the Northern Great Plains, the CPUSA, always a tiny, but vocal, minority with scant local support had virtually disappeared from the area. In large part it happened because of the Roosevelt administration's effective direct intervention, but it also collapsed from internal Party strife. Franklin Roosevelt's New Deal agricultural programs effectively stole the Communist's thunder. They had assumed that the farm crisis was permanent and bound to worsen. In 1932 there was no national old-age pension system, no federal unemployment compensation, no aid to dependent children, no farm subsidy, no national minimum wage law, and so on. Some Great Plains farmers sympathized with Communist economic doctrine, which seemed to offer a possible alternative to the dismal results of capitalism, but very few were swayed by Communist radical political dogma.[83] Arthur Schlesinger, Jr. said," The radical politicians, from Floyd Olson and the La Follettes to Sinclair and La Guardia, abhorred the Communists as troublemakers and doctrinaires. The radical ideologists had an equal abhorrence for Communist ideas."[84]

Several Pacific Northwest historians have suggested that Communists who moved there from the Great Plains increased radical agitation. Migrants may have continued their loyalty to liberal politics, but most already had abandoned Communism. By the time they arrived, moreover, the groundswell for

Communism had been stilled by Roosevelt's flood of liberal New Deal programs.

NOTES

1. Author's experience.
2. James C. Malin, *The Grasslands of North America: Prolegomena to Its History* (Lawrence, KS: Private Printing, 1947), passim.
3. John Gunther, *Inside USA* (New York: Harpers, 1947), 239.
4. Howard K. Lamar, "Comparing Depressions: The Great Plains and Canadian Prairie Experiences, 1929–1941," in *Experiences in a Promised Land: Essays on Pacific Northwest History*, ed. Thomas G. Edwards and Carlos A. Schwantes (Seattle: University of Washington Press, 1986), 175–206.
5. Examples: Great Plains Committee; Tweton and Rylance, *The Years of Despair*, 3–15; Francis Cronin and Edward Beers, *Areas of Intense Drought Distress, 1930–1936,* WPA Research Bulletin. Series 5, Number 1. (Washington, DC: United States Government Printing Office, 1937); R. S. Kifer and H. L. Stewart, *Farming Hazards in the Drought Area* (Washington, DC: United States Government Printing Office, 1938).
6. Palmer Skaare and Selmer Gafkjen, interviews, March 2000; Uff da, also spelled uuf da, is a popular Norwegian expression in the Dakotas and Minnesota that can be translated to "good grief."
7. J. A. Munro. "Grasshopper Outbreaks in North Dakota, 1808–1948," *North Dakota History* 16 (July 1949): 143–64.
8. D. Jerome Tweton and Daniel F. Rylance, *The Years of Despair: North Dakota in the Depression* (Grand Forks: University of North Dakota Press), 8.
9. Virlyn Norgard, conversation with author, January 2001.
10. Rolland Dewing, "The Roaring Twenties and the Dirty Thirties," in *Chadron-Chadron Centennial History*, ed. Rolland Dewing (Freeman, SD: Pine Hill Press, 1985), 111–12; Theodore Saloutos, "The New Deal and Farm Policy in the Great Plains," *Agricultural History* 43 (July 1969): 345–55.
11. Tweton and Rylance, *The Years of Despair*, 8.
12. David Nichols, ed., *Ernie's America: The Best of Ernie Pyle's 1930's Travel Dispatches* (New York: Random House, 1989), 117–18.
13. Sam Bloom, interview, March 2000.
14. R. S. Kifer and H. L. Stewart, *Farming Hazards in the Drought Area*, (Washington: U. S. Government Printing Office), 2.
15. Dewing, "Roaring Twenties," 112.
16. Herbert S. Schell, *History of South Dakota* (Lincoln: University of Nebraska Press, 1968), 289.
17. Theodore Saloutos, "The New Deal and Farm Policy in the Great Plains, *Agricultural History* 43 (July 1969): 345–55.

18. Gordon L. Iseminger, "The McIntosh County German-Russians: The First Fifty Years," *North Dakota History* 51 (Summer 1981): 8–14.

19. Con Marshall, "Chadron State College Grad Remembers When Edna Work Hall Was Being Built, " *Chadron Record* 24 September 2003; Con Marshall, *Continuing to Thrive after 75 Years—The story of Chadron State College* (Chadron, NE: Chadron State Foundation, 1986), 119–37.

20. Les Ferguson, *Smellin Like a Skunk,* (Hot Springs, SD: Private Printing, Undated—about 2001), 9–10; In the late 1920s Vern Lineback started his cattle operation in Nebraska's Sandhills with money from trapping skunks, badgers, and muskrats.

21. Paula Nelson, *The Prairie Winnows Out Its Own: The West River Country of South Dakota In the Years of the Depression* (Iowa City: University of Iowa Press), 119.

22. *Williston Herald,* June 18, 1931.

23. *Noonan Miner*, January 7, 1932.

24. Dorothy Schwieder, "South Dakota Farm Women and the Great Depression," *Journal of the West* 24 (October 1985): 10.

25. *Williston Herald,* August 6, 1931.

26. Foster Rhea Dulles, *The American Red Cross, a History* (New York: Harper, 1950), 277.

27. Ibid., 279.

28. Sam Bloom, interview, March 2000.

29. Schwieder, "South Dakota," 8.

30. D. Jerome Tweton, "The Politics of Chaos: North Dakota in the 1930s," *Journal of the West* (Fall 2002): 30–35.

31. *Williston Herald,* September 6, 1932.

32. *Noonan Miner,* October 6, 1932, and almost all other North Dakota newspapers.

33. Nelson, *The Prairie,* 135–138; Jeff Singleton. *The American Dole: Unemployment Relief and the Welfare State in the Great Depression* (Westport, CT: Greenwood, 2000).

34. Caroline Bird, *The Invisible Scar: The Great Depression and What It Did to American Life, From Then Until Now,* Tenth Printing (New York: David McKay Company, 1975), 50–51; Iseminger, "The McIntosh County," 8–14.

35. *Noonan Miner,* September 8, 1932.

36. *Noonan Miner,* September 13, 1933; Erling A. Erickson, "A North Dakota Farm Auction in the Great Depression," *North Dakota Quarterly* 39 (Winter 1971): 37–49; Maurice C. Latta, "The Economic Effects of Drought and Depression upon Custer County, 1929–1942," *Nebraska History* 33 (December 1952): 220–36; John L. Shover, "The Penny Auction Rebellion," *The American West* 2 (Fall 1965): 64–72.

37. Eugene Debs Lux, telephone interview, April 7, 2005.

38. Susan Winslow, *Brother Can You Spare a Dime? America from the Wall Street Crash to Pearl Harbor* (New York: Paddington Press), 63–83.

39. *Rapid City Journal,* September 24, 1932.

40. R. S. Kifer and H. L. Stewart, *Farming Hazards,* 35.

41. Tweton, "The Politics of Chaos," 30–35.

42. John F. Bauman and Thomas H. Coode, *In the Eye of the Great Depression: New Deal Reporters and the agony of the American People* (DeKalb: Northern Illinois University Press, 1988), 118.

43. Tweton and Rylance, "*Years of Despair*," 7.

44. Warren Christopher *Chances of a Lifetime* (New York: Scribner, 2001), 11–12; Eric Severoid, *Not So Wild a Dream* (New York: Antheneum, 1976).

45. Larry Remele, "The North Dakota Farm Strike of 1932," *North Dakota History* 41 (Fall 1974): 215.

46. Ibid., 216.

47. Bird, *The Invisible Scar,* 140–146; Irving Bernstein, *The Lean Years: A History of the American Worker, 1920–1933* (Baltimore: Penquin Books, 1966), 426–36.

48. John L. Shover, "The Communist Party and the Midwest Farm Crisis of 1933," *Journal of American History* 51 (September 1964): 261.

49. William C. Pratt, "Radicals, Farmers, and Historians: Some Recent Scholarship about Agrarian Radicalism in the Upper-Midwest," *North Dakota History* 52 (Fall 1985): 12–25.

50. *Noonan Miner,* November 12, 1933.

51. Pratt, "Radicals," 139.

52. Ella Reeve Bloor, *We Are Many* (New York: International Publishers, 1940), 266–67.

53. Sam Tanenhaus, *Whittaker Chambers* (New York: Random House), 91–205.

54. Arthur Schlesinger, *The Coming of the New Deal* Second Edition (Boston: Houghton Mifflin, 1958), 52–53.

55. Whittaker Chambers, *Witness* (Washington, D.C.: Regenery Publishing, 1952), 332–38.

56. Ibid. Chambers describes the leading members, 344–46.

57. Shover, "The Communist Party," 250–261

58. *Bowbells Tribune,* September 12, 1930.

59. Palmer Skaare, interview, March 2000.

60. Allan Mathews, "Agrarian Radicals: The United Farmers League of South Dakota," *South Dakota History* 3 (Fall 1973): 408–421.

61. Larry Remele, "The North Dakota Farm Strike of 1932," *North Dakota History* 41 (Fall 1974): 5–18.

62. *Bowbells Tribune,* June 10, 1932.

63. *Bowbells Tribune,* September 28, 1932

64. *Bowbells Tribune,* January 1, 1937.

65. William C. Pratt, "Rethinking the Farm Revolt of the 1930s," *Great Plains Quarterly* 8 (Summer 1988): 134; see also William C. Pratt, "Rural Radicalism on the Northern Plains, 1912–1950," *Montana* (Winter 2004): 69–74.

66. T. A. Larsen, "The New Deal in Wyoming," *Pacific Historical Review* 38 (August 1969): 266.

67. Pratt, "Rethinking," 137.

68. William D. Rawley. "The Loup City Riot of 1934: Main Street vs. the 'Far Out' Left," *Nebraska History* 47 (September 1966): 295–327.

69. Eugene Debs Lux, telephone interview, April 5, 2005. Lux remembers Bloor, Ware, and Harris stayed at the family home in Lincoln at one time. The wealthy Harris agreeably slept on the floor.

70. *Loup City Times,* June 22, 1934; see also *Grand Island Independent,* June 28, 1934.

71. Alice B. Howell, "B. O. Hostetler, District Judge," *Buffalo Tales,* Volume 6, Number 7, Buffalo County Nebraska Historical Society (July/August 1983).

72. Eugen Debs Lux, interview, April 7, 2005.

73. Pratt, "Rethinking," 139.

74. Husa family, interview, February 2004.

75. Pratt, "Rethinking," 139.

76. Charles Vindex, "Radical Rule in Montana," *Montana* 18 (Winter 1968): 2–18.

77. Ibid.

78. Lillian Husa Feist, interview, February 2004.

79. Vindex, "Radical Rule," 16–18.

80. Gerald Zahavi, " 'Who's Going to Dance with Somebody Who Calls You a Mainstreeter?': Communism, Culture and Community in Sheridan County Montana, 1918–1934," *Great Plains Quarterly* 16 (Fall 1996): 151–86.

81. Zahavi, "Who's Going to Dance," 255.

82. Vindex, "Radical Rule," 17–18.

83. Shover, "Communist Party," 261–62.

84. Arthur Schlesinger, Jr., *The Politics of Upheaval* (Boston: Houghton Mifflin, 1960), 162.

Chapter Four

The New Deal Responds

Rampant agricultural unrest resonated with newly elected Franklin Roosevelt and the heavily Democrat Congress. Many consider the flurry of liberal legislation during Roosevelt's first months in office to assist and regulate farm production as among the most effective of his sweeping New Deal program designed to provide relief, recovery and reform. No other economic group received as much help as the farmers. By leading a strong political turn to the left, Roosevelt essentially disarmed Communist aspirations in rural America and, at least temporarily, greatly expanded the political base of the Democratic Party. Agencies established in 1933 to alleviate the farm problem included: The Agricultural Adjustment Administration (AAA), designed to regulate farm production; The Commodity Credit Corporation (CCC), to support the Department of Agriculture; The Farm Credit Administration (FCA), to make long-term and short-term credit available to farmers; The Tennessee Valley Authority (TVA), to help develop the resources of the Tennessee Valley. Other more general programs that also directly assisted the farm community included: The Civilian Conservation Corps (CCC), to help unemployed young men obtain work; The Federal Emergency Relief Administration (FERA), to cooperate with the states to relieve hardships caused by unemployment and drought; The Public Works Administration (PWA), to increase employment and aid the economy through the construction of useful public works. Many more programs would follow the 1933 rush, but the new economic role of big federal government, willing to directly intervene to assist those in need, had been established firmly.[1]

In 1935, the federal government implemented the Works Progress Administration (WPA) which effectively took control of local work relief projects from local governments. They, especially in the Northern Plains, had demonstrated both an inability and an unwillingness to provide required matching funds for projects funded by the PWA. Regrettably, the WPA was designed more for unemployed laborers than property owning farmers, offering work for only about one-third in need.[2] The WPA also closed many rural projects in 1935, succumbing to demands from large farmers who wanted inexpensive labor. One report estimated only 11 percent of those affected by the shutdowns found harvest work.[3]

FDR had acquired an extensive background in forestry, both as a state senator and governor of New York and at his extensive Hyde Park property. Although certainly not the first to propose it, Roosevelt viewed tree planting on the Great Plains as a long-term solution for wind erosion. The many already established tree plantations had a demonstrated ability to modify the wind, protecting livestock and buildings and supplying habitat for wildlife. It was long understood that forestry could not change the climate utterly, but it had the potential to modify it. Roosevelt also envisioned the federal government could use massive tree planting as an employment relief project as well. Such a project also would dramatize institutional response to the drought problem.

Even though there were far more Democrats than usual among state-elected officials on the Northern Plains, the federal government encountered the ever-continuing difficulty of a readiness to accept federal support on the local level but either the inability or lack of conviction to provide equitable matching funds. In most cases matching funds would require politically ruinous new taxes. Democrat Tom Berry, a west-river rancher, was elected governor of South Dakota in 1932 on a pledge to balance the state's budget. Berry proposed a meager $8,033,000 for the biennium, $2,152,000 below the previous budget and his legislature trimmed $450,000 more.[4] South Dakota's congressional delegation, led by popular progressive Republican senator Peter Norbeck and newly elected Catholic Democrat senator William Bulow, helped funnel an impressive $24,432,688 in federal relief grants to South Dakota by March 1, 1935, even though their state failed to contribute a dollar. FERA Director Harry Hopkins wrote Berry warning that South Dakota must raise some matching funds or forfeit control of federal support. Berry pushed through a tax increase on business that raised $300,000, which helped lead to his defeat in 1936.[5] Strapped for money in 1935 the state legislature passed a four percent ore tax on the now prospering Homestake gold mine that provided one-third of the state budget. It was raised to 6 percent in 1937, then lowered to 2.5 percent in 1957.[6]

Norbeck, who was instrumental in securing WPA funds to help complete the faces on Mount Rushmore, died of cancer in December 1936 as South Dakota was beginning to regain some economic stability. The first native-born Governor and United States Senator, Norbeck is one of the most admired politicians in South Dakota history. Born to poor Norwegian immigrants, Norbeck made his fortune by inventing a drilling rig for artesian wells that was widely employed on the arid plains. The strapping Norwegian rapidly succeeded in politics, moving from the state legislature to Governor by 1917, then winning his Senate seat in 1920 at age fifty. Credited with the founding of the Black Hills' Custer State Park, Norbeck teamed with another much admired South Dakotan, historian Doane Robinson, to implement creation of the famous Mount Rushmore faces. Interestingly, most South Dakota leaders opposed the project as an unnecessary blot on the beautiful Black Hills. When the Teddy Roosevelt figure was dedicated in July 1939, conservative governor Harlan Bushfield lashed out against the general dependence upon government largess, even though the federal government had spent about $750,000, about three quarters of the total cost, on the project. Bushfield's effusion did not make a lot of sense, but it sounded good to conservative South Dakotans.[7]

In spite of its hostile and unstable political environment hard hit North Dakota also received a generous flow of federal relief dollars. Nonpartisan League Republican governor William Langer provoked most of the political headlines in North Dakota during the 1930s. His NPL associate and rival, Senator Gerald "Munitions" Nye, attained more national notoriety for his devotion to isolation and animosity toward President Roosevelt. Grandson of successful German Red River immigrants, Langer was president of the Columbia University class of 1910. He was described as "the biggest politician, noisiest student, most popular man, and most likely to succeed."[8] Maintaining he was "with Roosevelt all the way" Langer was elected governor in 1932. In office he proved to be a vitriolic Roosevelt critic and attempted to deal with the drought-depression crisis by slashing state spending, imposing a moratorium on mortgage foreclosures, and embargoing the shipment of grain and beef from the state in an attempt to raise prices.[9] A United States District Court declared the Embargo law void in January 1934. Langer's controversial administration ended when the North Dakota Supreme Court removed him from office later in 1934 on the grounds of diverting federal relief funds to his political newspaper, *The Leader*.[10] Langer appealed and his wife, Lydia, a New York City native, ran to replace him, but lost to Democrat D. Thomas Moody who was removed from office in five weeks for not meeting residency requirements. Thus, North Dakota had four governors in less than seven months.[11] After his appeal was upheld in 1935, Langer again was elected governor in 1936 as an Independent.

Drought disaster that summer had forced a mass exodus, and of those remaining, an estimated 70 percent were on relief.[12] North Dakota voters now were ready to accept some responsibility to alleviate the crisis. Langer backed an appropriation of $6 million for child welfare, old age pensions and general relief for the 1937–1939 biennium, which equaled *all* appropriations for the 1933–35 biennium.[13] Langer later served in the United States Senate until his death in 1959.

In 1936, William Lemke ran for President on the Union Party ticket backed by Reverend Charles Coughlin "The Radio Priest," Gerald L. K. Smith, and Dr. Francis Townsend. Louisiana Senator Huey Long, the intended nominee, was assassinated in 1935, swinging the nomination to Lemke. Republican Lemke had backed Roosevelt in 1932, but had fallen out with the President over his failure to support the Frazier-Lemke Bankruptcy Act of 1934. Congressman Lemke forced the bill out of the House Rules Committee through a public appeal to farmers to pressure their representatives to sign a petition. The petition effort succeeded and the bill promptly passed only to be declared unconstitutional by a unanimous vote of the United States Supreme Court. Lemke won less than two percent of the votes and no states as Roosevelt swept back in a landslide victory over Kansas Republican Alf Landon.

Nebraska enjoyed a much more cordial political relationship with the Roosevelt administration during the 1930s and suffered less from drought than the Dakotas. Although surely problematic, especially in south central Nebraska, the droughts of 1931–1934 were less severe and agricultural conditions less critical in most of Western Nebraska.[14] In contrast to the Dakotas, from 1933 to 1941 "only" 20 percent of Nebraskans received relief payments.[15] The Cornhusker State still reflected much of the Populist Democratic tradition of three-time presidential candidate William Jennings Bryan. Bryan's brother, Charles W. Bryan, and fellow Democrat Robert Cochran held the governor's office from 1932 to 1940. In 1932, the entire Democrat State ticket won and Congressmen John Morehead, Edgar Howard, and Ashton Shallenberger, re-elected consistently, effectively expressed rural dissatisfaction. Over 60 percent of voters supported the repeal of prohibition in 1934 and almost 60 percent supported pari-mutuel betting on horse racing. Nebraska also passed legislation creating public power and irrigation districts in 1933 that would eventually make it the only state with entire ownership of commercial electrical production.

Veteran Nebraska progressive Republican Senator George Norris, the undisputed father of public power, enjoyed a warm relationship with Roosevelt. He called the mild mannered and modest Senator "the very perfect gentle knight of American progressive ideals." An independent thinker with courage of his convictions, much like his good friend Idaho Senator William Borah, Norris had served in the Congress since 1902. His tenure included ten years in the House before his 1912 Senate election. Like Borah, Norris had opposed American entry into World War I and into the League of Nations. He supported Catholic Democrat Al Smith for president in 1928 because he was convinced the "monopolistic power trust" had dictated Herbert Hoover's nomination.[16] Norris also disagreed with Hoover's "trickle down" economic philosophy that opposed direct federal relief.

Known as the "Father of TVA" Norris sponsored legislation that created the Tennessee Valley Authority. As one of the few Republican leaders who supported public power, he was a strong backer of the New Deal's Rural Electrification Administration (REA).[17] Norris, from McCook in southwestern Nebraska, took special interest in extending the irrigation and hydroelectric potential of the North Platte River. The North Platte River Valley in Western Nebraska and southeastern Wyoming had prospered from irrigated agriculture since the Bureau of Reclamation finished the Pathfinder Dam in Wyoming in 1909. Sugar beets, corn and edible beans thrived and sugar beet leftovers and corn supported a substantial cattle-feeding industry that flourished during the drought years. In season, five sugar-beet factories employed 1500 men.[18] In 1936, livestock from Nebraska, Wyoming, and Montana was fattened in the Pathfinder District.

Norris strongly supported Nebraskans located farther east on the North Platte who long had sought another dam on the river for irrigation and electric power. He had introduced such legislation in the Senate as early as 1925, but received little support from a conservative Congress. In 1935, with federal money now flowing into such projects, the great Nebraskan overcame a number of local territorial disputes and skillfully guided through legislation that provided for a dam and reservoir at Keystone which would provide badly needed hydroelectricity and irrigation for much of south-central Nebraska. Finished in 1941, the Kingsley Dam which created Lake McConaughy Reservoir employed an average of 1500 workers during construction. The total cost was $43 million of which $24 million was an outright PWA grant and the balance a federal loan, which was fully paid back in 1995.

For successfully promoting Nebraska's one house legislature or unicameral, Norris made the cover of *Time*, January 11, 1937. The unicameral seemed to promote a Republican conservatism not favored by Norris, though.[19] By the late 1930s the Cornhusker State proudly proclaimed itself the "White Spot of the Nation" because it had no sales tax, no state income tax, no luxury tax, no bonded debt and all highways were debt free.[20] As late as 1952, visitors were greeted with billboards that still proclaimed Nebraska the "White Spot of the Nation." Many Nebraskans, however, resented the high property taxes needed to maintain the state even at a Spartan level of public service.[21] Nebraskans' parsimony, moreover, hampered the state's ability to build an infrastructure capable of taking advantage of future more favorable economic conditions. It was not until 1966 that Nebraskans voted to change their constitution to include both a state income tax and a state sales tax, allowing the state to dramatically improve its public services.

Until 1966, it was difficult for innovative ideas such as now nationally observed Arbor Day to gain state support in Nebraska. Arbor Day was co-founded by J. Sterling Morton, a Nebraska City newspaper publisher, farmer-politician and Governor Robert Furnas, also an enthusiastic horticulturist. Arbor Day had a profound effect upon the nation's ecology and encouraged enactment of the New Deal's much publicized Great Plain's shelterbelt plan. Nebraska's earliest nickname was "The Tree Planter State." Morton, a tree planting enthusiast, pushed the new state to proclaim the first Arbor Day in April 1872. The state government funded prizes to the groups and individuals that planted the most trees. Arbor Day is now observed by all fifty states.

Arbor Day's success helped pass the 1873 Timber Culture Act sponsored by Nebraska Senator Phineas Hitchcock. Originally it allowed individuals a free 160 acres of government land if they would plant and maintain 40 acres of trees. This grant could be added to the 160 acres allowed by the Homestead Act. The much too demanding requirements were modified to require 10 acres of trees and 675 per acre had to be alive after ten years. With modification the program still failed and was abolished in 1893. There were too many abuses and most farmers preferred to plant crops other than trees.

In 1902, under the leadership of conservationist President Teddy Roosevelt, the federal government established a 20,000–acre Nebraska National Forest in the Nebraska sand hills and a 30,000–acre Kansas National Forest near Garden City. Nebraska's Bessey Nursery was established as the oldest federal tree nursery in the country. Although troubled by fire and harsh climatic conditions The Nebraska National Forest, now totaling some 208,702 acres, remains as a unique example of prairie forestry. The Bessey Nursery has been a leading supplier of young trees adapted to the Great Plains for over a century. A harsh drought in 1911 killed 90 percent of the trees in the Kansas National Forest, prompting President Woodrow Wilson to abolish the Kansas program in 1915. The federal government further encouraged tree planting in 1924, passing the Clark-McNary Act which authorized the Secretary of Agriculture to cooperate with states for shelter belts, windbreaks, and wood lots.[22]

Although the 1930s Great Plains shelterbelt program was built on a long tradition of belief in the desirability of tree planting in the region, the New Deal proceeded on a much grander scale. In May 1934, the Forest Service announced a plan for a hundred-mile wide shelter belt system planted at the center of each section of land with a western boundary stretching the Canadian border to North Texas. In July, Roosevelt established the shelter belt project, also known as Prairie States Forestry. The original idea was for government purchase of designated land from farmers. When the courts denied funding, farmers were paid to plant and care for their shelterbelts with WPA and CCC funding. Sometimes WPA workers helped care for the trees. Because seedlings imported from outside the region had little chance to survive, the federal government operated twenty nurseries on the Great Plains by 1936. Most of the seedlings were red cedar, green ash, hackberry and elm. Although the original proposal was modified considerably, by 1942 the numbers involved were enormous. There were 30,233 shelterbelts extending 18,600 miles and containing 220 million trees on 30,000 farms.[23] The tree survival rate was estimated at 70 percent. In April 1935, Congress had declared soil erosion "a national menace" and established the Soil Conservation Service in the Department of Agriculture where the shelter belt project was transferred in 1942. Since three-fourths of the continental United States was privately owned, only active, voluntary support from landowners could make the program work. In 1937, FDR wrote all governors urging them to create local Soil Conservation Districts to channel all forms of assistance into natural resources concerns. Presently there are over three thousand conservation districts in the United States with one in almost every county.

In addition to funding projects to improve the physical infrastructure of the nation while providing sorely needed jobs, the WPA employed thousands of writers, artists, actors and musicians. Under the auspices of its Federal One program the WPA greatly expanded programs already undertaken by the FERA. At an average salary of twenty dollars a month their purpose was to widen and improve cultural opportunities and make Americans more acquainted with their grass roots heritage. The Federal Theater Project (FTP) established twelve regional centers from coast to coast. Each center launched its own productions and put together touring companies. The FTP helped other private and public theater groups produce their own shows. The FTP presented 64,000 performances of plays, musicals, operettas, folk and ballet dances, vaudeville skits and songs, and more over a five year period with an estimated attendance of more than thirty million. FTP participants included Arthur Miller, Arlene Francis, Will Geer, Joseph Cotton, and Burt Lancaster.[24] Although mostly middle class oriented, the FTP was viewed as leaning too far left by critics. Works like Sinclair Lewis's anti-fascist *It Can't Happen Here*, poverty oriented *One-Third of a Nation*, and *Power* (which celebrated the New Deal's commitment to building dams for hydroelectricity) drew heavy conservative criticism. But Communist Clifford Odet's 1935 sensation *Waiting for Lefty,* a call to power for the working class inspired by a taxi strike, drew the most ire.

Less controversial but still questioned as fiscally irresponsible, the Federal Music Project (FMP) and the Federal Arts Project (FAP) greatly democratized the arts, especially in rural areas. The FAP emphasized art education for children, and established one hundred community art centers. It employed almost six thousand artists who, besides teaching, turned out an enormous flood of murals, posters, sculptures, paintings, drawings and prints. Inspired by Mexican mural art of the 1920s FAP artists created murals, and other art for thousands of public buildings. Although mural work in county courthouses is most recognized, other tax supported buildings such as schools, libraries, and other edifices of government were included. Contrary to popular belief the numerous New Deal murals in post offices were funded by the Treasury Department, not the FAP. A pictorial and historical record of the daily life of the American people also was undertaken. Although much of the work was mediocre, some was outstanding. Roosevelt remarked that although some it was not so good, all of it was, "native, human, eager, and alive—all of it painted by their own kind in their own country, and painted about things that they know and look at often and have touched and loved."[25] Professional artists created much of the art after local committees carefully screened their anonymous proposals. As a result most of the winners, even in rural states, were from urban areas. FAP artists in Los Angeles painted the Ada County, Idaho, Courthouse murals for example.

South Dakota's Oscar Howe, the most highly regarded Sioux artist of the twentieth century, was a most notable exception. A Yanktonai Sioux born on the Crow Creek Reservation, Howe overcame severe childhood illnesses to attend the Santa Fe Indian School where he honed his artistic talent. After winning several art competitions Howe was employed by the FAP's South Dakota Artists Project in 1940 to paint the interior Dome of Mitchell's Carnegie public library. Just before his 1942 army induction, Howe completed ten large murals about the history of the Missouri River basin for the new civic auditorium in Mobridge. After the war Howe earned his bachelor's degree from South Dakota Wesleyan, followed by a Master of Fine Arts degree from the University of Oklahoma. Howe taught art at the University of South Dakota for more than twenty years and painted such outstanding modern interpretations of Sioux culture that in 1960 he was named Artist Laureate of South Dakota.[26] Howe's work is seen as a bridge between Euro-American and Native American cultures.

Indubitably the FMP raised the nation's musical consciousness. At the beginning of 1935 there were only eleven symphony orchestras in the United States. The FMP established another thirty-four by the end of 1936. All forms of American music —marching bands, swing bands, hillbilly, cowboy and jazz received support. The FMP sponsored 224,698 performances enjoyed by almost 150 million people. Music education also was provided for those who could not afford it. More than six thousand music teachers were employed and by June 1939 they had offered over a million classes.[27]

Although the FERA and the CWA previously had sponsored substantial research, the Federal Writer's Project (FWP) precipitated a massive increase in knowledge of the historical and cultural infrastructure of the nation.[28] From 1935 to 1941 the FWP published about 800 titles including fify-one state and territorial guides, thirty city guides, twenty regional guides, and 150 volumes in its "Life in America" series.[29] FWP writers also collected more than ten thousand first person life-history narratives that related life in the thirties plus reminiscences of earlier decades.[30] Run by ethnically diverse and cosmopolitan liberals enthused about ethnic, economic and regional diversity, emphasis was focused on cultural variation and "social forces."[31]

FWP director Henry Alsberg, a former *New York Times* editor who had led similar programs with the CWA and the FERA, was determined to tell Americans about America. The state and territorial guides were the most significant means of accomplishing this ambitious goal. Each state was assigned a general editor who selected a team to compile and compose guides that would interpret its history in the broadest sense. History, geology, economics, politics, culture, ethnicity, and demographics all were considered. Designed to capitalize on the authenticity of local knowledge, the guides were a worthy contrast to most studies that took a top-down approach. Local writers, nevertheless, were required to conform to complex standards and regulations set in Washington, D.C. Writers were told to avoid the romantic stereotypes found in most travel guides and to employ a documentary, objective style that included all pertinent issues including class and racial differences. Local editors frequently disagreed with policies dictated by their federal leaders, but in most instances they complied.[32] An invaluable, highly detailed study of every state and territory resulted. The guides were printed by commercial publishers and sold well in almost all cases. After more than sixty years they remain an important resource. Congress abolished the FTP in 1939 and mandated it would allow other projects to continue only if local sponsors would pay one-fourth of the cost. Every one of the states met the requirement for the FWP.[33]

To counteract the furious criticism of the many opposed to the myriad New Deal "socialistic" programs, the administration promoted their need to support the poor and dispossessed. Well-organized publicity efforts focused on photography, moving pictures, and journalistic assessments. Although much of her work involved internal communication, journalist Lorena Hickock, who from 1933 through 1936 served as the chief investigator for the Federal Emergency Relief Corporation, was one of the most influential individuals employed in the campaign. Affectionately known as "Hick," her in your face, tough approach had propelled the two hundred-pound, cigar-smoking, college drop out to top woman reporter of the Associated Press. Hickock was assigned to cover Eleanor Roosevelt during the 1932 election and immediately gained the future First Lady's confidence. Soon after Roosevelt's election Hickock quit the Associated Press for the FERA post, reporting directly to FERA head Harry Hopkins. She was quite well rewarded for her new job, earning $6000 annually plus five dollars a day per-diem and mileage.[34]

Hickock had served ten years with the *Minneapolis Tribune*, so was especially well acquainted with the Dakotas that she called the "Siberia of America." She thought the Twin Cities regarded Dakota farmers as peasants and the Saint Paul "money crowd" was unsympathetic. Hickock's reports from Western North Dakota during a 1933 fall tour alerted the White House to the reality of the tremendous suffering taking place. Bottineau County, North Dakota, had not harvested a decent crop in four years. Hickock wrote Hopkins, "Their houses have gone to ruins. No repairs for years. Their furniture dishes, cooking utensils have had no replacement in years. No bed linen. And quilts and blankets all gone. A year ago their clothing was rags." Hickock agreed with a number of other observers that the farmers were too willing to place the blame on themselves and were too reluctant to apply for relief. "My own impression is that they're damn slow asking for their allotments and do not ask for enough, she wrote.[35]

The Dickinson, North Dakota, area had much of the 1933 crop hailed out as well as an almost total failure for the hay crop. There, Hickock noted that much of their livestock would die in the winter even though Russian thistles were being harvested for feed. Although she had been told she would find a good deal of unrest, Hickok thought the many farmers applying for relief, a paltry six dollars per month per family, seemed almost too patient.[36] She alleged Twin Cities bankers seemed to be pocketing most of the relief loans and criticized Governor William Langer, "who seems to be wrong all around." Hickock further noted Reds of various types were talking to farmers, "but the feeling generally about the state seems to be that nothing violent is going to happen for the present."[37]

After touring North Dakota, Hickock drove east to examine conditions in Western Minnesota. Floyd B. Olson, the Popular Farmer Labor governor, had made headlines in 1933 by threatening to declare martial law and confiscate private wealth unless the legislature passed relief laws to deal with the Depression. Hickock found Minnesota in much better shape than the Dakotas. "So far as destitution is concerned, I can't see that there is any comparison between what I've seen in Western Minnesota and what I saw in the Dakotas," she wrote. Hickock indicated many families and transients had moved there from the burnt-up areas in the Dakotas. Some Dakotans obtained logging jobs in the Bemidji area.[38] Hickock additionally noted local newspapers' lack of concern. She reported that Republican newspapers in the Dakotas and Minnesota "don't do any more explaining or clearing up than they just have to!"[39]

Hickock toured South Dakota, Nebraska and Iowa in November. In western South Dakota she quoted a local welfare statement that in one county, "among the farmers eligible for relief road work, there probably are not half a dozen whose teams are fit to work." She further cited the report, "There have been cases where half-starved horses have dropped in the harness, right on the road job. . . ."[40] Besides the effects of the drought, Communist activity furnished Hickock a unifying theme. She reported that the County Attorney in Aberdeen, South Dakota, "Thinks Washington should send Department of Justice people." Hickock saw no difference there than in the rest of the country. "There's no doubt, however, that they are very, very busy. Getting right down among the farmers and working like beavers," she reported. Hickock added "Reds" were meeting constantly in Lincoln, Nebraska, and four Communists were indicted for destruction of property in the Sioux City, Iowa, area.[41] Hickock also was critical of Nebraska governor Charles Bryan opining, "Bryan and Langer have certainly messed things up in Nebraska and North Dakota. . . ."[42]

Well aware of the visual impact of pictures, the Resettlement Administration (RA), founded in 1935, and headed by Rexford Tugwell, funded film makers and photographers to deliver a visual message portraying the disaster of the Great Depression and the Dust Bowl. Columbia University economist Roy Stryker, "the apostle of the downtrodden," was selected to head the Historical Section. At Columbia, Stryker was noted for his generous use of photographs to enrich his classes. Young Stryker had collaborated with his former mentor Tugwell to write *American Economic Life*, (1924) which also included lots of photographs. Stryker's diligence and sound judgment left a lasting impression on Tugwell, who also liked the fact that Stryker was born in Kansas and grew up on a farm near Montrose, Colorado. Although he had little knowledge of photography, Stryker had a great sense for photo documentation combined with immense ability to lead and inspire.

Stryker hired a number of young photographers and filmmakers who made the public aware of Depression hardship through a barrage of over 270,000 photos and several widely viewed films showing everyday people in their everyday lives. One admirer referred to the collection as "endless fractions of reality."[43] Many of Stryker's crew later became leaders in photojournalism. Arthur Rothstein, became head photographer for *Look* magazine. He later was joined by John Vachon. Dorothea Lange, famous for her pictures of Dust Bowl migrants in California, and multi talented Gordon Parks joined *Life* magazine. Pare Lorentz became the leading American propaganda filmmaker during World War II.; Fortunately for the RA, photojournalism magazines such as *Life* and *Look* began shortly after its formation. Stryker cultivated them relentlessly and they published many RA and Farm Settlement Administration photos. The RA evolved into the FSA in 1937.[44]

Rothstein, by his own admission a provincial New Yorker, was hired just after graduation from Columbia. He planned for medical school, but his skills in photography, demonstrated while assisting Tugwell and Stryker with *American Economic Life*, earned an RA offer. Rothstein was directed to take pictures that created sympathy and encouraged public support for the dispossessed and showed evidence of land misuse and mismanagement to promote resettlement. Rothstein had to learn to drive so he could tour the Great Plains. Roosevelt was scheduled to tour the Plains in August and the national press was eager for background pictures. In April 1936, Rothstein took the iconic *Fleeing a Dust Storm* in Cimarron County, Oklahoma, where 40 percent of the population had already fled. A man and his two sons are pictured headed for the protection of a shed-like building in what appears to be a dust storm. *Fleeing a Dust Storm* quickly became the symbol for the Dust Bowl. Although Cimarron County had recently suffered a huge dust storm, Rothstein staged the famous picture when no dust was blowing.[45]

In May, Rothstein submitted several pictures of a steer skull on a parched alkali flat in the Badlands near Rapid City, South Dakota, changing its position several times. They were designed to illustrate the demise of the cattle industry and how farmers and ranchers were trying to live on sub marginal land and Stryker was delighted with them. The Associated Press used the skull picture as a symbol of the record drought that came later in the summer. Local leaders were outraged and charged Rothstein with faking the picture to promote New Deal farm programs. Residents of Fargo, North Dakota's largest city, located in the relatively prosperous Red River Valley, were especially complacent about the Depression. In 1935, only 10 percent of Cass County residents were on relief compared to 30 percent of all North Dakotans.[46] The editor of the *Fargo Forum*, a vehement critic of the New Deal, ran a front page story charging fraud just as FDR was coming through his state. He wrote, "There never was a year this scene couldn't be produced in North Dakota even in years when rainfall was far above normal." Other newspapers, *Time* and conservative journalists like Westbrook Pegler increased the flood of criticism, suggesting that Rothstein had carried the skull with him. He admitted relocating the skull strategically for maximum effect, but maintained the manipulation was done to dramatize the truth. One of Rothstein's supervisors advised, ". . . if you have that goddam skull, hide it for Christ's sake." Stryker and his staff absorbed the criticism with a sense of humor, even preparing a print of the skull picture to be used as a Christmas card.[47]

If the RA's photos troubled Great Plains conservatives, Pare Lorentz's *The Plow That Broke the Plains*, which premiered May 10, 1936, incensed them even more. To create the first film the United States government produced for commercial release Lorentz was paid $6,000 by the Resettlement

Administration. A strong supporter of the New Deal, Lorentz hailed from an affluent West Virginia background. He had written a book about Presidnet Roosevelt and an extensive article about the Dust Bowl for *Newsweek*, but this also was Lorentz's first film. The film employed only a three-man camera crew and no professional actors. Leftist eastern liberals Leo Hurwitz and Paul Strand structured *The Plow That Broke the Plains* on a rented typewriter in a hotel in Alliance, Nebraska. They wanted the entire focus to be on human greed and the ineffectual social system, but Lorentz refused, orienting the film more toward the role the government could play to ease the ecological and social disaster, especially emphasizing resettlement.[48]

The Plow That Broke the Plains was filmed in September 1935 in Wyoming, Colorado, Kansas, and Texas with later migrant shots in California. Citizens affected by the drought readily volunteered to participate as actors. Originally ninety minutes long it contained only seven hundred words of terse narration. The film begins with the inrush of speculators and cattle in the wake of the railroad. When the plains were plowed settlers are warned, "Plow at your peril." The economic boom created by World War I is summarized by the slogan "Wheat will win the War!" Temporary prosperity is followed by dust, drought, heat and winds, forcing thousands of refugees to head west in their dilapidated vehicles, "Baked out, Blown out, and Broke." It claimed the damage done to forty million acres could never be undone. The epilogue, which was later removed, an obvious pitch for the RA, shows 4,500 stranded families in new houses on small farms in ten states. Lorentz paid little heed to his tiny budget. The cost of *The Plow*, which was partly financed by his own money, more than tripled to $19,260.[49]

Although highly praised by liberals, *The Plow that Broke the Plains* never was largely distributed. Regular distributors refused to take the film, claiming it was too long for a short feature and too short for a long feature. The film's defenders suggested the real reason was their dislike for Lorentz and the New Deal. When *The Plow* did reach public theaters, mostly through Lorentz's personal efforts, its repetitive and tendentious style tended to bore urban audiences. In August 1938, *The Plow* was made available for educational distribution with a fifty-page study guide provided by the Farm Settlement Administration (formerly known as the Resettlement Administration). As an educational film it sold over six thousand copies in 1940.[50]

Criticism, mainly from the Great Plains, forced the government to withdraw *The Plow* in 1940, however. Texas state representative Eugene Worley threatened to punch Tugwell in the nose and asked Democrats to destroy the film. "It would have been as true to say a ship had caused an ocean storm as to say the plow broke the plains," said South Dakota farmer Harvey Reeves.[51] Kansas University history professor James Malin, a respected authority on the Great

Plains, described the film as only the most conspicuous of the excesses of political agitation, sensationalism, and lack of historical perspective that were designed to convince the public the Great Plains was becoming a desert.[52] Harlan Bushfield, South Dakota state Republican chairman, claimed *The Plow* would put South Dakota in the Republican column in November 1936. He said, "The picture in one savage blow ruthlessly destroyed all that South Dakotans have built up in a generation by picturing the state as a wasteland. Bushfield further asserted, "If there was any doubt about it before, *The Plow That Broke the Plains* has made South Dakota definitely Republican."[53] His prediction rang hollow when Roosevelt easily carried South Dakota in 1936.

South Dakota Congresssman Karl Mundt continued the attack in February 1939 when he demanded the film be withdrawn. "From beginning to end it is a drama of distress," said Mundt, who counted the South Dakota Education Association among his backers. The film went out of circulation in 1940 when the Congress refused to continue funding of the United States Film Service, created by Executive Order in 1938. *The Plow* again became available in 1961, "to be used for study as an art form only. Because the subject matter is long obsolete it is not to be used for public showing." In 1972 *The Plow* was made readily accessible to instructors and students.[54]

The Farm Security Administration which had evolved from the Resettlement Administration in 1937 became the Office of War Information in 1943. Stryker resigned after being assured the government would preserve the FSA picture collection. He was employed by Standard Oil of New Jersey as a publicist in an attempt to improve its tarnished image. Lorentz greatly enhanced his reputation by producing the highly regarded "Why We Fight" series for the Office of War Information.

Readily available for public use the some 270,000 FSA picture collection of the Great Depression now is considered a national treasure by many. Even though indisputably predisposed and at times manipulated for effect, they speak for the directly impacted, inarticulate minority by generally portraying the economic and ecological tragedy of the 1930s with accuracy. Those not severely affected by the Great Depression may argue otherwise, but the minority who suffered most should always be grateful for New Deal's effective efforts to publicize the catastrophe and push drastic measures to alleviate it.

NOTES

1. Leonard Arrington and Don C. Read, "New Deal Economic Programs," *The Centennial West: Essays on the Northern Tier States*, ed. William Lang (Seattle: University of Washington Press, 1991), 227–43.

2. Michael J. Grant, *Down and Out on the Family Farm: Rural Rehabilitation in the Great Plains, 1929–1945* (Lincoln: University of Nebraska Press, 2002), 80.

3. Ibid.

4. John E. Miller. "Restrained Radicals," in *Americans View Their Dust Bowl Experience*, ed. John Wunder, Frances Kaye and Vernon Carstensen (Nivot, CO: University of Colorado Press, 1999), 252.

5. Paul A. O'Rourke, "South Dakota Politics during the New Deal Years," *South Dakota History* 1 (Summer 1977): 254.

6. John R. Milton, *South Dakota: A History* (New York: W. W. Norton, 1977), 118–19.

7. Gilbert C. Fite. *Mount Rushmore* (Norman: University of Oklahoma Press, 1952), 206–11; see also Gilbert C. Fite, *Peter Norbeck: Prairie Statesman* (Columbia: University of Missouri Press, 1948).

8. Robert P. Wilkins and Wynona Wilkins, *North Dakota Centennial History* (New York: Norton, 1977), 115.

9. *North Dakota Blue Book,* Secretary of State Ben Meir Director (Bismarck: State of North Dakota, 1981), 27.

10. D. Jerome Tweton and Daniel F. Rylance, *The Years of Despair: North Dakota in the Depression* (Grand Forks: University of North Dakota Press, 1973), 23.

11. Wilkins, *North Dakota*, 118.

12. Federal Writers Project of the Works Progress Administration, *North Dakota: A Guide to the Northern Prairie State* (New York: Oxford University Press, 1950), 62.

13. D. Jerome Tweton, "The Politics of Chaos: North Dakota in the 1930s," *Journal of the West,* (Fall 2002): 30–35.

14. R. S. Kifer and H. L. Stewart, *Farming Hazards in the Drought Area* (Washington, D.C.: United States Government Printing Office, 1938), 41; Dorothy Wyler Creigh. *Nebraska: A Bicentennial History* (New York: W. W. Norton, 1977), 185–88.

15. James C. Olson, *History of Nebraska* (Lincoln: University of Nebraska Press, 1974), 321; House Select Committee to Investigate the Interstate Migration of Destitute Citizens, John H. Tolan, Chairman. *Hearings on House Resolution 63 and House Resolution 491, 76th Congress, July 29–December 11, 1940,* Preliminary Report. (Washington, D.C.: United States Government Printing Office, 1941) Volume 9, 3540.

16. John F. Kennedy, *Profiles in Courage* (New York: Harper and Row, 1961), 204–5.

17. Olson, *History of Nebraska*, 313.

18. Great Plains Committee, *The Future of the Great Plains*, House Document 144, 75th Congress (Washington, D.C.: United States Government Printing Office, 1937), 144–45.

19. Richard Lowitt, *George W. Norris: The Triumph of a Progressive, 1933–1944* (Urbana: University of Illinois Press, 1978), passim.

20. Carl Fleischhaurer, Carl, and Beverly Brannon, eds., *Documenting America, 1935–1943* (Berkeley: University of California Press, 1988), 94.

21. Salary levels for all public employees were among the lowest in the nation.

22. R. Douglas Hurt. "Forestry on the Great Plains, 1902–1942." http:// www .personal.KSU.edu/~jsherow/hurt2.htm. (accessed August 8, 2005)

23. William H. Droze, *Trees, Prairies and People: A History of Tree Planting in the Great Plains States* (Denton, TX: Texas Women's University, 1977), 222–23.

24. T. H. Watkins, *The Hungry Years* (New York: Henry Holt, 1999), 288–92.

25. William E. Leuchtenburg, *Franklin Roosevelt and the New Deal, 1932–1940* (New York: Harper, 1963), 128.

26. "Oscar Howe," http://www3.sdstate.eduAdministrator/SouthDakotaArtMuseum/Collections/HoweIndex-Textcfm. (accessed March 20, 2005)

27. David E. Kyvig. *Daily Life in the United States, 1920–1940: How Americans Lived Through the "Roaring Twenties" and the Great Depression* (Chicago: Ivan R. Dee, 2004), 253–54; Watkins, *The Hungry Years,* 282–84.

28. For FERA activity see Theodore Whiting, *Final Statistical Report of the Federal Emergency Relief Administration* (Washington, D.C.: United States Government Printing Office, 1942. A state example of FERA sponsored research is Rolland Dewing, "Depression on South Dakota's Indian Reservations: The SDERA Survey of 1935," *South Dakota History* 21 (Spring 1991): 84–96.

29. Leuchtenburg, *Franklin Roosevelt,* 127.

30. Ann Banks, *First Person America,* (New York: Alfred A. Knopf, 1980), Introduction, 11–25.

31. Susan Schulten, "How to see Colorado: The Federal Writer's Project, American Regionalism, and the 'Old' New Western History," *Western Historical Quarterly* 36, (Spring 2005): 49–70.

32. Schulton, "How to See Colorado," 66–70.

33. Watkins, *Hungry Years*, 286–87.

34. Richard Lowitt and Maurine Beasly, eds., *One Third of a Nation: Lorena Hickock Reports on the Great Depression* (Urbana: University of Illinois Press, 1981), 138.

35. Ibid., 70.

36. Ibid., 55–59.

37. Ibid., 71–74.

38. Ibid., 127.

39. John F. Bauman, *In theEye of the Great Depression: New Deal Reporters and the Agony of the American People* (DeKalb: Northern Illinois Press, 1988), 136.

40. Dorothy Schwieder, "South Dakota Farm Women and the Great Depression," *South Dakota History* 24 (October 1985): 9.

41. Lowitt and Beasly, *One Third of a Nation,"* 79.

42. Ibid., 125.

43. Kyvig, *Daily Life,"* 254.

44. Richard Doud, "Roy Stryker interview for the Smithsonian Institute," Montrose, Colorado, October 17, 1963. http://www.aaa/si/edu/oralhist/stryke63.htm. (accessed April 10, 2004): Bill Ganzel, *Dust Bowl Descent* (Lincoln: University of Nebraska Press, 1984), 4–12.

45. James Curtis, *Mind's Eye, Mind's Truth: FSA Photographs Reconsidered* (Philadelphia: Temple University Press, 1989), 78–89.

46. David Danbom, "Fargo and the Great Depression," *North Dakota History* 66 (Summer/Fall 1999): 42–43.

47. Curtis, "Mind's Eye," 72–75; Richard Doud, "Arthur Rothstein interview for the Smithsonian Institute," New York, New York, May 25, 1964. http://www.aaa/si/edu/oralhist/rothst64.htm. (accessed April 10, 2004)

48. William Alexander, *Film on the Left: American Documentary Film from 1931 to 1942* (Princeton, N.J.: Princeton University Press, 1981), 100.

49. Robert Snyder. *Pare Lorentz and the Documentary Film* (Norman: University of Oklahoma Press, 1968), 36–37.

50. Vernon Carstensen, "The Plow that Broke the Plains," in *Americans View Their Dust Bowl Experience*, ed. John Wunder, Frances Kaye and Vernon Carstensen (Nivot, CO: University of Colorado Press, 1999), 315–16.

51. George Reeves, *A Man from South Dakota* (New York: Dutton, 1950), 82.

52. James C. Malin, *The Grasslands of North America: Prolegomena to Its History* (Lawrence, KS: Private Printing, 1947), 134.

53. "Says a Film Loses a State," *New York Times*, 4 August 1936.

54. Carstensen in Wunder, *Americans View Their Great Depression*, 315–16.

Chapter Five

The Pacific Northwest: An Underdeveloped Favorite

When the question of acquiring the Oregon Territory emerged, New Englander Daniel Webster objected, "What do we want of this vast worthless area, this region of savages and wild beasts, of shifting sands and whirlpools of dust, of cactus and prairie dogs?. . . . Mr. President I will never vote one cent from the public treasury to place the Pacific Coast one inch nearer Boston than it is now."[1]

By the 1930s, this "worthless" area along with California had become by far the most highly rated region in the country in a *Fortune* magazine poll asking citizens where they preferred to go if they decided to move. More than a quarter chose the Pacific Coast, leading the second place East by almost 9 percent.[2] For most Northern Plains residents the first choice was the Pacific Northwest. It had much to offer. The mild climate and abundant rainfall in the west had created the most valuable temperate rain forest in the world and a premier fishery plus large and diverse agricultural production. Eastern portions offered huge expanses suitable for grazing, grain production and irrigated farming along with excellent timber in the moister areas. Only a small fraction of its enormous hydroelectric potential had been developed. Dams could be close to the region's excellent deep-water seaports that provided a prime location for world trade, especially the rapidly expanding Asian trade. The Pacific Northwest also featured a well educated, productive population that received a higher wage rate than most of country.[3] Much of the existing population, moreover, had roots in the Upper Midwest.

The need to increase employment of wage earners in manufacturing industries posed a major concern to the region which largely depended on exportation of raw and semi finished material from its timber, agricultural, mining and fishing resources. Few common manufactured articles were supplied from the home area. More manufacturing jobs were needed to provide an outlet for surplus labor and promote the economy. The new hydroelectric dams held great promise for needed future expansion in labor intensive industries. All industries benefited from a bounteous supply of low cost electricity and the Pacific Northwest offered the nation's greatest potential. Processing aluminum from bauxite used tremendous amounts of electricity and aluminum had replaced wood as a key element in the manufacture of airplanes. Seattle was the home of a small, but well-established airplane builder—Boeing. Shipbuilding, heavily dependent upon metal products and an important industry during the World War I period, had almost ground to a halt during the Depression, but many shipyards still existed along with the capacity to build more. The governments long-established Bremerton Naval Shipyard was undergoing major improvements as a part of the $237 million PWA appropriation for the navy in 1933.[4]

Pacific Car and Foundry (PACCAR), located in Seattle and Portland was the West Coast's only major supplier of steel after 1917. Founded by William Pigott in 1903 as Seattle Steel, its plants operated by electricity from the beginning. Besides producing steel for a variety of markets, the company specialized in log transportation equipment. In 1917, the company merged with Twohy Brothers of Portland and was renamed PACCAR. Its Renton plant built a variety of train cars and motor trucks in the 1920s. Pigott, active in community matters and an admired employer, stressed quality and built a highly competent and loyal work force. PACCAR survived the Depression by introducing Carcometal. A lightweight casting steel, twice the strength of basic steel with high elastic strength, it was ideal for tractor winches, hoists and arches used in rapidly increasing tractor logging.[5]

Plywood, paper and pulp manufacture all consumed large quantities of electricity. They were already expanding rapidly and would be quite mature by 1940, providing thousands of well paying jobs. Much of the expansion in pulp production was based on plentiful western hemlock, previously overlooked as unprofitable. Chemists unlocked the process of separating cellulose fibers from hemlock, for paper, particleboard, rayon and other products. Feeding a rapidly expanding market in the United States and Japan, nine new pulp and paper mills were established from 1930–1939.[6] Pulpwood consumption in western Washington and Oregon expanded from 400,000 cords in 1925 to 3,175,000 cords in 1940. By 1935, production of wood pulp for rayon at Shelton, Hoquiam and Port Angeles supplied a fifth of the world's output.[7]

Washington and Oregon's still adequate supply of quality old growth logs enabled the Pacific Northwest to dominate plywood manufacture in the 1930s. Split proof, light, versatile, with tremendous nail holding power, plywood enjoyed an enormous market. The plywood era was opened by the invention of a suitable-glue to replace the stinky, inadequate animal glue used in the 1920s. Dr. James Nevin, an eccentric Irish chemist, joined Aberdeen's Harbor Plywood in 1933 to find a suitable adhesive. Working nonstop with two assistants for a year Nevin perfected a waterproof-glue from coal tar, allowing exterior use of plywood. By 1938, twenty-eight plywood and veneer plants in Washington and fourteen in Oregon sustained substantial payrolls. Three years later Oregon had twenty-nine and Washington had thirty-three, by then operating twenty-four hours a day.[8] Not a "war babe," no new plants were built from 1942 to 1946. During the war the government gave plywood a top priority, even higher than most grades of steel.[9]

Although forest industries retain a significant position in all Pacific Northwest states, their pre-war dominance easily can be underestimated. In 1937, one-half of the total value of products in all Washington industries came from industries using the forest base. In lumber production it ranked first in the nation in Douglas fir, hemlock, cedar, spruce and alder besides being the leading producer of plywood and pulp.[10] By 1939, Oregon surpassed Washington in lumber production.

President Roosevelt was well acquainted with the Pacific Northwest and enjoyed strong support there. Convinced that it could supply the safety valve for the hundreds of thousands of Great Plains drought victims, Roosevelt used his considerable power and influence to encourage economic growth to accommodate that transfer. Speaking at the Bonneville Dam in 1934 Roosevelt said, "Out here you have not just space, you have space that can be used by human beings—a wonderful land—a land of opportunity."[11] As Under-Secretary of the Navy FDR first visited the area in 1914 to inspect naval bases at Portland, Seattle, and Bremerton. He made twenty-six speeches in two days in Washington as the 1920 Democrat candidate for Vice-President. Washington pledged its delegates to him first in the 1932 campaign and he swept Montana, Idaho, Oregon, and Washington in the election.[12] The new President was well aware of problems involving a lack of electrical power generation in World War I and had successfully waged a battle for public power companies as governor of New York.[13] Another close tie to the region evolved when John Boetigger.was appointed editor of the *Seattle Post Intelligencer.* A reporter assigned to cover Roosevelt's 1932 campaign by FDR's former schoolmate, Colonel Robert McCormick of the *Chicago Tribune*, Boetigger married Roosevelt's daughter Anna. Boetigger was appointed editor of Hearst's *Seattle Post Intelligencer* in December 1936. Hearst's hopes of building closer ties to FDR did not work out, however.[14]

Representative of the New Deal emphasis on regional planning, The Pacific Northwest Planning Commission was created in 1935 and headquartered in Portland. Noting the region's fortunate combination of low population and abundant resources the Commission suggested a much larger population could be accommodated in a temperate region containing 13 percent of the nation's land area and only 3 percent of its population.[15] It was estimated to contain three to seven million acres of fertile, undeveloped farm land, 40 percent of the nation's potential hydro-electric power and half of its standing timber.[16] An economy characterized as a seasonal extractor of raw materials would be transformed by bountiful electricity from the now under construction Columbia River dams. These dams were, "In all probability more far-reaching than any public work or group of public works heretofore planned or constructed by the nation."[17]

Roosevelt, who held a virtual blank check for authorization of federal projects, proposed that the solution to the Dust Bowl dilemma lay in the agricultural development of the Pacific Northwest. His speeches touting the advantages of the area heavily influenced many migrants.[18] As Grand Coulee Dam was being finished, Roosevelt said, "I have read a book recently; it is called *Grapes of Wrath.* There are 500,000 Americans that live in the covers of that book. I would like to see the Columbia Basin devoted to the care of the 500,000 people represented in *Grapes of Wrath.*[19] The President's vision for the Columbia Basin, however, could not be fulfilled because conservative estimates indicated a farmer needed at least $3000 cash to take over an eighty acre irrigated tract—a figure far beyond the reach of almost all migrants.[20] Cut over lands in Western Washington also rated too highly as an agricultural safety valve. Officials estimated that area could support fifteen thousand additional farms at a minimum income level but that was unrealistic because most could not produce anywhere close to a minimum standard of living.[21]

With war brewing in Asia and Europe, FDR undoubtedly perceived industrial expansion as a significant venue. He was well aware that the heavy concentration of industry in the East was not in the best economic and military interests of the nation.[22] The pressing need for strengthening West Coast military installations also had emerged. The roughly four hundred mile by fifty mile strip from Bellingham south along the Puget Sound to Seattle, Tacoma, and down to Portland and the Willamette Valley held special appeal. Huge quantities of inexpensive electricity could be delivered to tidewater to promote shipbuilding, pulp and paper production, airplane manufacture, and other industries. In the early 1930s, noted economic geographer J. Russell Smith cited its advantages for trade and commerce saying, "Nowhere in Europe nor in the Eastern United States is there any location for water power resources that rivals it." Smith accurately predicted the area, with about one million population at the time, would almost certainly increase to "5 or 6, perhaps 10 million. . . ."[23]

In the mid 1930s the nation was still strongly oriented toward the small family farm, however, and that was perceived, incorrectly in the long run, as the primary accommodation for Dust Bowl migrants. They could exploit the abundant, inexpensive cut over timberland west of the Cascade Mountains in Oregon and Washington and in Northern Idaho. Dairy farming, poultry, hay, small grains and a wide variety of berries and fruits would provide a livelihood as they had for earlier settlers in the area. The Soil Conservation Service estimated one million acres in Oregon, Washington and Idaho as suitable for crop production if cleared of brush and timber. Arid inland areas, moreover, would bloom when water from the new reservoirs reached the parched land. Irrigation had already transformed the Yakima Valley and the Wenatchee area, for example, and great expansion was anticipated in the Columbia River Basin, southern Idaho and eastern Oregon.

Officials estimated about half of the ten million acres of reclaimable land in Idaho, Oregon, Washington and Western Montana required irrigation. Sanguine estimations claimed water from the Grand Coulee Dam could supply 1.7 million acres alone. Other major projects on the Snake River and in the Willamette Valley drainage area could about equal that amount, making an estimated 150,000 new farms available. During the eighteen month period prior to July 1937 the report indicated 12,000 of the estimated 19,000 farm families coming into Washington, Oregon, and Idaho settled on some kind of rural land, much of which was undesirable cut over timberland.[24] Very few farmed in any organized irrigation project.

Between 1922 and 1930, the annual timber cut averaged over ten billion board feet. The best timber grew in the lower, more fertile areas, usually conveniently close to salt water or rivers, and was harvested first. Much of the more desirable lowland had been cleared for farming by the 1930s, but huge tracts of cutover land remained and were perceived as future farm sites. Although large corporations such as Weyerhaeuser, Pope and Talbot, and Simpson dominated, there were estimated forty thousand individual timber owners in Oregon and Washington. The big companies, especially the aforementioned, eventually realized that timber production could be sustained and retained their holdings by successfully lobbying for favorable tax considerations. Utilizing new technology employers cut wages, hours and employment, enabling them to lower prices that forced many small operators out. Rural sawmill towns disappeared as population increasingly concentrated in larger towns with more stable economies.[25] Many smaller operations abandoned their cutover land after selling the more desirable parcels.

Not all loggers showed such irresponsibility, though. The Bordeaux Brothers, who logged the Black Hills southwest of Olympia, pledged not to "renege, default, or avoid taxes." They sold most of their holdings to the state of

Washington in 1941 for a few cents an acre. This cutover land would eventually become the 91,659–acre Capitol Forest.[26] State ownership of Pacific Northwest timberland was dwarfed, however, by the enormous federal holdings. Estimated at 25.9 billion board feet, the federal government retained the most important block of commercial, mature timber.[27] Small private companies could bid to harvest select plots but because of the process and the required capital larger operators were much better situated to win.

When the vast Oregon territory was acquired from Great Britain in 1846, the federal government owned almost all of it and, as held true later on the Great Plains, offered generous grants of land to encourage settlement. After a four year struggle in Congress the Donation Land Claim Act of 1850 passed. Each white male settler who was a United States citizen or who had declared to become one before December 1, 1851, who arrived before December 1, 1850, received 320 acres of land. If married, his wife also was entitled to 320 acres. These generous grants lured a substantial number of settlers, either via the Oregon Trail or by making the long voyage around South America by ship.[28] Another option was to cross the Isthmus of Panama. Most of the settlers were New Englanders and their well located claims tended to evolve into cities and towns including Seattle, Tacoma, Bellingham, Everett and Vancouver. Grants were halved in the early 1850s, then changed in 1853 to require $1.25 per acre payment. All of this served as a precursor to the Homestead Act of 1863 that stipulated that the land had to be suitable for cultivation. In 1878, the Timber Claim Act permitted sale of 160 acres of government timberland unfit for cultivation for $2.50 and the applicant had to swear it was for his exclusive use. As happened with the Homestead Act, chicanery was common. Other large tracts of land were granted to the railroad builders who sold most of their acreage to large timber companies. Additionally the government granted the states of Montana, Idaho, Oregon, and Washington 16,988,799 acres. In 1936, Oregon retained only 14 percent, in sharp contrast with Montana's 84 percent, Idaho's 79 percent and Washington's 73 percent.[29] All would increase their acreage substantially by acquiring tax delinquent land or by purchase in the late 1930s

Even in the glutted timber market of the late nineteenth and early twentieth century 160 acres of old-growth forest contained an impressive amount of valuable wood which could be sold at a nice profit. After their property was logged many chose to stay and establish a farm by burning the debris and clearing the massive stumps.[30] Others sold to mainly first and second generation Scandinavians, many of who held regular jobs as loggers or mill workers.[31] Quite a few, never intending to farm or not as well located, sold the timber, then attempted to sell the logged over land; if not successful, they abandoned the property which became tax delinquent and reverted back to the counties.

When the timber industry declined drastically in the early 1930s, thousands of these stump ranchs were abandoned. Many owners migrated to other locations on the Pacific Coast, especially California. By 1934, Oregon had 2,601,827 acres in delinquency and Washington had about half that total.[32] In 1936, Oregon counties owned 1,778,273 rural acres as a result of tax foreclosure.[33] By the mid-1930s both states proposed to assume ownership from their counties. Rather than lose future tax revenues by having it taken over by the state, counties preferred to sell this land to private parties. This land was offered for as little as a dollar an acre for a forty-acre tract and many dispossessed farmers from the Dust Bowl assumed this "opportunity." Cutover land in northern Idaho could be obtained just as easily and also attracted a substantial number of migrants.[34]

In many cases the gamble did not pay. Farmers from the Great Plains tended to naively assume that the abundant rainfall and flourishing plant life promised success. Most of the cutover land was not cleared for good reason. Efficient removal of the large stumps required either heavy equipment or blasting powder, neither of which many newcomers could afford. Hiring a caterpillar tractor for clearing could cost as high as $300 an acre, dependent upon the difficulty. Blasting powder cost less but was slower and required lots of manual labor besides posing an inherent danger to its users. An official estimate indicated a farmer working alone required four hundred hours of his own labor, thirty-four hours of horse labor and $40 worth of dynamite (one acre required around two hundred pounds) to clear an acre of stump land.[35] Clearing also could be accomplished with hand tools, fire and animal power, but it was slow and laborious. Officials proposed that a settler should be able to clear about two acres a year by this method, but few did. In most cases the newcomers were forced to settle on less fertile higher land.

Many were disappointed when they found crops and pasture were not as bountiful as expected. The abundant rain leached out much of the soil's nutritional value. The frequently dry summers, characteristic of the modified Mediterranean/Marine West Coast climate, stunted crop growth, promoting a constant struggle with weeds, shrubs and young trees trying to reclaim the cleared spaces. Virtually worthless bracken fern thrived on cleared land. It could be subdued by regular plowing but much of the land was only semi-cleared and not ready for plowing. An abandoned farm taken over in the thirties averaged only $75 cash income a year.[36] Most rural migrants were forced to endure slum conditions with little access to quality education, libraries, health care and other amenities associated with an acceptable standard of living.[37] It was somewhat of a shock to many poor established residents that the Pacific Northwest was regarded as a land of opportunity.[38]

A federal report on migration downplayed the high expectations theme and emphasized the drought crisis. It said, "The recent migration into the Pacific Northwest has been primarily one of people seeking to escape from a more or less desperate situation elsewhere, not of people lured on by a reasonable expectation that larger opportunities awaited them in the region to which they are moving."[39] Possibly this assessment contained some element of self-promotion to encourage support for more government assistance. Most migrants, while acknowledging crisis conditions triggered their move, also anticipated improved economic opportunity in a much more temperate climate.[40]

The Resettlement Administration, noting the surge of rural newcomers and the problems of settling on cut over lands, distributed information throughout the Great Plains. It warned the drought farmer not to move unless he knew he had a farm job or unless he had enough capital to establish himself on a place or a job. A mimeographed bulletin designed to serve as a guide to incoming settlers was distributed at strategic points along the two main highways leading into the Pacific Northwest. It identified desirable and undesirable land and provided a directory of Resettlement Administration officials and county agents.[41] Twenty FSA camps such as the one portrayed in *Grapes of Wrath* were proposed and eight were built—four in Washington, two in Idaho and two in Oregon.[42] Government sponsored radio talks included "Our New Neighbors from the Drought Area" and "A New Family Settles on a Farm."

Migrants intending to farm in most cases knew good land from the less desirable, but usually were forced on poor stump ranches because it was affordable. About one fourth had a net worth of less than $100 on arrival. Few had anything close to buying a viable farm, forcing many to accept tenancy or purchase marginal land. Several families living together "doubling up" happened frequently.[43] Between 1930 and 1935 farm tenancy increased 22 percent in Idaho, 39 percent in Washington and 44 percent in Oregon.[44] Within the small farm group nearly all the increase took place in farms of less than fifty acres. By far the greatest expansion occurred in part-time farms of three to nine acres.[45] Many farms had less than one cleared acre when settled.[46]

An estimated 50 percent of the 460,000 1930s migrants to the Pacific Northwest settled in "rural problem areas," mostly in the ten most populous counties in western Oregon and Washington but with a substantial amount in Northern Idaho, also.[47] Richard White, a leader of the "new" Western historians, saw nothing but trouble: "Small farmers dispossessed by drought and Depression moved from the Northern Great Plains into western Oregon and Washington, where drought was unknown and lands were cheap and readily available. Many attempted to settle the logged-over-lands and in doing so participated in a much quieter ecological and social disaster in western Washington and Oregon."[48] Land tended to turn over rapidly as families moved around competing for scarce jobs or lacked income to retain their place. Primitive housing abounded, frequently consisting of one or two room cabins constructed of green lumber with no modern conveniences. Journalist Carey McWilliams toured the area in the late 1930s and observed, "Most of the homes are bare of furnishings. Boxes, stools, and benches serve in lieu of chairs. Here is the raw edge of poverty exposed like a sword."[49] Other migrants occupied poorer town and city residences, abandoned lumber camps, tourist cabins of all descriptions, even the berry shacks and apple growers' shacks. Some rented and some squatted. Schools reported many children inadequately clothed and malnourished.[50] Reports indicated compulsory school attendance was not enforced, especially for children of farm workers.[51]

A federal study of migration into the Pacific Northwest noted, "The cultural level in a sub marginal stump and brush area is usually low. School facilities have been inadequate; living standards are barely at the subsistence level; nutritional diseases are common; populations are ingrown. . . It is essential that recent settlers in such districts shall not become stabilized under these conditions."[52] The Tolan Report indicated migrant children as a rule were mentally alert but scholastically backward for the above reasons, but most of all because of their economic insecurity.[53]

In spite of the temporary reversal most migrants entrapped in poverty, somewhat like the many citizens of Japan and Germany after World War II, still retained values and skills that would enable them to escape. The federal government recognized their dilemma but state and local governments offered little help.[54] Historian Gordon Dodds suggested the migrants were not welcomed because they would compete for jobs, require higher taxes and possibly promote radicalism. "The older residents denied the migrants work relief, old age assistance, and medical services on the grounds that they were non residents. The ultimate relief for the great bulk of immigrants came with the outbreak of the Second War which gave employment either in the military or in the defense industries," said Dodds.[55] One of the federal official studies of migration stated, "There is a predominance of young, and middle aged persons in the prime of life. To permit this vigorous group of Americans to lapse into permanent poverty and insecurity will be a major national disaster."[56] The problem was recognized, but the solution to achieving social expectations rested on the ability of the dispossessed to persevere and to seize opportunities as they arose. Nearly all occupations from unskilled labor to highly trained professions were represented, although manual and semiskilled were over-represented. The latter required the most assistance to be assimilated into the Northwest's economy.[57]

Another government report recognized the urgency of the situation, stating, "Many of them are still ambitious enough to hope to acquire a foothold on the land. Whether they will keep up their fight and ambition is questionable unless rehabilitation measures are devised which will help them rise above the level on which they are now forced to live."[58] It was suggested but never implemented that WPA projects be employed to clear land for settlers and rural zoning laws be enacted, such as those in Wisconsin, to prevent occupation of unsuitable areas.[59]

Besides large projects such as irrigation, electricity, and transportation improvements designed to promote agriculture, the government proposed self-liquidating loans and cooperative clearing associations. The Resettlement Administration granted five thousand start-up farm loans. Five farmers in cooperation with The Farm Security Administration undertook a land clearing experiment near Sequim, Washington, called the Agnew Land Clearing Service. They were loaned $6500 to buy a small tractor, a bulldozer, and a truck. Eighty area farmers signed up for five thousand hours at $3.50 an hour. An estimated thousand acres were cleared roughly in a five year period at a low cost of around $25 per acre. Final costs per acre were estimated at between $38 and $60.[60] Rapid expansion of the industrial economy propelled by war, however, provided the badly needed economic safety valve and caused a decline of interest in clearing new farmland.

Newcomers to the Northwest found a less developed land than California containing many whom had arrived just before them, frequently with the same background. In 1930, only 44 percent of the inhabitants of the Northwest had been born there.[61] The majority of earlier migrants had been from the upper Midwest with similar backgrounds that eased the transition for the newcomers, in many cases with direct assistance because they were either related or acquainted. The 13.5 percent foreign born came largely from the Scandinavian countries and Canada, although there was also a substantial representation from all European countries such as Italy, England, Germany and Ireland plus a substantial number of Asians from Japan, China, and the Philippines.[62]

Unemployment remained high but the region did not have California's huge accumulated surplus of labor. The demand for labor in many of the Pacific Northwest's key industries—agriculture, lumbering, construction, fishing, and canning was highly seasonal. So, in spite of severe drops during the off season, employment during peak periods was obtainable for most able applicants, especially in the last half of the 1930s. By the second quarter of 1933 the all-important Pacific Northwest lumber industry was recovering, spurred by the dramatic increase in New Deal construction projects and increased foreign trade. In the last three-quarters of 1933 Washington lumber production increased 34.4 percent while Oregon lumber production increased 40.7 percent. Although the recovery continued throughout the 1930s and 1940s, production in Washington and Oregon did not exceed the 1929 level until 1950.[63] Turnover in jobs in these seasonal industries remained high, even in the Depression. Sawmills, regarded as one of the more stable employers in the region, experienced an impressive annual turnover rate estimated at two hundred percent.[64] Loggers rarely had both a stable residence and stable employment.

During the period 1929 to 1933, the Pacific Northwest experienced a more severe drop in income than the rest of the nation, but the rate of recovery between 1933 and 1937 substantially surpassed the national rate.[65] Several factors promoted the resurgence. The hard hit timber industry almost had regained its 1920s level. Large federally financed projects such as dams, roads, and bridges required huge quantities of labor and material. Drought had affected northwest agriculture in the early 30s, but mid-decade production stabilized, allowing excellent profits, especially in grain. Widespread failure of wheat in 1936 drove the price to $1.025, the highest price in the entire decade and Pacific Northwest producers marketed the best crop in a decade.[66] The Willamette Valley also had a record flax crop in 1936.[67]

The McGregor Land and Livestock Company, one of the largest wheat and sheep producers in southeastern Washington, kept detailed records. They indicated 1930 was the worst drought year in the Columbia basin with the area west of Ritzville producing no crops. The McGregors lost $48,000 that year, $14,000 in 1931 and $28,000 in 1932. By 1933, the worst was over and there were no more losing years. New Deal programs and improved conditions produced a profit of $33,000 in 1933. Using inexpensive wheat, hay, apples and horses (for food—now expendable because of mechanization), they fattened 3,300 hogs from Montana, North Dakota and Minnesota for a nice profit. Alexander McGregor, heir to and historian of the McGregor enterprise, noted the Columbia Plateau received hundreds from the Dust Bowl. "Most families had less that $500 and their chief asset was a car," he recalled.[68]

In 1936, WPA projects in the Northwest were cut back because of the demand for farm labor. The region's recovery was well underway. That year new car sales in the Pacific Northwest as well as the entire country broke records set in the 1920s. Production of cars and trucks both more than tripled at 3,669528 cars and 784,587 trucks.[69] The value of new construction in the nation also doubled from 1933 to 1936.[70] By 1938, the three Pacific Coast states had the highest median income in the nation.

For Oregon and Washington the emergence of the labor intensive paper and plywood industries absorbed more labor and helped push the timber cut back to 1920s levels.[71] Japan's rapidly expanding needs, based in part on their war with China, also created an expanded market for raw materials, especially forest products. Disturbing to many timber industry workers, but not to loggers and timber owners, the Japanese were allowed to purchase all the prime old-growth logs they wanted and ship them to Japan for processing. Military bases and shipyards were expanding and other huge federal construction projects such as Bonneville, completed in 1937, and Grand Coulee, completed in 1941, demanded large quantities of labor and materials, and, upon completion, generated an almost unlimited supply of inexpensive hydroelectricity. By 1938, the three Pacific Coast states enjoyed the highest median income in the nation and were poised for the dramatic economic boom precipitated by World War II.[72]

Alarming demographic studies that revealed the Pacific Northwest had an aging and possibly declining population convinced many that the influx of young, energetic populace bode well for the future. The area had one of the lowest birth rates per capita in the nation in 1930 with Oregon the third least fertile state and Washington fifth as measured by the number of children under five years old per thousand women between twenty and forty-four. Idaho and Montana, in contrast, ranked near the top.[73] Many males associated with the lumber industry had remained single and were now in their advanced years, making the rural areas where they tended to remain more elderly. Studies showed that 40 percent of the population was under nineteen in 1900 compared to 30 percent in 1940, while only two percent were over sixty-five in 1890, over 8 percent were in 1940.[74] Somewhat outrageous in retrospect, it was estimated that Oregon and Washington population would peak in 1950 and show a slow decline in the 1960s and 1970s as compared to 1950. The estimate for Idaho and Montana showed a consistent gain during each ten-year period.[75] A booklet sponsored by the state of Oregon suggested, "For the states of Washington and Oregon, fast becoming over-weighted with aging people and faced with a declining population by 1950, this coming of young blood is of considerable significance."[76]

Sparsely settled and blessed with enormous natural resources, the Pacific Northwest provided the most attractive safety valve for those fleeing the drought ravaged Northern Great Plains. Some have interpreted the Dust Bowl migration as the mere continuation of a steady migration from the Great Plains to the Pacific Northwest that had been a pattern for decades. The difference between the earlier period and the 1930s was that the Pacific Northwest was also in the throes of deep economic depression and less able to accommodate the flow of migrants. Their numbers were no greater than in previous decades, but their economic circumstances on average were far more desperate. Dust Bowl migrants, generally self-reliant and frequently assisted by relatives and friends, relied on federal assistance if their limited resources could not sustain them.

NOTES

1. Neil Morgan, *Westward Tilt* (New York: Random House, 1963), 207.

2. *Fortune* [poll] 16 (October 1937): 14; Leo A. Borah, "Washington the Evergreen State: The Amazing Commonwealth of the Pacific Northwest which Has Emerged from the Wilderness in a Span of Fifty Years," *National Geographic* (February 1933): 131–96,

3. Harvey Perloff, et al. *Regions, Resources and Economic Growth* (Baltimore: Johns Hopkins University Press, 1960), 189.

4. Harold Ickes. *The Autobiography of a Curmudgeon* (Chicago: Quadrangle Books, 1969), 279–98.

5. Alex Groner, *PACCAR, The Pursuit of Quality* (Bellevue, WA: Documentary Book Publishing Company, 1981), passim; Paula Becker. "PACCAR Inc—A Snapshot History," http://.historylink.org/-output.cfm?file-ID=4272. (accessed October 30, 2006)

6. W. Claude Adams, *History of Papermaking in the Pacific Northwest* (Portland: Binfords and Mort, 1951), 65–67; Donald H. Clark. "An Analysis of Forest Utilization as a Factor in Colonizing the Pacific Northwest and in Subsequent Population Transitions" (master's thesis, University of Washington, 1952), 135–36.

7. Jonathon Dembo. "The Pacific Northwest Lumber Industry during the Great Depression," *Journal of the West* 24 (October 1985): 51; Robert F. Ficken, *The Forested Land: A History of Lumbering in Western Washington* (Seattle: University of Washington Press, 1987): 184.

8. Donald H. Clark, "An Analysis," 135–36: Robert M. Cour, *The Plywood Age: A History of the Fir Plywood Industry's First Fifty Years* (Portland: Binfords and Mort, 1955).

9. Ibid., 133.

10. Calvin F. Schmid, *Social Trends in Seattle* (Seattle: University of Washington Press, 1944), 13, 23.

11. Gus Norwood, et al., *Columbia River Power for the People: A History of Policies of the Bonneville Power Administration* (Portland: United States Department of Energy, 1981), 40.

12. Frank Freidel, "FDR in the Northwest: Informal Glimpses," *Pacific Northwest Quarterly* 76 (October 1985): 122–31.

13. Frank Freidel, *Franklin D. Roosevelt: The Triumph* (Boston: Little, Brown and Company, 1956), Chapter 8, "Victory over the Power Magnates."

14. Frank Freidel, *Franklin* Roosevelt, 341; Albert A. Acena. "The Washington Commonwealth Federation: Reform Politics and Popular Front" (PhD dissertation, University of Washington, 1975), 168; Don Clark *What Depression? How America's Kids Beat the Blahs of the 1930s* (Victoria, Canada: Trafford Publishers, 2003), 19–21, 23–25. The Clarks were next door neighbors to the Boettingers in the exclusive Lawton Wood section. Clark enjoyed attempts to elude the FBI agents who were assigned to guard the two Roosevelt grandchildren day and night. Eleanor Roosevelt visited frequently. When Franklin Roosevelt visited, ". . . life became a little more

complicated, and a lot more fun." About a half-acre of Clark's heavily wooded backyard was illuminated by Secret Service floodlights.

15. William Dietrich, *Northwest Passage: The Great Columbia River* (Seattle: University of Washington Press), 269.

16. John Blanchard, *Caravans to the Northwest* (Portland: Northwest Regional Council, 1940), 5.

17. William Dietrich, *Northwest Passage,* 269.

18. Richard Neuberger, *Our Promised Land* (New York: Macmillan, 1938), 43.

19. David Wyatt, ed., *New Essays on the Grapes of Wrath* (New York: Cambridge University Press, 1990), 3.

20. Blanchard, *Caravans,* 5–9.

21. Campbell G. Murphy. "Farmers on Cutover Lands in Western Washington State" (master's thesis, University of Washington, 1954), 196.

22. William G. Robbins. "Persisting Reality: The Pacific Northwest and Northern Tier States as 'Plunder Provinces,' 1900–1948," in *The Centennial West: Essays on the Northern Tier States,* ed. William L. Lang (Seattle: University of Washington Press, 1991). 12–38.

23. Herbert A. Resner, *Power in the State of Washington* (Seattle: State Government, 1937), 1–2 (Introduction).

24. Willard Troxell and Paul O'Day, *Migration Into the States of the Pacific Northwest, 1930–1938* (Portland: Farm Security Administration, May 1940), 13–18; Leonard J. Arrington, "Western Agriculture and the New Deal," *Agricultural History* 49 (1970) 337–51; Carl P. Heiseg, "The Migrants II: New Farms on Newly Irrigated Land," *Land Policy Review* (November-December 1939): 10–16; David McEntire and Marion Clauson, "Migration and Resettlement in the Pacific Northwest, 1932–1940," *Social Science* 16 (April 1941): 102–15; Frederick Yonce "Public Land Disposal in Washington" (PhD Dissertation, University of Washington, 1969).

25. Jonathan Dembo. "The Pacific Northwest Lumber Industry during the Great Depression," *Journal of the West* 24 (October 1985): 51.

26. Margaret E. Felt, *Capitol Forest . . . the Forest that Came Back* (Olympia: Washington State Department of Natural Resources, 1975), 47–49. An excellent local publication, although Felt is unforgiving in her treatment of migrant stump ranchers.

27. Dembo, "The Pacific Northwest," 56.

28. Charles Miles and O. B. Sperlin, eds., *Building a State, 1889–1939.* (Tacoma: Washington State Historical Society, 1940), Donation Land Claims are listed by counties, 410–46; accomplishments of the 1018 claim holders, 447–52; and what became of the claims, 450–52.

29. Pacific Northwest Regional Planning Commission, *Migration and the Development of Economic Opportunity in the Pacific Northwest: A Report Prepared in Cooperation with the Pacific Northwest Land Advisory Committee* (Portland: Pacific Northwest Regional Planning Commission, 1939), 107. State land ownership in all three states increased dramatically after 1936. As a percentage of original federal grants the numbers are: Oregon, 42; Washington, 118; Idaho, 81. From Randal O'Toole, "Should Congress Transfer Federal Lands to the States?" Cato Policy

Analysis No. 26. http:///www.msn.com.should+congress+transfer+fedral+lands+to+the+states/. (accessed November 10, 2005).

30. Robert Ficken, *The Forested Land: A History of Lumbering in Western Washington* (Durham, NC: Forest History Association; Seattle: University of Washington Press, 1987), 25–26.

31. Richard White, "Poor Men on Poor Lands: The Back to the Land Movement of the Early Twentieth Century," *Pacific Historical Review* (February 1980): 291.

32. United States Forest Service, *Forest Land Ownership in Oregon and Washington. A Report* (Portland: United States Forest Service, 1934).

33. *Migration and the Development of Economic Opportunity*, 105.

34. Nelley P. Davis. *Stump Ranch Pioneer* (New York: Dodd Mead, 1942). The Davis Family migrated to Northern Idaho from Eastern Colorado.

35. White, "Poor Men," 296.

36. Ibid., 297; Author's experience.

37. Willard Troxel and Paul O'Day, *Migration into the States of the Pacific Northwest, 1930–1938* (Portland: Farm Security Administration, May 1940), see forward.

38. Michael K. Green, "Hard Times in the Promised Land: The Depression and the New Deal in Washington State," *Pacific Northwest Forum* 2 (Spring/Fall 1989): 4–5. Entire issue is devoted to the topic.

39. *Migration and the Development of Economic Opportunity*, 7.

40. Pacific Northwest Planning Commission, *Recent Migration into the Pacific Northwest: Land Problems, Requirements in Land Reclamation, Need for Coordinated Programs, Necessary Land Development and Settlement Policies* (Portland: Pacific Northwest Regional Planning Commission, 1938), 6–7.

41. Resettlement Administration, "Suggestions to Prospective Settlers in Idaho, Washington and Oregon," (Portland: Resettlement Administration, 1936).

42. Blanchard, *Caravans,* 43–45.

43. John Webb and Malcom Brown, *Migrant Families,* WPA Research Monograph 18 (Washington, DC: United States Government Printing Office, 1938), 11; author's experience.

44. *Migration and the Development of Economic Opportunity*, 103.

45. Ibid., 136.

46. Marion Clawson, David McEntire, and Carl P. Heisy, "Stump Ranching," *Land Policy Review* III (May-June 1940): 32; author's experience.

47. Carey McWilliams, *Ill Fares the Land: Migrants and Migratory Labor in the United States* (New York: Barnes and Noble, 1941), 54–56; *Migration*, 9; *Recent Migration*, 11–12.

48. Richard White, *"It's Your Misfortune and None of my Own": A History of the American West* (Norman: University of Oklahoma Press, 1991), 483.

49. McWilliams, *Ill Fares the Land,* 58. Author's experience, although furniture was not quite as Spartan as McWilliams' description.

50. *Migration,* 9–10.

51. James Sidel, *Pick for Your Supper: A Study of Child Labor among Migrants on the Pacific Coast* (New York: National Child Labor Committee, 1939), 13.

52. *Recent Migration*, 9.

53. Henry H. Collins, Jr., *America's Own Refugees: Our 4,000,000 Homeless Migrants* (Princeton: Princeton University Press, 1941), 262. An excellent summary of the eleven volume report of the Tolan Committee of the House of Representatives Investigation of the Interstate Migration of Destitute Citizens, 1941. The author observed migrant children were at least on a par with the native born in the rural schools, but as true with rural children in general, were behind students in urban schools.

54. John H. Tolan [Chairman], *Hearings on House Resolution 63 and House Resolution 491.* 76th Congress, July 29–December 11, 1940, 11 volumes (Washington, DC: United States Government Printing Office, 1941), Volume 10, page 4121.

55. Gordon B. Dodds. *The American Northwest: A History of Oregon and Washington* (Arlington Heights, IL: The Forum Press, 1986), 250–51.

56. Troxel and O'Day, *Migration into the States of the Pacific Northwest,* 28.

57. Ibid., 33–43.

58. *Migration and the Development of Economic Opportunity*, 84.

59. Ibid., 40–41.

60. *Ibid.*,141.

61. Troxell and O'Day, *Migration*, 33–43.

62. James E. Maxwell, *Preliminary Analysis of Population Data in Pacific Northwest States* (Portland: Northwest Regional Planning Commission, 1939), 2–8.

63. Jonathan Dembo, "The Pacific Northwest Lumber Industry during the Great Depression," *Journal of the West* 24 (October 1985): 53.

64. John H. Tolan, *House Select Committee,* Volume 10, 4140.

65. *Migration and the Development of Economic Opportunity*, 17.

66. "Midwest Drought Adds Millions to Coast Crop Value," *Ellensburg Record*, 18 July 1936; "Wheat Crop Will Be Best in Past Decade," *Ellensburg Record*, 31 July 1936.

67. *Salem* [OR] *Statesman,* July 9, 1936.

68. Alexander C. McGregor, *Counting Sheep: From Open Range to Agribusiness on the Columbia Plateau* (Seattle: University of Washington Press, 1982), 278–93.

69. United States Bureau of Census, *Historical Statistics of the United States, 1789–1945*, Series J, (Washington, DC: United States Government Printing Office, 1949), 223.

70. *Historical Statistics*, Series H, 168.

71. Blanchard, *Caravans,* 93.

72. *Migration and the Development of Economic Opportunity*, 157.

73. Blanchard, *Caravans*, 22–23.

74. Paul H, Landis, *Fifty Years of Population Growth in Washington*, Bulletin Number 419 (Pullman, WA: Washington Agricultural Experiment Station, 1942), 24–25.

75. Maxwell, *Preliminary Analysis*, 24–25.

76. Blanchard, *Caravans,* 17.

Chapter Six

Washington: The Evergreen State

In the late 1930s, James Farley, chairman of the Democratic National Committee and postmaster general of the United States reportedly said, "There are forty-seven states and the Soviet of Washington." Farley later denied the statement, but it has endured as an accurate assessment of the state in the Depression era because it had realized more than its share of publicity concerning radical labor confrontations and intense Communist activity. These much-reported events, however, did not reflect the conservative mainstream of the Evergreen State's politics. From 1889 statehood until the 1932 Democratic landslide, the state had elected only two Democratic Governors and the legislative branches were consistently dominated by mostly Progressive Republicans who, as in the Dakotas, predominated in towns and cities.[1] A strong and highly visible cadre of Communist supporters emerged in the 1930s, though. Of that decade, Harvey Klehr, a leading authority on American Communism, wrote, "No state proved as congenial to the Popular Front as Washington. In no other state did so many Party members win election to the legislature or wield so much power within the Democratic Party."[2]

Washington had built a solid foundation for 1930s radicalism but it was confined to a fairly small minority. As the timber industry boomed in the early twentieth century, pushing Washington‘s population from 518,103 in 1900 to 1,41,990 in 1910, Seattle became a hot bed of labor radicalism. This was another extension of a long history of confrontation between labor and management during the period of great industrial expansion after the Civil War. Highlights of labor strife included Chicago's Haymarket Square Riot (1886), The Homestead Steel Strike (1892), and the Pullman Railroad Strike (1894). The Federation of Western Miners (FWM), headed by violence prone Big Bill Haywood, waged a virtual war in the mining states of the Rocky Mountains.

In 1907, Haywood became a celebrity when famed defense lawyer Clarence Darrow won him a questionable acquittal for the bombing death of former Idaho governor Frank Steunenburg. By 1915, Haywood, an avowed Communist, headed the even more militant Industrial Workers of the World (IWW), commonly referred to as Wobblies. The name supposedly stemmed from a Chinese man's reference to them as the "I Wobbly Wobbly." Opponents frequently translated IWW into "I Won't Work."[3]

The IWW was formed when the FWM merged with several other liberal labor unions in Chicago in 1905. Its slogan "One Big Union" was intended to include everyone of the working class around the world. Critics viewed the IWW as a radical Communist organization. Miners, timber workers, textile workers and agricultural workers, many of whom were single and mobile, provided the bulk of membership in the United States. One way the IWW expressed their anti-establishment views was through protest songs. *Hallelujah, I'm a Bum*, a parody of a Salvation Army song *Revive Us Again*, especially annoyed critics.

An IWW hall was established in Seattle in 1905 and quickly gained a substantial membership, especially among timber workers. Given the harsh working conditions in the logging camps and sawmills, the timber industry provided a welcome environment for labor organization. Logging camps of the era were noted for their inadequate housing, food, safety precautions, low wages and long hours. Many loggers were single, moved frequently and retained little loyalty to their employer or their community. A large percentage was of liberal Scandinavian descent. In 1910, only two of ten Washington residents were born there. Mill workers, although more stable, suffered the same working conditions and frequently lived in tightly controlled company towns. When the WFM left the IWW to join the American Federation of Labor (AFL) in 1911, Haywood stayed with the IWW and became its leader in 1915, bringing his penchant for violence and confrontation. Militant labor activity in Seattle, Tacoma, Aberdeen, Centralia and other logging communities soon created vehement hostility toward the IWW.[4]

Three labor-related incidents in Washington before and after World War I gave the state notoriety. On November 5, 1916, five IWW members were killed and thirty-nine were wounded when two-hundred armed vigilantes led by the county sheriff engaged them in a gun battle when they attempted to land at the port of Everett. Two lawmen on shore were killed and nineteen were wounded. The IWW had been active in the lumbering and shingle-weaving town of Everett since 1914, much to the discomfiture of the mill owners. On September 30, 1916, forty-one IWW supporters from Seattle were taken from their boat at Everett and forced to run a gauntlet where most were badly beaten. Attempts to speak out about the injustices in Everett were quickly silenced by local authorities. That led to the fateful November gun battle when 239 IWW supporters from Seattle were met at the dock. All IWW supporters involved were acquitted later in a highly publicized Seattle trial.[5]

Logging companies, capitalizing on a labor oversupply, paid an average of thirty-five cents an hour and demanded ten hours a day, six days a week. World War I reversed the buyer's market for labor and the IWW, suffering no qualms about disloyalty charges, pushed for an eight hour day, much higher wages, and improved working conditions. When the owners flatly refused their demands, work stoppages and violence ensued, finally evolving into a general strike against the entire Pacific Northwest logging industry during the spring and summer of 1917. Not willing to sustain such a drastic reduction in the supply of a vital raw material, the government sent in about fifty thousand soldiers, known as the Spruce Army, to resume production. The soldiers were so named because they played a key role in logging spruce. It was the tough, light, wood preferred for building airplanes of that era.[6] The Army also organized about 100,000 loggers into the world's largest company union, the Loyal Legion of Loggers and Lumbermen, which prohibited all IWWs. The government further cracked down on radicals with the Espionage Act of 1917 and the Sedition Act of 1918.

Shortly after the War the Seattle General Strike of February 1919 stirred national attention. It provided fuel for the Red Scare of the era, and made Seattle mayor "Holy" Ole Hanson a national hero at least temporarily. Hanson had earned his nickname for leading the fight to close down the Meadowlands horse race track, describing it as a haven for criminals, gamblers and prostitutes. The strike began in the shipyards of Seattle and Tacoma where 35,000 workers demanded a raise after having their wage rate frozen during the war. The Seattle Central Labor Council backed them and completely shut down the city on February 6, 1919. Hanson threatened marshal law and called in federal troops who set up machine guns at strategic locations. After five days the strike was broken and Hanson declared, "Americanism has triumphed over Bolshevism." Most of the shipyard workers were left unemployed by post war cutbacks. On April 28, 1919, a bomb appeared on Hanson's desk, but it did not explode. Hanson, son of Wisconsin Norwegian immigrants, who had driven his family to Seattle from Butte, Montana, in a covered wagon, hoped to parlay his new found fame into the Republican nomination for President, but was ignored at the convention in favor of Warren G. Harding. Hanson moved to California and founded the city of San Clemente, but went bankrupt in the Great Depression.

Another deadly confrontation on Armistice Day, 1919, at Centralia, eighty-five miles south of Seattle, signaled the rapid decline of the IWW. Centralia and its close neighbor, Chehalis, were targeted by the IWW because they were located in the center of the area's thriving logging industry. Both communities had earned a reputation for conservatism. They had forced out Greeks and Italians in 1910 and bitterly opposed labor unions. Centralia showed its hostility to the IWW first in 1914 when it forcefully threw out over forty homeless IWW members. Not discouraged, the IWW opened a hall in Centralia in 1917, but was promptly evicted because of their outspoken opposition to the war, their support of Bolshivik Russia, and their attempts to organize the timber workers. Still not intimidated they opened another headquarters in 1918. It was wrecked and its occupants were run out of town in a manner similar to Everett.

Encouraged by the Seattle leaders, the IWW opened yet another hall early in 1919. This time they expected an attack and received no commitment when they requested police protection for what seemed inevitable. At the end of the Armistice Day Parade, Centralia Legionaires stormed the hall and broke down the door. This time armed Wobblies opened fire, killing three and wounding several others. Most, realizing the overwhelming odds, surrendered. Organizer Wesley Everest, a war veteran, fled and was cornered on a nearby river bank, where he shot and killed the leader of the pursuers before being captured and dragged back to jail. That night with the entire area in a state of anger, vigilantes easily removed Everest from his cell, drove him to a railroad trestle on the Chehalis River, mutilated him, hung him, and shot him. Everest joined IWW martyrs Joe Hill, executed for murder in Utah, and Frank Little, lynched in Butte, Montana. Unlike the other two, Everest's guilt was undisputed.[7]

Seven other Wobblies, defended by the Seattle lawyer who had won acquittal for those accused in the Everett incident, were convicted of second-degree murder and sentenced to 25–40 years. The trial was highly controversial and by 1939 all were either paroled or had died in prison.[8] As a result of the Centralia tragedy Washington passed a law making it illegal to belong to the IWW, causing its near disappearance in the conservative 1920s.

Logging camps provided good markets for meat, dairy products, poultry, vegetables, fruit, berries and other agricultural products. A number of canneries also were established to process the harvest. This led to a strong rural population in Lewis County concentrated in the fertile Chehalis River Valley. These areas, heavily populated by Scandinavians, especially socialistically inclined Finns, reflected liberalism akin to the rural Northern Great Plains . They supported organized labor, labor cooperatives, the Nonpartisan League and the League of Nations, but they did not support the IWW because of its radical inclinations.

The Grange, a key player in the Progressive politics of that era, tended to focus their political, social and economic interests. By 1910, Lewis County boasted nineteen granges.[9] Local antagonism to the Nonpartisan League and the Grange approached that directed at the IWW. Nonpartisan League organizers from North Dakota had achieved success in Idaho, but failed in Washington. In April 1918, two League organizers were tarred and feathered in the Winlock-Toledo area in Lewis County. In June 1918, Walla Walla citizens shut down the state Grange meeting because of its sympathy to the Nonpartisan League. State Grange leader William Bouck, a Dutch bulb grower from Sedro Wooley and a family man known as a loyal citizen, was arrested for opposing the sale of Liberty bonds to finance the war and advocating instead higher taxes on the wealthy. A Seattle grand jury indicted Bouck for violating the Espionage Act, but the case was dismissed.[10]

Washington's strong economy based primarily on a thriving, nation leading lumber industry, promoted robust growth until the 1929 collapse. The mammoth old growth trees that fed the industry produced an unprecedented yield. In 1899, the *Elma Chronicle* reported, "E. C. Stamper, a citizen of Elma, has completed working up a fir tree which grew on his place adjoining town. He received $12 for the bark, built a frame house 14 × 20 feet-8 feet high, with shed kitchen 8 feet wide; built a wood shed 14 × 20 feet, made 300 rails 10 feet long; made 334 railroad ties and 500 boards 6" × 2" by 2 feet and 15 cords of wood, all from one tree and has part of the tree left."[11] With a wealth of trees of this quality all over Western Washington, lumber's dominance of the economy was no surprise.

Proceeds from the sale of state timberlands supplied Washington a steady income and financed an impressive new state capitol. Unfortunately, Roland Hill Hartley, the first governor to enjoy it, alienated almost everyone and blocked or slowed nearly all forward advancement because of his fixation on cutting expenses. Frequently called "Rollin Hill" because of his practice of frequently "rollin' down the hill" from the executive offices to harangue the legislators in the statehouse. Republican Hartley said, "If I had my way I'd stop all legislation for 40 years and the state would be better off."[12] Everett historian Norman Clark, perhaps Hartley's most virulent critic, wrote:

> There was little about progress and nothing about the Progressive Age which Hartley could not hold up to wrath and condemnation. He detested prohibitionists, social workers, suffragettes, direct primaries and direct legislation. He hated radicals, internationalists, pacifists, unions, taxes, and progressive education. He was proud that as a legislator he had introduced laws against picketing and against teaching social science. He had voted against an eight-hour law for women.[13]

Much of Hartley's eight years as governor (1925–1933) were preoccupied with feuds, vendettas, and vetoes.[14] At a time when the state could have advanced dramatically, Hartley held his foot firmly on the brake.

Diminutive in stature with a limited education, Hartley, a hard worker, swore he never gave a man a job that he could not do better himself. He claimed to be a self made man, but his career was propelled by his 1888 marriage to Nina Clough, daughter of timber capitalist David Clough who was elected Minnesota's governor in 1895. Hartley was private secretary for Clough, who was convinced by railroader James J. Hill to move to Everett and establish a shingle mill. In 1890, Hill sold his St. Paul neighbor, George Weyerhaeuser (and fifteen partners), 900,000 acres in Washington for six dollars an acre and a promise of favorable railroad rates, prompting Weyerhaeuser to plan the largest lumber mill in the world for Everett. By World War I, Weyerhaeuser owned nearly two million acres, three quarters of it located in Washington.[15] Clough moved to Everett in 1900 and Hartley followed in 1902. They built the Clough-Hartley Mill, the greatest producer of red cedar shingles in the world.

Conservative Weyerhaeuser and partners waited until the 1890s economic collapse ended. St Paul neighbors and business leaders Chauncy and Everett Griggs and partners had purchased eighty thousand acres in Pierce County from the Northern Pacific Railroad in 1888. They formed the St. Paul and Tacoma Lumber Company and also invested in coal mining, shipping, a Tacoma smelter and banking. Partner Henry Hewett Jr. founded the town of Everett in 1890. After barely surviving the 1890s, St. Paul and Tacoma enjoyed prosperity by 1900, encouraging Weyerhaeuser and associates to make the largest private real estate investment in United States history up to that time. Young William Boeing also left Minneapolis for Hoquiam in 1903 to manage family timber interests.[16]

Hartley resolved he had a future in politics, becoming mayor of Everett in 1910. A fiscal crisis caused by closure of saloons led him to cut services and he was unseated after one stormy term.[17] Hartley was elected to the state legislature for one term in 1915, and after several tries became governor in 1924 on a rock-solid conservative platform that attracted the urban vote.

Determined to reduce the cost of government and lighten the burden of taxation, Hartley maintained services such as education and welfare should be funded at the local level. He vetoed a total of eighty-two bills during his eight-year reign. His veto of a state income tax further limited state support for vital services. Hartley opposed road improvement, child labor laws, promised to lower the cost of public education, and thought there were "too many libraries."[18] In 1925, Hartley vetoed a popular bill that would allow state normal schools to grant degrees. It suffered the same fate when it again easily passed the legislature in 1929. He also vetoed legislatively approved state parks budgets, causing severe deterioration of the system and forcing many to close by the end of his tenure. State roads received the same treatment and also suffered when Hartley appointed hard drinking Enoch "Baggy" Bagshaw as state supervisor of transportation in March 1930. Bagshaw shared Hartley's conservative philosophy and accomplished very little before he died of a heart attack in October. "Baggy" had enjoyed great success as the Everett high school football coach and had gained greater glory at the University of Washington. When a new university president restricted football scholarships the Huskies lost all of their conference games in 1929, causing Bagshaw's ouster. When the Hoover administration finally made some road construction loans available, moreover, Hartley refused to sign the necessary applications.[19]

Hartley's apparent role in the dismissal of Henry Suzzalo, the prominent president of the University of Washington, showed his unforgiving nature. Five Hartley appointed regents fired Suzzalo in October 1926 by a vote of five to two. No charges were presented and there was no hearing. Hartley denied all involvement, but the *Tacoma News Tribune* called it "the blind act of a dictator," and the *Wenatchee Herald* called for his dismissal. Hartley's animosity toward Suzzalo was well documented. Much of the feud involved the ambitious president's unwillingness to accept Hartley's harsh budget restrictions and his willingness to participate in politics not directly related to the university. Suzzalo also had served as chair of the National Defense Council Committee that arbitrated the 1917 timber strike, and, although he held no regard for the IWW, cast the deciding vote for an eight hour day for loggers, alienating lumberman Hartley. Additionally, in his ten years as president Suzzalo had pushed the university and himself into a position of national prominence and Hartley viewed him as a possible political rival.

Born in San Francisco to immigrant Italians from Trieste, Suzzalo completed graduate work at Columbia University and there became a professor of education under famed educator Nicholas Murray Butler, whose brother William was the leading banker in Everett. Upon William's request for a recommendation, Nicholas strongly endorsed Suzzalo. After obtaining the presidency in 1915, Suzzalo led the university forward with strong-willed aggressiveness. He established the country's first College of Fisheries. A number of impressive new buildings featuring uniform Tudor architecture were completed and the magnificent library, named for Suzzalo in 1933, was under construction. By 1922, his $18 thousand salary was considered excessive by many. Hartley, born in New Brunswick, Canada, wrongly called Suzzalo a "foreigner."[20] Ironically, when Hartley refused to provide money to celebrate the bicentennial of the birth of George Washington (1732), the DAR protested and blamed the governor's Canadian origins for his lack of patriotism.

In spite of loud objections Suzzalo's dismissal faded away quickly, largely because his dictatorial style had antagonized many. At a university faculty meeting a motion critical of the Regents' action failed for lack of a second. Faculty discontent had long simmered over the president's arbitrary style. He was accused of extreme favoritism in matters of salary, tenure and promotion. Determined that the faculty needed improvement, Suzzalo kept salaries low and hired new faculty with salary increases that were intended for existing faculty.[21] Many viewed his numerous political activities as self-promotional at the expense of the state.

Suzzalo's firing of football coach "Gloomy Gil" Dobie on the questionable grounds of failure to fully train character on the football field was not well received by Washington fans, either. Dobie, a former star quarterback at the University of Minnesota who held a law degree, came to Seattle after two undefeated seasons at North Dakota Agricultural College (now North Dakota State). The angular, acerbic Scot had not lost a game during his entire stay (1908–1916), the best record ever for any college football coach—but his bullheaded personality and anti-academic philosophy did not mesh well with the equally strong-minded new president. Dobie's demise helped prompt a number of alumni to suggest Suzzalo's departure was overdue.[22]

Like President Hoover, Hartley's conservative political philosophy, which appealed to many in the 1920s, offered little hope for individuals harshly impacted by The Great Depression. It reached the Pacific Northwest a little more slowly, creating some complacency among political leaders and the urban-elite, but it had a devastating impact when it arrived.[23] With construction virtually at a standstill, demand for lumber plummeted. Washington lumber production fell from a peak of 7.36 billion board feet in 1926 to 2.26 billion board feed in 1932.[24] By 1933 the number of wage earners was only half of the 1926 figure.[25] Between 1929 and 1933 the per capita income in Washington declined 33 percent compared to the national average of 28 percent. Shantytowns of the unemployed, derisively called Hoovervilles, sprang up in all Puget Sound Cities. Seattle had the largest with about six hundred residents.[26] Some Seattle residents killed their pets to save the expense of feeding them.

Tenino, a small logging town south of Olympia, became internationally known for making wooden money legal tender in the 1930s. Tenino was using paper scrip and decided to print it on wood with approval by the United States Comptroller of Currency. Sales of the wooden coins took off immediately with eight issues printed between 1932–1933. Egypt's King Farouk and Italian dictator Benito Mussolini were among the many collectors. Over $11,000 was sold and the city redeemed less than $1000, using the surplus to assist unemployed and for community improvement.[27]

Seattle had no organized relief effort until 1931. Communists had formed active Unemployment Councils (UC) in New York, Chicago, and Detroit in 1930 and began organizing in Seattle. In response Seattle non-communist labor leaders organized the self-help Unemployed Citizens League (UCL) in 1931. With support from local authorities, the UCL set up neighborhood commissaries that dispensed food, firewood and clothing in return for matching labor from the unemployed. It succeeded dramatically and soon received national attention. A coalition of the Communist Unemployed Council and the UCL marched on Olympia, July 4, 1932. Hartley refused to meet with them but met with a small delegation two days later. In Olympia, hostilities between the two groups erupted into an angry fistfight. Lack of support for the Seattle UC convinced them the best strategy was to bore from within and they began joining the UCL, soon giving it a far more radical tone.[28]

Although the Washington State Treasury showed a surplus in 1932, over 200,000 were on relief. Of the total of $57,736,876 provided for relief during 1932–1934, the federal government provided two-thirds.[29] Unpopular even in his own party, Hartley was eliminated from the governor's race in the 1932 primary elections. His parsimonious administration helped fuel another hunger march on Olympia, January 1933. Estimated at between five hundred and one thousand the marchers' list of demands included unemployment insurance, relief for rural families, and prohibition of foreclosures or tax sales.[30] On January 25, a relief bill was passed, establishing a five-member commission to administer funds from President Hoover's Reconstruction Finance Commission.

Another more massive demonstration led by the UCL, March 1, 1933, shook Olympia just as the new governor was taking office. The marchers were greeted by a group called the "American Vigilantes of Thurston County," who directed them with broom handles to Priest Point Park, where they spent the night surrounded by over eight hundred vigilantes. A small delegation of demonstrators was allowed to see the new governor the next day.[31] That spring, state officials withdrew $60,000 from the Parks and Parkway Fund to employ laborers in state parks, but it was minute compared to federal efforts. From June 1933 until the close of 1938, CCC workers developed fourteen Washington State park sites. The FERA and the WPA finished eight others. Major state park developments included Beacon Rock, Deception Pass, Gingko, Lewis and Clark, Millersylvania, Moran, and Riverside.

Washington Democrats, following FDR's lead, had swept every important state office. Herbert Hoover carried every county in Washington in 1928 and lost them all in 1932. Governor elect Clarence Martin, a slender, mustached, moderate Democrat from Cheney, promising a concern for human need and human dignity, appealed to Republicans as well. Only the third Democratic governor in Washington's history, Martin won an even larger percentage of votes than did Roosevelt. In his Inaugural Address Martin proclaimed, "Surely with such resources at hand we need only the spirit to seek, to determine, to build, the genius to create, and the readiness to cooperate toward a common development." The new governor embarked on a program of bipartisan progressive reform. On March 2, he closed the banks, as the vast majority of states had done prior to FDR's inauguration and announcement of a National Bank Holiday.

Martin had earned a law degree from the University of Washington and was hailed as its first graduate to become governor. Although true, he was much more defined by Cheney, a college town located a few miles from Spokane. Martin's father had established a successful grain elevator-flour milling operation there and was also involved in banking. Clarence, extremely active in a variety of activities, graduated from young Cheney Normal in 1906.[32] After obtaining his law degree, Martin ran the family business and became mayor in 1928, a position he maintained as governor. He personally funded Cheney's municipally owned street lighting project and also his campaign for governor. Farmers knew him as a fair dealing businessman and supported him politically.

Martin's faith in agricultural expansion as a viable solution for the many new migrants was expressed in a 1936 state publication. Martin said, "In 1900 there were 33,202 farms in 1935, 85,202. Surely another 156 per cent gain is possible in the next 35 years."[33] The publication claimed the Puget Sound Basin was the greatest producer per acre of hay and grains—with oats running heavier per acre than any place on earth. Martin foresaw tremendous expansion in manufacturing and agriculture triggered by the Grand Coulee and Bonneville projects. He estimated that 2,000,000 acres of arid lands could be irrigated and Washington would host another million habitants. North Dakota migrant Lennie Husa, whose family raised strawberries, remembers being part of a 1938 busload of Rochester students driving to Olympia to visit Governor Martin. The Governor was especially enthused about the annual Rochester strawberry festival.[34]

Several new Democrat office holders offered a somewhat zany contrast to the staid Martin and undoubtedly contributed to the state's eccentric reputation. In the legislature three new Democrats were charged with statutory offenses and one resided in jail for the rape of a twelve year old girl. Victor Meyers, the colorful incoming Lieutenant Governor, was a popular Seattle bandleader who ran for Mayor of Seattle in the robes of Mahatma Gandhi and promised "a hostess on every streetcar."[35] He lost, but was bit by the political bug and decided to file for governor in 1932. Allegedly because Meyers did not have the sixty-dollar fee required to run for Governor, he paid the twelve dollars required to run for Lieutenant Governor.

Meyers, "The Clown Prince of Washington Politics," taken too lightly by many, remained Lieutenant Governor until 1953 and also served as Washington Secretary of State from 1957 to 1965. Born in Little Falls, Minnesota, he was the fifteenth of sixteen children. The family moved to Oregon when Meyers was in his mid-teens. A gifted musician, his band played at the lavish Rose Room at Seattle's prestigious new Hotel Butler, then at the popular Trianan Ball Room. Noted for his offbeat sense of humor Meyers once said, "I won't tell any lies about my opponent, if he won't tell the truth about me."[36]

Polish born Marion Zioncheck, supported by Seattle's radical Unemployed Citizen's League, was elected to the United States House of Representatives in 1932 and made headlines mostly for his extracurricular antics. In January 1936, he was arrested for drunk and disorderly conduct. Three months later he received two speeding tickets in a week. By late June, he was placed in a mental hospital. Zioncheck returned to Seattle in August and leapt to his death from his fifth floor office a week after his friend, young Seattle state representative Warren Magnuson, filed to run for his seat.[37] Also elected to the House of Representatives in 1932 was Democrat Monrad (Mon) C. Wallgren, Magnuson's drinking and card-playing friend. A gregarious jeweler and optical goods dealer from Everett and the 1929 national three-cushion billiard champion, Iowa born Wallgren later became a United States Senator and governor.[38]

Strong rural-based conservatism, albeit, remained vigorous across the nation as well as the Pacific Northwest.[39] There were an estimated 120 fascist organizations in the United States in the 1930s and 1940s mostly stimulated by liberal policies of the New Deal which they viewed as a threat to the independent farmer and small businessman. Fascism also was promoted by nationalist conservatism in Germany and Italy.[40] William D. Pelley's pro-Nazi Silver Shirt organization was organized in twenty-six cities in Washington. Seattle, Olympia, Centralia, Chehalis and Tacoma led, but their numbers stayed low at an estimated 1600.[41] "Down with the Reds and Out with the Jews," was their motto. Orville Roundtree, a Chehalis insurance man, was the most significant leader in the state. Although it was only several hundred dollars a month, Centralia-Chehalis Silver Shirts led the United States in contributions based on community size.[42] In 1936, Washington was the only state that allowed Nazi sympathizer William D. Pelley on the ballot, refusing the same opportunity for the Communist Party. Pelley, though, received only 1,598 votes for president of the almost 700,000 cast in the state.[43]

Section 7A of the National Industrial Recovery Act (NIRA) encouraged union organization, creating a flurry of union activity. With the severely depressed lumber industry offering little promise, the IWW focused on agriculture and mining workers in rural, conservative central Washington. Since World War I, agricultural workers in the fertile Yakima Valley had engaged in a series of disputes over wages and working conditions.[44] Even though a labor surplus existed in the Depression, owners brought in Filipino workers to keep wages low. Trouble spread from the fruit orchards to the hop fields in 1933. Spurred by legalization of beer, hop prices had leapt from 11–14 cents a pound in May to 40–50 cents a pound before harvest. The owner's pay rate of 12.5 cents an hour was challenged by the IWW who wanted 35–50 cents an hour for workers. That was refused flatly and provoked a confrontation. The National Guard, state patrol, and local law enforcement crushed an IWW led strike on August 24. Described as the "Congdon Orchards Battle" local officials after a fifteen minute clash herded 60–70 pickets into a makeshift "prison." Held briefly, they were ordered out of the county.[45]

Coal to supply fuel for the steam locomotives of the era had made the Cascade Mountain communities of nearby Cle Elum and Roslyn. In early 1934, members of the Western Miners Association, after a bitter, violent struggle to gain bargaining rights, struck to protest federal mediators' decision in favor of the United Mine Workers led by John L. Lewis. The strike was suppressed harshly by local officials, the state patrol and immigration officers. Many of the coal miners were foreign born, mostly Slavic or Italian, so were vulnerable to charges of criminal behavior. The repressive environment in Cle Elum received more national publicity when *The New Republic* ran a May article, "A Little Nest of Fascists." The piece evolved around the observations of an Oxford University economics professor and his wife, who visited Cle Elum-Roslyn and Yakima to study area labor relations. They reported they were illegally held by the state patrol and their traveling companion, a young black labor organizer, was placed under arrest and jailed most of an afternoon with no reason given. He was released late in the afternoon and warned next time he would be "handed over to the vigilantes. Remember Yakima."[46]

Essentially a rural, moderate conservative, Martin showed strong, progressive leadership early in his first term. Pledging full cooperation with the New Deal, the new administration gained approval for numerous projects aimed at reducing relief rolls.[47] Realizing their dependence upon county relief was failing, the FERA required states to form a unified comprehensive program to handle unemployment relief and public welfare. Martin appointed Harvard graduate, Republican Charles Ernst, director of the Washington Emergency Relief Administration (WERA). In order to take advantage of federal funding of new programs and benefits Ernst shifted the relief burden from county and local governments to the state. He helped Washington become a model of timely, professional and efficient social services. In 1935, the legislature established the Department of Public Welfare that Ernst headed. When it evolved into the State Department of Social Security in 1937 Ernst stayed at the helm.[48] A modest old-age pension system was established to abolish the poor farm. Martin also pushed through a $10 million bond project for public works. In 1934, the State Department of Public Welfare helped an estimated 600,000 people in one way or the other in 1934.[49]

Impending federal funding of Bonneville Dam allowed Martin to include $377,000 in the 1933 state budget to explore the possibility of building a dam at Grand Coulee for irrigation and electric power. The state contracted the Bureau of Reclamation to do the planning, obtained water rights, and purchased land around the proposed site. Ground was broken as a state project. It was understood that federal funding and control would follow, though.

Roosevelt vowed that the federal government "would never part with its sovereignty or with its control of its power resources while I am President of the United States." FDR advised Washington Senator Clarence Dill that the project would be funded if Washington State came up with the seed money and Dill would refrain from emphasizing the land reclamation aspect. Roosevelt wanted more emphasis on hydroelectric generation because of adamant resistance from Mid-western politicians who opposed huge expansion of irrigated farmland that threatened to further swell the oversupply of farm commodities. In 1933, FDR first allocated $63 million for a low dam at Grand Coulee and then $31 million for Bonneville.[50] The Army Corps of Engineers began construction on Bonneville immediately. By December, led by the Bureau of Reclamation, construction of Grand Coulee was underway.[51]

In contrast to Hartley's support of rigorous admissions policies to keep enrollment down, especially at the University of Washington, Martin believed in an "open door" policy for public colleges and universities. Tuition and admissions requirements were lowered, curriculums were expanded, faculty salaries were increased and normal schools finally became colleges in 1937.[52] With federal assistance many new buildings were erected at state institutions. The University of Washington especially benefited, receiving federal grants for seven new buildings and a wind tunnel with classrooms and offices to study aerodynamics. Enrollments at state institutions of higher education increased dramatically by the end of Martin's second term as a result of these progressive measures. [53] Washington institutions of higher learning continued to maintain a tight lid on liberal activism, though. Of the 1930s, Seattle historian Richard Berner said, "When it came to abridging first amendment rights, the University of Washington was second to none." It required employees to sign a Yellow Dog Contract that prohibited union membership. The university banned all controversial political speakers. Second-income married women were threatened or dismissed.[54]

These many new programs mandated new taxes which, given the desperate times, received approval by the state legislature. After the state Supreme Court declared a state income tax unconstitutional, a state sales tax replaced it in 1936. The tax was two percent on retail sales with exemptions for gasoline, milk, and bread. For taxes less than a penny, aluminum tax tokens worth one-third of a cent were used. As war approached, aluminum was needed, so plastic and paper tokens were substituted. After receiving their fair share of ridicule, tokens eventually were eliminated.[55]

Huge federal expenditures combined with an expanding economy and population allowed the state to maintain a balanced budget throughout the Depression. Part of the favorable balance resulted from Washington's lack of full cooperation in providing matching funds for federal programs. Much was made over the increased taxes needed to support the stream of incoming migrants, but they furnished a substantial contribution in sales, property, and other taxes besides providing a labor force that benefited employers' incomes and a substantial new consumer base. Federal relief dollars provided a large portion of the capital involved. The Evergreen State, for example, hosted an estimated 250,000 CCC volunteers.[56]

Repeal of prohibition, and the restoration of horse racing with on-track pari-mutuel betting and ten round professional boxing, provided not only new employment opportunities but additional substantial tax revenues. When the federal government ended prohibition, Washington quickly did, too. The Schmidt family built a $300,000 brewery for Olympia beer (actually located in Tumwater). Emil Sick, born in Tacoma from a prominent brewery owning family, moved back to Seattle from Canada and founded a brewery that produced Rainier beer, named for the famous mountain. Other, smaller breweries were built, too. The demand for hops, long a staple in the Yakima Valley, skyrocketed. Soon wine was legalized and Washington's berries and grapes became more valuable. Taverns sprang back to life in every city and hamlet with the state retaining exclusive licensing of beer and wine sales. When hard liquor was legalized later, Martin successfully proposed an exclusive state monopoly on its control and sale. State-run liquor stores brought in huge revenues, as they still do. In their first full year of operation they sold $10 million. Then, a fifty cent a year liquor purchase permit was required.[57]

Horse racing in Washington had enjoyed a long tradition. When the ban on pari-mutuel betting was lifted, primarily to gain more revenue, the response was immediate. Longacres, built on 107 acres of former hop and potato fields in rural Renton, became the center piece for Pacific Northwest horse racing for almost sixty years.[58] It immediately became a major track on the racing circuit and attracted nationally known horses, riders and trainers. Joe Gottstein, a successful Seattle realtor, directed his money and energy into Longacres. Blessed with a huge labor force of three thousand motivated by others standing in line for their jobs and inexpensive materials, Gottstein built the facility in twenty-eight days. They erected a track, thirty-seven barns with 854 stalls, a clubhouse and a large grandstand, consuming some two million board feet of lumber.

Longacres opened August 3, 1933, with barns so full some horses were turned away. Many participants lived in tents, heating water over open fires in fifty-gallon tanks. Gottstein lived at the track where he maintained a competitive personal racing stable. [59] In 1934, Tom Smith, a down-on-his-luck trainer, raced at Longacres. Smith went on to attain fame and wealth as the trainer of Seabiscuit. A long shot horse from California, Seabiscuit came to symbolize an ability to overcome adversity during the Depression. .[60] The inauguration of the $10,000 Longacres Mile in 1935 firmly established Longacres as one of the nation's leaders. In 1936, at least seventy-five horses were turned away because of lack of stable space and the crowds set new attendance records.[61]

With the improved economy and an election pending, Martin turned farther to the right politically late in his first term. The rise of the left-leaning Washington Commonwealth Federation (WCF) and a wave of labor strikes pushed Martin to the right. He no doubt also was influenced by the election of extremely conservative governors in Oregon and California. The Great Maritime Strike of 1934 affected the entire West Coast and in mid 1935 the Pacific Northwest suffered the most significant lumber strike since 1917. Martin, no friend of organized labor, sent the National Guard to Tacoma and other lumbering communities to protect workers crossing the picket lines. Workers, discouraged by the hostility of local government and encouraged by the federal Wagner Act that authorized union organization, soon unionized the majority of big Pacific Northwest lumber companies. By 1937, the new Congress of Industrial Organizations (CIO) had 50,000 members in its International Woodworkers affiliate. When the Newspaper Guild struck against the *Seattle Post Intelligencer,* Martin proposed a Washington State Industrial Tribunal (like Taft-Hartley), but it died in committee.[62]

Founded in 1935, the WCF evolved out of the Unemployed Citizens League and several other socialist organizations. It was a Bellamy-like group akin to Upton Sinclair's End Poverty in California (EPIC) organization and its technocracy motto was "Production for Use." In theory Communists were not allowed, but in fact they dominated the WCF.[63] The WCF nominated King County Commissioner John C. Stevenson to compete with Martin for the 1936 Democratic nomination for governor. A shady character, Stevenson had built his reputation on the radio advertising the Painless Parker chain of dentists. He had served as a pilot for Canada in World War I and was wanted for stock fraud in New York. Martin refused to extradite his rival, fearing the political consequences. As the campaign heated up Martin attacked him on the radio, ". . . do you know that the leaders of the Communist Party, the so-called Commonweath Federation and their candidate for the Democratic nomination for governor—the spearhead of their Communist drive—proposes to destroy that system by substituting a revolutionary plan for government?"[64] Martin was saved by the new blanket primary which allowed Washington voters to cross party lines and vote for any candidate. It was clear that the unpopular Hartley would gain the Republican nomination, so many Republicans crossed over to support Martin. The WCF, seeing Stevenson had no chance to win, dropped its support and nominated another candidate. Running as "the governor of all the people," Martin smashed Hartley 466,550 to 189,141 in November. Initiative 119, the WCF's "Production for Use" proposal lost 370,140 to 97,329.[65]

From 1936, Martin and the state legislature stayed to the right of the New Deal and pursued a policy of avoiding taxes on business and maintaining a balanced budget. Business had made a strong recovery.[66] By 1936, industrial payrolls reached $235 million compared to $129 million in 1933.[67] Much of the increase emanated from the lumber industry that showed spectacular gains after the 1935 strike. After a drop in 1938 payrolls rose to $303,602,603 in 1939.[68] Yet, because of federal contributions, residents paid fewer taxes in 1938 than in 1931. It was estimated that in 1938 for every $70 paid in federal taxes $478 returned to the state. Toward the end of the 1930s, Washington ranked seventh among eight western states in average pension payments and last among six western states in aid to dependent children.[69]

After his landslide 1936 victory FDR cut back federal spending, creating the "Roosevelt Depression" of 1937 with unemployment jumping to eleven million. Tied closely to construction, Washington's timber oriented economy dropped hard. Martin responded by cutting 24,000 from relief rolls in 1937 just after the 1936 flood of Dust Bowl migrants arrived. Historian Norman Clark wrote, "Thousands of people were suddenly arriving from the Dust Bowl states—five thousand families were counted in January 1937 and when state agencies attempted to respond to their plight, their directors discovered that federal money they anticipated was not forthcoming and that the state was sinking rapidly again into the quicksand of depression."[70] By 1938, 240,00 sought relief, a number approaching that of 1935. Martin called the recession problem a good thing saying people "had been going too fast since the last depression."[71] Perhaps he did not realize the real hardships some faced. When all WPA work closed in Roslyn, for example, Anton Adams and Pete Thomas asked if it could be continued because "some people were starving."[72]

Martin supported the attempt to purge "irresponsible radicals" from the legislature and other areas of public service. The legislative drive achieved little, but Martin did support the successful ouster of Charles H. Fisher, the president of Western Washington College of Education at Bellingham since 1923. A native of Pennsylvania, Fisher had established Western as the strongest of the three state colleges of education. But his liberal ideas led to an increasing cacophony of conservative criticism. In 1936, Frank Sefrit, the editor of the *Bellingham Herald*, wrote, ". . . numerous executives and members of subversive organizations and of free love, atheistic and un-American pacifist organizations have been invited to address the student body in recent years, while pro Americans have not appeared on invitation in assembly." Sefrit, also the Grand Dragon of the local Ku Klux Klan, complained that the flag was seldom displayed on campus, and that student funds were misapplied. Fisher's board of trustees originally found the charges false. Sefrit's allies complained to Martin, and the governor summoned the trustees who then supported Fisher's dismissal. This heavy-handed move unleashed a storm of protest that attracted national attention.[73] Fisher's firing played an important role in denying Martin the 1940 Democratic gubernatorial nomination. Support for Communism in the United States withered with the August 1939 Nazi-Soviet Union nonaggression pact followed by the Soviet invasion of Finland. By 1940, radicalism in Washington politics essentially was mute.

New governor Arthur B. Langlie, Seattle's young, moralistic mayor, returned Republican conservatism to Olympia, winning the 1940 election by less than six thousand votes. Martin turned so conservative he had supported Langlie in his 1938 bid for Seattle mayor. In the open primary disillusioned Democrats chose former Senator Clarence Dill over Martin as their candidate for governor.

Langlie's background typified that of many Washingtonians. His father, Bjorne, had migrated from Norway to Lanesboro, Minnesota, where Langlie was born in 1900. Bjorne homesteaded three miles north of Noonan, North Dakota, in 1905. When the Soo Railroad arrived, he managed a hotel at nearby Kermit. In 1909, fire destroyed the hotel and Bjorne decided to move to Montana. When he found a ticket to Seattle cost no more, he took it and established a small grocery store at Charlottetown, a hamlet adjoining Bremerton. Langlie starred in sports and was a student leader at Bremerton High School. At the University of Washington he gained undergraduate acclaim as a baseball and tennis star and earned a law degree in 1926. Langlie joined a group of young reform-minded leaders called the New Order of Cincinnatus and with their backing ran unsuccessfully for mayor in 1936 but won in 1938. Langlie won the governor's race in 1940 and eventually became the only three-term governor of Washington. Quiet, retiring and soft-voiced, Langlie, "a fiscally responsible conservative," appealed to the electorate with his honesty, conservatism and strong anti-Communist views.[74] After losing the 1944 gubernatorial election to Wallgren, Langlie was re-elected in 1948 and 1952. Langlie served as keynoter of the 1952 GOP convention that nominated General Dwight D. Eisenhower for president. In 1956, Langlie ran for United States Senator against Magnuson, but was defeated soundly in a mudslinging contest.

Scandinavians with Great-Plains ties dominated Washington politics for decades after 1940. That year Norwegian Henry Jackson, the reform minded prosecuting attorney of Snohomish County, won the Congressional seat his Everett neighbor, Mon Wallgren, had vacated to move up to the Senate. Jackson became the youngest member of the House at age 28. After sixteen years there, Jackson went on to a distinguished career in the United State Senate, teaming with Warren Magnusen to earn the label "Gold Dust Twins." Jackson also was described as "Boeing's Senator" because of his strong support of national defense and home state economic giant Boeing. Jackson grew up in Everett but his father, Peter, had worked in Montana twice before settling in Everett. Nicknamed "Scoop" by his older sister, Gertrude, a single elementary teacher who avidly supported him, Jackson, a hard working straight arrow, attended the University of Washington and earned a law degree there in 1935.[75]

Magnuson had a similar ethnic background and followed the same academic path as Langlie and Jackson, but enjoyed a far more colorful personal life. Magnuson's adopted parents ran a bar in Moorhead, Minnesota. Quarterback of his high school football team and a good student, Magnuson started college at the University of North Dakota at Grand Forks, then transferred to North Dakota State before moving to Seattle in 1925. Stories that he was lured by a football scholarship or that he "rode the rods" do not hold up. The most accepted theory is that he followed his girl friend west. He did play a down or two at quarterback in the 1926 Rose Bowl, though.

Backed by the Washington Commonwealth Federation, union leader Dave Beck, and Dorothy Stimson Bullitt, the wealthy widow of Scott Bullitt, the state's leading Democrat until his untimely death in 1932, Magnuson never looked back. A drinker, card player, and playboy with a predilection toward pretty Hollywood starlets, Magnuson overcame his personal peccadilloes with arguably the best political instincts of any Senator of his era. "Maggie," a consummate backstage operator, avoided confrontation and won a host of friends on both sides of the aisle. Although they disagreed politically, Senator Joe McCarthy called him "the most popular Senator." Jackson and Magnuson formed one of the best teams ever for obtaining federal support for their state.[76]

William O. Douglas, appointed to the Supreme Court in 1939, also had a Minnesota background. In 1872, his mother's family moved from New England to Maine, Minnesota, twenty-three miles from North Dakota. The Douglas family left Minnesota in 1902 when the future Justice was four. After his father, a Presbyterian minister, died in California in 1904, the family moved to Yakima, Washington, where Douglas grew up. He worked his way through Whitman College in Walla Walla, holding several jobs at a time. After teaching high school English a few years at Yakima, Douglas headed east on a sheep train to study law at Columbia University. He finished in the top six of an illustrious class that included twice nominated Republican presidential candidate Thomas Dewey. Douglas, prone to embellish his record, claimed he finished second. As a law professor at Yale, Douglas established his reputation as an expert on corporate law, bankruptcy law and securities law. Roosevelt appointed Douglas to the Securities and Exchange Commission in 1934, where he built a reputation as a tireless enemy of business corruption and was appointed chairman in 1936. Pushed by western senators who supported dams, irrigation, and public power, Douglas took Louis Brandeis's Supreme Court slot. A legal realist, that is one who interprets law as an instrument of social policy, Douglas stayed on the Court thirty-six years and seven months, the longest continuous service in history. Brilliant, eccentric, and independent, Douglas advocated liberal causes throughout his long tenure.[77]

Not nearly as radical as James Farley's "Soviet of Washington" description, the Evergreen State had established a more liberal, progressive tradition in the 1930s and was well positioned to meet the industrial demands of World War II. Washington enjoyed the enormous natural advantage provided by deep saltwater ports on Puget Sound combined with an almost limitless potential for hydroelectric power. Its great timber industry remained healthy and Boeing would lead in wartime bomber production. Additionally, a number of shipyards and many other businesses were well established and set to expand. They stood ready to benefit from a vastly increased labor force. In late August 1936, Walter Duffey, the regional director on the National Resettlement Administration, estimated that since 1930, 42,000 had come to Washington from the drought area as permanent settlers and further indicated many more were coming.[78] More than anticipated came and eventually the many opportunities in manufacturing displaced the popular theory that agricultural expansion would provide the economic safety valve for Dust Bowl migrants.

NOTES

1. Third party candidate Bull-Moose Progressive Theodore Roosevelt carried Washington, South Dakota and Minnesota in 1912. Washington approved a direct primary (1907, a strong workmen's compensation law (1911), an eight-hour day for women (1911, and suffrage for women (1910).

2. Harvey Klehr, *The Heyday of American Communism: The Depression Decade* (New York: Basic Books, 1984), 252–55; Eckard V. Toy, Jr., "Silver Shirts in the Northwest: Politics Prophecies and Personalities in the 1930s," *Pacific Historical Quarterly* 80 (October 1989): 139–46. Toy disagrees with Farley and stresses the region's conservatism; see also David A. Horowitz, "The Klansman as

Outsider: Ethnocultural Solidarity and Antielitism in the 1920s," *Pacific Northwest Quarterly* 80 (January 1989): 12–20.

3. Melvin Dubofsky, *"Big Bill" Haywood* (Manchester: Manchester University Press, 1987).

4. Robert L. Tyler, *Rebels in the Woods: The I.W.W. in the Pacific Northwest* (Eugene: University of Oregon Books, 1967).

5. Norman H. Clark, *Milltown: The Story of Everett, Washington, from Its Earliest Beginnings on the Shores of Puget Sound to the Tragic an Infamous Event Known as the Everett Massacre* (Seattle: University of Washington Press, 1970).

6. The Museum of Flight, adjacent to Boeing Field in Seattle, contains an outstanding exhibit demonstrating early airplane construction.

7. Mary L. Stough, "Centralia's Union Mural," *Columbia* 13 (Fall 1989): 24–26.

8. Robert Tyler, "Violence at Centralia," *Pacific Northwest Quarterly* 45 (October 1954) 116–24; John M. McClelland, *Wobbly War: The Centralia Story* (Tacoma: Washington State Historical Society, 1987).

9. Marilyn P. Watkins, *Rural Democracy: Family Farms and Politics in Western Washington, 1890–1925* (Ithaca: Cornell University Press, 1995), passim.

10. Carlos A. Schwantes, "Farmer-Labor Insurgency in Washington State: William Bouck, the Grange, and the Western Progressive Farmers," *Pacific Historical Quarterly* 76 (January 1985): 2–11.

11. Washington State Planning Council, *The Elma Survey* (Olympia: Washington State Planning Council, 1941, mimeographed), 21.

12. Gordon Newell, *Rogues, Buffoons and Statesmen: The Inside Story of Washington's Capital City and the Hilarious History of 120 Years of State Politics* (Seattle: Superior Publications, 1975), 327–28.

13. Clark, *Milltown*, 164.

14. Dan McGovern, "The Ungracious Intolerant Governor," *Renton Chronicle*, 22 October 1936.

15. Paul W. Rodman, *The Far West and the Great Plains in Transition, 1859–1900* (New York: Harper & Row, 1988), 290.

16. Albert Gunns, "Roland Hartley and the politics of Washington State" (master's thesis, University of Washington, 1952).

17. Ibid., 20–23.

18. Ibid., 78–102.

19. Norman H. Clark, *Washington: A Bicentennial History* (New York: W. W. Norton, 1976), 156–57.

20. Edgar I. Stewart, *Washington: Northwest Frontier*, Four Volumes (New York: Lewis Historical Publishing Company, 1957), Volume II, 272–77.

21. Charles M.Gates, *The First Century at the University of Washington, 1861–1961* (Seattle: University of Washington Press, 1961), passim.

22. Robert Welch, "The Loser Who Won: The Story of the Legendary Gil Dobie," *Columbia* 1 (Fall 1987): 38–45; Stewart, *Washington*, Volume II, 272–77; Gunns, "Roland Hartley," Chapter Five, "Hartley Versus Suzzalo," 134–62.

23. Phyllis W. Bultmann, *The Great Depression and Its Fifty Year Shadow: Proceedings of a Conference Held at Western Washington University* (Bellingham, WA:

Western Washington University, 1981), 21; Michael K. Green, "Hard Times in the Promised Land: The Depression and the New Deal in Washington State," *Pacific Northwest Forum* 2 (Spring/Fall 1989): 3. Entire issue is devoted to the Depression; Grays Harbor Regional Planning Commission, *The History of Aberdeen, 1775–1982* (Aberdeen: Grays Harbor Regional Planning Commission, 1982), 5.

24. Jonathan Dembo, "The Pacific Northwest Lumber Industry during the Great Depression," *Journal of the West* 24 (October 1985): 51.

25. Clark, *Washington*, 155.

26. Donald Francis Roy. "Hooverville: A Study of a Community of Homeless Men in Seattle." (master's thesis, University of Washington, 1952); The Washington State Historical Society in Tacoma has an excellent Hooverville exhibit.

27. Arthur Dwelley. "Wooden Money: The Depression-era Scrip from Tenino," *Columbia* (Spring 1997): 41–44.

28. Arthur Hillman, *The Unemployed Citizens' League of Seattle* (Seattle: University of Washington Press, 1934).

29. Lancaster Pollard, *A History of the State of Washington*, Four Volumes (New York: American Historical Society, 1937) Volume 4, 544. Green, "Hard Times," 3–5.

30. Shanna B. Stevenson, *Lacey, Olympia and Tumwater* (Norfolk, VA: The Downing Company, 1985), 175.

31. Newell, *Rogues, Buffoons and Statesman*, 369–72; Richard C. Berner, *Seattle in the 20th Century* (Seattle: Charles Press, 1991), 319–21.

32. Cecil P. Dryden, *Light for an Empire: The Story of Eastern Washington State College* (Cheny, WA: Eastern Washington State College, 1965), 194–95, 202–03.

33. Clarence Martin [Governor], *Washington on the Threshold of Prosperity* (Olympia: State of Washington, 1936) 5; Richard E. Fisch. "A History of the Democratic Party in Washington, 1854–1956" (PhD dissertation, University of Oregon, 1975).

34. Interview, February 2004.

35. Carlos Schwantes, *The Pacific Northwest: An Interpretive History* (Lincoln: University of Nebraska Press, 1996), 310–11.

36. Ate van Deldon, "Vic Meyers from Dance Hall to City Hall," http://www.vjm.biz/articles3.htm (accessed October 8, 2005).

37. Fayette F. Krause, Jr, "Democratic Party Politics in the State of Washington" (PhD dissertation, University of Washington, 1971).

38. Fisch, "A History of the Democratic Party," 298.

39. Norman H. Clark, *The Dry Years: Prohibition and Social Change in Washington* (Seattle: University of Washington Press, 1988). Illustrates the inherent conservatism of Washington, the most liberal state of the Pacific Northwest.

40. Catherine M. Stock, *Rural Radicals: Righteous Rage in the American Grain* (Ithaca: Cornell University Press, 1996), 140–41.

41. Eckard V. Toy, "Silver Shirts in the Northwest: Politics, Prophecies and Personalities in the 1930s," *Pacific Northwest Quarterly* 80 (October 1989): 141.

42. Karen E. Hoppes, "William Dudley Pelley and the Silvershirt Legion: A Case Study of the Legion in Washington State, 1933–1942" (PhD dissertation, City University of New York, 1992), 174–77; Lawrence J. Saalfelt, *Forces of Prejudice in Oregon* (Portland: Archdiocean Historical Commission, 1984): 175–77.

43. Toy, "Silver Shirts," 173.

44. For background concerning the issue of local control, see Calvin Coulter, "Victory of National Irrigation in the Yakima Valley," *Pacific Northwest Quarterly* 42 (April 1951): 99–122.

45. James G. Newbill, "Yakima and the Wobblies, 1910–1936," in *At the Point of Production: The Local History of IWW*, ed. Joseph R. Conlin (Westport, CT: Greenwood Press, 1987), 165–80. Wilma Carroll Groeschell, then a teenager in Zillah, near Yakima, remembers the incident as being a topic of discussion at the time, but not that momentous—conversation with Wilma Groeschell, July 2004.

46. John C. Shideler, *Coal Towns in the Cascades: A Centennial History of Roslyn and Cle Elum, Washington* (Spokane: Melior Publications, 1996), 118–23.

47. "Drought Sends Thousands to Washington,"*Renton Chronicle*, 26 November 1936.

48. "A History of Human Service." http://www/.dshs.wagov/:indetail/3history .html. (accessed September 11, 205); Jan Ordos, *History of Medical Care for the Poor in Washington, 1833–1988* (Olympia: State Department of Social and Health Services), 19–21.

49. Clark, *Centennial History*, 159–60.

50. William Dietrich, *Northwest Passage: The Great Columbia River* (Seattle: University of Washington Press, 1996), 266; Craig Wallner, *Electrifying Eden: Portland General Electric, 1889–1965* (Portland: Oregon Historical Society, 1990).

51. Paul C. Pitzer. *Grand Coulee: Harnessing a Dream* (Pullman: Washington State University Press, 1994), 72–73.

52. Dryden, 181–82; Fisch, 241; Vernon Carstensen, "The Good Old Days or the Bad Old Days?: History and Related Muses in the Northwest in the 1930s," *Pacific Northwest Quarterly* 68 (July 1977): 105–11. Carstensen was a young history professor at Central Washington College of Education in the 1930s. Also see Samuel R. Mohler, *The First 75 Years: A History of Central Washington College* (Ellensburg, WA: Central Washington State College, 1967), 170–71.

53. United States Public Works Administration, *America Builds: The Record of the PWA* (Washington, DC: United States Government Printing Office, 1939), 107–08.

54. Richard Berner, *Seattle in the 20th Century* (Seattle: Charles Press, 1991), 282–83.

55. James R. Warren, *Seattle: 150 Years of Progress* (Carlsbad, CA: Heritage Media Group, 2001), 143–45; Phil Roberts, *A Penny for the Governor, a Dollar for Uncle Sam: Income Taxation in Washington* (Seattle: University of Washington Press, 2002), 3–6, 73–85.

56. Washington State Historical Society, *Building a State: Washington, 1889–1939* (Tacoma: Washington State Historical Society, 1940), 10–15.

57. Newell, *Rogues*, 374–80; Clark, *The Dry Years*, passim.

58. Boeing bought the site in 1990 for $90 million. Emerald Downs, a new track nearby, replaced Longacres.

59. Stephen Sadis, *The Miracle Strip: A Story of Longacres Race Track*, Documentary-80 minutes. (Seattle: Perpetual Motion Pictures, 1992); Shawn Clymer, "Longacres to Hollywood Park: The Horse Racing Family of Jack Leonard," *Renton*

Historical Society Quarterly, 30 (May 1999); Dan Aznoff. *Renton: The First 100 Years, 1901–2001* (Renton: King County Journal Newspapers, 2001), 31–33; Conversation with racehorse owner Bill Harris, September 3, 2005.

60. Laura Hillenbrand, *Seabiscuit: An American Legend* (New York: Ballantine Books, 2003), 34 and passim.

61. "Longacres Stables Full," *Renton Chronicle*, 25 June 1936.

62. Krause, "Democratic Party Politics," 166–68.

63. Albert A. Acena, "The Washington Commonwealth Federation: Reform Politics and Popular Front" (PhD dissertation University of Washington, 1975), 125; Krause, "Democratic Party Politics," 129.

64. *Daily Olympian*, September 2, 1936.

65. Krause, "Democratic Party Politics," 156–58.

66. Berner, *Seattle*, 407.

67. Krause, "Democratic Party Politics," 156–158; "New Year Looks Good in Renton," *Renton Chronicle*, 31 December 1936.

68. Washington State Historical Society, *Building a State: Washington 1889–1939* (Tacoma: Washington State Historical Society, 1940), 291.

69. Fisch, "A History of the Democratic Party," 242.

70. Clark, *Centennial History*, 66.

71. Krause, "Democratic Party Politics," 182.

72. History Committee, *Spawn of Coal Dust: A History of Roslyn, 1886–1955,* Revised Edition (Roslyn, WA: Private Printing, 1979), 160.

73. "I'm AginYou," *Time* (July 10, 1939): 14.

74. George W. Scott, "Arthur B. Langlie: Republican Governor in a Democratic Age" (PhD dissertation University of Washington), 1971.

75. Robert G. Kaufman, *Henry Jackson: A Life in Politics* (Seattle: University of Washington Press, 2000); Conversation with Doug Kyes an Everett native well acquainted with the Jackson family, March 2004 and April 2006.

76. Shelby Scates, *Senator Warren Magnuson and the Shaping of Twentieth Century America* (Seattle: University of Washington Press, 1997); Delphine Haley, *Dorothy Stimson Bullitt: An Uncommon Life* (Seattle: Sasquatch Books, 1995), 165–68. Bullitt greatly expanded her already considerable fortune by obtaining the rights for Seattle's first television station, KING.

77. Bruce A. Murphy, *Wild Bill: The Legend and Life of William O. Douglas* (New York: Random House, 2003).

78. William S. Hopkins, *Seasonal Unemployment in the State of Washington* (Seattle: University of Washington Publications in Social Science, Volume 8, Number 5, 1936), 102 footnote.

Chapter Seven

Oregon: The Land of Promise

In 1930, Oregon, although much larger in area than Nebraska and blessed with impressive attributes for agriculture, trade, and industry, still had a population of less than one million. They were almost all thrifty and energetic Protestants, born in the United States, but over half had migrated from other states. Oregon's low rate of adult illiteracy placed it second only to Iowa. Almost all children age six to seventeen attended school.[1] A little over 10 percent were foreign born, mostly from Canada, Germany, and Sweden. Small towns predominated with Portland the only city exceeding 100,000.[2] Much of Oregon's vast timber resources still remained intact. The Willamette Valley, a rectangular trough of level and rolling farm and timber lands larger than Maryland, held special appeal to agriculturally oriented drought victims. Advantages over Washington's Puget Sound river valleys included a milder climate, more fertile land, and less inclination for flooding. Western Oregon's initial appeal resulted in more acreage in improved farmland in 1880 than it contained in 1930. An enormous amount of inexpensive abandoned and cutover land thus beckoned devastated Great Plains farmers from both north and south. An estimated 200,000 migrated to the Beaver State in the 1930s while about 80,000 Oregonians left, mainly to California.[3]

Oregon led the Pacific Northwest in the nineteenth century, becoming a state in 1859, long before Washington (1889) and Idaho (1890), but later than California (1850). *Hail to the Land of Promise, My Oregon* appropriately was adopted as the state song in 1927. From the 1820s until a final northern border was established at the 49th parallel in 1846, American settlers, mostly serious, sober Protestants from Missouri and Illinois, flowed into the fertile Willamette Valley via the famed Oregon Trail. A married couple was entitled to 640 free acres and many established claims before the land was surveyed.

When the California Gold Rush created demand for food and wood products, Oregon Territory, in the middle of the largest temperate rain forest on earth and with rapidly increasing agricultural production, prospered.[4] Located where the Willamette River joins the Columbia, Portland dominated banking and business in the region. Operating from Portland, Yankees controlled much of the trade. But when the transcontinental railroads chose the deepwater ports of Tacoma and Seattle as their western terminals Portland's dominance ended.[5] Alaska's Klondike Gold Rush of 1898 confirmed Seattle's ascendancy.

Compared to Seattle's image as a wide-open, aggressive, lumbering city with a colorful and volatile political scene, Portland, more oriented to commerce in agriculture, seemed old even when it was new. Reflective of its New England origins, Portland's conservative bankers, traders, and mill operators, closely linked by marriage and business partnerships appeared content with sober stability. They promoted business expansion more aggressively than critics conceded, though. Often called "the city where it's always afternoon," Portland reflected more of a village mentality according to some observers.[6] Wags in Seattle liked to tell about a woman who told a census taker, "I have three sons, two living and one living in Portland." Earlier, Portlanders were flattered when a famous visitor, Samuel Bowles of the *Springfield* (Massachusetts) *Republican,* said, "They keep Sunday as we do in New England, and as no other population this side of the Missouri now does." To Bowles, Portland in 1865 had "the air and the fact of a prosperous energetic town, with a good deal of eastern leadership and tone to business and society and morals."[7]

Geographical factors, always critical, worked against Portland. Although Portland served the productive Willamette Valley and agricultural areas to the east, Seattle was the natural gateway to Alaska and, along with other Puget Sound seaports, preferred for the lucrative Asian trade. Because James Hill had close personal and economic ties with Tacoma and Seattle, they received preferred treatment in freight rates for over thirty years. Finally in 1921 the Interstate Commerce Commission granted Portland lower rates, but the Puget Sound area retained its trade leadership.[8] Portland's location on the Columbia River placed it at a disadvantage to the deepwater ports of the Puget Sound. The immensely difficult and dangerous bar at the mouth of the Columbia awaited ships bound for Portland. Often called the "Graveyard of the Pacific" the bar has claimed over two thousand vessels, including two hundred major ships during recorded history.[9]

William U'Ren, a frail, tubercular Populist, provided the impetus that transformed Oregon politics. His "Oregon System," featuring the initiative, referendum and recall plus a host of other progressive reform measures, gave Oregon a reputation as a leader in progressive reform. "Referendum U'Ren" came from a Wisconsin English immigrant family of blacksmiths and preachers. They had moved to Nebraska to farm and were wiped out by grasshoppers. After a stay in Colorado, the U'Rens returned to Wisconsin. But William U'Ren decided to move back to Colorado for his health and became a lawyer. After brief stays in Hawaii and California he moved to Oregon City in 1889. His Populist single tax political ideology and spiritualism gained the support of the Lewelling brothers who had laid the foundation for the deciduous fruit industry in Oregon. The brothers were Quaker abolitionists from North Carolina who had moved to slave-free Indiana, then to Iowa where they formed a wagon train to Oregon in 1847. The Lewellings hauled several hundred boxes of grafted fruit and nut trees, vines, and berry bushes that thrived in the productive Willamette Valley. They made U'Ren a partner in their prosperous nursery and orchard business and backed his drive for more direct democracy in Oregon.

With an established base U'Ren gained the support of the Farmers Alliance and Industrial Union which also viewed Oregon as a corrupt state in need of change through laws that allowed direct participation of its citizenry.[10] Elected to the House of the Oregon legislature in 1896, U'Ren served only one term, but achieved his goals. Called the "Holdup of 97" U'Ren, a master strategist, achieved his goal by having all Populists refuse to take their oath of office in 1897, thus stopping all official business because of lack of a quorum. In 1898, U'Ren used a Republican gold-silver split concerning selection of a United States Senator to coerce Democrats and Republicans into passing his "Oregon System." He accomplished this by bargaining a mere thirteen Populist votes to support silver interests. Reforms included initiative, referendum, and recall plus direct election of United States Senators. In 1902, they were included as amendments to the Oregon constitution, the first amendments since 1859.[11] Up to World War I Oregon was renowned as the leader in progressive legislation and government reform. Although opposed by Teddy Roosevelt and Woodrow Wilson, U'Ren's Oregon System was held up as a model for the rest of the country and adopted by most Western states.

In 1903, Oregon passed a law limiting women to ten hours of work in factories and laundries. It was upheld unanimously by the United States Supreme Court in 1908 in the landmark case *Muller v. Oregon.* Much of the popular support for reform government emanated from the surge of newcomers who arrived around the turn of the century. During the first decade of the twentieth century seventy thousand came from Illinois with New Yorkers second and Missourians third. By 1910, Iowa led.[12]

World War I reversed Oregon's political image from populist progressivism to Ku Klux Klan bigotry. Ironically, both inclinations were inspired by rural restlessness created by economic stress. Permeated with rural attitudes,

Oregon was ninety percent Protestant and over ninety-eight percent white in the 1920s. The 1920s concerns focused on Communism, Catholics and foreigners but were also fueled by economic depression in lumber, shipbuilding and agriculture. The state preserved its maverick reputation, however, by electing a Jewish governor by the end of the 1920s. The base for the KKK was built by the Federation of Patriotic Societies of Oregon that began in 1917. The Klan entered Oregon from California in 1921 and was vigorously promoted by Protestant churches and the Masonic Lodge, growing to fourteen thousand members by 1922.[13] In 1923, there were an estimated sixty-five chartered Klans in Oregon.[14] Portland served as virtual headquarters of the Klan west of the Rockies. For years the Portland police department maintained a red squad devoted to squelch Communism, similar to that of Los Angeles.[15] The high water mark for the KKK came in the election of 1922. When incumbent Republican governor Ben Olcott publicly denounced them and evoked an old Oregon law prohibiting the wearing of masks in public places. In retaliation the Klan supported Walter Pierce, a populist Democrat from Pendleton, Oregon, who won easily. Pierce grew up on an Illinois farm and moved to eastern Oregon as a schoolteacher and then superintendent. After earning his law degree from Northwestern University, Pierce practiced law in Pendleton, and also became a leading businessman and farmer before entering state politics.

The popular perception that the enigmatic Pierce was a reactionary KKK governor is deceiving. In 1919, as an Oregon State Senator Pierce alone voted against a criminal syndicalism act which made advocacy of revolutionary class struggle a felony. The Klan voted for Pierce because they had no alternative. Like urbane Senator Charles McNary, Pierce remained silent on the Klan issue and accepted Klan support for political gain. Pierce in fact ran on progressive issues: consolidation of state offices, a severance tax on timber holdings, a gross earnings tax on certain utilities and a state income tax. Republicans claimed Pierce was a secret member of the Nonpartisan League and was trying to "Sovietize" Oregon. Populist, anti-Catholic Pierce did back the compulsory public school law.[16] After gaining office, he proved so unreceptive to Klan patronage demands, which they thought the wily Pierce had guaranteed for their support, that the KKK led an unsuccessful attempt to recall him during his first year.[17] The Klan also successfully backed Democrat Elton Watkins for Congress over Republican C. N. McArthur who had condemned the KKK. Watkins, the first Oregon Democrat elected to the House since 1879, was a leading spokesman for immigrant restriction. The Klan also endorsed several successful candidates for the state legislature.[18]

Passage of the Klan-sponsored "One Flag! One School! One Language!" Initiative gained most national attention, though. Directed especially at

Catholic schools, it abolished private and parochial schools for children between the ages of eight and eighteen and carried 115,506 to 103,685.[19] Scheduled to go into effect in 1926, the law was declared unconstitutional in 1924 by a 9–0 vote of the Supreme Court. Oregon newspapers, sensitive to loss of advertising and subscribers, mostly remained silent during the school debate, but several objected to court intervention. *The Grants Pass Spokesman* editorialized, "We cannot understand why foreign minorities in America are ever listened to by our courts, when they endeavor to cancel issues Americans vote in with which to protect their institutions, be these issues right or wrong."[20] Washington, with a Klan chapter in every major city, but more Scandinavian and Catholic and with strong opposition from the press, soundly rejected a public schools only law in 1924. Idaho, more Mormon and Catholic than either Oregon or Washington, showed limited interest in the Klan.

Anti-Catholic, anti-foreign, anti-Communist sentiment flourished from 1923 to 1925 to the extent *The Washington Post* estimated (perhaps inflated) the Oregon contained 150,000 Klan members.[21] *The Klamath Falls Herald* reported that Catholics celebrated the birth of boys by burying guns and ammunition underneath churches "in preparation for the day when the government is to be overthrown on behalf of the Pope."[22] Klansman Kaspar K. Kubli, an aptly named Harvard educated lawyer and printer, served as speaker of the Oregon House of Representatives during this period. In 1923, the legislature unsuccessfully proposed a bill to eliminate Columbus Day as a state holiday and substitute Armistice Day. Bills to tax church property and to prohibit the import of wine for sacramental use also lost.[23] The Alien Property Act, which prohibited Japanese from buying or leasing land in Oregon, did pass with Pierce's endorsement.

Discouraged by Oregon's intolerance, Catholics, foreigners, and minorities tended to choose other destinations if they relocated. Although not enforced, an 1844 territorial law banned African Americans from the state. It officially was repealed by the 1926 state legislature. No doubt some of the fifty thousand who left Oregon in the 1920s were influenced by the narrow political climate as well. Not everyone left Oregon voluntarily. In the Finnish community of Astoria, editors and staff of *Toveri*, a Communist linked newspaper, were arrested and deported.

In 1924, Kubli challenged incumbent Charles McNary for the Republican nomination for the United States Senate but was easily defeated. After 1925, the Oregon Klan declined sharply, following the pattern of the national organization that was tarred by scandal, violence and corruption.[24] In 1924, Pierce divided his party by supporting third party Progressive presidential candidate Robert La Follette. As expected, Pierce lost in 1926 but was elected to Congress in 1932 at age seventy-two and served ten years in the House of

Representatives. Pierce consistently supported the New Deal and supported public power. Kubli also abandoned the Klan and remained Speaker of the House through 1929.[25]

Unusual events propelled Julius Meier, Jewish co-owner of Meier and Frank, Portland's largest retail store, into the governor's seat in 1930. Meier previously had participated in Oregon politics but never as a candidate. When his close friend, Basque attorney Clarence Joseph, the Republican gubernatorial candidate and a strong public power advocate, died unexpectedly, Republicans replaced him with a private power supporter. Incensed, Meier ran as an independent on a public power platform and won 55 percent of the vote. Although personally difficult at times, Meier proved a wise choice, skillfully guiding his state through the worst four years of the Depression. The Depression devastated the timber industry, by far Oregon's leading employer. Production fell from 4.45 billion board feet in 1926 to 1.6 billion board feet in 1932.[26] Meier moved on unemployment by forming a planning committee and substantially increasing state highway funding. He left the state in sound financial condition by cutting state budgets and actively seeking federal assistance. Even more significantly, Oregon, unlike Washington, re-approved a state income tax in 1930.[27] Poor health forced Meier to retire in 1934.

Under the leadership of long-time Mayor George Baker, Portland faced the Depression with remarkable early diligence, attracting much national recognition. By late 1930, Baker ordered immediate cuts in city budgets and directed that all savings go into a relief fund for the unemployed. Additionally he ordered city departments to create public works jobs—the most noted being an urban renewal project that replaced old buildings with new ones. "I'll wreck the town if it will give employment," said Baker.[28] A large Civic Emergency Committee was formed to administer emergency relief funds. Portland voters approved a $2 million bond issue for relief in April 1931 and followed that with a community chest drive in the fall that raised $744,000. Portland's laudable and much publicized effort, however, proved much too meager to handle the economic disaster that peaked in 1932.[29] Driven by the dramatic decline in the timber industry, at the depth of the Depression more than fifty thousand families and more than eight thousand single persons were unemployed.[30] Per capita income in Oregon dropped from $668 in 1929 to $358 in 1933.[31] Reflective of Oregon's dire economic circumstances, the ill fated 1932 Veteran's Bonus March to Washington, D.C., originated in Portland.

Baker, also a public power advocate, was rewarded in 1932 with a futile attempt to recall him on the grounds he was associated with underworld graft, despite being completely cleared of the charges by a grand jury. Portland elected an anti-New Deal mayor in 1932 and voted down most progressive legislation the rest of the decade, including a badly needed measure to establish a Housing

Authority in 1938. State government followed the same pattern. After the Bonneville Dam every public works project was initiated only upon voter approval of a specific bond issue, of which the proceeds had to match whatever federal funds were available in the proportion the government set for the project.[32]

Meier's departure allowed two-term Democrat Congressman Charles Martin to make a successful bid for governor, establishing a Democrat Governor Martin (not related) in both Olympia and Salem. Although Washington's Clarence Martin had begun to lean more to the right by the time Charles Martin was elected, their approach to the office differed dramatically. Clarence Martin provided sympathy for human needs that moved Washington forward. Oregon's Charles Martin, much like Roland Hartley, brought a caustic, reactionary approach to Salem that accomplished little and ended in political rejection. Born in 1863 in rural Illinois, Martin graduated from the United States Military Academy at West Point and ended an outstanding forty-five year military career as a major general in 1927. In 1897, while stationed at Vancouver Barracks, he married the daughter of Ellis Hughes, one of Portland's wealthiest business leaders. Martin, a registered Republican, retired in Portland to manage the vast properties of the Hughes estate.[33]

Republicans controlled the state senate and the two United States Senate seats throughout the 1930s. In 1932, 57 percent of Eugene voters supported Herbert Hoover's reelection.[34] Voter registration in Oregon ran two to one Republican during this period and good Democrat candidates were few. Martin, capitalizing on anti-Hoover sentiment and good Portland connections, won a Congressional seat in 1930 as a write-in Democrat, serving two terms in the House before his 1934 election as governor. Much of his popularity was based on his significant role in the funding of the Bonneville dam in 1933.

Revered Republican Charles McNary, Senate minority leader and a close friend of Roosevelt, led the effort to get the project funded.[35] An enthusiastic and innovative farm owner who developed the American filbert and the Imperial prune, McNary was noted for his devotion to agriculture. He was coauthor of the failed 1920s McNary-Haugen bill, a far-reaching proposal to create federal price supports for agricultural products. Politically pragmatic, McNary had opposed Hoover Dam, fearing its approval would jeopardize Columbia River dam proposals.

Martin's reputation as a strict law and order advocate also won support because Oregon had experienced considerable labor unrest, highlighted by the devastating eighty-two day Pacific Coast strike of the International Longshoreman's Union in 1934.[36] Most crucial, the Republican split allowed Martin to win the three-man race with only 39 percent of the vote. Blunt and insensitive, Martin spewed a stream of provocative declarations. Reporters loved to quote him, often calling him "Iron Pants" because of his military demeanor.

Even though Martin pledged to be "the FDR of Oregon," he opposed the New Deal and public power as "socialistic." Martin referred to Oregon union leaders as "pestiferous peewees" who would go to any length "to embarrass me and my administration." He believed in survival of the fittest and was often quoted for rephrasing FDR's famous saying on fear. Martin said, "We have nothing to fear from the future except our own fear and laziness." He opposed plans for assistance to the able-bodied unemployed and although extremely wealthy maintained that the physically and mentally disabled should be able to make it on ten dollars a month. Even more callous, Martin supported a plan to chloroform "the aged and feebleminded wards of the state" to help balance the budget.[37]

In spite of Martin's hostility to New Deal "socialism" Oregon received more than its share of federal programs. New Dealers were justifiably convinced its large, lightly settled area and abundant natural resources provided an economic safety valve for those nature had forced to relocate. Most of Oregon's large forest reserves were owned by the federal government, which retained 60 percent of Oregon's land, and FDR was determined not to surrender federal control of Oregon's vast hydroelectric potential. Some 87,000 CCC's in forty-nine camps helped conserve government forests and build parks and recreational facilities.[38] They also served as front line firefighters to help quell the rash of forest fires that erupted throughout the region. Some were man-made to create jobs.

Of the many CCC ventures in Oregon accomplishments at then neglected Crater Lake National Park, Oregon's only National Park, show the New Deal at its best. Inadequate funding had brought building deterioration, inadequate roads and trails, poor landscaping, and an insufficient Rim Campground. Additionally, thousands of acres of neighboring pine forest were dying of beetle infestation and blister rust. Two CCC camps were established at Crater Lake that employed up to four hundred men. In 1933, around two hundred were assigned to beetle control work, completely eradicating the problem by 1934. The battle against white pine blister rust continued throughout the 1930s. Even though the CCC cleaned up debris and other fire hazards, from 1931–1941 over one hundred fires, mostly caused by lightning, struck anyway and the CCC helped fight them. They also built fire trails, two fire detection lookouts and installed an extensive telephone and radio system. More visible accomplishments included new buildings, dramatic improvement of camping facilities, impressive landscape work around the lodge, and paved roads with stone curbs.

The CCC's significant and direct and indirect contribution to the region's economy was and continues to be under appreciated.[39] Young men who greatly valued the opportunity for meaningful work made lasting, significant improvements to the infrastructure at minimal taxpayer expense. Many of the CCCs, young and single, came from out of state and, as held true in neighboring states, a fair percentage were so impressed that they stayed or returned later. Almost all remember the CCC it as a positive turning point in their life.[40]

WPA workers were local, mostly family men, and were required to accept private employment if available. After obtaining basic skills in construction and other fields many accepted jobs in the private sector. The WPA also encompassed a broad cross-section of skilled unemployed including teachers, lawyers, writers, artists and architects. An estimated 25,000 WPA workers were employed in Portland alone from 1935 to 1942. Building the Portland airport employed over one thousand from 1936 to 1941, but numerous smaller projects like roads, bridges, sewage systems, flood control and public buildings absorbed many more, not only in Portland but around the state. WPA workers built five impressive bridges over estuaries along the Oregon Coast and also graded and paved Highway 101.[41]

One of their most magnificent and highly publicized efforts was the construction of Timberline Lodge at the base of Mount Hood. With the support of Portland businessmen, the entirely hand-made lodge utilized native Oregon materials wherever possible. Even the draperies were hand-loomed from Oregon wool and flax. Started in June 1936, it was erected in only fifteen months at a bargain cost of $2 million. Oregon conservatives accepted the CCC but many vocally opposed the "socialist-boondoggle" WPA in spite of its significant contribution.[42]

The collapse of the timber industry in the early 1930s created its share of discontent in Oregon. It was estimated that the Unemployed Citizen's League enrolled more than six thousand in Portland in 1932. Many were lumber workers who were ripe for union organization. Both the American Federation of Labor (AFL) and the new Congress of Industrial Organizations (CIO) actively sought support during the New Deal. Martin, who viewed union leaders as Communists, sent state police to break up strikes, resulting in a number of arrests and convictions.[43] Radicalism was muffled by the 1919 Oregon Criminal Syndicalism Law prohibited advocacy of "any unlawful acts or methods as a means of accomplishing or effecting industrial or political change or revolution." The United States Supreme Court struck down the law in 1937 in the case of *De Jong v. State of Oregon.* Dirk De Jong, once a Communist candidate for mayor of Portland, had been convicted for advocating Communism at Portland public meetings. After repealing the law the Oregon legislature substituted a conspiracy law.

"Iron Pants'" authoritarian ways alienated much of his constituency. When public power interests formed the Oregon Commonwealth Federation in

1936, Martin referred to them as "young Jews, Communists, CIOs and Crackpots."[44] He told a group of farmers who approached him to veto possible sales tax legislation it "was none of their business," and to "go home and listen to the birdies sing."[45] After giving a speech dedicating the new state capitol building, the crowd moved forward, causing Martin to bark, "Get back you bastards, get back."[46]

Martin stayed in form concerning the surge of impoverished migrants from the Dust Bowl. He called them "alien paupers" and advised that if they wanted to eat, selling their "rattletrap automobiles" should provide enough funds. Martin viewed the newcomers as an unneeded tax burden and as "socially dangerous malcontents." He closed the federal transient camp in Roseburg, near the California border, saying transients "should be kept moving out of our state the same as criminals."[47]

By 1934, all three West Coast governors were conservative, although Washington's Martin was not in the same league as the other two. Oregon's bombastic leader had much in common with Frank Merriam, the reactionary governor of neighboring California. A former auditor of the state of Iowa, Merriam moved to Long Beach in 1910 at age forty-five and gained the support of archconservative newspaper publisher Harry Chandler. Upon the death of Governor James Rolph, Merriam became governor in 1934. He promptly activated the National Guard to suppress the International Longshoremen's strike in San Francisco, then won a bitter election battle for governor against Socialist-turned Democrat, Upton Sinclair. "Central Casting could not have sent a more rightward adversary to place against the recent Socialist Sinclair than the exacting, humorless, Red-baiting numbers cruncher from Iowa," said California historian Kevin Starr.[48] Hurt by the National Democratic Party's lack of support and an all-out Republican effort to defeat him, Sinclair lost quite badly.

Like Hartley and Merriam, Martin's tightfisted ways and strict anti-unionism retained a coterie of conservative admirers, but by 1938 most Oregonians were ready to dump their intemperate seventy-five year old incumbent. His constant criticism of the New Deal, refusal to pursue federal support, hostility to public power, and incessant labeling opponents and critics "Red" proved too dogmatic for most. Roosevelt and insiders in his administration, Harold Ickes and George Norris, supported a successful state coalition against Martin that defeated him in the primaries.[49] Martin claimed he was the victim of a Communist conspiracy and gave his support to the winner, Charles Sprague. Sprague was a moderate Republican newspaper man who was born in Kansas, grew up in Iowa and moved to eastern Washington before moving to Oregon in 1925. Ironically, Sprague backed public power and labor unions and opposed a loyalty oath. The Beaver State again displayed its political independence in 1940. Even though their popular Senator McNary ran for vice president on the Republican ticket, Roosevelt still carried Oregon.

In spite of Martin's criticisms an estimated 200,000 chose to relocate in Oregon in the 1930s, featuring a dramatic surge during the 1935–37 period. Although exact numbers could not be established, one-fourth to one-third came from the Northern Great Plains . Probably few migrants were aware of Martin's hostile remarks and relied upon recommendations from friends and relatives and Oregon's well publicized favorable resources and climate, which, along with New Deal programs, had created a marked improvement in the state's economy. In addition to the many federally funded projects, the federal Farm Security Administration granted some eight thousand rehabilitation loans and grants to migrants and aided another one thousand families through community and cooperative services.[50] Those who migrated from the Northern Great Plains to the Pacific Northwest, moreover, held little sense of inferiority to their new neighbors. Most were confident in their abilities and only wanted an opportunity to use them.

The rain-blessed western portion especially offered much that was attractive. *Three Faces West* (1940), starred John Wayne as the leader of a group of farmers moving from Dust Bowl "Ashville Forks," North Dakota, to Oregon. Wayne stressed that they intended to own their own farms and were not interested in becoming itinerant farm laborers, a counterpoint to the California bound Jodes of *Grapes of Wrath* fame. "We are not fruit pickers. We are farmers," Wayne declared. In Oregon the migrants built houses and plowed fields, apparently on their way to prosperity. Also concerned with the rise of Nazi Germany, *Three Faces West* was not one of Wayne's best efforts, but it contained some pertinent scenes, especially of the Dust Bowl and the recreation of the trek to Oregon.

Many Oregonians viewed the migrants in a much more positive light than their governor, but opposed huge New Deal expenditure to assist them. On July 9, 1936, at the peak of the Dust Bowl crisis, the *Salem Statesman* commented that the drought effects were over exaggerated and complained about generosity with other people's money. "Established agencies of the Red Cross and the county farm agents could probably handle what emergency measures are required." A week later the *Statesman* allowed that the newcomers from the plains should fit. It ran an editorial "Westward Trek," saying ". . . their culture is about the same . . . they will be right at home as far as people go." The editorial concluded, "With cooperation and patience much may be accomplished in the settlement of Oregon."[51] A government sponsored study showed more enthusiasm, saying, "Those from the Northern Great Plains come from an area in which educational levels have been relatively high, where the general standard of living has been relatively good, and where culture patterns are similar to those of the Pacific Northwest. Most of them are about as well qualified for ready assimilation into the social system of the region as any group that might be attracted to it."[52] Some rural merchants provided "special information for drought people" at the end of their mimeographed bargain-day bulletins.[53]

The Oregon WPA Writer's Guide (1940) portrayed the Great Plains drought migration in historical perspective:

> If symbolism may be needed to complete the picture, let there be two symbols for Oregon: a pioneer of the covered wagon epoch, and beside him likewise grim and indomitable, the plodding figure of a modern farmer driven from middle-western soil by years of drought. Thousands of dust-bowl refugees have drifted into Oregon since 1930. If hunger and hardships and uncertainty are the essences of the pioneer tradition, they are part of it already; and as the bearded early immigrants brought a first cohesion to the territory, those latter day American pioneers may strengthen that cohesion and make their own distinctive contribution to the future of the state.[54]

Although most migrants to Oregon came from neighboring Washington, Idaho and California as well as other regions, a Farm Security Administration study found about one-third were from the Northern Great Plains. Among the Plains states Nebraska was represented most heavily. Nebraska's [55] population dropped 62,129 from 1930 to 1940. In spite of steady growth in Oregon, Oregon's population stood at only 1,062,656 in 1940. In 1936, an estimated 10,272 came from the Great Plains—tripling that of 1934 and more than doubling 1935. Those from the Great Plains states usually came as young families and were prone more toward agriculture, tending to settle in rural areas, especially in the southern Willamette Valley and the Rogue River Valley.[56]

Good farmland in Western Oregon cost more than most migrants could afford and Oregon officials preferred that migrants start as farm laborers. An official Oregon publication told the story of "Mr. G." who hitchhiked to Eugene from Nebraska and worked as a farm laborer before sending for his family. "Today (1940) he has 80 acres, 12 cows, a barn, and 95 pullets." "Mr. R." from North Dakota made a down payment of $200 for 60 acres (total cost $1500). He lost the property when he could not make the payments and was forced to go on relief.[57]

The Oregon State Planning Board, a fact finding committee created in 1935 to make recommendations for conservation and development of Oregon's natural resources in cooperation with the National Resources Committee and the WPA, made an outstanding study of migrants. Funded through the WPA as a successor to the Reconstruction Advisory Board, which was created in 1933 to present proposals to the Reconstruction Finance Corporation and supervise the construction and management of such projects, the OSPB employed three specialists and sixty technical and clerical workers. Altogether the OSPB completed forty studies and many were shared nation-wide. Their work is summarized in its *Oregon Looks Ahead.* Unfortunately, the state legislature abolished the OSPB in 1939.

Under the heading, "Blessing or Curse," the OSPB said, "Migration indicates vitality and hope. Each new family (not on welfare) consumes about $1000 annually." The capital value of each new farm family was estimated at $15,000. On the negative side it suggested desirable agricultural lands were already owned, which left only undesirable stump lands, abandoned farms or expensive to acquire developed farms for prospective settlers. It noted migrants created increased competition for work and more need for taxes for relief and other social services. To alleviate the migrant problem the OSPB recommended more public works projects and work relief programs.[58] Their study of migrants concentrated on public schools and the Oregon State Employment Service. Although not all-inclusive, the data is considered reliable. It showed migrants tended toward youth, 85% were under 45, more than half were under 30.[59] Urban areas attracted more singles, whose numbers steadily increased throughout the decade. True of all western states, migration in and out was heavy. In 1930, an estimated 60% of Oregonians were born outside the state. During peak Dust Bowl migration years, 1930–37, Oregon gained an estimated 81,000 from migration but two left for every three who entered.[60]

Analysis of incoming residents contradicted the common perception that they were predominantly farmers and unskilled laborers. The charts consistently showed that the newcomers possessed a range of skills and vocational experience very similar to that of the resident population.[61] Impartial authorities agreed that Dust Bowl migrants should not be considered unskilled itinerant tramps, intent on grabbing whatever government handouts they could. Most brought considerable skills and were determined to relocate permanently and carve a respectable economic and social position in their new community. A disproportionate number registered as truck drivers, hoping to qualify for one of many trucking jobs available at federal projects. Most banked upon their farm experience with trucks and other machinery, but many did not qualify for the more rigorous standards required at construction sites. By 1938, Oregon passed Washington as the leader in lumber production, not only attracting lumber workers from neighboring states but offering opportunities to Dust Bowl migrants whose strong work ethic and mechanical background allowed rapid adjustment to logging, mill, and factory work. This transition meant more than half of the incoming migrants settled in cities and towns, which also attracted a much larger percentage of single males over fifteen than single females over fifteen.[62]

A large percentage of migrants, especially those from the Dust Bowl, intended to make a living in agriculture in western Oregon, where every plant and animal known to exist in a temperate climate would thrive. Leaders among the wide variety of crops included pears, peaches, grapes, cherries, strawberries, apples and nuts. Wheat, primarily from eastern Oregon, remained the principal crop, contributing about thirty percent of the combined value of all crops in 1937.[63] As held true in Washington, the Oregon wheat crop, blessed with high prices, yielded well in 1936 and 1937. The 1936 Oregon wheat crop was 33% higher than 1935 and 64% higher than 1934.[64] Eighty -two Great Plains migrants families settled in the Vale-Owyhee irrigation project in eastern Oregon, but the land supply was too limited to accommodate many.[65]

Abandoned farms and cutover land were readily available, but newcomers rarely had the capital to buy the most desirable properties, so were forced to accept upland or shoestring valley locations, especially concentrated in southwestern Oregon. Unscrupulous land agents and real-estate salesmen frequently took advantage of the newcomers' lack of understanding of local conditions, selling unproductive land at inflated prices.[66] Many attempted low-grade dairy production or small-scale sheep raising with marginal results because of lack of suitable forage and pasture.[67] Most eked out a bare subsistence utilizing food from the farm, wild berries and fruit, and hunting and fishing. It much resembled the nineteenth century, except almost all owned an automobile and most had a home radio, frequently battery powered because electrical power lines still did not reach more poorly located farms. As late as 1938–39 an estimated fourteen thousand migrant families wintered in rural Oregon.[68] Like western Washington and northern Idaho a large percentage of these stump ranchers ultimately obtained full time jobs in the resurgent lumber industry. World War II created a massive labor demand that soaked up the existing labor supply and promoted recruiting forays to the Middle West by companies such as Boeing and Kaiser.

Funding of the $62 million Willamette Valley federal flood control project in June 1938 also created a multitude of opportunities. This massive undertaking was promoted by the Willamette Valley Waters Association, created in 1933 by nine Willamette Valley counties to gain support for a plan for seven United States Army Corps of Engineers dams in the river system. Besides helping avert catastrophic floods, the reservoirs would provide much needed irrigation capacity to counteract the valley's dry summers, plus power, conservation and recreation capability. Governor Martin, in spite of his general opposition to New Deal "socialism," had formed the Oregon State Planning Board primarily to advance the plan. The federal Flood Control Act of 1936 allocated $2,430,000 for construction of bank protection works and channel clearing for flood control and erosion prevention on the Willamette River system. The act also empowered the Corps of Engineers to make a preliminary examination of the Willamette River system and the Corps strongly recommended construction of the dams. The 1938 bill called for construction of the seven dams with a local contribution of only $1 million. Besides the Corps scientific evidence, Oregon lobbyists achieved their goal by emphasizing its usefulness in accommodating the migrant surge. An official publication said, "Intensive development of an area so eminently suited to agriculture and forestry is also desirable from the standpoint of national progress in order to provide opportunities for those who are steadily migrating from less favored region to the Pacific slope."[69] It suggested that the amount of new agricultural land made available by irrigation and reclamation might create "possibly 10,000 new farms." Only two dams, Cottage Grove and Fern Ridge (near Eugene) were completed before World War II stopped construction.[70] After the war eleven more dams were constructed—the two most expensive each cost about the same as Grand Coulee.

In 1940, the WPA *Guide to Oregon* described it as "still the most unspoiled and uncluttered spot in America."It warned, "Soon, perhaps, it will be changed by the coming of power, the in rolling immigration from the dust bowl, the devastation of timber-cutting and forest fires, and the boosting activities of chambers of commerce."[71] Heavily influenced by the New Deal's massive improvement of infrastructure which included dams, powerhouses, electric transmission lines, roads and bridges and much more, Oregon's population increased 50 percent from 1940 to 1950, a higher percentage than Washington.

NOTES

1. United States Bureau of the Census, Sixteenth Census 1940, *Oregon Changes of Population*, Volume II, Part V. (Washington, DC: United States Government Print Office, 1943), 172; WPA Writer's Program. *Oregon: End of the Trail.* (Portland: Binfords and Mort, 1940), 76–77.

2. Sixteenth Census, *Oregon Characteristics*, 980.

3. Oregon State Planning Board. *Oregon Looks Ahead.* (Salem, OR: State Printing Department, 1938), 23–25.

4. William G. Loy, *Atlas of Oregon* (Eugene: University of Oregon Press, 2001), 22–23.

5. Stewart H. Holbrook, *The Yankee Exodus: An Account of Migration from New England* (New York: Macmillan, 1950), passim.

6. Dorothy O. Johansen, "A Working Hypothesis for the Study of Migration," *Pacific Historical Review* 36 (February 1967): 1; Kimbark E. MacColl, *The Growth of a City: Power and Politics in Portland, Oregon, 1915 to 1950* (Portland: The Georgian Press, 1979), passim.

7. Paul W. Rodman, *The Far West and the Great Plains in Transition, 1859–1900* (New York: Harper & Row, 1988), 115–20; Dorothy O. Johansen, *Empire of the Columbia* Second Edition (New York: Harper & Row, 1966), 286.

8. Gordon B. Dodds, *Oregon: A Bicentennial History* (New York: Norton, 1977), 162–63.

9. The Columbia River Maritime Museum, Astoria, Oregon, visited August 2005.

10. Jerry A. O'Callaghan, "Senator John H. Mitchell and the Oregon Land Frauds, 1905," *Pacific Historical Review*, 21 (August 1952): 255–61; Senator Mitchell was indicted and convicted of having received fees for expediting land claims of clients. Almost all of Oregon's public school lands fell into private hands during this period. Mitchell died in 1905 while his conviction still was under appeal. This was only the most sensational of many Oregon land fraud cases. The rest of the West experienced similar corruption in the disposal of public lands. Cultural historian Vernon Parrington called the disposal of public lands "The Great Barbecue." See also Johansen, *Empire of the Columbia*, 351,356.

11. Richard L. Neuberger, *They Never Go Back to Pocatello: The Selected Essays of Richard Neuberger,* ed. Steve Neal (Portland: Oregon Historical Society Press, 1988), 162–63; Thomas C. McClintock, "Seth Lewelling, William S. U'Ren and the Birth of the Oregon Progressive Movement," *Oregon Historical Quarterly* 68 (June 1967): 197–220. South Dakota was the first state to adopt the initiative, referendum and recall in 1898.

12. Johansen, *Empire of the Columbia,* 2–3.

13. Dodds, *Oregon*, 296; Lawrence J. Saalfelt, *Forces of Prejudice in Oregon, 1920–25* (Portland: Archdiocean Historical Commission, 1984), 1–4.

14. Eckard V. Toy, "Robe and Gown: The Ku Klux Klan in Eugene, Oregon, During the 1920s," in *The Invisible Empire in the West: Toward a New Historical Appraisal of the Ku Klux Klan,* ed. Shawn Lay (Chicago: University of Illinois Press, 1992), 272.

15. MacColl, *The Growth of a City*, 483–85.

16. Johansen, *Empire*, 496.

17. Walter M. Pierce and Arthur H. Bone, *Oregon Cattleman/Governor, Congressman: Memoirs and Times of Walter M. Pierce* (Portland: Oregon Historical Society, 1981); David A. Horowitz, "The Klansman as Outsider: Ethnocultural Solidarity and Antelitism in the 1920s," *Pacific Northwest Quarterly* 80 (January 1989): 18.

18. Horowitz,"The Klansman," 18.

19. Toy, "KKK in Eugene," 182; Scottish Rite Masons also opposed parochial schools; Paul Halsinger, "The Oregon School Controversy, 1922–1925." *Pacific Historical Review* 37 (August 1968): 327–41.

20. *Grants Pass Spokesman,* April 26, 1924. Quoted in Saalfelt, *Forces of Prejudice,* 91.

21. Schoenberg, Wilfred P. *A History of the Catholic Church in the Pacific Northwest* (Washington, DC: Pastoral Press, 1987), 827.

22. Vivian C. Atterbury, *The Oregon Story* (Portland: Binfords and Mort, 1959), 51.

23. Saalfelt, *Forces of Prejudice*, passim.

24. Eckard V. Toy, "The Ku Klux Klan in Oregon," in *Experiences in a Promised Land: Essays on Pacific Northwest History*, ed. G. Thomas Edwards and Carlos A.

Schwantes (Seattle: University of Washington Press, 1986), 282–83; Toy, "Robe and Gown," 153–84; Jeff La Lande, "The Jackson County Rebellion: Social Turmoil and Political Insurgence in Southern Oregon During the Great Depression," *Oregon Historical Quarterly* 95 (Winter 1994–95): 406–71.

25. Malcom Clark, Jr., "The Bigot Disclosed: 90 Years of Nativism," *Oregon Historical Quarterly* 75 (June 1974): 109–83.

26. Jonathan Dembo. "The Pacific Northwest Lumber Industry during the Great Depression," *Journal of the West* 24, (October 1985): 51.

27. Dodds, *Oregon*, 298; Roberts, *A penny for the Governor,* 69–72.

28. William H. Mullins, "I'll Wreck the Town If It Will Give Employment: Portland in the Hoover Years of the Depression," *Pacific Northwest Quarterly* 79 (July 1988): 111.

29. William H. Mullins, *The Depression and the Urban West Coast, 1929–1933: Los Angeles, San Francisco, Seattle, and Portland* (Bloomington: Indiana University Press, 1991), 42; T. H. Watkins, *The Hungry Years,* (New York: Holt), 84.

30. Lancaster Pollard, *Oregon and the Pacific Northwest* (Portland: Binfords and Mort, 1946), 266–69.

31. Vivian C. Atterbury, *The Oregon Story* (Portland: Binfords and Mort), 60.

32. MacColl, *The Growth of a City*, 504.

33. Ibid., 431–33; Gary Murrell, "Democrats Disintegrate: No New Deal for Governor Charles Martin," *Columbia* 41 (Fall 2003): 5–12; Robert E. Burton, *Democrats of Oregon: The Pattern of Minority Politics, 1900–1956* (Eugene: University of Oregon Press, 1970): 70–71.

34. Paul Shinn, "Eugene in the Great Depression, 1929–1935," *Oregon Historical Quarterly* 86 (Spring 1985): 345.

35. Steve Neal, *McNary of Oregon: A Political Biography* (Portland: Western Imprints, 1985), Introduction 11–12 and passim.

36. MacColl, *The Growth of a City*, Chapter 15, "Violence at the Port: The Depression Years," 453–86; Paul G. Hummanti, "Finnish Radicals in Astoria, Oregon, 1904–1950," PhDdiss., University of Oregon, 1975; William Bigelow and Norman Diamond, "Agitate, Educate Organize: Portland, 1934," *Oregon Historical Quarterly* 89 (Spring 1988): 5–29.

37. Murrell, "Democrats Disintegrate," 10.

38. Martin, Grace Brandt, *An Oregon Schoolma'am, Book Two: The Depression Years* (Brownsville, OR: Calapooia Publications, 1981), 180. Unique insight of a young, Prineville teacher encountering mostly New York CCCs.

39. No public recognition of the CCC effort at Crater Lake was observed during the author's June 2005 visit.

40. Edwin G. Hill, *In the Shadow of the Mountains: The Spirit of the CCC* (Pullman: Washington State University Press, 1990), passim. Norman A Myers, *Letters to Home: Life in C.C.C. Camps of Douglas County, Oregon, 1933–1934*, ed. Gerald W. Williams (Roseburg, OR: USDA Forest Service, Umpqua National Forest), 1983.

41. "Oregon WPA," http://bluebook.stateor.us/culural/history/history25.htm. (accessed January 2006)

42. MacColl, Chapter 16, "The Depression Years: Some Federal Projects and Pitfalls," 487–518.

43. Floyd McKay, *An Editor for Oregon: Charles A. Sprague and the Politics of Change* (Corvallis: Oregon State University Press, 1998), 73.

44. Murrell, "Democrats Disintegrate," 9.

45. Burton, *Democrats of Oregon*, 70–71.

46. Murrell, "Democrats Disintegrate," 5

47. ——, *Iron Pants: Oregon's Anti New Deal Governor, Charles Henry Martin* (Pullman: Washington State University Press, 2000), 158.

48. Kevin Starr, *Endangered Dreams: The Great Depression in California* (New York: Oxford University Press, 1996), 149–50.

49. McKay, *An Editor*, 78; Murrell, "Democrats Disintegrate," 11.

50. WPA Writer's Program, *Oregon: End of the Trail* (Portland: Binfords and Mort, 1940), 101.

51. *Salem Statesman,* July 18, 1936.

52. Pacific Northwest Regional Planning Commission, *Migration and the Development of Economic Opportunity in the Pacific Northwest. A Report Prepared in Cooperation with the Pacific Northwest Land Advisory Committee* (Portland: Pacific Northwest Regional Planning Commission, 1939), 8.

53. Richard L. Neuberger, *Our Promised Land* (New York: Macmillan, 1938), 54.

54. WPA Writer's Program, *Oregon*, 8.

55. Willard Troxell and Paul O'Day, *Migration Into the States of the Pacific Northwest, 1930–1938* (Portland: Farm Security Administration, May 1940), 7; Oregon State Planning Board *Oregon Looks Ahead* (Salem, OR: State Printing Department, 1938), 15–16.

56. Oregon State Planning Board, *Study of Migration Into Oregon, 1933–1939* (Salem, OR: State Printing Department, 1939), 5–6, 10, 16–19.

57. John Blanchard *Caravans to the Northwest* (Portland: Northwest Regional Council, 1940), 28.

58. Oregon State Planning Board, *Oregon Looks Ahead,* 17–18.

59. Ibid., 15–16.

60. Oregon State Planning Board, *Study,* 26.

61. Ibid., 182–83, 219–20; Oregon State Planning Board, *Migration,* 8.

62. Oregon State Planning Board, *Study,* 25–26.

63. WPA Writer's Program, *Oregon,* 53–55.

64. *Salem Statesman,* July 16, 1936.

65. Carl P. Heisig. *New Farms on New Land* (Washington, DC: United States Department of Agriculture, Bureau of Agricultural Economics, 1941), 114.

66. Neuberger, *Our Promised Land*, 58.

67. Oregon State Planning Board, *Study*, 10.

68. James Sidell, *Pick for Your Supper: A Study of Child Labor among Migrants on the Pacific Coast* (New York: National Child Labor Committee, 1939), 13.

69. Oregon State Planning Board, *Oregon*, 64.

70. Merlin Blais, "Willamette: Rebel River," *Portland Oregonian*, 28 February 1943.

71. WPA Writer's Program, *Oregon*, Preface.

Chapter Eight

Idaho: The Gem State

Bordered by six states and Canada, Idaho, "The Gem of the Mountains," larger in area than Nebraska and either of the Dakotas, presents a north-south division. The northern area is associated more with the Pacific Northwest than the southern area that is more aligned with the Great Basin. A popular early twentieth century quip claimed Idaho was the only state with two capitals—Spokane and Salt Lake City. Logging and mining prevail in the mountainous north while agriculture, much aided by irrigation, pre-dominates in the arid south. The north is more German, French (Canadian), Catholic and Democrat while the south is more English, Swedish, Mormon and Republican. An estimated one-third of Idahoans is Mormon. In 1930, Idaho had a population of only 445,000, whose demography in terms of race, educational level, and marriage and divorce rates compared with neighboring Oregon. The federal government retained 63.7 percent of Idaho, an amount that exceeded the total acreage of twenty-three other states. Extremely rural, only Pocatello and Boise contained a population over ten thousand in the 1930s.

The Utah connection created a long history of anti-Mormon sentiment in Idaho. Encouraged by Brigham Young, Mormons settled in southeastern Idaho by the 1860s and spread into the upper Snake River Valley by the 1900s. Tight knit, hard working and generally prosperous, Mormons soon predominated southern Idaho.[1] Ironically, the now solidly Republican Mormons created political resentment in territorial times and early statehood because they block-voted for Democrats who controlled the Territory before the 1880s. Mormons opposed the Republican Party because they had suffered constant repudiation from every Republican convention since its founding in 1856. Besides overall resentment against Mormon theocracy, much Republican criticism focused on their practice of polygamy or plural marriage. By

1880, the Republican controlled Congress passed the Edmunds Act, barring polygamists from voting, holding office or serving as jurors in cases involving plural marriage.

Led by ambitious Republican Fred Dubois, whose Illinois family was connected closely to both Presidents Abraham Lincoln and Benjamin Harrison, Idaho passed a Test Oath in 1885. It required individuals to testify under oath whether they belonged to the Mormon Church or believed in its doctrines. The Test Oath, essentially disenfranchising Mormons, was included in Idaho's state constitution in 1890. After Mormon leadership announced plural marriages were no longer acceptable Mormons were allowed to vote in 1893, but officially the Test Oath was not removed from the state constitution until 1982.[2]

Dubois, a free coinage of silver Republican and anti-imperialist, switched to the Democratic Party and won appointment as one of Idaho's first United States Senators. Dubois' silver devotion was such that the cattle on his ranch were branded 16 to 1, the silver to gold ratio demanded by Populists. In the Senate, Dubois continued his anti-Mormon stance highlighted by his unsuccessful attempt to unseat Utah Senator Reed Smoot.

William Borah, another Illinois native, headed his future father-in-law William McConnell's successful run for governor in 1892. Borah, Dubois' bitter rival, welcomed Mormons into the Republican Party that won about half of the Mormon vote in 1894. His unsuccessful, but much publicized, 1906 murder prosecution of IWW leader Bill Haywood established Borah as a national figure and made him an odds-on-favorite for the Republican nomination for United States Senate. Mormon support was also crucial for Borah's victory over Dubois in his 1907 Senate election by Idaho's Republican State Legislature.[3]

Southern Idaho greatly benefited from the 1894 Carey Act (Desert Land Act) which gave each of sixteen western "reclamation states" a million acres with the requirement that the land had to be irrigated. Named for Wyoming Senator Joseph Carey, it was designed to lure settlers and private capital. Carey land was free to the state. The states contracted with individuals or commercial companies to build and operate the irrigation systems. No lands were to be leased or sold except for reclamation and settlement, and not more than 160 acres could be sold to one person. Settlers paid fifty cents an acre, creating a development fund, but that proved inadequate and states did not manage their Carey Grants adequately. Although Idaho offered little support, local irrigation districts, comparable to school districts, proved more successful than in any other state. About sixty percent of all Carey Act lands irrigated in the United States are in Idaho.[4]

Western Congressmen, with Senator Dubois a key leader, dissatisfied with Carey Act progress, wanted the federal government to use receipts from the sale of public lands to build irrigation and hydroelectric power projects in their states. Eastern and Mid-Western congressmen opposed this development of western competition. In 1901, Westerners flexed their increased political muscle in the Senate by filibustering and killing a bill containing rivers and harbors projects favorable to the East. In a 1902 compromise Congress approved the Newlands or Reclamation Act for the seventeen Western states which directly involved the federal government in reclamation. Named for Nevada Democrat Francis Newlands, it was, "An Act appropriating the receipts of public lands in certain states and territories to the construction of irrigation works for the reclamation of arid lands." Its three main purposes were (1) to federally plan and construct major improvements; (2) to provide maximum benefits for the entire area in which it was located; (3) to make these federally financed self-liquidating. The latter was to be accomplished by charging costs against the lands they served and eventually transferring ownership and management of the canals to associations of water users.[5]

Few acts of Congress have had such sweeping results. Many consider the National Reclamation Act the key that truly unlocked the West. Critics quickly noted the Act's tendency to favor big farms and direct public funds toward improvement of private land held within the various projects. In 1910, in response to mounting criticism, Senator Borah said, "The law as it was passed was intended to be, as was said in the public prints and as was generally understood, a poor man's law; that is to say, it was designed that men of most moderate means might go upon the public lands and, under these projects, initiated and carried on by the government, obtain homes."[6] As it evolved, unfortunately, the Reclamation Act never provided the safety valve for the poor that Borah and his colleagues envisioned. Only a small minority of the first generation of project farmers succeeded. Much of the proposed land was either difficult or unsuited for irrigation Getting started required a fair amount of capital and successfully establishing an irrigated farm required expertise and grueling work that forced many out.[7]

Federal dollars ignited an explosion in dam construction, power plants and canals. Now a branch of the Interior Department, the Bureau of Reclamation (USBR) operates 180 projects in seventeen states containing more than six hundred dams and reservoirs. It provides agricultural, household and industrial water to about one-third of the American West and is the second leading supplier of hydroelectric power. Now lands irrigated by the USBR supply a major portion of the nation's food and fiber. Other significant benefits include flood control and enormously expanded recreational opportunities. Sale of water, electricity and land has repaid about 97 percent of the cost. Although originally passed with an irrigation emphasis, most large population centers in the Far West owe much of their growth to USBR power. Hoover, Grand

Coulee, Shasta and Glen Canyon dams are among the better known dams operated by the USBR. The Army Corps of Engineers, the USBR's natural rival, operates Bonneville and a number of other dams. Although the Corps is more oriented toward flood control and navigation, dams controlled by the Corps also generate a substantial amount of hydroelectricity.

Especially before the surge in New Deal construction, Idaho again was perhaps the major beneficiary of the Newlands Act. Authorized in late 1902 and completed in 1906, the Snake River Minidoka Project provided irrigation for 120,000 acres in the Burley-Rupert area and began the first federal dam to generate hydroelectricity in 1909. At its 1915 completion the picturesque 350 foot high Arrow Rock Dam on the Boise River, about twenty miles northeast of Boise, was the tallest concrete dam in the world. The American Falls Dam finished in 1927 furnished Idaho's largest water storage facility, opening 115,000 irrigated acres and supplementing one million more. It also generated electricity. Completed in 1932, the Owyhee Dam, located on Oregon's Owyhee River along the Idaho state-line, rose sixty-seven feet higher than Arrow Rock. Irrigation infrastructure put in place during the New Deal provided water for 105,00 acres of which about 30,000 were located in southwestern Idaho. Problems associated with Owyhee Dam construction were analyzed to help build Hoover Dam which towered three hundred feet higher than Owyhee.

In spite of the dramatic increase in irrigated agriculture Idaho did not prosper in the 1920s. New settlers were attracted by the dramatic increase in irrigated land, but it required capital and skills not possessed by the average working man. Qualifiers frequently were discouraged by unexpected difficulties. Prices for potatoes, grain, and livestock stayed low because of oversupply. Other extractive industries such as mining and lumbering suffered the same fate. Many elected to leave, mainly to the West Coast, making Idaho second only to Montana in the percentage of people who moved out in the 1920s.[8]

If not all was well with the American economy in the 1920s, the sports world did not reflect it. The 1920s were known as the Golden Era in American sports and sports minded Idaho took enormous pride in the exploits of jockey Earl Sande. "The Idaho Hot Potato" was to horse racing what Jack Dempsey was to boxing and Babe Ruth was to baseball. Hard working Sande won racing's Triple Crown in 1930 after being the top money winner in 1921, 1923 and 1927. He finished in the money in over sixty percent of his races, an all-time record. Sande was born in Groton, South Dakota, to impoverished Norwegian immigrants who moved to American Falls in 1908 when he was nine. In 2005, both the South Dakota and Idaho State legislatures passed resolutions commemorating the seventy-fifth anniversary of Sande's Triple

Crown feat. After injuries forced Sande to retire early as a jockey, he became a leading trainer. Sande spent his last years in Oregon where his parents made their final home.

Idaho was ill prepared to host the stream of dust bowl migrants who came from the entire Great Plains area. There was an abundance of non-irrigated low priced farmland in the southern region and cut over forestland in the north, though. During the period 1929–1932 Idaho experienced severe drought that maximized the economic depression making it sixth in percentage decline in income for that period. Mining output dropped from $32 million in 1929 to $9 million in 1933. Farm income declined from $116 million in 1929 to $41 million in 1932.[9] Only North and South Dakota, Oklahoma, Mississippi and Montana decreased more.[10] In 1934, southern Idaho suffered the most severe drought in its recorded history. Prompt action by the FERA, providing over $1 million that summer, prevented a disaster.[11] Idaho's mining output also dropped from $32,000,000 in 1929 to $9,000,000 in 1933. With drastically reduced tax revenues the state was hard-pressed to maintain basic services. A notice posted by the State Department of Public Assistance along a highway in southern Idaho at the peak of the depression warned, "No relief funds available in Idaho to non-residents."[12]

Fortunately, Idaho's political leadership effectively worked New Deal programs to maximize benefits for their state. On a per capita basis Idaho ranked fifth in New Deal outlays from 1933–1939.[13] State spending remained so tight that by 1936 three term Democrat governor "Cowboy Ben" Ross considered his reduction of state indebtedness by one-third the proudest achievement of his six years in office. "We got by for two years and Uncle Sam paid the bill," said Ross.[14] As held true in neighboring Washington and Oregon, Idaho was well on the way to recovery by 1936. New Deal policies helped the mining and timber industries and Pacific Northwest agriculture, especially grain, benefited from the massive crop failures of the drought stricken Great Plains.

Although popular and able, Ross was overshadowed by the iconoclastic Progressive Republican Borah, who served as United States Senator from 1907 until his death in 1940. Frequently and inaccurately portrayed as a provincial, Borah was considered the best orator in Congress and possibly the best debater as well. Popularly known as "The Lion of Idaho," Borah had attained international celebrity by the 1930s. A statue of Borah represents Idaho in the United States Capitol. In 1936, *Time* Magazine declared him "the most famed Senator of this century," and "the great Moral force of the Senate, the one member who could arise and deal with Right and Wrong in an electric way." A champion of local self-government, Borah supported progressive reforms including the income tax, the direct election of senators and labor legislation, but he was known best for his opposition to the League of Nations and the World Court which earned him another more pejorative nickname, "The Great Opposer."

In 1932, Borah ingratiated himself with Roosevelt by opposing the re-election of Herbert Hoover because Hoover did not support direct relief. Borah blamed the Depression on lack of purchasing power, lamenting that four percent of the population controlled eighty-four percent of the wealth. He supported most New Deal domestic reform measures and attracted federal money to Idaho, but aligned with his Great Plains colleagues as a strong isolationist.[15] "The Great Opposer" showed his independence, however, by championing recognition of the Soviet Union in the early 1930s.

Borah grew up in Illinois, took his legal training at the University of Kansas and moved to Boise in 1891. Four years later the ambitious young lawyer married Mary McConnell, the governor's daughter. By the 1930s, Borah, a lone wolf whose focus was opposition to monopoly, had become a political giant. His powerful position in the Senate combined with his support of New Deal domestic policies promoted the generous flow of federal money into Idaho. Borah confidently predicted that the Dust Bowl migration would involve millions of people who would help develop Idaho and the rest of the Pacific Northwest.[16] After an unsuccessful try for the Republican presidential nomination in 1936, Borah again declined to endorse the party nominee, Alfred Landon.

James P. Pope, Idaho's Democrat senator from 1933 to 1939, also was instrumental in securing federal support. Pope consistently supported the New Deal, including public power and opposition to neutrality legislation. Eager to retain a supportive liberal Democrat from Idaho, Roosevelt favored Pope's wishes, which were especially evident in generous federal funding of Idaho CCC, WPA and Rural Electrification (REA) programs. Like Oregon and Washington, Idaho was accustomed to political leaders who grew up in other states, especially Midwestern. Pope, who grew up on a Louisiana cotton plantation, was one of several exceptions, though. The most notable was Bavarian born Governor Moses Alexander, a Boise clothing-store owner. Alexander became the first elected Jewish governor in the country, serving two terms (1914–1918). After starring in football at Louisiana Tech, Pope earned his law degree at the University of Chicago. Supposedly the future senator stopped at Boise in 1909 when his money ran out. Pope went on to become mayor of Boise and won the senate seat in the 1932 Democratic landslide. Idaho voters rejected Pope in 1938, choosing eventual winner isolationist D. Worth Clark in the 1938 Democrat primaries. Pope then left Idaho to become Director of the Tennessee Valley Authority.

In addition to the two effective senators, T. A. Walters, a reclamation lawyer from Caldwell, was appointed Assistant Secretary of Interior under

Ickes, wielding considerable influence for Idaho. Walters, the former Chair of the Idaho Democrat Central Committee, enjoyed a close relationship with both Pope and Borah, but quarreled with Governor Ross over patronage. With two-thirds of its acreage in federal ownership Idaho managed to procure a total of 163 CCC camps, twice as many as its population warranted.[17] A total of 86,775, only about one-quarter from in state, served in the Idaho CCC. Each camp lasted about three years so the number in operation peaked at eighty-two in 1935. In its ten-year history the CCC spent over $80 million in Idaho which ranked second nationally in CCC expenditures.[18]

Especially well administered in Idaho, the CCC planted trees; built roads, buildings, fences and phone lines; developed conservation and reclamation projects; fought fires, insects and diseases; and provided numerous other services. Not only did the labors of the "tree army" greatly benefit the state and the CCC members, many others directly benefited as well. The CCC required enrollees to contribute twenty-five dollars of their thirty-dollar a month income to dependants.[19]

By February 1936, the WPA, which specialized more in road building, also had 510 projects in Idaho that employed 22,000.[20] Besides roads, the WPA built dozens of schools and community centers, the Black Canyon Irrigation Project, and the Arrowhead Dam. Historically conservative, Idahoans willingly accepted New Deal assistance. A detailed study of the New Deal in Pocatello by Mervin Swanson explored the attitudes of local businessmen toward the New Deal and found they practiced a sophisticated selectivity, favoring programs that promoted their own interests. Not one Pocatello city council member voted against a single work relief project in the 1930s. Nor did any individual group speak out publicly against any work relief project in Pocatello. Consistently, Pocatello requested more money, more projects and more jobs.[21]

Idaho native Vardis Fisher spearheaded arguably the most successful WPA federal writer's project in the nation. The WPA sought qualified writers to head the state programs and Fisher had the necessary credentials. Fisher's father, a Mormon bishop, was sent by Brigham Young to establish a colony in the isolated upper Snake River Valley. After graduating from Rigby high school Fisher attended the University of Utah and went on to earn an honors Ph.D. in English from the University of Chicago. (Incredibly, fifteen-year old Philo Farnsworth outlined the plan for television at Rigby high school in 1922.) Fisher pursued an academic career at the University of Utah and New York University, championing self-knowledge and reason and never failing to acknowledge his atheism. Already the author of six novels, Fisher returned to Idaho in the early 1930s to write full time. With a family to support and little income Fisher won the state directorship in 1935 at an annual salary of $2300.

Handicapped by inadequate facilities, untrained assistants, and persistent intervention from Washington superiors, Fisher pushed to finish the first WPA guide. Leaders of the national project did not want "a small unimportant state to be first," and unsuccessfully attempted to slow Fisher's progress by demanding revisions and additions that Fisher mostly ignored. He wrote 374 of the 405 pages of the text and had *Idaho: A Guide in Word and Pictures* printed by Caxton Printers of Caldwell, Idaho, in 1936.

Fisher was not the only gifted writer from Idaho. Lawrence Henry Gipson, whose family established Caxton Printers, was selected in the first class of Rhodes scholars to study at Oxford. After earning a Ph.D. in history at Yale, Gipson enjoyed a distinguished career at Lehigh University, winning a Pulitzer Prize in 1962 for *The Triumphant Empire: Thunderclouds Gather in the West, 1763–1776,* the tenth volume of his fifteen volume work on the British Empire before the American Revolution.

Idaho received rave reviews and was sent to all state directors in the United States as a model. Fisher was appointed director of Writers Project for the entire Rocky Mountain Region.[22] After his stint with the Writer's Project Fisher continued publishing prolifically, writing a weekly column in the *Idaho Statesman* from 1943 to 1950 and authoring a number of books. His most profitable effort was *Mountain Man,* which was used as the basis for the popular movie *Jeremiah Johnson.*

Governor Ross, like his fellow Democrat governors in Washington and Oregon, was not dedicated to the New Deal, but expediently supported what benefited his state. Idaho's first native-born governor, he grew up on a ranch in Bannock County, and only attended school for six years, but later studied at a business college for three years. Ross founded the Idaho Farm Bureau and built a rural political base with his message, "the cow, the pig, and the hen." Colorful "Cowboy Ben" was the mayor of Pocatello, at that time one of the strongest union towns in the nation, when he became the first three term governor (1931–1937). Ross, never known for underestimating himself, believed he was fated to become president. Forest fires in 1931, set by arsonists wanting jobs putting them out, provided Ross an immediate crisis. He declared the involved central Idaho counties in a state of insurrection, proclaimed martial law, and employed the National Guard to prohibit public access.[23] In 1935, Ross furthered his conservative, take charge image by again declaring martial law in the Teton County pea picking rebellion. There some 1500 mostly Mexican workers struck over wages. They demanded $1.00 per hundred weight instead of seventy cents and a fifteen cent bonus for staying. Authorities arrested 125 Mexicans and escorted them to the county line.

In 1935, the federal government, tired of the parsimony of state governments, insisted they provide matching funds to support New Deal projects.

Ross temporarily stopped support for eighty thousand needy persons to gain support for a 2 percent sales tax to raise matching funds. His tactics brought political disaster for "Cowboy Ben." Every Idaho Democrat except Ross won in 1936. His challenge for Senator Borah's senate seat was smashed by almost two to one in spite of Roosevelt's overwhelming Idaho vote. The sales tax also lost on referendum. By 1938, Republicans regained control of Idaho and the West.[24]

Idaho gained almost eighty thousand residents in the 1930s, an increase of more than 18 percent, but, unlike its more western neighbors, only gained 64,000 during the 1940s. Many Dust Bowl migrants, who had stopped in Idaho simply because they had run out of money, were moving west by 1939, attracted by higher wages and steady employment promoted by the boom in military contracts.[25] A large percentage of those making the transition to the Pacific Coast states had pursued a subsistence style of living in Idaho. Many of the estimated 6700 casual workers who had migrated from the Southwest into southern Idaho never established deep roots. Of these about one third were listed as farm laborers who followed the harvest cycle. A typical pattern might include working the fruit orchards of Yakima, picking ferns near Centralia (WA), digging clams at Copalis and Ocean City, harvesting peas and cherries at the Dalles, then reaping fruits, vegetables, sugar beets and potatoes in the Snake River Valley.[26]

Most of the Northern Great Plains migrants settled on cheap cutover land in Bonner and Boundary counties in northwestern Idaho. Only in Idaho did over fifteen percent of migrants seek a farm on logged over land.[27] A 1939 study of 172 farmers from other states in northern Idaho revealed that all but four had settled since 1929. Sixty percent were from the Great Plains and fewer than one third had owned their own farms before moving. Thirty percent were engaged in non-agricultural work before moving. Sixty percent of the "farms" had less than one acre of cleared land when migrants settled and half or more of the recent settlement had occurred where land-use areas were acute. Clearing land in northern Idaho was somewhat easier than in western Washington and Oregon because pine stumps were smaller and rotted faster, but plentiful brush and lack of capital kept the process slow. The vast majority of homes lacked electricity and only 8 percent had running water in the house. In spite of Spartan conditions and a tribute to their self-reliance, less than one quarter of these settlers received public assistance.[28]

Several unique Idaho entrepreneurial ventures were stimulated by Depression conditions. Frank Bruce Robinson, a Moscow pharmacist, made a fortune through his mail order religion called "Psychiana." Born in England, he had studied theology in Canada and served in the Salvation Army then rejected all organized religion and becoming a drunken drifter before establishing himself as a pharmacist in Portland, Oregon. Upon moving to Moscow Robinson said, "I talked with God and experienced a New Thought religious conviction that emphasized spiritual healing, prosperity, and physical and material happiness." Those who read and followed his mail order lessons were promised the same results with a money back guarantee. Using astute advertising in newspapers, magazines, and the radio Robinson's lessons seemed to hold special appeal to Depression weary people around the world. By the late 1930s, the self-proclaimed "archbishop of Psychiana" received sixty thousand pieces of mail a year and was reported to be the richest man in Idaho.[29] Psychiana quickly declined upon Robinson's death in 1948.

Another Idaho enterprise had a more permanent impact. Still an international icon, Sun Valley became the first destination ski resort in the United States in 1936 and a model for those that followed. Averill Harriman, chairman of the Board of Directors of the Union Pacific Railroad, asked his friend Austrian count Felix Schoffgotich, a skiing expert, to find the perfect spot for a European style winter resort. After searching several months Schoffgotich recommended Ketchum, a remote old mining town in south-central Idaho known for its abundant snow and winter sunshine. Harriman paid a destitute rancher about ten dollars an acre for his three thousand-acre spread in a sheltered valley adjacent to the Sawtooth National Forest. Soon twelve hundred more acres were added.

Harriman budgeted $3 million to build a year around resort that would project an aura of elegance described as "roughing it in style." Depression conditions in rural Idaho subsidized this monument to conspicuous consumption. Capitalizing on low prices for material and an abundance of low-wage labor the luxurious resort was completed by Christmas, providing a much-needed economic boost to the area. The glamorous resort quickly became a favorite of Hollywood movie stars and other luminaries, including author Ernest Hemingway who became a full-time resident and while there wrote the last two chapters of *For Whom the Bell Tolls*.[30]

Celebrities gave Sun Valley visibility but with eight chair lifts serving more ski runs than anywhere else in the world, customers with more limited budgets were essential. Illustrative of Depression era prices regularly featured "learn to ski weeks" offered seven days and six nights for $75. The package covered accommodations, meals, six days of ski lessons, and the use of ski lifts and ice-skating rinks.[31] In spite of its impressive reputation Sun Valley consistently lost money and eventually was sold by Union Pacific in the 1960s.

Unlike Sun Valley the Morrison-Knudsen Heavy Construction Company enjoyed Depression prosperity that helped propel them to international leadership by the 1940s and 50s. Founded in Boise in 1912 by Morris Knudsen,

50, and Harry Morrison, 27, the company grew steadily under their sound leadership. Knudsen was a Danish immigrant who had farmed in Nebraska and Idaho. He started a small construction firm using a couple of horses for power. Morrison grew up on an Illinois farm, starting as a seventeen-year old water boy for a Chicago construction firm. The job took him to Idaho where he joined the Bureau of Reclamation and learned surveying. By nights he earned an engineering degree from a correspondence school. Knudsen accepted Morrison's bid to become a partner even after Morrison admitted he had no capital other than himself. After engaging in some small dam and canal building subcontracts, they won a construction bid with the Union Pacific Railroad and they were on their way. A tireless worker and an organizational genius, Morrison conceived the idea of a consortium to build dams that were too large an undertaking for just one company. Their firm teamed with five others called the Six Companies to build Boulder and Bonneville Dams. Between 1933 and 1940 Morrison-Knudsen worked on twenty major dams, plus numerous other irrigation, reclamation and flood control projects.[32] In 1954, *Time* magazine called Harry Morrison the one builder in history whom had done the most to change the face of the earth.

Another Midwesterner J. R. "Jack" Simplot moved to southern Idaho from Iowa as a child. In 1923, Simplot quit school at age fourteen, supposedly because he was tired of milking cows. After gaining a stake raising hogs, Simplot began his potato empire in the 1930s using advanced techniques in seed, fertilizer and marketing. By 1940, he shipped ten thousand cars of Idaho potatoes across the United States. During World War II Simplot made a fortune selling dehydrated potatoes and onions to the military. By the late twentieth century Simplot, now known to many as the "French Fry King" because of his lucrative contract with the McDonalds Corporation, made *Forbes* magazine's fifty wealthiest in the country. Simplot's empire extended far beyond potatoes. His Company is one of the top ten suppliers of cattle and beef in the country, a major supplier of minerals and chemicals, a major supplier of fertilizer and livestock feed and supplements. Simplot also is a key investor in Micron Technology, the owner of over 150 trucks and six hundred railroad cars, major holdings in real estate, and involved in numerous other ventures. Many incorrectly assume Simplot is Mormon. Neither was his friend and fellow Boise billionaire, grocery magnate Joe Albertson.[33]

By 1939, Idaho was well on its way to economic recovery—lumbering, mining and agriculture all showing strong improvement.[34] But many, especially in the crowded mountain valleys of northern Idaho and also western Montana, were trapped in a low-income subsistence lifestyle and were receptive to change. Greatly benefited by New Deal programs in the 1930s, Idaho did not receive the enormous defense contracts awarded to manufacturers in more advantageously located Oregon, Washington and California. Attracted by the almost unlimited demand for high paid workers, many Idahoans moved to the West Coast.

NOTES

1. Paul Rodman, *The Far West and the Great Plains in Transition, 1859–1900* (New York: Harper & Row, 1988), 175–82.

2. Leonard Arrington, *History of Idaho* (Moscow, ID: University of Idaho Press; Boise: Idaho State Historical Society, 1994) Volume I, 429–31; Rodman, *The Far West*, Chapter 8, "Self-Proclaimed 'Peculiar People,'" 169–82.

3. Rufus G. Cook, "The Political Suicide of Senator Fred T. Dubois of Idaho," *Pacific Northwest Quarterly* 60 (October 1979): 193–98.

4. *Idaho Yesterdays* 30 (Spring/Summer 1986): Special issue devoted to Idaho water history; Dorothy O Johansen, *Empire of the Columbia*, Second Edition (New York: Harper & Row, 1966), 388–92.

5. Johanson, *Empire*, 392–98.

6. Donald J. Pisani, *Water and American Government: The Reclamation Bureaus, National Water Policy, and the West, 1902–1935* (Berkeley: University of California Press, 2002), 2; Donald Swain, "The Bureau of Reclamation and the New Deal, 1933–1940," *Pacific Northwest Quarterly* 61 (July 1970): 137–46.

7. Pisani, *Water*, 27–28, 32–64.

8. Carlos Schwantes, *The Pacific Northwest: An Interpretive History*, (Lincoln: University of Nebraska Press, 1996), 189.

9. Merle Wells and Arthur Hart, *Idaho: The Gem of the Mountains* (Northridge, CA: Windsor Publications, 1985), 127.

10. Arrington, *History of Idaho*, Volume II, 42.

11. Michael P. Malone, *C. Ben Ross and the New Deal in Idaho* (Seattle: University of Washington Press, 1970), 76.

12. Carlos Schwantes, *Hard Traveling: A Portrait of Work Life in the New Northwest*, (Lincoln: University of Nebraska Press, 1994), 210–11.

13. Don C. Reading, "New Deal Activity and the States, 1933 to 1939," *Journal of Economic History* 33 (1973): 794–95.

14. Malone, *C. Ben Ross*, 99.

15. Schwantes, *The Pacific Northwest*, 378–80.

16. Richard Neuberger, *Our Promised Land* (New York: Macmillan, 1938), 34.

17. Elmo R. Richardson, "Western Politics and New Deal Policies: A Study of T. A. Walters of Idaho," *Pacific Northwest Quarterly* 54 (January 1963): 9–18.

18. Arrington, *History of Idaho,* Volume II, 56–57; Kelly Roberts, "CCC in Idaho" http://www.idptv.state.id.us/outdoors/shows/ccc/showtranscript.html. (accessed November 10, 2005)

19. Judith Austin, "The CCC in Idaho, *Idaho Yesterdays* 27 (Fall 1983): 13–18.

20. Malone, *C. Ben Ross*, 76–90.

21. Mervin R. Swanson, "Hope Restored: The New Deal in Pocatello," *Idaho Yesterdays* 23 (Summer 1979): 53–57.

22. Ronald W. Tabor, "Vardis Fisher and the Idaho Guide: Preserving the Culture for the New Deal," *Pacific Northwest Quarterly* 59 (April 1968): 68–76.

23. F. Ross Peterson, *Idaho: A Bicentennial History* (New York: Norton, 1976), 147.

24. Malone, *C. Ben Ross,* 86–129.

25. Charles McKinley, *Uncle Sam in the Pacific Northwest* (Berkeley: University of California Press, 1952), 11.

26. David Glaser, "Migration in Idaho's History," *Idaho Yesterdays* 11 (Fall 1967): 26–27.

27. John Webb and Malcom Brown, *Migrant Families,* WPA Research Monograph 18. (Washington, D.C.: United State Government Printing Office, 1938), 21.

28. Marion Clawson, David McEntire and Carl Heisig, "Stump Ranching," *Land Policy Review* 3 (May-June 1940): 32–38; Pacific Northwest Regional Planning Commission *Migration and the Development of Economic Opportunity in the Pacific Northwest: A Report Prepared in Cooperation with the Pacific Northwest Land Advisory Committee* (Portland: Pacific Northwest Planning Commission, 1939), 9.

29. Frank B. Robinson, *The Strange Autobiography of Frank B. Robinson* (Moscow, ID: Psychiana Incorporated, 1941). Arrington, *History of Idaho,* Volume II, 70.

30. Hal Rothman, "Tourism as a Colonial Industry," in *Power and Place in the Pacific Northwest*, ed. Richard White and John Findlay (Seattle: University of Washington Press, 1999) 177–203.

31. Federal Writers Project, *Idaho: A Guide in Word and Picture*, Second Edition (New York: Oxford), 194–95.

32. Glen Barrett, "Reclamation's New Deal for Heavy Construction: Morrison-Knudsen in the Great Depression," *Idaho Yesterdays* 22 (Fall 1978): 21.

33. Louie Attebury, *J. R. Simplot: A Billion the Hard Way* (Caldwell, ID: Caxton Printers, 2000), 201–02.

34. Peterson, *Idaho*, 155–58.

Chapter Nine

Baked Out, Blown Out and Broke

Even though New Deal programs provided massive assistance to drought stricken areas, they could not prevent the destructive drought that propelled hundreds of thousands of despairing migrants off the Northern Great Plains. As New Dealers were well aware, most of those who left would have to rely primarily upon federal programs if they needed help. No doubt a substantial number stayed on the Plains because of federal support. Many tenant farmers, however, were forced to leave because landowners now preferred to farm their own land while taking advantage of the benefits offered through the Agricultural Adjustment Act and other New Deal farm support programs.

The shift of surplus population from the Plains to areas capable of sustaining a population increase had begun long before the 1930s. The Northern Great Plains had become over-populated by the 1920s with more people than the agriculturally oriented economy could support and bore a well-earned reputation for periods of severe drought. The allied conditions of larger farms and more mechanization meant fewer farmers and less demand for hired labor. Thus the traditional path of starting as a farm laborer to eventually become an independent owner became increasingly difficult. Because very few large towns existed, moreover, it was not as easy to find jobs in town, a common practice for rural people in more populated areas.[1] As rural areas shrank, so did the need for the goods and services from towns. During the early thirties more youth were maturing in the United States than ever before. In 1935, there were approximately 20,800,000 youth, 16–24 years old, almost ten million living in rural areas. This constituted a record figure in each case.[2] The Great Plains, where most married early and had large families, contained a disproportionately high percentage of young people ready to enter the work force.[3]

Accordingly, migration accelerated to areas that provided more economic opportunity, especially the West Coast.[4] Always transitional, the Northern Great Plains experienced about the same amount of outward migration in the 1930s as in the 1920s and 1940s.Much of the 1930s pilgrimage, however, was spurred by unprecedented natural disaster, and was not as well planned or financed. It entailed a sense of desperation not experienced to that degree before or after. The Farm Security Administration estimated 36,000 families migrated from drought areas into rural communities of the Pacific Northwest between 1930–1937 and lack of financial ability kept more from leaving.[5] As historian Walter Nugent suggests, "It took a little *something*, in the 1930s, to be able to buy gas or a bus ticket."[6] Those who had migrated earlier enjoyed abundant economic opportunities in timber, agriculture, mining, and other areas that no longer existed during the Great Depression.[7]

Popular stereotypes of those who left portray them as foot-loose country hayseeds, "baked out, blown out, and broke." Some writers referred to them as "Northern Okies," others called them "Dokies," a play on Dakota origins of many. As is true of much stereotyping, some basis of truth exists, but major exceptions should be noted. A large percentage of the migrants had never engaged in farming and had no intention of beginning. The Depression also withered the need for townspeople on the Northern Plains. Merchants, professionals, and skilled tradesmen also left, supplying an incalculable amount of human and material capital to their new locations, which were usually towns and cities. Of the estimated ten thousand migrants who moved to the Pacific Northwest from North Dakota farms during 1936–37, 7,500 entered towns and cities.[8] Most of these farm migrants had not experienced grinding poverty their entire lives by any means. Many of the migrants earlier actually had experienced comparable or even better incomes than those previously established in their new locations. During the period 1924–1928 the Northern Great Plains enjoyed a considerably higher gross income per farm than either the Pacific Northwest or the Southern Great Plains. From 1920 to 1931 the figures for the Northern Great Plains and the Pacific Northwest were very similar.[9] Most farm migrants were established families who held property, livestock, machinery and at least one automobile when they left.[10]

Unlike the Southern Plains migration, which largely but not nearly as overwhelmingly as portrayed by many, consisted of poorly educated share croppers and farm laborers, those who departed the Northern Plains exited with an educational and values level quite similar to that found in their new environment.[11] Historian James Gregory found Californians tended to have a higher regard for Dust Bowl migrants from Kansas, Nebraska and the Dakotas than for those of the Southwest.[12] The percent of illiteracy among those ten years and over in 1930 found Oregon and Washington at one percent tied for second behind Iowa, and Idaho ranked fourth at 1.1 %. Following closely, however, South Dakota and Nebraska tied for fifth at 1.2% and North Dakota tenth at only 1.5%. In contrast Arkansas and Texas tied at thirty-sixth with 6.8 %. Surprising to many, Oklahoma tied Colorado at twenty-third with 2.8 percent.[13] Most of the migrants from the Northern Plains left with some capital and never intended to become itinerant farm laborers, although a number took that path temporarily.

They had acquired skills that would allow them to succeed either as farmers or in the industrial work force. By the 1930s, Northern Plain's agriculture ranked among the most technologically advanced in the nation, requiring men and women farmers to be mechanically capable and self-sufficient. These attributes enabled them to adapt quickly to job requirements in the mills, factories, forests, and fields of the Pacific Northwest. Already acquired skills plus a strong, in many cases remarkable, work ethic bode well for their economic survival.[14]

Moving to seek better opportunities elsewhere had become an American tradition and was not considered that socially negative until the Great Depression. Although more highly publicized and therefore more visible, Depression migration was not confined to the Great Plains. From its inception the United States was a nation on the move, usually east to west. The 1930 census revealed about one-third of the entire population of the United States was living in different states than those in which they were born. Combined with rural hardships and increased job opportunities in more urban areas, one person in eight was living in a different location in 1940 than they were at in 1935.

Only in the Dakotas was farming failure of principal importance for migration.[15] In the 1930s, the assumption that landowners could assume large debts because of capital appreciation of land collapsed. Between 1926 and 1940, North Dakota and South Dakota bore the highest foreclosure rates in the country, averaging seven thousand annually.[16] They also received by far the greatest dollar value in commodities through 1936. South Dakota received almost triple Oklahoma's share, North Dakota well over twice and Nebraska stood about equal to Oklahoma.[17] Families in the West moved much more readily than eastern families. The Far West, with 22.7%, had the highest percentage of movement to non-contiguous states and the west north central followed with 21.6%. California continued to be the favorite state destination of most migrants, gaining 300,000 in the 1930s. Migrants from the Northern Plains, however, preferred Washington, Oregon and Idaho.[18]

The Pacific Northwest gained an estimated 460,000 during the thirties with about twenty-five percent originating from the Northern Plains.[19] Although not all headed west, some sixty-two thousand Nebraskans left along with an estimated 119,000 South Dakotans and around 120,000 North Dakotans.[20] Only five states lost population in the 1930s—the Dakotas (South Dakota 7 percent, North Dakota 4.5 percent), Nebraska (4.5 percent), Kansas (4.3 percent), and Oklahoma (2.5 percent).[21] Many Northern Plains migrants made at least one stop, usually in western Montana or Idaho, before reaching their final destination farther west. Large numbers eventually settled in western Washington or Oregon, especially when West Coast defense industries such as shipbuilding and airplane manufacturing created an almost unlimited demand for labor. Younger, better-educated migrants tended to move farther. Family mobility tended to be greatest soon after marriage and before the families had gained a foothold in the community.[22] Accordingly, family size was small and 80 percent of the children were under fifteen, providing a capacity for both greater fecundity and productivity. Most migrants were native-born Caucasians, allowing them to more easily blend in with their new environments.[23]

Consistent with migration patterns throughout the country, migrants from the Northern Plains usually set out with a specific destination in mind. More than half of the families had a definite contact at their destination, either relatives or close friend whom more or less were obligated to assist them. Many Dust Bowl migrants found government assistance difficult to obtain and virtually owed their survival to friends and relatives. One survey of drought migrants, however, calculated about 50 percent had received public assistance after moving to Washington.[24] It did not differentiate between federal and state and local support, but one would assume much of it was federal.

Each state had different settlement laws with common characteristics of antiquity, complexity and their inappropriateness to present conditions. Migrants were forced to wait at least a year to establish residency—Oregon had a three-year provision and California raised their requirement to five years. Legal residency in the states of departure ended quickly—South Dakotans lost residency in thirty days.[25] Those caught in the limbo did not qualify for assistance or relief employment from state and local governments. The Hoover-established Public Works Administration (PWA) hired in the general labor market instead of focusing on the relief rolls. The PWA also required local matching funds which tax-strapped citizens frequently denied.[26] Run by local administrators, these agencies shunned outsiders while attempting to meet the great demand from established local residents. The 1933 Federal Emergency Relief Administration required one year's residence throughout the United States.

Well aware of the situation, the federal government shifted from funding local proposals to retaining federal control. The Civil Works Administration (CWA) was entirely a federal operation that employed up to 4,230,000, but

Roosevelt thought it too expensive and phased it out early in 1934, hoping the states would assume more of the burden. They did not and when FERA efforts proved inadequate to stem the rising tide of misery, the Emergency Relief Appropriation Act of 1935 sanctioned the greatest single appropriation in the history of the world and anchored Roosevelt's "Second New Deal."

The new law allowed Roosevelt to spend the money mostly as he saw fit and, with an election looming, the incumbent President spent generously. Much was funneled through the Works Progress Administration (WPA) , which drew bitter opposition.[27] Some more socially acceptable barbs were, "WPA—We Putter Around," and "What's that statue over there?"—"That ain't no statue it's a WPA worker." Critics complained that irresponsible, politically oriented New Deal spending was driving the country to bankruptcy and placing an unfair tax burden on its citizens. Those charges are ironic within the framework of contemporary federal spending and taxation. Four percent was the highest federal income tax rate before World War II and all New Deal programs cost a total of $45 billion, or about $57 per capita.[28]

The WPA's myriad accomplishments speak for themselves. After seventy years their net value, besides providing invaluable work relief and training, far exceeds the original investment. The WPA included 3.5 million workers and built or improved thousands of miles of highways, roads and bridges. It built more than 2,500 hospitals, 5,900 school buildings, 1,000 airport landing fields, almost 13,000 playgrounds, and much more.[29] Established to provide employment relief for family men, the WPA favored those who were established property owners, especially on the Great Plains, so both those who migrated and were not established and those who remained and were not established found it difficult to qualify.[30]

WPA achievements in North Dakota typify a comparable pattern throughout the West and illustrate the magnitude of permanent contributions to the nation's infrastructure. In North Dakota the WPA, between July 1, 1935, and June 30, 1942, built 20,373 miles of highways and streets, 721 new bridges and viaducts, 166 miles of sidewalks. Also constructed were 15,012 culverts, 503 new public buildings, 61 additions to public buildings, 680 outdoor recreational facilities, 809 water wells, 2 irrigation projects, 39 sewage treatment plants, and 9 water treatment plants. It rebuilt 1,002 bridges and viaducts, 2,180 public buildings, and 1,721 culverts. It repaired 6426,207 books, served 3,653,392 school lunches, and sewed 2,078,451 garments.[31]

Affiliated with WPA, the National Youth Administration (NYA) provided work opportunities for 700,000 youths between ages 16 and 25 who wanted to continue their education. They repaired, renovated and maintained school buildings and undertook other community improvement projects. In Redfield, South Dakota, fourteen NYA boys landscaped the new artificial lake built by the WPA. They also built a two hundred foot boardwalk, a sixteen foot pier, two rafts, two diving towers, a safety line of buoys, a guardrail and seats for spectators. Redfield paid only $500 for materials.[32] Many NYA beneficiaries later became outstanding leaders. A sterling example, Leigh Gerdine, a future Rhodes Scholar and university president, worked his way through the University of North Dakota on a NYA grant.[33]

Altogether, federal programs injected over $266million into North Dakota's economy during the Great Depression.[34] "Massive federal expenditures for relief and farm programs saved North Dakota," said respected North Dakota historian Elwyn Robinson.[35] South Dakota received a similar amount of federal help. Although the government's intention was to maintain population stability, and it did to a degree, many still elected to leave the Plains. Without federal aid the additional exodus no doubt would have been even more disastrous to the Great Plains infrastructure. Those who left faced the customary criticism from who stayed or "stuck" and were often described as "quitters." Departure meant abandoning a familiar rural lifestyle for an unknown future. It meant breaking relationships with extended family and longtime friends. It meant starting over at the lower rungs of the economic and social ladder while adjusting to a much different environment. It also created a serious decline for support for Great Plains infrastructure such as schools, hospitals, roads, libraries, churches and the like. The implication of moral weakness, however, had another side. Studies showed that migrants were younger and better educated than non-migrants, and the highest migration rates were for those on top of the occupational ladder. By leaving the home environment the individual was forced to become more self-reliant and less provincial, promoting personal growth and economic advancement.[36] Conversely, the states they left lost an enormous amount of human capital, most of whom they had paid to educate and train.

As the decade long drought continued the flow of migrants became a torrent, leaving behind withered farmsteads and communities. Local newspapers and business organizations urged all to stand pat and show courage because better times were just around the corner. Local journalists were inclined to emphasize a business as usual policy, with minimal coverage of the ravages of the drought. It was insightful that major league baseball deals frequently were featured on the front page in 1935 and 1936.[37] In many towns businessmen sponsored free movies once a week to attract trade. Business and professional leaders in Crosby organized a "Gloom Dispellers" group in 1931 to stage cost-free community celebrity programs. Williston and Crosby later formed "Gloom Chasers" organizations to little avail.[38]

Great Plains Dust Bowl victims continued to vote with their feet in alarmingly high numbers. Farm population for the country as a whole held almost constant during the thirties, but the west north-central states lost 7.3 percent, the highest rate of any area. North Dakota and South Dakota led with 17.5 percent and 21.3 percent respectively.[39] An estimated 86,699 North Dakotans left the state between 1935 and 1940.[40] In contrast to the rural depletion, many towns in western South Dakota gained population.[41] The opportunity to take over abandoned farms and to acquire livestock, machinery and household goods at bargain prices, albeit, provided a significant opportunity for many who "stuck." They anticipated many migrants would return, but the vast majority did not.

In spite of the immeasurable advantages of receiving so much new human and material capital to benefit their large, under-populated areas, the Pacific Northwest states offered an unusually cool welcome to the flow of newcomers. They, too, were experiencing a severely depressed economy and saw problems in accommodating a flow of unemployed newcomers. Many were concerned about increased relief rolls, more competition for jobs that would lead to lower wage rates and problems with housing and sanitation. Migrants also increased the need for more taxation for schools, police and fire protection. Some critics even expressed concern about their possible radical political inclinations.[42] These concerns probably were magnified by the problems California and other western states were experiencing accommodating the flood of incoming migrants. Early in 1936, Colorado Governor Edward Johnson proclaimed martial law in a mile-wide strip along the southern border. Johnson dispatched the National Guard to "prevent and repeal the further invasion of aliens, indigent persons or invaders." Johnson added, "Jobs in this state are for our citizens."[43] County officials in Island County, Washington, who had welcomed new settlers in the early 1930s, reversed their thinking by 1934 when the federal government asked about settling more dust bowl migrants. The county chamber of commerce decided migrants required too much tax money. They did not want any more "dole seekers."[44]

Migration from the Northern Plains in the 1930s exhibited a number of unique qualities. Given such a large area, understandably specific areas experienced different weather and different difficulties at differing times. Michael Grant, a leading authority, suggests "The timing and locale of drought conditions during the 1930s defy generalization."[45] Concerning droughts, historian David Danbom suggests, "What was different in the thirties was the scale, scope and frequency "[46]

The Western Dakotas were hit hard early. In July 1930, the Kadoka, South Dakota, area, sizzled with six days in a row of 104–110 temperatures combined with hot winds. Grasshoppers made their first appearance in May 1931, signaling the beginning of "bare earth farming." The hard winter of 1931–32 decimated livestock. More rain fell in 1932 but crops were limited by the return of heat and grasshoppers along with flies and cutworms. Money was so scarce in 1932 that both the *Kadoka Press* and the *Bison Courier* advertised they would take wheat in exchange for newspaper subscriptions. The *Courier* indicated farmers could dump the wheat in specially constructed bins and could keep the sacks because they were more valuable than the wheat.[47] In June 1933, Bison endured temperatures of over ninety from June 4–20 accompanied by hordes of grasshoppers. On July 13, the area reported its first dust storm and Kadoka's water supply went dry during a torrid August. The "black blizzard" of November 13 signaled the beginning of more years of dust storms combined with abnormal heat and drought.[48]

Neighboring North Dakota suffered similar disaster, especially in the wheat-oriented northwest. The *Bowbells Tribune* reported on July 11, 1930, almost no crops would be harvested because of hot weather and drought. Conditions remained so bad in 1931 that Red River farmers gave truckloads of potatoes and other vegetables to their western neighbors through the Red Cross. Yet the more fortunate easterners tended to encourage their western neighbors to tighten their belts and tough it out. Located near Grand Forks, the *Northwood Gleanor* reprinted an editorial from Nebraska's *Hastings Democrat* about "Hard Times." It said, "Who are you to be hollerin' about hard times? . . . Dad and mother reared a family around a cook stove in the kitchen and bathed themselves and you children in a wooden washtub, but you've got to have furnace heat, inside toilets, and porcelain bathtubs, and yet you holler your heads off about times being hard."[49] That indictment may have been convincing for the comfortable residents of the more humid eastern regions of the states involved, but the reality was that those amenities never were achieved by most on the arid Northern Great Plains.

Hope that the Great Plains disaster would end rapidly was smashed in the ensuing three years. Drought and grasshoppers combined with the collapse of farm products prices continued to trouble North Dakota and the Northern Great Plains in 1932 and 1933. In July 1932, the still sanguine *Northwood Gleanor* ran an editorial from the *Amarillo Globe News* entitled "I Like the Depression." Again, the implication was that it was manageable. It said, "I have had more fun since the depression started than I ever had in my life: I had forgotten how to live, what it means to have real friends, what it was like to eat common everyday food. Fact is I was getting just a little high hat. . . ."[50] In 1933, the per capita income in South Dakota dropped to a dismal $129, but the worst lay ahead, even as the rest of the country started recovering. When the FERA was ended in July 1935, North Dakota was second only to New Mexico in percentage of population on relief rolls. South Dakota followed closely while Nebraska had considerably less.[51]

By 1935, approximately 40 percent of farm operators in western North Dakota were tenants who tended to be younger and more mobile and with less interest in conservation and community building.[52] Nebraska had the highest percentage, 49.3, of farms operated by tenants. South Dakota, more cattle oriented, had 62 percent of land under lease in 1935. An estimated 28 percent of tenancy involved young farmers who could not afford to own their own land and were related to the landlord. Disastrous drought conditions encouraged them to relocate to more promising environments. In 1935, no Great Plains' state had 25 percent or more of tenants who had occupied their farms for over ten years.[53]

If Lorena Hickock's 1933 reports found her aghast at the economic and social disaster occurring on the Northern Plains, she would be even more outraged during 1934–1936. Drought, grasshoppers, and dust storms prevailed in 1934. The dust began to blow in early April, turning day into night. May was severely hot and bone dry with the most severe dust storms seen in the country. An estimated eighty-percent of the nation faced severe drought and almost the entire state of North Dakota suffered severely with Grafton baking at 107 as early as May 30.[54] It was almost July before the Noonan, North Dakota, area received its first serious rain. "It will not save crops," opined the *Noonan Miner*.[55] By late 1934, 89 percent of all Divide County residents were on direct relief.[56]

Grazing and feed supply for livestock collapsed to the extent that by late July the government had bought 2,797 railroad carloads of cattle in North Dakota alone. In Divide, Hettinger, and Sheridan counties the government purchased almost all livestock sold. Because of mortgages and liens only a few farmers could retain more than a third of the price of government purchased stock.[57]

Western portions of South Dakota and Nebraska suffered a similar fate. South Dakota had a higher percentage on relief than any other state—39 percent and over 50 percent of farm families.[58] Farmers grumbled that, "Everything blew away except the mortgage." From 1925 to 1939, South Dakota endured by far the highest number of mortgage foreclosures and assignments to avoid foreclosure, followed by North Dakota and Nebraska.[59] Nebraska's most severe drought came in 1934. By July 15, Central Nebraska had over twenty days of over temperatures over one hundred degrees, reaching a one-day high of 112.[60] Between December 7, 1933, and July 19, 1934, Scotia, Nebraska, received less that two inches of precipitation. Three quarters of the area's crop acreage produced nothing and over half of the cattle in Valley County were sold.[61] By August 1934, the government declared thirteen West (of the Missouri) River South Dakota counties sub marginal and established programs to move families out. The federal reclamation officer for the area asserted that both of the western Dakotas should be evacuated at once, creating a wave of criticism that forced a retraction.

The Federal Emergency Appropriation Act of June 1934 provided $525 million for drought relief for the entire country. About 80 percent of the drought relief loans went to the ten Great Plains states, with the spring wheat belt of the Northern Plains receiving more than any other area. By December 1934, South Dakota had the highest percentage on relief in the country with over half of the state's farm families receiving public assistance.[62] North Dakota followed closely—89 percent of farmers in Divide County were on relief rolls by spring 1935.[63] The spring wheat area had the highest percentage of recipients who were "normal" families with children under ten.[64]

Communities throughout the region lamented the departure of many "good" families with many holding sales before sad departures from friends and other family members. Frequently rural communities held large farewell parties. Those who left experienced relief and also sadness. South Dakotan Rose Van Schaak, who moved to Idaho, said, "A feeling of panic clutched at my heart; I was leaving my childhood home . . . the figure of my mother waving goodbye to us will in my memory forever." Citizens were encouraged to stay and tough it out, but many had had enough and felt compelled to seek opportunity elsewhere—mainly Oregon and Washington, but many also moved east, especially to Minnesota and Iowa.[65] The state of Oregon had set aside twenty thousand acres for migrants in two western counties—Columbia and Douglas, and a Dakota Colonization Association was organized to attract five hundred settlers from North Dakota. A meeting was held at Dickinson, North Dakota, in November 1934, but apparently lured few takers in part because the North Dakota organizers wanted to charge fees.[66]

Enough rain fell in 1935 to allow at least a modest spring wheat crop throughout most of the area, however, Divide County had a five inch deficit resulting in meager crops. North Dakota also experienced the worst year for hail loss in its history.[67] The price dropped to seventy-nine cents a bushel and late rains caused yet another problem with black wheat rust.[68] Meanwhile farmers east of the 100th meridian enjoyed near normal crops. Departure from the western area of the Northern Plains continued at a steady pace. Paula Nelson, commenting on improved conditions in the Kadoka area, nonetheless noted, "Fine families continued to leave the area in troubling numbers."[69] As held true in cotton growing states, a number of moves were triggered by increased federal advantages to large landowners who now profited more by accepting government subsidies than by renting or leasing.

If the first half of the 1930s offered disaster for many, 1936 brought the worst weather in 350 years of recorded history with fierce, unmerciful, record setting blasts of winter cold followed by devastating dust storms and scorching summer heat. North Dakota froze in subzero cold every day from January 12 through February 21. From February 2 through February 19 the thermometer stayed below zero. Many farmers recorded temperatures well below freezing *inside* their homes with stoves going. Some stacked manure against their outside walls for better insulation. Hot dry weather in the spring was accompanied by severe dust storms. "May is the year's driest so far at .62 inches and no rain forecast," the *Williston Herald* reported on June 1. By June, hordes of grasshoppers spread throughout the plains. By June 4, the *Beach Advance* noted, "blistering rainless heat and high winds . . . excessive growth of thistles."

The back breaker for almost all plant life came during the hellish period between July 5 and July 11 when temperatures sizzled at over one hundred daily. Eight other days in July reached one hundred and most of the rest were in the nineties. In a thirty-one day period from July 2 to August 1 the mean temperature soared to 81.48 compared to a normal mean of sixty-nine. Farm families huddled in their cellars to escape the brutal heat.[70] It was also the driest year on record with only 7.17 inches of precipitation. More weather records were broken in North Dakota in 1936 than any other recorded year.[71] Strong winds blew the parched soil away creating more severe wind erosion than any other state.[72] On July 6, the *Williston Herald* lamented, "The last hope of a grain crop is gone today after the latest searing weekend. By July 10, most crops in Western North Dakota were incinerated. On July 10, the *Divide County Journal* reported, "It is estimated that in an area covering three-quarters of the state not a binder will be pulled into the fields this fall." On July 30, the *Beach Advance* said less than half of wheat seeded on summer fallow land was fit for harvest, leaving four hundred farm families without income. In 1936, 104 of 122 North Dakota counties suffered from "extreme drought distress."[73]

Heat and drought in the entire central United States dominated the news throughout the country. For example the catastrophe consistently made front-page headlines in the small town *Aberdeen* [WA] *Daily World* from July 2 through July 20.[74] An estimated 4,400 Midwesterners perished in the heat wave.[75] Noted correspondent Ernie Pyle wrote from Bismarck in late July, "You arrive at a point where you no longer look and say, 'My God, this is awful!' You gradually become accustomed to dried fields and burned pasture; it stretches into a dull, continuous fact. . . The story is the same everywhere."[76]

State and local governments offered scant help, making federal programs the last resort for public assistance. North Dakota and South Dakota ranked first and second in allocations from the Agricultural Adjustment Act (AAA) and also ranked the same in disbursements from the Farm Security Administration. During the period 1933 through 1939 the Farm Credit Administration loaned $144 million to North Dakota and $122 million to South Dakota. In Divide County 72 percent were on relief.[77] By late 1936, half of North Dakota's population received some form of stipend from the government.[78] A July 21 *New York Times* article stated, "In the Dakotas, hardest hit of the drought states, about 20,000 farmers are on WPA."[79] Although this aid allowed many to retain their farms and stay, the brutal conditions convinced many others it was time to leave.

Shattered weather records were tallied throughout the region but were worst in the Dakotas. In January and February of 1936 the temperature did not rise above zero for thirty-five straight days at Bison, South Dakota. That torrid summer many West River residents slept outside on hay wagons or truck beds to avoid rattlesnakes.[80] Few goods or services were purchased. Economies included making clothing from flour and sugar sacks, making soap, and canning food. A South Dakota rancher complained, "Since I came to this god damn country in 1880, there's only been two good years—1916 and next year." He stayed.[81] The Rapid City airport reported a record average temperature for July of 82.4 combined with a record low of 0.27 inches of precipitation and annual low of 7.5l. This compared to an annual mean of 17.34 and a July mean of 2.31. On July 10, after seven days above 100, Mitchell, South Dakota, residents held a mass prayer for rain. The White River went dry for the first time since 1911 and even Russian thistles failed. That summer Grace Martin Highly, a welfare worker and relief director in western South Dakota, drove from Belle Fourche, to Buffalo, to Lennon, and down to Philip and never saw a cow.[82]

The *Literary Digest.*reported extreme drought in almost the entire state of North Dakota and South Dakota, "much worse than Oklahoma or Texas."[83] By August, 34 percent were receiving public assistance in the spring wheat section of the Great Plains compared to thirty-three percent in the Southwestern Great Plains.[84] Whistling in the dark, the *Dickinson Press* editorialized, "In a few instances families will leave the area but no exodus will be general."[85] Two weeks later the *Press* noted 75 percent needed aid in the Dakotas. Ads for farm sales flooded area newspapers along with accompanying accounts of ever-increasing family departures, which rose from a steady stream to a torrent by August.[86]

President Roosevelt announced an immediate increase in federal aid and the formation of six man group led by Rural Electrification Administration head Morris L. Cooke. The group was charged to conduct a broad study called the Great Plains Drought Area Study.[87] Its purpose was disaster rehabilitation and prevention of another. "We should face the fact that climatic conditions make special safeguards absolutely necessary. . . ." Roosevelt noted in his letter of instructions.[88] Public hearings were held at McCook and

Chadron, Nebraska, and Rapid City and Bismarck. Letters of suggestion were welcomed. FDR also announced he would personally tour the drought-stricken area in late August.

Rexford Tugwell, head of the Resettlement Administration, announced plans for immediate relief and led a preliminary study group to the region in July. The group found the area between Bowman, North Dakota, and Belle Fourche, South Dakota, the worst they had seen in two thousand miles of travel. Cactus was the only vegetation, the few milk cows left were going dry, but there were no grasshoppers because of the heat and drought. Even though their land was devastated, South Dakota farmers, more oriented to livestock production, protested the government's "4–4–2 rule," which required they had to be down to four cows, four horses, two brood sows and twenty chickens to qualify for assistance. About one-third of the area's population had departed to the Pacific Northwest.[89] North Dakota, South Dakota and Nebraska all received generous WPA, RA, and other grants and government cattle purchase resumed. Free hay was shipped in to feed livestock and mutton and cornmeal were distributed to needy people. The mutton, barely palatable, was despised by all.[90] The *New York Times,* never that enthusiastic about government spending in the West, suggested, "Much of the federal activity in the drought relief area is possibly unconstitutional."[91]

Rain was falling when Roosevelt's special train arrived at Jamestown, North Dakota, on August 26. It seemed symbolic but eastern North Dakota was enjoying a normal crop year. Large crowds greeted the charismatic President and his entourage as his train headed west. If FDR was dismayed by the same scenes that shocked Ernie Pyle and other reporters, he remained outwardly jaunty and confident as he communicated his concern and delivered pep talks. "Keep your chin up," he urged. "And again I say that you are not licked," promising immediate increases in federal aid.[92] For a large percentage, though, the battle already had been lost and they had decided to continue the war for survival at another, more promising location which meant the Pacific Northwest for many.[93]

Permanently settled on the Northern Plains for only less than half a century most of the migrants were either first or second-generation residents, so their roots in the area were still shallow. A fair number of those who left were first-generation European immigrants and their families. Many had first stopped in states like Minnesota, Iowa and Wisconsin before moving to the Great Plains during the early twentieth century rush. Having experienced at least one major move already, another change was not as daunting. Possibly because of lack of capital or perhaps stronger family ties, rural Norwegians and Germans tended to stay. Many of those who left, however, came from families who were as much as ninth generation Americans whose families had started on the eastern seaboard and worked their way west.

Some opinion among those who stayed thought the migrants fled too soon and should stay and fight it through. Many, especially among those who left, however, viewed the flight as a logical response to an untenable situation, even though it meant separation from family and friends and coping with a new environment. T. E. Hays, who had served two terms in the South Dakota state legislature and was selected an "Eminent Farmer" by South Dakota State College, left for Oregon in late 1936 to work as a carpenter. At a gathering of Dakotans in Oregon, Hayes reported many of the migrants "felt rather hurt because some of the papers referred to them as quitters because they had moved out west." One elderly woman said, "Give us in Dakota half the rain they get in Oregon and we will surprise the world."[94] A. D. Burns, who had moved to the irrigated Yakima Valley, liked it but missed "those faithful relatives and friends who are still hanging on . . . always hoping for better luck next year." Burns added, "If it's ever possible to return to our old home, we won't be from South Dakota anymore."[95]

New Deal proposals to assist moving farmers from the drought stricken areas to more productive areas were ridiculed by many. Pierre, South Dakota, mayor John Hipple, also editor of its *Capitol Journal*, wrote, "The latest government move suggesting to depopulate North and South Dakota in particular by moving families of these states to other states on account of soil erosion is so damnably ridiculous that the plan should be preserved and carved in stone to contribute to a monument of folly that may be erected in future ages when the history of political horseplay is finally collected. . . ."[96] Possibly because of the hostility of states affected, New Deal programs to assist movement out of the drought area fell far short of expectations and of those who moved very few received any direct government assistance for the change.

Arthur Rothstein's prescience enabled him to take the best known picture of Dakota migrants just three months after his Oklahoma classic *Fleeing a Dust Storm*. While sleeping in a government car near Missoula, Montana, in mid July 1936, Rothstein was awakened by honking from a Model T Ford carrying five passengers with "Oregon or Bust" painted on the back. Rothstein pursued, stopped the car, saying he represented the Resettlement Administration and asked if he could take some pictures. Rothstein captioned the best known photograph, "Vernon Evans and his family of Lemmon, South Dakota . . . left for a new start in Oregon or Washington. They expect to arrive at Yakima, Washington, in time for hop picking. They live in a tent and make about 200 miles a day in a Model T Ford." Forty-one years later Evans, now back on the family farm in South Dakota, recalled the event of his lifetime, "Well we was all without jobs here at the time. The jobs was so few and far between that you couldn't buy a job. We had friends that we knew out in

Oregon, we decided we was going out there and see if we could find work." Evans continued, "We got out around Missoula and we was having a good time. There was this car sitting alongside the road and a guy sleeping in it, so we honked and hollered at him, having a big time. Pretty soon this car was after us. Well, we seen he had an emblem on the side of the car and we'd heard they was sending'em [migrants] back, wasn't letting them go through. So, we thought, 'Here's where we go back home.' . . . He asked us if we cared if he took some pictures of us. That fall or winter, why, these pictures started showing up in different magazines and papers." [97] After nine years in Oregon, Evans returned to the family farm upon his father's death.

Marie (Braught) Johnson and Frank Braught, Evans' sister and brother-in law were also pictured. Johnson recalled, "We had friends who had come out to Oregon the year before, and they'd write back what a great country it was. There was grass up to a cow's belly and there was fruit free for the picking. And there was work in the fruit orchards. We had nothing, came with nothing." They settled near Lebanon and established a comfortable lifestyle. Like most migrants Johnson preferred her new home and stayed. "We go back to South Dakota every once in a while to visit, but I wouldn't want to live there. No way! No way! I just get that feeling every time I go back, like it used to be. I know it's not quite that bad any more, but . . . no way. I tell Vern and Flora all the time they should have stayed out here," she said.[98]

Besides sending many letters to family and friends who stayed, several migrants wrote letters to their hometown newspapers, usually expressing concern about the drought at their former location and enthusiasm for their new home. A letter to the Scotia, Nebraska, newspaper from the Yakima Valley said, "To the friends we left behind us we give our sympathy. We sincerely hope the hard times let up back there and that you all prosper as we have since we have been out here. We have all been working steady since we got here and good wages, too. All of us are making from 2.50 to 4.00 per day. The climate here just suits us. It is warm during the day and cool during the nights and a person can get a good night's rest."[99]

Not everyone experienced such success. Harold and LaDeen Shepherd and their nine month old son, Allen, accompanied by Harold's brother John and sister-in-law Marge left Madrid, Nebraska, for Oregon in late summer 1939, planning to stay if work could be found. Harold drove a 1936 four-door Chevrolet, towing a two-wheel trailer. In Portland, they stayed the first few nights with Elmer and Annabelle Dunham. Elmer was a carpenter who Harold knew when he was teaching at Palisade, Nebraska. They slept on the kitchen floor until they rented a little room at a motel for five dollars a week. Harold and John found jobs with the Meier and Frank department store selling vacuum cleaners for a five dollar commission, but quit after managing to sell only one. Harold sold it by telling a customer "I am Meier from Shepherd and Frank." They went to Kelso and Longview across the Columbia River in Washington to apply for a job with Weyerhaeuser. There, they encountered huge lines of unemployed workers eager for any work and were not successful.

Harold responded to an ad in the Denver paper that promised teachers could receive a $25 travel loan. They returned to Nebraska on that loan, driving day and night. While driving at night through the Umatilla-Cayuse Indian reservation in eastern Oregon, a horse reared up and kicked out their windshield. With no money to replace the windshield, a piece of cardboard sufficed. LaDeen filled a one-quart jar with boiling water, two tablespoons of dark Karo syrup and canned milk for little Allen's daily ration. Back in Madrid Harold taught for several years before becoming high school principal. He became Madrid's postmaster in 1944 and retired from that position in 1972. Allen earned a Ph.D. in history at the University of Nebraska and has been a professor of history at Chadron State College since 1972.[100]

At Chadron State, Shepherd worked with another Dust Bowl descendant who had also obtained a Ph.D. The author's family exited North Dakota in August 1936. His twenty-five year old father, Lloyd Dewing, a ninth generation American, traced his roots back to colonial Massachusetts from a family tree that had achieved much. Successful farmers, business and professional leaders, war heroes, Ivy League professors, a famous artist, a Rhodes Scholar, and many other Dewings had helped build the country.[101]

Lloyd's great-grandfather, Charles C. Dewing, left Cambridge, Massachusetts, for Cincinnati, Ohio, in 1820 at age twenty. After twenty years as a river boatman, Charles took advantage of land opportunities in Illinois and Iowa for another twenty years—finally homesteading near Hutchinson, Minnesota, in 1862. Charles and his sons, Samuel, Fergus, and William immediately faced the crisis of the Minnesota Indian War. They all enlisted in the Minnesota Citizens Regiment. Samuel wrote, "This was the year made famous by the bloody outbreak of the Sioux Indians; we almost lived on our horses, engaged in scouting and fighting the savages."[102] William's obituary made the front page of the Hutchinson newspaper when he died in 1917. At age fourteen he had enlisted and stood guard that earned him the title "Last of the Stockaders."

In 1900, William's son Jacob (Jake) homesteaded near Portal in Burke County in extreme northwestern North Dakota. Most of the first settlers in that area came from central and western Minnesota and had grown up on grain growing farms. Jake's boyhood friend, Archie Curtis, homesteaded nearby. Soon Jake's two sisters and brothers-in-law moved from Minnesota also. Jake lived in a homestead shanty the first year. He returned to Minnesota and married Elsie Bowyer from Glencoe, Minnesota, in 1901. Elsie came in 1902 with her father and infant daughter. A railroad immigrant car brought farming basics including a team of horses, one colt, two cows, thirteen chickens, a walking plow, household goods, and lumber for a wood-frame home.[103]

High wheat prices and good crops soon brought prosperity the Dewings had never known in Minnesota. By 1918, the family moved into a large, comfortable home built next to the much smaller original. Considered a showplace for the area, it had windmill-generated electricity, indoor plumbing, central heat and, before long, a telephone. Economical heating fuel came from the coal mine near Noonan that contained "the best quality lignite in the state of North Dakota." By 1933, its 200,000 ton annual production ranked third in the state. The price dropped from $1.99 a ton in 1929 to $1.30 a ton in 1939.[104]

A large barn was added to accommodate about thirty horses that were used to till the now one thousand-acre wheat farm. Horses were indispensable in those times. Six horses pulling a two-bottom plow could plow only about six acres a day. Plowed land was then disked to prepare it for seed. Six horses pulling a ten-foot drill could seed about twenty acres a day. After planting season came haying season. Two horses could pull a hay mower, but it was usually only a five-foot cut. Then the hay had to be raked and stacked, either outside or in a barn if available. As time allowed, fields left for summer fallow were disked to keep out weeds and preserve moisture for next year's crop. Horse drawn binders harvested the grain in August and September. The twine bound grain bundles were stacked in shocks and hauled by wagon to a steam-powered thresher. Marketable grain then was transported by wagon to elevators located along the Soo railroad line. Much work, equipment and technical skill were required, as was the ability to make acute business decisions.[105]

Jake enjoyed considerable status as a shrewd, successful farmer who never overextended himself by purchasing too much expensive equipment. He took an active role in local politics, serving as county commissioner, helping establish a rural school, and hosting William Langer and other politicians a number of times, but he was not above stretching the law occasionally. Their property bordered Canada in the "three corners" area where Manitoba, Saskatchewan and North Dakota meet, a location that lent itself to illegal trade in liquor and wheat. Bootlegging Canadian liquor from Saskatchewan into the Portal area was highly profitable during prohibition and even with the end of prohibition in 1933 because North Dakota delayed legalization of hard liquor until 1936. State highway 52 from Portal to Minot became known as "Whiskey Gap" and at times cars loaded with Canadian liquor parked overnight in Jake's garage. Saskatchewan's leading bootlegger later became famed international distiller Seagrams.

Wheat prices declined and crops only were average in the 1920s. But the Dewing family's well established farm plus six capable sons and two daughters allowed them to maintain an affluent lifestyle by western North Dakota standards. Chet Johnston, Lloyd's first cousin, who later moved to Seattle, remarked, " The Dewing house seemed so huge when we visited."[106] The Dewings employed a full time maid and during harvest season a large threshing crew consisting of mostly transient laborers was hired.

Recreation activities were strongly oriented to family and friends. Card playing, listening to the radio, social gatherings, barn dancing, ice skating, hunting and impromptu boxing matches were favorite pastimes, but, in season, baseball provided the focus for men and boys.[107] Every town and many townships had a baseball team that typically played every Sunday during the summer. The Dewing and Johnston boys were avid participants. Chet's brother, Les, achieved almost legendary local status as a pitcher, catcher, and second baseman. He was invited to try out for the professional Spokane Indians in the mid-1930s. Radio reception was so good reception from the East and West Coasts almost was the rule.[108] Broadcasts of major league baseball games demanded high priority. Johnny, the father, was so intent on a World Series game that he let a shed on his property burn while he listened to the broadcast.

If the 1920s were a good time to grow up on a thousand-acre wheat ranch, the 1930s proved a terrible time to reach adulthood. Competent and ambitious, Lloyd grew up with no reason to suspect he would not become a successful wheat farmer like his father. Although a good student he preferred farming and, like many others in the 1920s, declined to attend high school. He was working on the family farm in 1929 and hoping to eventually own one. Unlike Jake's good timing, the ensuing economic crash and the drought sabotaged the best of abilities and intentions.

In 1932, Lloyd married Mary Dalebout, daughter of Dutch immigrants from Goes, Holland. Karel, her father, had followed his father, Cornelius, who had migrated to Minnesota in 1890, then moved near Noonan, North Dakota, in neighboring Divide County, to help his terminally ill son Mike. Karel took over his brother-in-law, John Westdorp's 320–acre farm in 1911.[109] Westorp had migrated to the United States in 1906, working on farms in Iowa and North Dakota, then taking care of Mike's farm until Cornelius arrived. Westdorp used his inheritance to purchase the 320 acres along the Canadian border.

When Westdorp left for Canada to break army horses, Karel took over the farm. There were few buildings and the house could only be described as a shack, affording little protection from the area's biting cold and blistering heat. Fortunately the land had been planted to flax which yielded a good crop and earned a huge price per bushel, allowing Karel to buy the farm for eight hundred dollars. Mary, born in 1912, was the fourth child of six and the first born in the United States.[110] Nicholas, Karel's younger brother, came to North Dakota alone to work in the harvest and returned to Holland to bring his family back to Noonan.

The Dalebouts fit into a Dutch-Belgian enclave and earned a decent living until the Great Depression. At one time Karel owned over twenty workhorses and retained part ownership of a steam threshing machine. Karel and his four sons were tireless workers, rising at four in the morning to feed and water the horses so they would be ready to work the fields by sunrise. Canadian farmers, taking their grain to Noonan for a better price, frequently stopped at the Dalebout farm to water and feed their horses and enjoy a coffee break. Perhaps an augury, mother Cornelia, who came from a comfortable Dutch background and never adjusted to the rigors of North Dakota, died unexpectedly in 1929 at age fifty-one. Mary had moved to Columbus where she worked as a nanny for newspaper publisher Leo Mahoney. She graduated from Columbus high school in 1931 with Lloyd's brother, Ralph.

The virtually penniless newlyweds moved into a house on Jake's farm, called "the honeymoon house" because several older brothers and an older sister had lived there when first married. Later used as a grain-storage shed, it had no modern conveniences. To help ward off winter cold, manure was stacked along the outer walls. When the weather warmed, dust from the frequent windstorms permeated its interior. Two children, Cornelia (1932) and Rolland (1934) were born there. Lloyd farmed some of his parent's land as well as some of Karel's for four futile years. He supplemented his meager income by driving a horse drawn school bus during the 1935–36 school year.[111]

By 1936, Lloyd and family had moved to Karel's vacated farm. As one who owned no land, he did not qualify for most of the federal aid programs. They did receive some mutton and cornmeal, though. The mutton, doled out as a result of federal sheep purchasing, was almost inedible. They survived on a subsistence basis with a Spartan lifestyle and help from the extended family. Several of Lloyd's close friends joined the Young Communist League and attempted to recruit him, but he had no interest, partly because of his parents' adamant opposition.

After the crop failure of 1932 Karel decided to take a look at Western Washington upon the invitation of a Swedish neighbor, Ed Moline, who had recently moved to a "shoestring valley" south of Olympia upon the advice of his bachelor brother Orville. Orville worked as a cook at the nearby Bordeaux logging camp. Moline indicated there were several good properties available near him at bargain basement prices. Karel and his son Joe drove out in a

Model A Ford and liked what they saw—especially the mild climate and green countryside.

Karel bought forty acres with a house and large root-cellar-woodshed for only $400. About eight acres were cleared and contained several varieties of fruit trees and berries. Waddell Creek, a substantial stream, formed much of the northern boundary. Its streambed had yielded enough gold that it attracted some attention during the depths of the Depression, but the amount was never substantial. For this reason recent developers have referred to Waddell Creek as "Treasure River." Karel's eldest son John soon bought five acres in the Southeast corner of the property and moved there with his wife and infant son, working on a local farm, where they stayed until he finished building his house.[112]

Devastated by the heat and drought and encouraged to move west by those who were already there, the young Dewings decided to join the exodus. Lloyd's older brother, Warren, had started farming in 1929, never had a crop for three years, took work with the WPA, and then departed for Washington finding work in Alaska with a Minnesota relative.[113] Lloyd's uncle, Eugene, Jake's younger brother, had established residence in Spokane and encouraged him to move there. The sale was held August 22, 1936, at the Dalebout farm. Another uncle, Odin Stompro, the Columbus postmaster, married to Jake's sister, handled the sale. Coffee and doughnuts were served to the group of mostly friends and relatives who purchased equipment, furniture, livestock, hay, grain, and more for a total of $430. Only about half went to the Dewings because others had offered items for sale as well.[114]

As plans for the President's North Dakota visit were finalized, the motley caravan of four vehicles and fifteen people rolled out to the west. The Dewings rode with Mary's older brother Cornelius in his Model A Ford sedan with a homemade trailer in tow. Karel and Eugene drove a Model A coupe. Karel's brother Nicholas, and half brothers Edward, Mike, and Eddie were in a Model T Ford converted into a small open truck. A neighbor Manley Hanson, his wife and two children, and Nicholas's daughter, Mary, came in another Model A, also towing a homemade trailer. Several small tents and kerosene camp stoves went along for cooking food and providing shelter. Clothes, silverware, dishes, and bedding represented most of the remaining cargo.

The group planned to cover about two hundred miles a day, stopping at noon for sandwiches. In the early evening they pitched their first camp near Wolf Point, Montana, on U.S. Highway 2. The evening meal usually consisted of freshly purchased hamburger, ever-present bread and "whatever else was available." Breakfast was always oatmeal or pancakes and bread. Several adults slept in the cars because the tents were too small to accommodate everyone. Recalling the trip, Lloyd took special pride in the efficiency the self-reliant group showed in making and breaking camp.[115]

Few problems arose during the trek. The summer weather cooperated and rather than posing difficulties as portrayed in Steinbeck's *Grapes of Wrath,* Montana authorities and citizenry proved understanding and sympathetic. The migrants had reason for concern, though, because earlier in the year authorities in both Colorado and California had attempted to physically close their borders to "unqualified transients." In April 1936, Colorado Governor Edwin Johnson had sent the state patrol to close southern entry to his state to stop "alien laborers from other states." That lasted about two weeks. More dramatic and even more unconstitutional, Los Angeles Police Chief James Davis early in 1936, assuming authority from somewhere unknown, ordered 126 officers to sixteen crucial highways and railroad entry points to turn back all indigent transients who could not prove California residence.[116] These blatant attacks on citizens' rights were quickly rectified by public ridicule and court decisions. It was also reported that in Washington State private agencies sometimes arranged for the return of transients to their state of legal residence with the state paying the cost.[117]

Heavy cargoes, rough roads, and worn equipment did create a problem with flat tires, though. When yet another flat plagued Manley Hanson, who could not afford to replace it, Hanson sat down in despair and broke into tears. His fellow North Dakotans, accustomed to helping each other in time of need, quickly chipped in enough money to buy a new tire. Hanson eventually successfully settled on a farm near Twin Falls, Idaho.

After almost a week on Highway 2 the migrants camped near Priest River, Idaho, to rest, do laundry and prepare for the final push to Spokane. The Dewing family and Eugene and Karel made the fairly short trip to Spokane. Lloyd rented a small house in Dishman, a Spokane suburb. Unlike their North Dakota home, it had electricity and running water, but the toilet was still outside. After working in the fruit harvest along with Mary, Lloyd found a job at a paper mill in nearby Post Falls, Idaho. Karel returned to his place on Waddell Creek that fall. Life in Dishman was quite pleasant, especially compared to the grimness of the Dust Bowl. The little house always seemed crowded with visiting relatives and the Spokane area, not drought devastated like the Great Plains, offered numerous attractions.

Nicholas and Edward found an eighty-acre tract bordering Priest River so attractive they decided to buy and stay. Nicholas returned to Columbus, North Dakota, to move his large family to Idaho. Their departure merited a short article in the Columbus newspaper. There were twelve children in all, but the two eldest, already married, stayed in North Dakota and Mary had stayed in Idaho. Family members delight in relating an incident during their trip to Idaho. The brakes on their old Hudson were so weak that, while crossing the Rocky Mountains, a child rode on each running board holding a large block of wood to jam under the rear tires, just in case. On at least one occasion they were needed. Nicholas sold his Hudson at Priest River and never owned another vehicle. Used to living in a comfortable house, mother Maajte struggled to adjust to caring for her large brood in a converted chicken coop.[118]

Because he was adept at handling horses, Nicholas was hired at a pole yard in Priest River where he worked until moving to Spokane during World War II. The pole yard provided just enough income for his large family to get by, but doing so required maximum efficiency and economy. Breakfast seldom varied. Nicholas bought oatmeal in large economy-sized containers and every morning it was cooked in a large kettle placed directly over the open wood fire in the kitchen stove. A milk cow, some chickens, a large garden, wild berries, and lots of fish from the river helped them scrape by. Several sons enrolled in the CCC, which required them to send home twenty-five of the thirty-dollar salary.[119] Soon, a fairly large colony of relatives and married children formed a small hamlet near Priest River.

Nelley Davis, who had moved from western Nebraska to a ranch near Pueblo, Colorado, migrated with her family to the nearby Bonner's Ferry area during the same time and wrote *Stump Ranch Pioneer*, published in 1942. Much like the North Dakotans the Davises left eastern Colorado with $160 and traveled for six days in a car towing a home made trailer. Davis noted a cardboard sign on a migrant's truck:

> Idaho we're busted flat
> Here we come in spite of that
> Not expecting wealth or gain
> Just want our kids to see the rain

Davis summed up her feelings about the move, saying, "We felt as any sturdy, self-respecting people would feel, driven by the forces of the elements to forsake the chosen pattern of their lives, and pushed into a mode of living foreign and unexpected to their prairie-bred instincts."[120]

They bought forty acres of cut over land near others from Colorado and built an 18 × 27 house. They gardened and owned goats and chickens, but relied heavily upon forest products for their income. Old cars and trucks were converted into buzz saws or substitutes for tractors. Cordwood, the staple cash crop, was supplemented by cedar posts and shakes and boughs and Christmas trees. In 1939, they received an average of 1.5 cents a tree which retailed at between 50 and 85 cents. Women often helped with the Christmas tree harvest.

Davis enthused about their new environment. Abundant moisture nurtured a variety of useful plants and flowers and there were no poisonous snakes.

She canned four to eight hundred quarts of fruits, vegetables, and berries a year. A strong sense of community soon evolved with participation in the Grange and 4–H and competition and socialization at local fairs. Their self-reliance and ebullience offered a marked contradiction to the many critics of the Dust Bowl experience.

Not all migrants shared the Davis's success and enthusiasm, however. Lumber companies circulated advertisements describing sub-marginal land in northeastern Washington and the northwest Idaho panhandle. They said, "Soil sub-irrigated, black, silt and loam; abundant water supply; numerous trout streams: A farmer can start with a small capital and work into a beautiful farmhouse with all modern advantages close at hand." One farmer wrote the WPA Division of Social Resources, "A certain lumber company (which advertised its properties as productive farm land) was responsible for more bankrupt farmers in Eastern Washington and Northern Idaho than the depression itself."[121]

North Dakotans Ivar and Sofia Husa resettled about twelve miles south of Waddell Creek. They and three of their four children left Belden, North Dakota, in April 1936, also driving a Model A Ford pulling a trailer. It took them seven days to reach East Stanwood, Washington, where older son, Leo, who was working as a choker setter in the logging industry, had made arrangements to lease a small farm for them. After about a year there, the family purchased a small farm in Independence Valley, a Finnish community near Rochester, where they raised strawberries and kept a few cows and chickens. Ivar, who emigrated from Finland in 1900, wanted to live in a Finnish area, and a friend whom he had met while commercial fishing near Vancouver Island in the early 1900s helped him find the property. Youngest son, Lennie, recalls, "My memories of North Dakota during the dust bowl days are vivid and sad. . . My parents had met in North Dakota as young homesteaders in 1906. . . The dry years in the early 30's wiped out their resources and efforts. It was difficult for them to abandon their home and move to a new location to begin their life anew. This, however, they did and with a lot of hard work they established a new home in Independence Valley."[122] The Husa's story followed a pattern followed by thousands of other migrants. Family members and friends who had moved earlier provided assistance and the newcomers worked hard to succeed.

Self-reliance, perseverance and ambition hardly fit H. L. Mencken's acerbic perception of Dust Bowl victims. The well known, cynical Baltimore journalist tarnished his reputation with intemperate attacks on Roosevelt and his New Deal programs. Never an admirer of small-town and agricultural life Mencken did not spare Dust Bowl residents, whom he felt were receiving far too much aid. A December 1936 effusion against victims of the upper

Midwest drought in *American Mercury* plumbed the depths of Mencken's callousness. Mencken, perhaps partly inspired by North Dakotan William Lemke's failed 1936 presidential campaign, raged, "There will never come a day when the one-crop clodhoppers of the land will cease to howl and beat their breasts, or the politicians to salvage them out of the public till—these mendicants call themselves farmers, and appear in statistics under the style. . . .They are simply land speculators who sent out on the wrong limb and got skinned." Mencken claimed that frauds began to swarm as one crossed the 94th meridian into the Dakotas. He punched, "They outnumber actual farmers by at least five to one. Here is the actual Zion of the eternal but bogus Farm Problem. Here is the Holy Land of locusts, droughts, whirlwinds, and big freezes. Here the only sound ever heard to issue from human throats is the piteous wail of 'Gimme!' " Mencken complained that the handouts came from earnings "from the rest of us." He suggested that the entire region be emptied of its present hopeless population and be turned back to the Indians.

According to Mencken they came to get land for nothing, hoping to grow a crop of wheat in two months and then, as earlier charged by the *Chicago Tribune,* "loll at ease the other ten." They hoped to take advantage of rising land prices and sell out to "real farmers" at top prices. He further suggested that remote inhospitable land was settled by "misfits and failures, speculators and deadbeats," inferior people who were incapable of supporting themselves in the best of conditions. Mencken proposed sterilization "on a wholesale scale" to save taxpayer money and "scrap their biological potency."[123]

Unlike the 1932 *Chicago Tribune* piece, Mencken's bomb elicited little comment, perhaps because it sank under its own weight. Dust Bowl victims tended to blame themselves for their plight and showed surprising apathy toward radical politics as writers William Saroyan and Lorena Hitchcock noted. Those who stayed on the Plains and made it through the Depression tend to believe the government had helped others, but, in their own cases, they thought they toughed it out on their own.[124] Even many of those who left maintain they received little if any government assistance.[125] The criticism that the transients were abnormal people was dismissed by government studies that recognized mobility as one of the basic characteristics of the American population, only now lack of opportunity and capital made the reabsorption process more difficult. Interestingly, transient families proceeded in this process at a much faster rate than individuals on the resident relief roles.[126]

The government's official study of the problem, *The Future of the Great Plains,* addressed issues raised by New Deal critics. "The Nation can afford such relief when it is needed. It cannot afford *not* to give it when it is needed," it noted. "The Committee has been impressed during its field trips by the certainty that in the Great Plains area it was dealing with people who desired nothing else than to earn their own living by their own efforts," the report said. Seeming to specifically address Mencken's criticisms, it recognized the enormity of losses incurred, "It is a cruel error to regard any large portion of the population as some uninformed commentators have done, as speculative investors whose calculations have gone wrong. Not in money alone, but also in labor and endurance, they have paid for better fortune than has yet been theirs."[127]

The Committee made nine major recommendations called Lines of Federal Action: 1. Expand investigations and surveys; 2. Federal acquisition of land in range areas; 3. Control and use of lands acquired by federal government in range areas should be in cooperation with local grazing associations; 4. Institute measures to increase size of farms through federal credit and purchase; 5. Development of water resources; 6. Resettlement with federal assistance; 7. Compensation to local governments who lose tax revenues because of federal acquisition; 8. Control of destructive insect pests such as grasshoppers and Mormon Crickets; 9. Development of other resources such as the abundant lignite coal reserves that could be used to generate electricity.[128] All of the recommendations eventually were instituted to a certain extent. In the first three years of the New Deal, for example, the government acquired more than twice the acreage in national forests as had been purchased in the previous history of national forests.[129] Although these measures did not stop the flow of population out the Great Plains, their influence remains highly visible and one can not help speculating about the fate of the region if they had not been implemented.

New Deal planners also addressed problems in the Pacific Northwest. Regarding the migrant problem, the Pacific Northwest Planning Commission suggested, "This is not the first, and by no means is it the greatest influx of people that the region has experienced, but the problems of economic assimilation are different and in many respects far more difficult than they have been heretofore." The Commission noted there were some seven million acres of not replanted cut over and burned land which could employ 2000 men for the next ten years.[130] Most Dust Bowl migrants to the Pacific Northwest, however, received little assistance for resettlement. There were some federal resettlement camps, especially in California, but most were still on the drawing board when the rush of 1936–37 occurred.

Even though they were United States citizens migrants were greeted with an unusual amount of suspicion and some hostility. "We heard some critical talk about us, but nothing serious," said Lloyd Dewing. Their skills, outstanding work ethic, and reliability helped fuel antagonism towards them from the Pacific Northwest workforce, many of whom were also unemployed or struggling to hold jobs. Dust Bowlers were also willing to take lower wages, had fewer inclinations towards labor unions, and tended to see things from the farmers' viewpoint. These factors created a depressing effect upon wages and working conditions for farm labor and fueled antagonism against the newcomers, especially in areas like Yakima and Wenatchee that grew large specialty crops.

Northern Great Plains migrants, however, did not envision themselves as transient farm laborers and were determined to re-establish in permanent jobs and locations.[131] Generally young, ambitious, and unpretentious, they encountered little open hostility although there may have been more covert opposition, such as that from labor unions, than was realized. The New Deal preserved an economic floor for many via programs like the WPA and CCC and other work relief programs. Federal support for unions also meant that most of the industrial workers in the Pacific Northwest were unionized and the newcomers benefited from the more favorable work environment unions provided when they were able to break into the industrial work force. Few migrants anticipated the profound impact of the upcoming world war or fully appreciated the striking economic potential the government's huge investment in Pacific Northwest infrastructure portended. Voracious demand for industrial labor would soon convince most who had not already done so to make the transition from farm to factory.

NOTES

1. Great Plains Committee, *The Future of the Great Plains*, House Document 144, 75th Congress (Washington, DC: United States Government Printing Office, 1937), 66–67; Berta Ash and A. R. Mangus. *Farmers on Relief and Rehabilitation* (Washington, DC: United States Government Printing Office, 1937).

2. Bruce L. Melvin and Edna N. Smith, *Rural Youth: Their Situation and Prospects* (Washington, DC: WPA Division of Social Research, United States Government Printing Office, 1938), Page 13 of Summary.

3. Ibid., 2–3.

4. Raymond D. Gastil, "The Pacific Northwest as a Cultural Region," *Pacific Northwest Quarterly* 64 (October 1973): 150–51. Charts show high percentage of migrants from the western north central states to the Pacific Northwest.

5. Geraldine Moun, conversation, March 2000.

6. Walter Nugent, *Into the West: The Story of Its People* (New York: Knopf, 1999), 241.

7. Pacific Northwest Regional Planning Commission, *Migration and the Development of Economic Opportunity in the Pacific Northwest. A Report Prepared in Cooperation with the Pacific Northwest Land Advisory Committee* (Portland: Pacific Northwest Regional Planning Commission, 1939), 5.

8. Ibid. Dorothy Hubbard Schwieder, *Growing Up With the Town: Family & Community on the Great Plains* (Iowa City: University if Iowa Press, 2002), 67.

9. David L. Carlton, and Peter A. Coclanis, eds., *Confronting Southern Poverty in the Great Depression: The Report on Economic Conditions of the South with Related Documents* (New York: Bedford Books of St. Martin's Press, 1996), 120.

10. Michael J. Grant, *Down and Out on the Family Farm: Rural Rehabilitation in the Great Plains, 1929–1945* (Lincoln: University of Nebraska Press, 2002), 12; Marion Clawson, David McEntire, and Carl P. Heisy, "Stump Ranching," *Land Policy Review* III (May-June 1940): 32.

11. United States Bureau of Census, Sixteenth Census, "Characteristics of Population," Volume II, Part 6 (Washington, DC: United States Government Printing Office, 1930); Arthur Mangus, *Changing Aspects of Rural Relief* (Washington, DC: United States Government Printing Office, 1938), 81–Chart, "Percent of Rural Relief Persons without Schooling."; James N. Gregory, *American Exodus: The Dust Bowl Migration and Okie Culture in California* (New York: Oxford University Press, 1989) 15–16.

12. Gregory, *American Exodus,* 104.

13. Carlton and Cocolinas, *Confronting Southern Poverty*, 119–126.

14. Dwight Sanderson, *Research Memorandum on Rural Life in the Depression*, (New York: Social Science Research Council, 1937) 32–33; Great Plains Committee, *The Future of the Great Plains* (Washington, DC: House Document 144, 75th Congress, 1937), 6; Charles F. Ernst, *Migrants: Our Potential New Settlers* (Olympia: State of Washington Department of Social Services, 1939).

15. John H. Tolan (Chairman, House Select Committee to Investigate the Interstate Migration of Destitude Citizens), *Hearings on House Resolution 63 and House Resolution 491*, July 29 to December 11, 1941 (Washington, DC: United States Government Printing Office, 1941), Volume 10, 4198; John Webb and Malcom Brown. *Migrant Families*, WPA Research Monograph 18 (Washington, DC: United States Government Printing Office, 1938) Page 23 of Summary.

16. Grant, *Down and Out*, 17.

17. Whiting, Theodore, *WPA Final Statistical Report of the Federal Emergency Relief Administration* (Washington, DC: United States Government Printing Office, 1942), 105–7 and Tables I though X, 127–227.

18. Edmund Brunner, "Internal Migration in the United States, 1935–1940," *Rural Sociology* 13 (March 1948): 9–22.

19. Donald Worster, *Dust Bowl: The Southern Plains in the 1930s* (New York: Oxford, 1979),

20. James Sellers, "Nebraska-One Hundred Years," *Nebraska History* 34 (December 1953): 262; Carey McWilliams. *Ill Fares the Land: Migrants and Migratory Labor in the United States* (New York: Barnes and Noble, 1941), 66–67; Robert P. Wilkins and Wynona Wilkins (New York: W. W. Norton, 1977), 104.

21. Nugent, *Into the West, 243.*

22. McWilliams, *Ill Fares*, 21.

23. Everett S. Lee, "The Turner Thesis Re Examined," *American Quarterly* 13 (Spring 1961): 20–29; Webb, Summary 18, 27–28; Dorothy Schwieder and Deborah

Fink, "Plains Women: Rural Life in the 1930s," *Great Plains Quarterly* 8 (Spring 1988): 79–88.

24. Richard White, "Poor Men on Poor Lands: The Back to the Land Movement of the Early Twentieth Century," *Pacific Historical Review* (February 1980): 299.

25. Henry H. Collins, Jr., *America's Own Refugees: Our 4,000,000 Homeless Migrants* (Princeton: Princeton University Press, 1941), 235–36.

26. Arthur M. Schlesinger, *The Politics of Upheaval* (Boston: Houghton Mifflin, 1960), 265–67; T, H, Watkins, *The Hungry Years* (New York: Holt, 1999), 244–46.

27. Carroll Van West, "The Best Kind of Building: The New Deal Landscape of the Northern Plains, 1933–42," *Great Plains Quarterly* (Spring 1994): 136.

28. Leonard J. Arrington and Don C. Reading, "New Deal Economic Programs in the Northern Tier States, 1933–1939," in *The Centennial West: Essays on the Northern Tier States*, ed. William Lang (Seattle: University of Washington Press, 1991), 227–43.

29. William E Leuchtenburg, *Franklin D. Roosevelt and the New Deal, 1932–1940* (New York: Harper & Row, 1963), 125–26.

30. Grant, *Down and Out*, 90–101.

31. Elwyn B.Robinson, *History of North Dakota* (Lincoln: University of Nebraska Press), 408–9.

32. Betty Lindley, *A New Deal for Youth: The Story of the National Youth Administration*, (New York: Da Capo Press, 1972), 16–27.

33. Ibid., 174–75.

34. D. Jerome Tweton and Daniel F. Rylance,*Years of Despair: North Dakota in the Depression* (Grand Forks: University of North Dakota Press, 1973), 13–16.

35. Robinson, *History of North Dakota*, 397.

36. Everett S. Lee, "The Turner Thesis Re Examined," *American Quarterly* 13 (Spring 1961): 16–25.

37. See *Noonan Miner*, *Bowbells Tribune*, *Beach Advocate*, summer 1936.

38. *Williston Herald*, August 5, 1936.

39. Howard Ottoson, et al., *Land and People in the Northern Plains Transition Area* (Lincoln: University of Nebraska Press, 1966), 90.

40. Tweton and Rylance, *Years of Despair*, 16. Wilkins, *North Dakota,* estimates a total of 120,000 from 1920–1939, 104.

41. Paula Nelson, *The Prairie Winnows Out Its Own: The West River Country of South Dakota In the Years of the Depression* (Iowa City: University of Iowa Press, 1996), 174.

42. McWilliams, *Ill Fares*, 339.

43. "Basically Jobs," *Literary Digest* (May 2, 1936): 134.

44. Richard White, *Land Use, Environment and Social Change: The Shaping of Island County, Washington* (Seattle: University of Washington Press, 1980), 134.

45. Grant, *Down and Out,* 21–22. For detailed long term grain production figures see R. S. Kifer and H. L. Stewart. *Farming Hazards in the Drought Area* (Washington, DC: United States Government Printing Office, 1938), Supplemental Tables, 132–47;

46. David B. Danbom, *Born In the Country: A History of Rural America* (Baltimore: Johns Hopkins University Press, 1995), 223;

47. Nelson, *Prairie*, 124

48. *South Dakota History* "The Enduring Frontier: The Impact of Weather on South Dakota History" (Spring-Summer 1985): 29.

49. *Northwood Gleanor,* August 7, 1931, Quoted in Gordon M. Bakken. *Surviving the North Dakota Depression* (Pasadena: Wood and Jones, 1992), 44; See also James Beddow, "Midwestern Editorial Response to the New Deal, 1932–1940," *South Dakota History* 4 (Summer 1977): 140–53.

50. Bakken, *Surviving*, 45–46.

51. Berta Ash and A. R. Mangus, *Farmers on Relief*, 5–6.

52. R. S. Kifer and H. L. Stewart, *Farming Hazards*, 37.

53. Great Plains Committee, 44–48

54. Carter Goodrich, et al, *Migration and Economic Opportunity* (Philadelphia: University of Pennsylvania Press, 1936), 237–38.

55. *Noonan Miner*, June 28, 1934.

56. Tweton and Reylance, *Years of Despair*, 7.

57. Theodore Saloutous, "The New Deal and Farm Policy in the Great Plains," *Agricultural History* 43 (July 1969): 345–55; C. Roger Lambert, "The Drought Cattle Purchase, 1934–1935: Problems and Complaints," *Agricultural History* (April 1971): 85–93.

58. Nelson, *Prairie*,157; Jean Choate, "Debt, Drought, and Depression: South Dakota in the 1930s," *Journal of the West* 31 (October 1992): 33–44.

59. Lawrence A. Jones and David Durand, *Mortgage Lending Experience in Agriculture* (Princeton: Princeton University Press, 1954), 28.

60. Maurice C. Latta, "The Economic Effects of Drought and Depression Upon Custer County, 1929–1942," *Nebraska History* 33 (December 1952): 220–36.

61. Richard G. Bremer, *Agricultural Change in an Urban Age: The Loup Country of Nebraska, 1910–1970* (Lincoln: University of Nebraska Press, 1976), 84.

62. Nelson, *Prairie,* 149–50

63. R. S. Kifer and H. L. Stewart, *Farming Hazards*, 113–15.

64. Ash and Mangus, *Farmers on Relief*, 56, see also chart on 37.

65. Webb and Brown, *Migrant Families*, 43–48, for patterns of migration see maps on 29–31, 34.

66. *Dickinson Press*, October 25, 1934; November 29, 1934; March 7, 1935.

67. *Noonan Miner*, August 29, 1935; *Beach Advance*, January 9, 1936.

68. *Dickinson Press*, July 25, 1935.

69. Nelson, *Prairie*, 152.

70. Geraldine Moun, conversation, March 2000.

71. Philip Kress, "North Dakota Weather: An Analytic Summary of Conditions over the Last Century," *North Dakota History* 34 (Summer 1967): 258–71.

72. Great Plains Committee, 134.

73. Van West, "The Best Kind of Building," 129.

74. *Aberdeen Daily World*, July 2, 1936, through July 20, 1936. Special thanks to the staff at the Aberdeen Public Library who untangled the microfilm so it was readable, March 10, 2005.

75. Local examples among many—*Modesto Bee*, July 8, 1936; *Ellensburg [WA] Record*, July 17, 1936.

76. David Nichols, ed., *Ernie's America: The Best of Ernie Pyle's 1930's Travel Dispatches* (New York: Random House, 1989), 125–26; Alfred Klauser, "It Can't Rain Here," *Nation* (August 8, 1936): 152.

77. Don Reading, "The New Deal Activity in the States, 1933 to 1939," *Journal of Economic History* 33 (1973) 792–810; Wilkins, *North Dakota,* 103.

78. Ibid.

79. "Minnesota Farms Slash Mortgages." *New York Times* , 21 July 1936) 6.

80. Nelson, "*Traveling*," in Lang, 253.

81. George S. Reeves, *A Man from South Dakota* (New York: Dutton, 1950), 13.

82. *South Dakota History.* "South Dakota in the Great Depression," Special Edition (Summer 1989).

83. West in Black Crisis of Drought," *Literary Digest* (July 18, 1936, 122–23+; Kifer and Stewart, *Farming Hazards,* 14–21; Pacific Northwest Regional Planning Commission, "Migration," 240.

84. Great Plains Committee, *The Future*, 59.

85. *Dickinson Press*, August 6, 1936.

86. Nelson, *The Prairie*, 163–74; Rolland Dewing, "The Great Depression: A Dust Bowl Migrant's Memoir of Coming to the Pacific Northwest," *Columbia* 10 (Spring 1996): 30.

87. Morris L. Cooke, a wealthy Philadelphia mechanical engineer, had led the fight for rural electrification for Governor Gifford Pinchot in Pennsylvania and Governor Franklin Roosevelt in New York. Cooke found private utilities so hostile to the idea that he became a champion of public power.

88. Great Plains Committee, 131.

89. "Desert in Dakotas Bears only Cactus," *New York Times*, 22 July 1936, 6.

90. Mary Dewing, conversation with author, September 2004.

91. *New York Times*, July 30, 1936.

92. *Divide County Journal*, September 4, 1936.

93. Tolan Committee, Volume Ten, 4119–20.

94. Nelson, *The Prairie*, 178.

95. Ibid. 179.

96. Quoted in *Salem* [Oregon] *Statesman*, July 7, 1936.

97. Bill Ganzel, *Dust Bowl Descent* (Lincoln: University of Nebraska Press, 1984), 24–27; James Curtis, *Mind's Eye, Mind's Truth: FSA Photography Reconsidered* (Philadelphia: Temple University Press, 1989), 16.

98. Ganzel, *Dust Bowl Descent*, 26–27.

99. *Scotia* [Nebraska] *Register*, September 17, 1936. Quoted in Bremer, *Agricultural Change in an Urban Age*, 84–85.

100. Letter from Allen Shepherd, July 19, 2004.

101. Adam R. Dewing, *The Descendants of Andrew Dewing, 1638–2002* (Green Lake, Wisconsin: Private Printing, 2002); Susan Hobbs. *The Art of Thomas Wilmer Dewing: Beauty Reconfigured* (Washington: Smithsonian Press, 1996); Arthur Stone Dewing, *The Financial Policy of Corporations* (New York: Ronald Press, 1953).

102. Benjamin Franklin Dewing, *Descendants of Andrew Dewing of Dedham, Mass.* (Boston: Privately Printed, 1904) 75–76.

103. Burke County Committee, *Pioneers and Progress*, Volume 2 (Rugby, North Dakota: Burke County Historical Society, 1989).

104. Colleen A. Oihus, *A History of Coal Mining in North Dakota, 1873–1982* (Grand Forks: North Dakota Geological Survey, 1983), 47–50.

105. Conversations with grain farmers in North Dakota, South Dakota and Nebraska, including many close relatives. Harvest time was an annual ritual lasting 30–35 days. Many Great Plains farms have virtual museums of outdated horse drawn equipment. Much of the old equipment was collected for scrap iron in World War II, though. For an excellent overview see Thomas D. Isern, *Bull Threshers and Bindlestiffs: Harvesting and Threshing on the North American Plains* (Lawrence: University of Kansas Press, 1990); A personal account is June Osterberg, "Threshing Time," *North Dakota Horizons* 16 (Fall 1986): 25–27; See also Carrie Young, *Nothing To Do But Stay* (New York: Delta, 1993), 70–74.

106. Chet Johnston, conversation with author, August 1986.

107. "Farming in the 1930s: Having Fun," *Wessells Living History Farm*, http://www.livinghistoryfarmorg/farminginthe1930slife-14–html. (accessed February 9, 2004)

108. Bennie Bengston, "Radio Comes to the Farm," *North Dakota Horizons* 20. (Winter 1990): 25.

109. Kathe L. Lemmerman, *Columbus/Noonan Study: The Impact of Coal Development on Two North Dakota Communities* (Minot, ND: Minot State College, 1974). A significant lignite coal mine played an important role in the local economy.

110. Joyce Dalebout and Mary Dewing Dalebout, *Dalebouts, 1631–2000* (Olympia: Private Printing, 2000), 127–34.

111. For a personal account of rural North Dakota Schools in the Great Depression see Enid Bern, "Memoirs of a Prairie Schoolteacher," *North Dakota History* 42 (Summer 1975): 5–18.

112. For a discussion of migration chains see Gregory, *American Exodus*, 29–35.

113. Pearl Stompro Berget, letter, September 24, 2001.

114. Dewing, "Depression," 37.

115. Author conversations with Lloyd and Mary Dewing, Cornelia Dewing Peabody, Cornelius Dalebout, Mary Dalebout and Karel Dalebout.

116. Kevin Starr, *Endangered Dreams: The Great Depression in California* (New York: Oxford University Press, 1996), 177.

117. Eric Beecroft and Seymin Janow, "Toward a National Policy for Migration," *Social Forces* (May 1938): 475–92.

118. Maajte Dalebout, *Memoirs* (Private Scrapbook, 1912–1967), courtesy of her daughter Jenny Dalebout Dillon.

119. Edwin G. Hill, *In the Shadow of the Mountain: The Spirit of the CCC* (Pullman: Washington State University Press, 1988), Chapter 7, "The Pacific Northwest," 97–133.

120. Nelley P. Davis, *Stump Ranch Pioneer* (New York: Dodd Mead, 1942), 38–39.

121. Webb and Brown, *Migrant Families*, 12.

122. Lennie Husa e-mail message to author, October 18, 2004.

123. H. L. Mencken, "The Dole for Bogus Farmers," *American Mercury* 39 (December 1936): 400–408.

124. Nelson, *Prairie,* 200.

125. Conversations with author.

126. Webb and Brown, *Migrant Families*, 125–26.

127. Great Plains Committee, *The Future of the Great Plains*, 6

128. Ibid., 1–89.

129. William E. Leuchtenburg, *Franklin D. Roosevelt and the New Deal, 1932–1940* (New York: Harper and Row, 1963), 174.

130. Pacific Northwest Planning Commission, *Migration*, 5, 23.

131. Author's experience. This is a consistent theme in government sponsored studies.

Chapter Ten

Adapting in Eden

By early 1940, concerns about the surge of unemployed Dust Bowl migrants to the Pacific Northwest subsided. An article, "Promised Land" in the *Reader's Digest* by well-known writer Frank J. Taylor said, "It is amazing how completely they have lost themselves in this vast evergreen country. . . Few of them are asking for relief." Emphasizing the role of agriculture, Taylor suggested, "Most of those who have been in the Northwest for two years or more have realized their dream of a plot of ground, a vegetable garden, and some chickens. . . The newcomers are welcome here in the Northwest."[1] Taylor claimed people from the Northern Prairie States were preferred for farm labor and quoted a Wenatchee apple grower, "These Dakotans are real farmers." A study confirmed that migrants from the Great Plains were less likely to claim relief than those from the coastal states because they were preferred as farm laborers.[2] A sample of migrant drought farmer in 1937, nevertheless, showed 48.3% received some form of public assistance before leaving the drought area, and 38.5% were receiving assistance after entering Western Washington with the percentage increasing with length of residence.[3]

Taylor estimated a family could put up a one-room shelter and a small barn for $100, indicating he had seen thousands of them around the Puget Sound and in Oregon's Willamette Valley.[4] Most of these were located on small acreage. Between 1930 and 1940 the number of farms under fifty acres in western Washington increased from 26,627 to 48,389.[5] By 1940, few were on relief, but they needed much more income than the estimated average annual net profit of $75 per stump ranch, when it was estimated $901 a year was required for a decent rural standard of living. A Farm Security Administration official praised the migrants, "Those people from the Dust Bowl never complain or whimper. I haven't heard a squawk from them. All they ask for is a chance. Give it to them, and they'll make good."[6] Those accustomed to the dreary hardships of the Dust Bowl temporarily might accept such a Spartan lifestyle, but ultimately most found a viable economic base in industry rather than agriculture.[7]

The Pacific Northwest indeed must have seemed like the Promised Land to those fleeing the drought devastated Northern Great Plains. Blessed with natural wonders including fresh and salt water, mountains, beaches, the best and largest temperate forests in the world, an abundance of inexpensive land, and ample reliable rainfall in most areas, the Pacific Northwest had much to offer. Although their new environment was more accommodating, it was hardly Eden as many learned quickly. Even though they shared similar values and educational levels as those already there, they were still migrants, most of whom arrived almost empty handed and received little assistance from state and local government, which favored established residents. As Taylor suggested, adjustment to their new environment proved remarkably efficient given the circumstances. For most the only option left was to adjust in the best manner possible.

The government's idea that the transplanted farmers could re-establish themselves on small farms in cutover areas and newly irrigated land, never worked as well as expected. Irrigated farms cost too much and most migrants had no experience with the complexities of irrigated agriculture. Forced to farm marginal cutover land, most earned far too little from this unproductive land to be self-sufficient. The solution involved what many called "working to support the farm," farming part time and holding an outside job, usually in some aspect of the timber industry, a pattern similar to that of their already established neighbors.[8]

Agricultural experts estimated enough farmland to support an average family in the rainy portions of the Pacific Northwest required at least eighty acres, of which a minimum of thirty should be cleared.[9] As late as 1931 the Washington State Director of Agriculture advised settlers to choose land with big stumps because the land was bound to be fertile. Since farm land in the Willamette Valley cost much more, most migrants seeking land moved to the Puget Sound area which gained 53 percent in population during the period 1930–1940.[10] Farmland in Lewis County was valued on average at only thirteen dollars and acre in 1935, but very few migrants could finance a purchase of eighty acres.[11] In 1939, a sample study in Washington showed 35.5% of 104 drought migrants settled on cutover land less than forty acres in size. Only 9.3 % of 48,389 farms in Western Washington contained seventy acres or more. Another study of 1051 upland cutover farms indicated one-third had less than two acres of cleared land. In Thurston County 69% of all farms contained less than seven acres of cleared land. Contrary to higher expectations, farmers averaged less than one-half acre of newly cleared land per year.[12]

Clearing stumps and brush was a difficult and frequently not very rewarding task. Heavy machinery and blasting powder cost too much for those of limited means and banks were cautious about extending loans for land clearing. The state passed a bill to subsidize local units for clearing land, but no local agencies supported it. A bill proposed in the state legislature to create a state powder factory that would sell explosives to settlers at cost failed.[13] Most farmers practiced forms of agriculture such as dairy, poultry and berries that could be adapted to land with stumps still there. Grain and hay became the largest single expense for most stump land farmers.[14] As late as 1942 a federal plan to assist land clearing was still in the planning stage. The proposal was dropped because of the massive migration to defense jobs and wartime priorities.[15]

Remarkably, high school students were instrumental in conducting the most comprehensive accurate local survey of conditions in the Pacific Northwest in the 1930s. Under the auspices of the Washington State Planning Council, Elma High School students distributed and collected 1,600 questionnaires in the eastern two-thirds of Grays Harbor County and one-third of southwest Mason County. They represented rural areas with a large influx of Dust Bowl migrants. The Planning Council, greatly impressed, published the survey in December 1941. The small towns of Elma, McCleary, and Oakville, bordering the Black Hills west and southwest of Olympia, were the leading population centers. The Chehalis River, which flows into Grays Harbor at Aberdeen, drains the area.

For forty years lumbering in the Black Hills had furnished the economic base, but the old growth forests were almost gone. By fall 1941, all major logging in the Black Hills ceased and some 70,000 acres, now known as Capitol Forest, were sold back to the state.[16] In 1929, Grays Harbor County had thirty-four sawmills and thirty-seven other wood-using plants. By 1939, only ten mills remained, leaving 20,000 acres of tax delinquent lands, and payrolls that equaled only 25 percent of the 1929 figure.[17]

Many loggers, aware of the inevitable, had moved on to other sites in Washington, Oregon, and northern California, selling their small stump ranchs at bargain prices, or merely abandoning them. Although many grew at least part of their own food, most displaced loggers and unemployed mill workers, in contrast to recent migrants, showed little interest in farming full time and preferred to move where new jobs in the timber industry opened. In contrast to this instability, surveys indicated that three-quarters of the drought migrants stayed in the county where they first settled.[18]

The Elma Survey affirmed Midwestern roots for the majority of students. The survey indicated, ". . . if the town of Elma were to be picked up bodily and deposited in the midst of rural Ohio, it would probably go serenely on its rural-city way without attracting noticeable attention."[19] Typically, their parents were Scandinavians born in North Central States who moved to the Northern Great Plains as children, then migrated to Washington during the lumber boom between 1890 and 1910. They achieved an average of one year of high school education while most of their children graduated from high school. The majority preferred to live on a small tract of land out of town. There, they raised a few cows and chickens and established an orchard and a vegetable garden. Most established families had electric lights, running water, wash machines, autos and either a piano or a phonograph, but most lacked an indoor toilet, ice box or refrigerator, telephone, an oil heater or furnace. As was true of recent migrants most families did not participate in organized group activities such as church, clubs or civic organizations.[20]

As one would expect, most of the recent Dust Bowl arrivals experienced a lower standard of living. The best acreage was already taken and those good sites that were available were unaffordable for most migrants. The survey said, "Along the roads above the flood plains of the Chehalis lie the farmsteads while up the adjoining valleys are the small farm plots of the onetime lumberjacks. Farther back migrants have built their shacks on what seems to them better farmlands than the dry unfriendly plains of the Dust Bowl."[21] Of the 2,400 persons who moved into the region since 1930 an estimated 40 percent of the new settlers came from the Great Plains and Rocky Mountain regions. During same period 2,700 left with a disproportionate number of young women among them.[22] Most of these migrants preferred to pursue what they knew best—farming. The vast majority, lacking the required capital to acquire an adequate farm, relied upon outside employment, mainly in the lumber industry, frequently working in government relief programs before finding private employment. The survey found only half of those whose occupation was farming ten years ago now identified farming as their chief source of livelihood.

Cooperation between assistance and rehabilitation agencies was lacking.[23] The Resettlement Administration combined with the FERA and the Soil Conservation Service, could purchase marginal lands and help farmers on that land to relocate, but very little was accomplished. The Resettlement Administration did not purchase any marginal land in the Pacific Northwest, and it resettled only 173 farm families in Western Washington.[24]

Much of the meager agricultural production was home consumed in a subsistence living style. Most of the "farm" units had only one or two cows and butterfat production per cow averaged 208 pounds a year in the area considered compared to an average of 306.2 in Western Washington. Poultry flocks were small and not a major source of income.[25] The Elma Survey found only 42 percent of present mill workers lived in the area ten years ago and suggested, "This can be partially explained by the immigration of non-unionized workers from Mid-western farms. . . ."[26] Competition for jobs in part hindered social acceptance for Great Plains migrants. Lack of participation in organized group life by the long-time residents and by the newcomers also limited assimilation. It was estimated about forty-five percent of those moving into the entire western Washington cutover area after 1929 came from the Northern Great Plains, most of the rest had lived in the state before moving.[27] Social interaction between migrants and established residents was quite limited. Both groups tended to stay to themselves and pursue social outlets through immediate family, relatives, and perhaps a few close friends.[28] Many migrants moved together and lived in the same localities. For example, over eighty migrants from one small town in South Dakota settled in nearby Kitsap County.[29]

Recent migrants faced economic and social challenges inherent to their transition. But the survey found, "Although recent migrants have come during a period of restricted opportunities, their problems and successes are little different from those of long-time residents. There appears to be no relationship between unemployment and length of residence, and the annual incomes of newcomers average only fifty dollars below those of long-time residents." About half of those surveyed had annual incomes under $750.[30] The study granted that migrants' planes of living were ten to fifteen percent under the area average but maintained they were probably higher than they would have been had they remained in their former location.

Unique aspects of employment in the timber industry explained this exceptionally close economic parity. About half of the jobs in the timber industry, an unusually high percentage, were classified as unskilled labor, allowing easy entry. Yet entry-level wages were competitive because of the historical high turnover rate and demanding and dangerous nature of the work.[31] School authorities, nonetheless, reported many cases of malnutrition among migrant families.[32] Migrants loss of "psychic income," values received from non-material goods of life which are mostly conditioned by education and cultural environment, definitely existed, too, but can not be quantified.[33]

Not only were there more job opportunities, the mild, usually wet climate promoted an easier lifestyle and a wide variety of plant life which could help sustain a family through home consumption and outside marketing. Trees of many varieties were still everywhere and were used primarily for construction and firewood with Douglas fir and western red cedar favored for construction. Using good fir for firewood was common because the market for small timber stands was so limited. In hindsight the practice was a serious mistake. Even then the Elma Survey noted, "Good stands of poles and piling-size timber are being cut for fuel at a fraction of the market price possible through higher utilization."[34] Cedar, noted for its straight splitting and durability, was used for shakes, shingles and fence posts, especially. Bolts from downed old growth cedar still were easily obtainable, sometimes pirated from unoccupied land. Although fir firewood burned well and produced a high level of heat, deciduous red alder, considered a weed tree at the time, was favored by many because it contained no pitch, burned quietly, lasted well, and produced a good heat level. Western big leaf maple, also abundant in lower areas, shared alder's qualities. Fir cones for the growing demand of tree nurseries and Christmas trees, both primarily from Douglas fir, also were marketable.

Bark from the cascara tree, also described as a tall shrub, used to treat constipation and upset stomachs, was peeled and dried by thousands of youths, unemployed adults, and those seeking supplementary income. A member of the buckthorn family, cascara usually grows only fifteen to twenty feet high, but sometimes much taller. It thrives in the western lowland areas from British Columbia to northern California. Distinguished by its bright yellow inside, the bark peels easily during spring and early summer. An average yield per tree is about ten pounds, but large specimens have been known to yield over two hundred pounds. Much of it was stripped barehanded with a jack knife or a hunting knife. Popularly called "Chittum Bark," it was a much-sought commodity at ten to fifteen cents a pound for dried bark. Owners considered the presence of cascara in their wood lots a valuable asset. Every rural resident knew about cascara, and like other forest products, it was pirated extensively. One year in the late 1930s Portland alone shipped over 500,000 pounds of dried cascara bark.[35]

Irresponsible harvesters frequently stripped the reachable bark and left the tree to die. Destruction of cascara was so great British Columbia banned peeling in the 1920s. States began requiring that the tree to be cut down and at least the bottom foot of bark had to be left on the stump to allow the peeled tree to regenerate. The price went to twenty cents a pound in World War II and reached thirty for a while after the war until effective synthetics ruined the market. Some demand still persists, however, most of the annual harvest of around 200,000 pounds of dried bark is supplied by professional harvesters, who also pick brush, mushrooms, fir-cones, ferns, berries and other forest products.[36] Most forest owners now thin cascara trees as a bothersome weed. Thinning and leaving cascara on my wood lot always brings back memories of peeling, packing out, drying and selling my then primary source of income.

A variety of shrubs and ferns used in floral arrangements and landscaping flourished. Salal and Oregon grape abounded especially. Salal, an attractive evergreen with thick shiny leaves, grows in almost all soil types and is probably the most dominate shrub west of the Cascades. Picking selected salal sprigs or "picking brush" provided income for many Depression era residents. Another widespread, popular evergreen, Oregon grape, closely related to the barberry family, has a fruit the looks like bright blueberries and leafs that resemble holly. Its dainty yellow blossom has been the Oregon State Flower since 1892. Among the largest of all evergreen fern types, the shade loving and bountiful western sword fern's delicate fronds are also used in many floral arrangements. The western hazelnut, the parent of the domestic filbert, was also plentiful and easily harvested if you were fortunate enough to beat the squirrels and chipmunks.

Berries, both wild and domestic, thrived and represented an important part of the diet both fresh and canned. Domestically, strawberries and raspberries led, although a great range of other berries grew well. Wild blackberries, huckleberries, elderberries, black caps (a dark raspberry), and strawberries were readily available. The native blackberry or dewberry, source of the domestic Loganberry, Youngberry, and Boysenberry, was highly favored for its delicious sweet flavor and firmness. It thrived on cut over land, so huge patches had sprung up and logging companies did not restrict access to berry pickers. Frequently an entire family participated and could harvest gallons of delectable fruit in one outing. Some marketed the much sought after berry for several dollars a gallon.

Less desirable, but seemingly everywhere, the aggressive Himalaya blackberry also provided excellent and much larger fruit. Noted for its astonishing vigor and vicious thorns, it was introduced to America by Luther Burbank in 1885 and can be found in any soil as well as most shade and light intensities. Burbank brought the plant to the United States by exchanging seeds with a horticulturalist in India. Extremely aggressive, its canes can shoot out over thirty feet during one growing season and it can be a major nuisance. Open land in western Washington and Oregon contained large masses of these bothersome but productive pests, Seattle having more than its share. The Himalaya blackberry ripens in August and September allowing a natural harvest sequence to the native blackberry that ripens in June and July in lower elevations. The more-seedy Evergreen or cut-leaf blackberry, introduced from England in the 1850s, although less aggressive, was widespread, also. Salal and Oregon grape berries, although earlier quite popular with the Native-Americans, were abundant also but seldom harvested.

Huckleberries abounded and also were an important food source. Red huckleberry abounded in lower cut over areas west of the Cascades, frequently establishing itself on rotting stumps and down logs. The berries looked much like salmon eggs and had a tart flavor that limited their fresh consumption, but they made excellent jelly and pies. The more palatable blue huckleberry tastes much like a domestic blueberry, but its unique, sharper flavor makes it greatly preferred. It is found at higher elevations throughout the Pacific Northwest and was a staple for many migrants who settled in their proximity. Besides large domestic use, the wild blue huckleberry enjoyed immense commercial demand, leading many Depression bound Pacific Northwest residents to supplement their income by harvesting the succulent berry. The wild blue huckleberry harvest is still vital today, featuring an increasing number of commercial harvesters who expect at least eighteen dollars a gallon for them.[37] The wild huckleberry is so prevalent in northern Idaho that it is honored as the official state fruit. Priest Lake and Bonners Ferry host annual Huckleberry Festivals.

Domestic vegetables and fruits supplied a healthy and wide variety of nutrition. Almost everybody maintained a substantial garden. Early producers such as peas, beans, lettuce, cabbage, rhubarb, and squash grew readily. Root crops such as potatoes, carrots, beets, onions and turnips could be consumed fresh, stored, or canned. Most households canned hundreds of glass jars of fruits, berries, vegetables and meat for year around use. Canning season usually began with peas and possibly rhubarb in spring and ended with apples, meat and root crops in the fall.

Abandoned orchards were widespread and their crop usually was picked freely by those not fortunate enough to have an orchard of their own. Apples of diverse varieties, pears, cherries, and plums were the most common fruits. They were consumed fresh or canned and in some cases, culls were fed to livestock and poultry. Several varieties of apples stored well so could be available throughout the winter.[38]

Fish and other wildlife also supplemented many larders. Salmon, the equivalent of the buffalo to the indigenous population of the Pacific Northwest, still abounded. All Pacific salmon return to their home streams to spawn and die. There they are especially vulnerable to predators including man. Although not as thick as in pioneer days when farmers used pitchforks to pitch them out of smaller streams by the dozens for food and fertilizer, the runs remained fairly substantial. Spawning salmon varied in quality, becoming bruised and tasteless during their spawning run, but salmon still fairly fresh from the sea were quite acceptable and fairly easy to catch with a gaff or a spear, an illegal but common practice. Other freshwater fish, especially trout, provided additional food. Those who were fortunate enough to live close to saltwater beaches could rely on an abundance of shellfish. "When the tide is out, the table is set," was a popular pioneer slogan. Deer thrived on the brush and vines of cut over land and were quite abundant. Legal deer hunting was one of the favorite and much anticipated sports in the Pacific Northwest and a good deal of poaching also occurred. Many of the recent migrants took little interest, however, possibly because many did not hunt deer while living on the plains.[39] Additionally, hunting rifles, unlike a spear or a gaff, were quite expensive and considered an unnecessary luxury.

In 1946, Betty McDonald's's *The Egg and I* (1946) became a blockbuster book. A humorous memoir of her and her new husband's attempt to establish a chicken farm on the northern Olympic Peninsula near Port Townsend. (1927–1931) It bore striking similarities to the experience of later rural Dust Bowl migrants. The movie version, starring Claudette Colbert and Fred MacMurray, was a hit also. Besides cleverly portraying the many challenges and frustrations of establishing a successful operation with no modern conveniences, McDonald aptly describes the area's vegetation and physical characteristics. The McDonald's cultural and financial depth was much greater than the typical migrant, though. Her husband had graduated from an agricultural college and she came from an affluent New York background. McDonald's father, a mining engineer, had established the family in Seattle's elite Laurelhurst neighborhood.

McDonald's upper middle class viewpoint did not mesh with the locals, whom she tended to mock and belittle. Her approach was similar to that of Presbyterian minister's son Erskine Caldwell whose ribald fictional accounts of Southern poverty typified by *Tobacco Road* (1932) and *God's Little Acre* (1933) were national hits but considered atrocious misrepresentations by many Southerners. *Egg and I* characters "Ma and Pa Kettle" evolved into a movie series that portrayed the rural northwest as a haven for backward hicks. This image was not totally untrue, but not as harsh as portrayed by the young woman who left her husband and the chicken farm in 1931, returning to Seattle and future fame. McDonald's former rural neighbors still deeply resent her unflattering portrayal of them.

Our family returned to a similar rural lifestyle by moving to the Puget Sound area in 1937 when Lloyd's job at the paper mill in Post Falls ran out. We moved to grandfather Karel's place on Waddell Creek, about fourteen miles south of Olympia and about two miles northwest of the village of Littlerock. Founded along the Black River in 1853 by New Englanders who mostly came via the Oregon Trail, the town became a thriving, raucous logging center with the coming of a railroad in 1890. At one time Littlerock boasted seven shingle mills seven saloons, a confectioner's store, general store, post office, hotel and livery stable, a barber shop, several garages, and a train depot. But the area's magnificent old growth forest was depleted and Littlerock was in rapid decline as symbolized by the 1932 closure of its high school, which existed for only a decade. One peripheral legacy of the high school was a new grange hall. R. A. Alm, the high school principal, was also the first Grange master and took the lead finishing a hall the same year the high school closed.[40]

The Mima Mounds, scattered on some thirty thousand prairie-like acres west and south of Littlerock, were the most significant geographical factor in the neighborhood. Sometimes described as "Paul Bunyan's Potato Patch," they consisted of regularly spaced hills, about thirty feet across and four to six feet high. Although thought to be a result of glacial action, no definitive explanation for the mounds exists. The Washington State Department of Natural Resources recently has established a 445 acre park known as the Mima Mounds Natural Area.

Our new home had no modern conveniences, no neighbors in sight, and the climate and vegetation were vastly different. The trip from Spokane took all day, so it was dark when we arrived. Mary, accustomed to the openness of North Dakota and eastern Washington, recalls that it seemed as if we traveled through a dark jungle to get to the house. Our family of four used one large bedroom; Karel and sons slept in the other. The main room ran the distance of the two bedrooms and served as a combined kitchen family room and dining room. Kerosene lamps provided illumination and wood burning stoves were used for heating and cooking. Mary did most of the cooking and housework as the young men came and went seeking work. Males wore bib overalls and females wore dresses, usually hand sewn from flour and feed sacks that were decorated with different patterns as a sales incentive.

Seasonal agriculture work, principally in haying and berry production, provided most of the income at first. The surplus of drought-migrant labor had a depressing effect upon wages and working conditions, a situation not always appreciated by established residents.[41] Wages for berry picking, mainly strawberries, were based on the amount picked and a good picker made about two dollars a day. Women were naturally better at this and male adults shunned picking if at all possible, preferring maintenance jobs such as hoeing and hauling. One dollar a day plus lunch was the standard wage for farm work such as haying, harvesting, and planting. A neighboring Norwegian widow who ran a fairly substantial dairy provided much of the farm work for the Dalebouts. Cream sales provided her main source of income. The North Dakotans fell and cut up a huge old growth Douglas fir on her property in 1937 that provided several years' supply of firewood for two households.

If the little colony of migrants suffered misgivings about their hard scrabble, threadbare lot, it was well camouflaged. A positive, good-natured optimism prevailed, combined with expectance that their new environment would ultimately provide an adequate living standard. No one went hungry but we did live "lean." Overall, the diet featured more variety than North Dakota's. Potatoes, bread and oatmeal still dominated, though. In season, fruit from several large orchards, wild and domestic berries and nuts, and vegetables from a carefully tended garden balanced the menu. Produce also was canned for the off season and stored in an excellent root cellar along with bushels of potatoes, carrots and beets. Animal products were scarce—a few chickens provided eggs and an occasional chicken dinner. Homegrown pork supplied most of the meat, though. It was eaten fresh, canned, smoked or preserved in a barrel of lard. Although deer were plentiful, venison never appeared on the table. Fish from Waddell Creek frequently did, however. The salmon run was eagerly anticipated. Returning salmon negotiated the Chehalis and Black Rivers before entering Waddell Creek. Prone to flooding because its drainage area almost all had been logged, it was more like a small river from October through June. By that time many salmon were badly beat up and inedible. Brighter fish were gaffed or speared, however, and were quite palatable either fresh or smoked in a smokehouse that was there when Karel purchased the place.

Recreation focused on activities that were inexpensive and close to home. Single deck pinochle was the favorite past time with much repartee and occasional good-humored attempts to bend the rules. Some pick up ball games were organized using home made vine maple bats and the larger "kitten ball" or softball, but lack of an adequate playing field hindered that activity. In the warmer months everybody fished for trout and women and children swam in the creek almost daily. The men rarely swam. On special occasions, such as the Fourth of July, everyone in the neighborhood gathered for a picnic along the creek. Indoor gatherings frequently were highlighted by violin or accordion music.

Later, the Fourth of July gathering shifted to Millersylvania State Park at Deep Lake, about six miles east of the Waddell Creek community. John H. Miller (Johann Mueller), a former general in the Austrian Army, willed the 842–acre site to the state as a park in 1921. It served as the area headquarters for the CCC in the Great Depression. During the period 1934–1935 the CCC built four kitchen shelters, 125 unsheltered and thirty sheltered picnic tables, a bathhouse, a swimming dock, trails, water fountains and other improvements. The park was used for end of school picnics by many rural schools, 4–H summer camps and a variety of other functions. Entrance for public use was free as was true for all 125 Washington state parks and other publicly owned recreational areas, furnishing a great benefit for everyone, but especially the underprivileged.

There were very few books and magazines and no daily newspaper so communication with the outside world relied upon a battery powered radio, which picked broadcasts out of the air for free. In the 1930s, the radio, whose higher priced versions were encased in elaborate wood cabinets, frequently served as the centerpiece of living room furniture. By the late 1930s an estimated 90 percent of the nation's homes had radios, arguably creating the first true mass culture in the world.[42] Newscasts and President Roosevelt's Fireside Chats were followed closely, as were daytime serial broadcasts such as *Our Gal Sunday*, *Kate Smith* and *Ma Perkins*. Favorite adult evening programs included *Amos'n Andy*, *Jack Benny*, *The Grand Old Opry* and *Phil Harris*. Children were fascinated by *Jack Armstrong*: *The All-American Boy*, *Little Orphan Annie*, *Flash Gordon*, *Tom Mix*, *The Lone Ranger, The Green Hornet,* and a number of others. The weekly boxing matches, broadcast live from Madison square Garden, held special interest. All were elated when Joe Louis, "The Brown Bomber," demolished the German, Max Schmeling, in their storied 1939 rematch. Other than the late arriving *Grapes of Wrath* (1940), movies, newsreels and other media played down Great Depression difficulties.[43]

Baseball was the pre-eminent sport on the Great Plains. And the Pacific Coast League Seattle Rainiers, known as the most popular minor league team in the United States, quickly became radio favorites with Washington's Plains migrants. With major league baseball confined to sixteen teams in ten cities northeast of the Mississippi River, the Pacific Coast League had emerged as the strongest of the many minor leagues of the 1930s. Pacific Coast League boosters viewed the league as a third major league and derisively referred to the major leagues as the "Eastern League." The mild climate allowed for a longer season and complemented implementation of night baseball. All Pacific Coast League parks were lighted for night baseball by the late 1930s. A series usually consisted of five night games and a double header on Sunday. Attendance for weekday night games almost tripled that of weekday day games.[44]

Because minor league teams were not forced to sell their stars to the major leagues, many talented players spent their entire careers in the Pacific Coast League. They preferred to stay because they enjoyed their status in the league and earned considerably more than paid for rookies or substitutes in the major leagues.[45] Sale of outstanding players to major league teams, nevertheless, was an important source of revenue. A few Pacific Coast League standouts who later gained fame in the major leagues included: Joe DiMaggio (San Francisco Seals), Ted Williams (San Diego Padres), Frankie Crosetti (San Francisco Seals), Fred Hutchinson (Seattle Rainiers), Vernon "Lefty" Gomez (San Francisco Seals), Ernie Lombardi (Oakland Acorns) and Bobby Doerr (Hollywood Stars and San Diego Padres).

Brewer Emil Sick purchased the Seattle franchise in 1937, supposedly upon the advice of his friend teamster union leader Dave Beck. Sick immediately built a modern stadium that held up to 16,000. The Rainiers, named for Sick's beer brand name, not the mountain, won the pennant in 1939, 1940, and 1941. Their spirited rivalry with the Portland Beavers, who had won six league champions between 1906 and 1936, usually attracted sellout crowds at both ballparks. Lucky Beaver Stadium, known by locals as the Vaughn Street Stadium, was an ancient wooden firetrap with buckets of sand at the end of each aisle to prevent fires. From 1938 to 1952 the Rainiers led the minor leagues in attendance.

The Rainiers' roster included stars such as Hutchinson, Jo Jo White, Bill Lawrence, and "Kewpie" Dick Barrett. They also featured Leo Lassen., an irrepressible, unique, colorful broadcaster known as "The Voice of Summer." Lassen was a legend in the Seattle area. He had a sharp, high pitched, staccato style backed by an encyclopedic knowledge of the game and a passion for accuracy. Although he read the classics and could compose and play classical music on the piano, he only talked baseball. Lassen's dramatic style was typified by his description of a homerun, "It's a long high fly ball back to the left field wall—BACK, BACK, BACK AND IT'S OVERRR!" A play at first base was "closer than the wallpaper on the wall." Almost every youth in the area had an imitation of Lassen who was on the air from 1931 to 1960.[46] Now nationally renowned sportscaster Keith Jackson replaced Lassen. Then Jackson was a recent graduate of Washington State College's Edward R. Murrow School of Communication.

The Dutch have a special relationship with Christmas and St. Nicholas (or Sinterklaas) and no effort to observe the holiday was spared. A fine fir Christmas tree was carefully decorated and lit with real candles and presents for all were placed under the tree. Relatives and friends gathered at Karel's house for Christmas Eve. After everyone enjoyed a hearty dinner, Karel appeared in a complete Santa Claus outfit to distribute gifts and good cheer. He relished his role and it seemed everyone had a terrific time. In spite of the interest in Christmas, no one participated in organized religious activities.

Although they tended to stay to themselves, the migrants were accepted readily by working class neighbors and associates. Imbued with a tradition of hard work, self-reliance, honesty and Great Plains neighborliness the migrants caused little friction. Relations with the business and professional community were more formal but not strained. Once the newcomers established their reliability, small general store owners quickly extended credit. Well-established community members displayed more indifference rather than open hostility. Many expressed virulent hostility to New Deal programs and organized labor, however. In this sense they directly opposed policies that most benefited the migrants.[47] Those with a steady income, moreover, tended to not even recognize the depression's existence. In a noted study of the children of the Great Depression one third of the women and more than half of the men said they were essentially unaware of the Great Depression. One whose father was employed steadily said he guessed the Depression was over when he was born in 1928! [48]

Olympia had a large cannery that employed hundreds of women during summer and fall, running three shifts a day at peak periods. The canning schedule was geared to the ripening of berries and fruit with demand for labor peaking in late summer and early fall when trainloads of pears and apples from eastern Washington were processed for the world market. Standard pay of thirty-four cents an hour for an eight-hour shift attracted many more candidates than could be employed. Hundreds of women lined up and the lead supervisor walked down the line indicating her choices by pointing her finger and saying "you." Mary and several neighbors were selected much to their delight. As a condition of employment they were required to join the CIO. After canning season ended, Mary usually worked about a week picking turkeys for Thanksgiving. She had to be careful not to exceed the maximum income allowed before WPA rules disqualified him. That limitation soon ended when he became a railroad section hand for Weyerhaeuser, staying in camp during the week and returning home on weekends.

In 1938, Lloyd paid seventy dollars for forty acres of cutover timberland near Waddell Creek. The land had once been the home site of a local pioneer family, whose only legacy was two mature apple trees, a hand dug well, a small rock garden, and some rusted out machinery. The surrounding area reminded one of a World War I battlefield scenc. Enormous blackened old growth snags and a few living old-growth Douglas fir dominated the scene. Old growth stumps, notched for springboards that allowed fallers to avoid the tree's butt swell, were everywhere. Several acres were stacked three or four feet high with the blackened remains of second growth fir ruined by a recent fire. Young trees mingled with a thick brush cover, featuring a wide variety of plants and flowers. Salal, Oregon grape, hazelnut and bracken fern constituted much of the brush. Flowers included trillium, bleeding heart, Indian paintbrush, lupine, skunk cabbage, columbine, wild rose, fireweed and many others, creating a botanist's delight. Old roads, still passable in many cases, crisscrossed the area.

Lloyd obtained lumber for a basic house by logging with a Model A Ford and borrowing a neighbor's truck to haul the logs to the mill. Much of the logging was done with a crosscut saw, an ax, a few wedges, and a peavey to roll the logs. Using a home made shillelagh and a steel froe Lloyd split cedar shakes from downed old growth logs found on the property. Lumber and other building materials were also salvaged from Bordeaux's recently abandoned logging town, called Hollywood. Later, wall telephones from Hollywood were used for a private neighborhood-only hookup. Ed Moline helped build a brick chimney for the wood stoves. Throughout the war years the house had no electricity or plumbing. When the well went dry in the summer, water had to be hauled from the creek.

We started with some goats and a few chickens. The goats soon gave way to a small dairy herd. Other than brush and small trees, very little pasture existed on the property, but it was located in an area with an open herd law, which meant the cattle could be allowed to run free and property owners protected their crops with fences. They migrated to the open fields of an abandoned farm along Waddell Creek and usually could be found there, but occasional searches for wayward animals provided some interesting adventures.

The property was developed substantially as the family's income improved. The well was professionally drilled and never ran dry again. In addition to the original house and small barn/chicken house a large barn, a huge building designed for producing fryer and broiler chickens, a two car garage and several other outbuildings were built. New amenities included running water and electricity generated by a gasoline home generator. The place deteriorated rapidly after we moved out in 1953, selling at a modest price. Barely a trace of fifteen years of effort and investment remains. Several families retained their property much longer, though, and realized substantial value increases, as holds true for the twelve-acre farm where the Dewing family moved. Ironically developers have built luxury homes in the immediate vicinity of the original home and the need for accurate surveys revealed most of the family buildings were outside the true property lines.

Lloyd transferred to Weyerhaeuser's Olympia plywood plant in 1940 and worked there for twenty-five years. Before and after retirement he successfully invested in real estate. Always a farmer at heart, Lloyd became one of the better known polled Hereford breeders in Washington.

Mary took a full-time job at the Cedar Creek State forestry nursery in 1950. After working in the field for several years, she became secretary of the new L. T. Webster nursery, retiring in 1977. Mary also actively participated in the cattle operation and remains remarkably active and productive at age 93.

The coming of the war in Europe ended the Great Depression, and the other young North Dakotans quickly assimilated into the burgeoning economy. After working briefly for the Bordeaux Logging Company as it finished its Black Hills logging, Uncle Cornelius took a job as a bucker at Weyerhaeuser's nearby Vale logging operation. Uncle John had already been working for the Northern Pacific Railroad for several years and stayed until retirement, establishing a substantial poultry operation on his permanent location where Waddell Creek flows into the Black River. Uncle Peter took over management of his new wife's family dairy farm, a pioneer eighty-acre tract along the Black River, near his brother John's property. Several years after the war Peter and his family moved to Sweet Home, Oregon, where he found employment in the plywood industry. Uncle Joe married John's sister-in-law and returned to North Dakota to farm. Those employed in the timber industry were required to join the union and benefited from its quest for fair wages and equitable working conditions and benefits, but they were anything but incendiary revolutionaries. Happy to hold jobs with a decent income, they were punctual, hard working, and loyal to their employer.

Karel had become a citizen in the 1920s, but his three older sons, John, Joe, and Cornelius were born in the Netherlands and had never acquired citizenship. This became an issue with the national draft law passed in 1940 and also in a far more practical sense because Karel wanted to visit his brother-in-law, John Westdorp, in British Columbia and Cornelius always drove. If any of his three sons left the United States, they, as non-citizens, would have a problem returning. Karel knew that newly elected governor Arthur Langlie had once lived in Kermit, North Dakota, near his farm in the Noonan area, and made an appointment at the governor's office to obtain his sons' citizenship. When he arrived, the sturdy, mustachioed Dutchman, dressed in bib overalls, high-topped black work shoes, a clean work shirt, and carrying his battered gray felt dress hat, immediately was ushered into Langlie's office. The two spent almost an hour discussing developments and mutual acquaintances in North Dakota and the citizenship matter was taken care of immediately. Karel enjoyed telling the story of his visit with Langlie and was most grateful. But he had seen enough of life's vicissitudes that he never overplayed it, which would be out of character for him, anyway.

In his later years, Karel moved to Littlerock to a small house adjoining Cornelius's. It was just down the road from his brother, Nick, who had also moved there from Spokane after the war. Karel died in humble circumstances in 1959. He had led his family west, though, and his human legacy is enormous. Ultimately, there were eighteen grandchildren whose many children are now having grandchildren and great grandchildren of their own. Brother Nicholas died in 1971 leaving an even larger number of direct descendants. Most of their descendants still live in Western Washington and enjoy a comfortable lifestyle far removed from Depression era poverty.

Although most of these Dust Bowl descendants meet middle class criteria such as income, education, and housing, lingering, deep-seated "scars that do not show" remain. This is especially the case for the generation born in the late 1920s or 1930s, who either moved to the Pacific Northwest or were born there. The adults who moved had matured in the rural, small town environment of the Northern Great Plains. They were "planfully competent" by sociologist John Clausen's definition in his *American Lives: Looking Back at the Children of the Great Depression*. Clausen's criteria included self-confidence, dependability and intellectual investment. These qualities equipped the adolescent with an ability to accurately evaluate personal efforts and recognize options and maintain the self-discipline to pursue those goals. This individual could also accurately interpret the intentions and responses of others.[49] Migrants who reached maturity before the 1930s in most cases had acquired this competence although many were temporarily among the "worthy poor." Their children faced an uphill social and economic struggle that challenged their character and perseverance. Generally they were on the outside looking in at the established institutions and they had to make their way in spite of poorer housing, clothing, transportation, and cultural opportunities. Established family values provided the rudder that helped guide them through an extremely adverse environment.

Medical and dental problems among young and old were neglected. Inadequate diet and lack of professional attention, either because it was not available or not affordable, took a heavy toll. Dental caries, pyorrhea and crooked teeth were much too common. Dentures provided the ultimate solution for many and some migrants required them while they were still teenagers. Medical examinations that might allow early detection of illness were unknown for most. Much of the health assessments for the young came from the schools, who were concerned about communicable diseases and where inoculations for smallpox and diphtheria were administered.[50]

Migrants who settled in rural areas generally attended small rural elementary schools that had inadequate physical facilities and faculty. One journalist caustically and inaccurately in most cases described the migrants as "a horde of wretched families with children who never saw the inside of a school."[51] Most migrant children attended elementary school but many encountered difficulties at the secondary level. Students fortunate enough to have a rural high school in their district could adjust much easier than those forced to commute to urban high schools. In comparison to their urbane counterparts, they were poorly prepared to compete in basic subjects such as science, mathematics, English and history. Participation in extracurricular activities such as sports and fine arts not only was limited by lack of preparation, but also by the physical distance from the individual's home to the activity. Furthermore, urban high schools of the 1940s and 1950s catered to the middle class values of their communities and seldom went out of their way to accommodate rural students.[52] Communities like Olympia, Everett,. Bellingham, and Vancouver had only one public high school, which encouraged compliance with the status quo.

Most school personnel did not directly disparage children from lower socioeconomic backgrounds. Their emphasis on status and cultural conformity, nevertheless, made the disadvantaged painfully aware of their inadequacies and challenged their sense of pride and identity. Faced with different standards and expectations many rebelled against the rural lifestyle that had worked for their parents. After finishing the required eighth grade education many students in rural schools dropped out. High school students also were flunked out at a high rate and, although no formal studies exist, it seemed as if the failure rate for those from rural areas was much higher.[53]

The increased tax burden for schools created by migrant children received considerable attention. Local forest historian Margaret Felt wrote, "They moved in with a family and demanded construction and/or maintenance of a road, and also presented the county and school district with the problem of getting their children back and forth to school."[54] "In *Land Use, Environment and Social Change: The Shaping of Island County, Washington*, Richard White, now Margaret Byrne Professor of History at Stanford, said, "The social cost of these farms went well beyond the relief payments and personal suffering. Because of the scattered nature of much cut over land settlement, the cost of providing essential services such as roads and schools, was often far higher than in the more prosperous regions."[55] The significant migrant contributions in property taxes, sales taxes, support of local business and industry and the infusion of more, mostly able students into declining school systems, has not been recognized adequately.[56] Because of population depletion and a dramatic decline in tax revenue, rural schools in the Pacific Northwest were being closed and consolidated rapidly. Even with the Dust Bowl migration, the rate of population growth between 1930 and 1940 was the lowest in any decade of the twentieth century.[57] Migrant children not only supplied much-needed enrollment and a fresh outlook for the schools, but their children and their children's children continue their support. Littlerock elementary school, for example, enrolled its first North Dakota migrant children in 1938 and since has had them and their descendants enrolled on an almost continual basis. Most of the roads, school bus routes and instructional facilities already existed before the migrants came, and the increased use they caused barely increased the local tax burden, which should be balanced against the increased revenues from the newcomers.

Growing up in rural isolation with limited socialization opportunities also affected choice of marriage partners and the chances of success in this all-important venture. Married couples who migrated rarely parted, but, based on empirical evidence only, their descendants seem to have experienced a higher than normal divorce rate. Marriage often occurred among individuals who had not known each other for long and whose families in many cases had never met. Unlike the rural heritage of the previous generation marriages now faced the pressures of urbanization, industrialization, both working, women's changing roles and easier divorce. These factors along with disparate backgrounds, tastes, and values often led to separation.[58]

If early doubts persisted about the benefits of the Dust Bowl migration to the Pacific Northwest, they have long since vanished. The migrants made a relatively seamless adjustment, demonstrated strong family values, an impressive work ethic, strong character, and a sense of tolerance. They sank deep roots and stayed, leaving a record of remarkable achievement. Of the many successful migrants a few outstanding examples follow.

Dr. Donald Strandness, Jr. moved to Olympia from Bowman, North Dakota, in 1938 at age ten. Strandness, an outstanding student and a star gymnast and halfback, graduated from Olympia High School in 1946. He starred in the classroom and on the gridiron at Pacific Lutheran University in Tacoma and went on to graduate from the University of Washington School of Medicine in 1954. From the early 1960s until his retirement in 1995 Strandness served with great distinction on the medical faculty of his alma mater becoming head of vascular surgery. Characterized as having a "magnetic personality, a twinkle in his eye, a broad smile, infectious laugh, great sense of humor, and a commanding presence, he was known as "the father of non-invasive vascular diagnosis," a technique for diagnosing obstructions of veins and arteries. Strandness published 176 book chapters, 451 scientific papers, fifteen books, and served on the editorial board of thirteen journals, winning numerous awards and professional offices. He credited much of his success to his Norwegian Lutheran upbringing in North Dakota where the "rules of God and the fallibility of man" were continually impressed upon him.[59]

North Dakota native Lois Phillips Hudson joined the English faculty at the University of Washington in 1969. Hudson spent her first nine years on a farm near Jamestown, North Dakota. Her reputation was based upon *Bones of Plenty* (1962) her highly regarded biographical novel about the economic injustice of trying to survive as a wheat rancher in drought stricken North Dakota. Her companion non-fiction work *Reapers of the Dust: A Prairie Chronicle* relates personal experiences mainly in North Dakota. A chapter, "Children of the Harvest," however, deals with the family's migration from North Dakota to Fox Island, Washington, (just west of Tacoma) in 1937 when she was nine and with their adjustment to their new home. Hudson effusively praised her watery, lush new environment. She practically lived on berries and fruit during her less than a month's stay. The family purchased a tent and camping equipment to work in the harvest, first in the Yakima Valley, then at Wenatchee. Hudson wrote astute descriptions of the life of itinerant farm laborers and the process of harvesting hops and fruit for minimal wages. As a ten-year old she complied with the mandatory school attendance law and related the harsh difficulties and outright discrimination schools imposed on North Dakota "Okies." At Wenatchee, Hudson was told she was the first child of itinerant laborers placed in the "A" (best) group. The family settled on a twenty-acre farm in Sammamish Valley that they bought for $1800 in back taxes. Hudson's mother taught school at Redmond and earned a master's degree in remedial reading from the University of Washington.[60]

Born in 1922, Fran Agnes moved to Wenatchee from Haynes, in southwestern North Dakota, during the Great Depression when his father found work there with the WPA. After graduating from Wenatchee High School, Agnes joined the Army Air Force in 1940. He survived the Bataan Death March and served three and one half years as a Japanese Prisoner of War. After the war Agnes returned to Wenatchee briefly. Saying he "did not want to pick apples the rest of life" Agnes re-enlisted in the Air Force, retiring as a captain in 1961. Agnes worked for the Washington State Job Service until 1987, becoming actively involved in veterans issues. He was instrumental in establishing the Tahoma National Cemetery in Kent in 1997 and played a key role in gaining legislation to guarantee a color guard at veteran's funerals and helping veterans obtain disability payments.[61]

Lennie Husa, the youngest of the Husa children, graduated from Rochester High School in 1943, joined the army and served in the Europe with the 87th infantry division. Husa attended Washington State College on the GI Bill, obtaining a degree in Agricultural Engineering in 1950. He spent his career with the United States Department of Agriculture and Soil Conservation Service in Washington State. After retirement Husa became president of the Northwest Chapter of the Finlandia Foundation.[62]

Born on a Divide County wheat farm near Ambrose, North Dakota, in 1920 Aggie Andreason Willis moved to Port Angeles, Washington, with her family in the early 1930s. In 1941, young Aggie bought the "Doghouse," a restaurant with six stools and two booths for $250.00. Aggie had virtually no knowledge of the restaurant business but she was a fast learner and a trim, attractive blond with a tooth paste smile and an outgoing personality. With advice from the previous owner, she tripled her business in two months. Between 1941 and 1961, Aggie's grew to fifty motel units with an indoor swimming pool, a coffee shop, and a popular restaurant and cocktail lounge. In 1946, she married Jim Willis, a chief petty officer in the navy. In 1961, Aggie was the only woman who sat on the Board of Directors of the Washington State Restaurant Association.[63] She was inducted into the National Restaurant Association Hall of Fame later. At her untimely death from cancer in 1975 Aggie's motel had 120 rooms and the restaurant had been further expanded.[64]

Of the many educators in Port Angeles who grew up on the Great Plains, George Ellis stood out. After his family's sheep operations in South Dakota, Colorado and Wyoming failed in the early thirties they moved to the small town of Rainier, Washington, where employment was available at Weyerhaeuser's new Vale operation. Ellis graduated from Rainier High School in 1932 and worked his way through college with logging jobs in the summer.

In 1939 he started his education career in a one room schoolhouse near Shelton. After serving as an elementary principal at several schools in the Olympia area, Ellis became an elementary principal at Port Angeles in 1945. His homespun manner, good judgment, and hard work moved him steadily upward in the administrative ranks. Ellis became the junior high school principal in 1953, the high school principal in 1960, district curriculum director in 1965 and the district superintendent in 1968.[65]

Hardly a typical migrant, Alfred Fleury grew up in Zurich, Switzerland, and liked to tell of his two-hour visit with Albert Einstein in a bar where Einstein tried to explain the theory of relativity to him. After earning a degree in business from New York University, Fleury moved to South Dakota and started a hotel in 1928. When it went bankrupt in 1930 Fleury who described himself as "now an Okie" moved to Seattle. There he bought a substantial lot on the south end of Mercer Island for $1000., Fleury used a twelve-foot rowboat to go back and forth to improve his lot. The Fleury family moved to Mercer Island in 1933, where he became known as "Mr. Everything." After a stint working for the WPA, first as a laborer, then as timekeeper and accountant, Fleury became the storekeeper for the Richfield Oil Corporation Construction Department. Mercer Island had a population of only twelve hundred when the Lacey Murrow floating bridge, connecting it with Seattle, opened on July 2, 1940. Fleury helped build the infrastructure for the now booming community. He was active in developing a library, roads, schools, a fire department, and served on the first City Council. His wife also took an active role in the community.[66]

Royal Donelson was born in Farnum, a small community in southwestern Nebraska in 1927. He and his family moved to Bothell, Washington, in 1937 where he graduated from high school in 1944. After serving over twenty years in the United States Army Signal Corps, Donelson returned to Bothell where he opened a shoe store on Main Street. He became a prominent leader in the Bothell business community, serving nine years on the city council, including four years as mayor. For over almost four decades Donelson helped promote a number of Bothell's significant on-going community activities.[67]

Robert "Bud" Olson was born in Columbus, North Dakota, in 1918. After spending his childhood in nearby Minot, Olson hopped a freight train to the West Coast and settled in Everett with his father. He won a basketball scholarship to at Washington State College where he led the team in scoring from 1938 to 1940. After military service in World War II Olson embarked on an outstanding career in sales in Seattle.[68]

Ida (Hays) Rhonemus was born in 1913 in Streeter, North Dakota, the seventh of eleven siblings. She loved to tell the story about hopping a freight train in North Dakota during the Great Depression with a brother and an uncle. They rode to Seattle in a boxcar. Ida died in October 2005 survived by three children, five grandchildren and four great grandchildren.[69]

This small sampling of the achievements of Dust Bowl migrants from the Northern Great Plains provides insight into their widely diverse contributions. Some, like Fleury, were thoroughly prepared before migrating. Others, like Strandness, Hudson, Willis, Olson, Ellis, Husa, and Donelson acquired much of their formal education in their new location. For many other migrants the first several years in the Pacific Northwest were focused on the hard business of surviving. As opportunity presented itself precipitated by international politics, and enhanced by impressive natural resources and a well-established infrastructure such as transportation facilities, timber, agriculture, shipbuilding and airplane manufacturing, most eagerly took advantage and permanently established themselves.

April 22, 1940, the United States House of Representatives appointed Democrat California Congressman John Tolan to head a five member committee, The Select Committee to Investigate Interstate Migration of Destitute Citizens. Critics might suggest the timing was a year or two late and publication of *The Grapes of Wrath* forced the issue. Regardless, it resulted in an outstanding analysis of a situation that President Roosevelt told Congress ranked with the rise of unemployment as the most important unforeseen factor to intrude into the federal relief situation. Tolan's background made him well qualified to head the committee. Born in Minnesota, he had moved to Anaconda, Montana, at age 20; graduated from the University of Kansas law school and practiced law in Montana until moving to Oakland in 1914. A nation-wide effort, the committee traveled 20,000 miles, interviewed 500 witnesses, and recorded three million words of testimony, published in eleven volumes in April 1941.[70]

As the committee's title implied, migrants received sympathetic treatment. Migrants were encouraged to discuss their problems and goals in their own words. The committee concluded that most tended to be younger families who migrated for economic reasons rather than for better welfare which was difficult to obtain locally because most states based eligibility for assistance on the number of years the individual has spent in the community. Most migrants did not become transient farm laborers, but settled permanently in their new locations within a year.[71] As resident unemployed, transients could be eligible for federally funded work projects such as WPA, CCC, and others. For many these federal programs provided the crucial economic base needed to become re-established.[72]

By early 1941, with war raging in Europe and Asia, the United States had emerged from the Depression spurred by an enormous increase in defense spending and war contracts. The commission noted the dramatic increase in employment in explosives, chemicals, aircraft, ships and machine tools and urged decentralization of manufacturing for strategic reasons and also to provide employment for workers forced out of agriculture. The commission noted that in World War I almost all of the war contracts went to states in the triangle northeast of the Mississippi River.[73] Domination in airplane manufacture and an established ship building capacity combined with the war in the Pacific to assure the West Coast a prominent position in World War II defense spending. Now most employable workers migrating from the Great Plains to the West Coast were moving directly into defense oriented jobs, creating problems providing adequate housing, schools and other infrastructure in urban areas.[74]

NOTES

1. Frank J. Taylor, "Promised Land," *Reader's Digest* (February 1940): 29.
2. Ibid., 32: Paul H. Landis and Melvin Brooks. *Farm Labor in the Yakima Valley, Washington*, Bulletin Number 343 (Pullman, WA: Washington State College Agricultural Experiment Station, 1936).
3. Campbell G. Murphy. "Farmers on Cutover Timber Lands in Western Washington State" (master's thesis, University of Washington, 1943), 41.
4. Taylor, "Promised Land," 31.
5. Richard White, *Land Use, Environment and Social Change: The Shaping of Island County, Washington* (Seattle: University of Washington Press, 1980), 118.
6. Richard Neuberger, *Our Promised Land* (New York: Macmillan, 1938), 56.
7. White, *Land Use*, 140–41.
8. Murphy, "Farmers," 167–68.
9. Ibid., 20.
10. Calvin F. Schmid, *Social Trends in Seattle* (Seattle: University of Washington Press, 1944), 5.
11. Thomas Pressly and William Scofield, *Farm Real Estate Values in the United States by Counties, 1850–1859* (Seattle: University of Washington Press, 1965).
12. Murphy, "Farmers," 25.
13. White, *Land Use*, 126.
14. Ibid., 126–29; Author's experience.
15. Murphy, "Farmers," 192.
16. Margaret E. Felt, *Capitol Forest . . . the Forest that Came Back* (Olympia: Washington State Department of Natural Resources, 1975), 48–49.
17. Carsten Lien, *Olympic Battleground: The Power Politics of Timber Preservation* (Seattle: Mountaineers, 2000), 91.
18. White, *Land Use*, 120–21.
19. Washington State Planning Commission, *The Elma Survey* (Olympia: Washington State Planning Commission, 1941), 18. Hereafter referred to as *The Elma Survey.*
20. *The Elma Survey,* 157–58.

21. Ibid. 19; Murphy, "Farmers," 36–37.

22. Murphy, "Farmers," 162.

23. Ibid.

24. White, *Land Use*, 132–41; Murphy, "Farmers," Chapter 4, "The Lewis County Special Area Project of the FSA," 167–95. Lewis County contained an estimated one fourth of cut over land in western Washington suitable for agricultural development.

25. *The Elma Survey*, 71–83.

26. Ibid., 42.

27. Murphy, "Farmers," 48

28. Dwight Sanderson, *Research Memorandum on Rural Life in the Depression* (New York: Social Science Research Council, 1937), 44; Author's experience.

29. McWilliams, *Ill Fares*, 54.

30. *The Elma Survey*, 162–64.

31. Ibid., 32.

32. Pacific Northwest Regional Planning Commission, *Migration and the Development of Economic Opportunity in the Pacific Northwest. A Report Prepared in Cooperation with the Pacific Northwest Land Advisory Committee* (Portland: Pacific Northwest Regional Planning Commission, 1939), 9–10.

33. Sanderson, *Research*, 128; White, *Land Use*, 132–33.

34. *The Elma Survey*, 28.

35. Vivian C. Atterbury, *The Oregon Story* (Portland: Binfords and Mort, 1959), 37.

36. Author's experience; *The Elma Survery.*

37. Tan Vinh, "Hunt's on for Rare, Wild Huckleberry," *Seattle Times.* (14 August 2005), 1,18. Asking price for one gallon of wild huckleberries at the Roslyn, Washington, farmer's market was $28 on September 3, 2005.

38. Author's experience.

39. Rolland L. Dewing, "The Great Depression: A Dust Bowl Migrant's Memoir of Coming to the Pacific Northwest," *Columbia* 10 (Spring 1996): 29, 31.

40. Dale Rutledge, *Littlerock Community: United Methodist Church, Early History* (Littlerock, WA: Privately Printed, 1989); Bernadine Dafoe *History of Maytown, Washington* (South Thurston County Historical Society, 1985).

41. *Migration and the Development of Economic Opportunity*, 10.

42. Laura Hillenbrand, *Seabiscuit: An American Legend* (New York: Ballantine Books, 2003), 152–53.

43. Arthur F. Wertheim, "Relieving Social Tensions: Radio Comedy and the Great Depression," *Journal of Popular Culture* 10 (Winter 1976): 501–09; Ralph A. Brauer, "When the Lights Went Out: Hollywood, the Depression and the Thirties," *Journal of Popular Film and Television* 8 (Winter 1981): 18–29; Fred MacDonald, *Don't Touch that Dial: Radio Programming in American Life, 1920–1960* (Chicago: Nelson-Hall, 1979).

44. Charles C. Alexander, *Breaking the Slump: Baseball in the Depression Era* (New York: Columbia University Press, 2002), 24–25, 283.

45. Ibid., 12; Rookies and substitutes in the 1930s major leagues earned around $3500.

46. Emmett Watson, *Digressions of a Native Son* (Seattle: Pacific Institute, 1982), 73–93; See Also Steve Cohen, "Portland Baseball's Golden Age," in *Great Moments in Oregon History*, ed. Win McCormack and Dick Pintarich (Portland: New Oregon Publishers, 1987), 159–67.

47. Frank H. Lamb, *Fifty Years in Hoquiam: Memoirs of Frank H. Lamb* (Hoquiam, WA: Private Printing, 1948), 299.

48. John A Clausen, *American Lives: Looking Back at the Children of the Great Depression* (New York: The Free Press, 1993), 504.

49. Clausen, *American Lives*, Forward, 7.

50. Murphy, "Farmers,"148–49.

51. G. R. Leighton, "Seattle Washington: The Edge of the Last Frontier," *Harpers*, Part II (March 1939): 440.

52. Lois Phillips Hudson, *Reapers of the Dust: A Prairie Chronicle* (Boston, 1984); Author's experience.

53. See Clark, *Milltown: The Story of Everett. Washington*, (Seattle: University of Washington Press, 1970), 82–83. A large percentage of the author's rural elementary school classmates either did not go on to Olympia High School or dropped out quickly. James M. Gregory, *American Exodus: The Dust Bowl Migration and Okie Culture in California* (New York: Oxford University Press, 1989), 128–36—An excellent account of migrant children's difficulties in California's public schools.

54. Felt, *Capitol Forest*, 48.

55. White, *Land Use*, 134. Between 1930 and 1940 Island County had a net growth of 731.

56. Sanderson, *Research*, 43.

57. Calvin F. Schmid and Stanton E. Schmid, *Growth of Cities and Towns: State of Washington* (Olympia: State Planning and Community Affairs Agency, 1969), 7.

58. Glenda Riley, *Building and Breaking Families in the American West* (Albuquerque: University of New Mexico Press, 1996), 113–44.

59. David S. Sumner, "In Memoriam: Donald Eugene Strandness, Jr. M.D. (1928–2002)," *Annals of Vascular Surgery* 16–2 (2002): 139–40; Carol Ostrom, "Gene Strandness, 73, Innovative Surgeon," *Seattle Times*, 11 January 2002, B 8.

60. Hudson, *Reapers*, 99–113; E-mail from Lois Phillips Hudson November 9, 2005.

61. Sarah Wright, "Fran Agnes, World War II POW, Dies at 80," *Seattle Times*, 20 February 2003, B 4.

62. Lennie Husa, interview, February 2004; Lennie Husa e-mail to author, September 18, 2004.

63. John D. McCallum and Lorraine Wilcox Ross, *Port Angeles, U.S.A* (Seattle: Wood and Reber, 1961), 176–78.

64. Obituary of Aggie Willis, *Peninsula Daily News*, 15 October 1975.

65. Esther Webster, "Dedicated Educator Balances His Work with Education," *Peninsula Daily News* 1 September 1972; Obituary of George Ellis, *Peninsula Daily News* 28 February 1988. Special thanks to Beth Witters and Genie DeVine for research assistance. Telephone interviews with Ellis' widow Frances Hanson and his son Tom Ellis, November 2004.

66. Alfred J. Fleury, *Memoirs: Mercer Island, Washington, 1930–1975* (Mercer Island, WA: Privately Printed, about 1975) 105 mimeographed pages. Obtained for author by Barbara Pozner of the Renton Public Library; Judy Gellatly, *Mercer Island Heritage.* (Mercer Island, WA: Mercer Island Historical Society, 1989), 93–100.

67. Obituary of Royal Donelson, *Seattle Times*, 8 August 2005.

68. Obituary of Robert Olson, *Seattle Times*, 3 March 2006.

69. Obituary of Ida (Hays) Rhonemus, *Seattle Times*, 23 October 2005.

70. Henry H. Collins, Jr. *America's Own Refugees: Our 4,000,000 Homeless Migrants* (Princeton: Princeton University Press, 1941) an excellent summary of the Tolan Report.

71. John H. Tolan (Chairman). House Select Committee to Investigate the Interstate Migration of Destitute Citizens. Hearings on House Resolution 63 and House Resolution 491, 76th Congress, July 29–December 11, 1940, 11 volumes. (Washington DC: United States Government Printing Office, 1941), Volume 9, 3585–86. Hereafter referred to as Tolan Report.

72. Ibid., Volume 10, 4179.

73. Ibid., Volume 9, 3858–77.

74. Walter Nugent, *Into the West: The Story of Its People* (New York: Knopf, 1999) 255–59; David M Burerge, *Renton: Where Water Took Wing* (Chatsworth, CA: Windsor Publications, 1989; Ted Van Arsdal, *Vancouver on the Columbia* (Northridge, CA: Windsor Publications, 1986); Tolan Report, Volume 9, 3707–3709.

Chapter Eleven

Prosperity Returns

As late as November 1937, even though the economies in the Pacific Northwest were much improved, 292,740 in Idaho, Oregon and Washington registered as unemployed in a mail census. Field samples indicated these returns were low.[1] Prosperity seemed a distant goal, but war brought immediate, unprecedented economic growth for the entire nation, with the West Coast experiencing the most dramatic gains. Although California expanded most, Washington and Oregon also were poised for swift and continuous industrial expansion based on the necessities of a two front war. The four war years brought a maturation that would have taken much longer in peacetime.

Prosperity for the plains, still heavily dependent upon agriculture, came, too, with the return of good weather and high prices. The average gross income per farm in North Dakota climbed to $8,000 in 1945.[2] South Dakota's output of farm products increased 81 percent from 1940 through 1950, compared to a national rise of 31 percent over the same period.[3] After a decade of good times, though, as agriculture became more mechanized and the supply of commodities again met or exceeded demand, prosperity could not be sustained. Rural population waned as many continued to be forced off the farm for employment in cities and towns. Large numbers sought employment in the Pacific Northwest, but now, unlike the 1930s, most quickly found well paying jobs.[4]

By the end of the 1930s private entrepreneurs and enormous federal investment had established an infrastructure enabling massive economic growth in the Pacific Northwest. Grand Coulee and Bonneville dams symbolized the New Deal's big government approach. The Columbia River carried ten times more water than the Colorado, offering the nation's greatest potential for hydroelectric power and that was being realized. Almost unlimited inexpensive electricity from the monumental Columbia River dams supported economic activities from powering a farmer's milking machines to supplying the enormous electrical demands of newly established aluminum manufacturing plants.

Bonneville, built by the Army Corps of Engineers forty-two miles east of Portland for $43,900,000, was really not one but two dams situated cater-corner to each other on opposite sides of Bradford Island. It was started in 1933 and finished in 1937. Although sharing a border with Washington, Bonneville was considered "Oregon's Dam" by Oregonians. A Washington critic wrote, "The real difficulty in the economic distribution of Bonneville power is the fact that Oregon, and especially Portland, is suffering under the delusion that the Bonneville plant is for their exclusive advantage, and that Washington is uncommonly brazen in harboring the idea that they, too, should benefit by the development."[5] Bonneville was designed to generate electricity and included a lock that permitted navigation for ocean-going vessels as far as the Dalles. Puget Sound business leaders justifiably worried that their ports would lose trade from their eastern hinterland to Portland and lower Columbia cities. About five thousand men were employed in its construction at a wage rate considered among the best for the time. F. L. "Bud" Williams, an Oregon native, expressed his appreciation for being hired for $.75 an hour as a twenty year old electrical worker in 1935. He had been employed as a logger for $.15 an hour.[6] Williams' salary rested in the middle of a scale ranging from $.50 an hour for unskilled labor to $1.20 an hour for skilled labor.

Grand Coulee Dam, at completion the largest concrete structure in the world, twice as wide, more than twice the cost, and almost three times as high as Bonneville, still staggers the mind of first time visitors. Symbolic of New Deal willingness to finance projects private enterprise shunned and local government could not afford, Grand Coulee profoundly impacted the Pacific Northwest and heavily influenced the course of the nation as well. In 1933, after the state of Washington spent a little over $400,000 for preliminary planning, Roosevelt authorized $63 million in PWA funds for a low dam. In June 1935, FDR authorized expansion to a high dam at Grand Coulee. The Bureau of Reclamation, the Corps of Engineers natural rival, hired a consortium of private construction companies to build Grand Coulee Dam. They employed over 12,000 men and women supplemented by additional 2000 CCC and WPA men in seven major government camps. CCC and WPA cleared 54,000 acres for the Grand Coulee reservoir, moved 1200 buildings and other infrastructure and built roads and transmission lines.[7]

Completed in 1942, two years ahead of schedule, Grand Coulee generated more than fifteen billion kilowatt-hours of low priced electricity during World War II. A high voltage line built by the WPA and CCC to connect Grand

Coulee and Bonneville enabled creation of the Bonneville Power Administration (BPA). It supplied the enormous amounts of power required by the new aluminum plants scattered around the region and the war-inspired atomic energy works at Hanford. Bonneville Power supported myriad other industries and activities including the Boeing Aircraft Company in the Seattle area and Kaiser Shipyards in the Portland area. Although prices for electricity were kept lowest in the nation, the dams were able to pay their own way.

Generation of electricity became Grand Coulee's most significant role, instead of Roosevelt's concept of a "Planned Promised Land" for thousands of Dust Bowl migrants created by irrigated acreage in the Columbia Basin.[8] Canny Roosevelt surely realized the limitations of the Columbia Basin Project as a solution for the Dust Bowl tragedy. Previous Bureau of Reclamation projects had demonstrated clearly that the financial and technical demands of irrigation projects such as the Columbia Basin provided an opportunity for the few rather than the many.[9] Patently the almost unlimited hydro-electricity supply, which promoted industrial expansion, created jobs and enhanced national defense, held the most immediate promise. Roosevelt knew Harold Ickes, his influential Secretary of Interior, which includes the Bureau of Reclamation, had been won over by Boulder Dam (later Hoover Dam) and favored hydroelectricity more than irrigation.[10] The Bureau of Reclamation's farm requirement of at least $2000 in capital and previous experience in irrigation, moreover, precluded most migrants. As held true for the jobs involved in building the dam, most of the irrigated acreage went to individuals already established in the general area.

Portraying the controversial dam as a solution for the Dust Bowl migration made sense politically, though. Fort Peck in drought stricken eastern Montana, the greatest earthen dam in the world when completed, was as costly as Grand Coulee. It received far less criticism in part because as a WPA project it provided work for thousands of Great Plains drought victims. Also, Fort Peck originally was designed for navigation, water supply and flood control only although hydroelectric generators were added later. *Life* magazine gave Fort Peck favorable publicity when it debuted November 23, 1936, with famed photojournalist Margaret Bourke-White's photograph of the Fort Peck Dam project on the cover.[11]

Irrigated agricultural expansion remained the prime goal of local Grand Coulee supporters, such as Wenatchee newspaper publisher Rufus Woods and Washington Congressman William O'Sullivan. Citing the success of irrigated agriculture in the Yakima Valley, they envisioned the same for the much larger Columbia Basin. Fearing competition, farm interests in the Midwest and other areas including Washington State and Idaho opposed Grand Coulee as did private power providers in the area.[12] When Germany invaded Poland in 1939 the federal government made Grand Coulee a national defense project, officially switching the emphasis to electrical generation.

Both Bonneville and Grand Coulee dams suffered a barrage of criticism. Roosevelt's concept that regional resources were also national resources received little credibility. Locally, the *Bellingham Herald* and the *Yakima Daily Republic* opposed. Oregon Senators Charles McNary and Frederick Steiwer, concerned about funding for Bonneville, also opposed Grand Coulee.[13] In July 1935, a *Saturday Evening Post* article suggested Grand Coulee Dam would become as equally a useless monument as the Egyptian pyramids. In June 1937, as Bonneville was nearing completion, *Colliers* ran an article calling it a "Dam of Doubt."[14] An eastern engineer reportedly said, "The Columbia is certainly a wonderful river. It waters four states and drains forty-eight!"[15] New York Republican Congressman Francis Culkin, a persistent critic, commented, "Up in the Grand Coulee area there is no one to sell the power to except the jack rabbits and the rattlesnakes, and they are not amenable, as you know, to the ordinary processes of an electric meter."[16] Even the government sponsored study on migration and economic opportunity doubted. It maintained the cost of fuel and purchased electricity for manufacuturing in general was only 3 percent of the total cost of production. The study questioned whether the attraction of cheap energy alone could offset the advantages of markets, transportation, connections, labor supply, and often cheap raw materials enjoyed by established eastern manufacturing centers.[17]

Huge expenditure for dams made Washington one of the highest per capita recipients of federal expenditures during the period 1933–1939. Of the fourteen states comprising the Pacific and Mountain regions, however, Washington ranked only thirteenth.[18] Per capita federal expenditures in the East were lower because of the region's much greater population, but the total volume of expenditures was as impressive as in the West.[19] In the long run the Grand Coulee Project handed taxpayers a bargain. Labor costs, high by Depression standards, averaged only eighty cents an hour, and building equipment and material had dropped to twentieth century lows. Grand Coulee was built on the premise that receipts from all sources would repay the entire cost within fifty years plus 4 percent interest with interest paid on cost of power development only.[20] These goals have been reached. Besides Grand Coulee's immeasurable past and future contribution, the government owns a facility that has increased in value multiple times. In comparison, McNary Dam, completed in 1954, cost $285 million, more than twice the original cost of much larger Grand Coulee. Increasingly, though, critics suggest that positive benefits provided by the Columbia River dams must be measured against the huge environmental and social costs.

Indisputably, the more immediate goal of providing badly needed jobs succeeded. From 1933 to 1943 over 12,000 men and women were employed, working night and day. By 1935 the Grand Coulee Project employed over 3000, the largest payroll in the state. In the late 1930s employment peaked at 7400.[21] Although workers came from all forty-eight states, employment preference was given to Washington residents. Those in Grant and other neighboring counties received top priority but populous King County provided more workers than any other.

Whether electricity generated by the Columbia River dams should have public or private ownership and distribution was being decided by votes throughout the region with alarming results for public power advocates. In March 1941, voters in Spokane, Portland, Eugene, and Tacoma, content with their established private systems, rejected switching to electrical lines connected to the Bonneville Power Administration.[22] The BPA made a short film called *Hydro* to promote public power, but wanted a full-length feature film to show how power from the Columbia dams could bring the good life to common people if publicly distributed.

Early in 1941, charismatic folksinger Woody Guthrie was hired by the Department of Interior to promote Bonneville public power. Guthrie, an Oklahoma native, would come to symbolize the Dust Bowl migration from Oklahoma to California. His ballads included *So Long It's Been Good to Know Ya*, *Dust Bowl Blues* and *Oklahoma Hills*. But in 1941 his cousin Jack Guthrie, who had a radio show in Los Angeles, was perhaps better known.[23] Woody's greatest popularity would come decades after the Depression. Guthrie expressed his sympathy for social protest by inscribing, "This machine kills fascists," on his guitar. Considered a Communist by the FBI, he never joined because of his distaste for authoritarianism of any kind. While in New York, however, Guthrie contributed to the Communist *Daily Worker* and traveled in a radical political circle including Mother Bloor and Pete Seeger. He was just what working class and urban radicals sought, a honest-to-goodness laboring man with a gift for writing and singing in a folk idiom with a strong radical tone.[24]

Guthrie left New York for the Oregon job in the spring of 1941. He was paid at the skilled labor rate of $266.66 for thirty days as a federal employee. Beginning in May 1941, Guthrie toured the area in a chauffeured 1940 black Hudson drawing angry protest letters from citizens who wondered why their tax dollars were being squandered to squire a scruffy fellow with a guitar. Visiting a different site each day the Oklahoman wrote twenty-six songs in thirty days. Guthrie closely related to the workers and viewed the dams as a means of improving the lives of the poor. Among his better-known songs were *Roll on Columbia*, *Pastures of Plenty*, and *Grand Coulee Dam*. They were played over loud speakers at meetings to sell bonds to carry power lines from the dams to the region's towns and cities. In 1987, *Roll on Columbia* became

Washington's official state folk song. The film *Columbia* was not released until 1948 because of the war.[25]

Inexpensive electricity from the Bonneville Power Administration provided a boon for all recipients. By 1943, per capita use of electricity in the service area surged to 3,500 kilowatt-hours annually compared to a 1,410 national average. The rate of $17.50 per kilowatt year anywhere on the transmission system represented the lowest regional rate in the country.[26]

Of all the beneficiaries of abundant, inexpensive public power the Boeing Aircraft Company ranked among the highest. Already established and competitive, Boeing benefited enormously and its explosive expansion during the war made it synonymous with Seattle. Although many Dust Bowl migrants eventually found employment at Boeing in the 1940s, it had not been true during the 1930s. The company had no new job openings because many skilled employees had been laid off and were eager to return. Boeing, the largest single industrial employer in Seattle with 1700 employees early in 1934, cut that number to six hundred by August. Wages at Boeing were 25 to 75 cents an hour and workers, hired by the day, were fortunate to work three or four days a week.[27] As late as 1935, workers lined up outside the plant and foremen picked those needed for the day. Late in 1934, the board of directors in an historic gamble voted to design and build a plane to compete for an Army Air Corps contract for a plane that would carry 2000 pounds of bombs over 2000 miles. In 1935, Boeing built Model 299 (B-17), a four engine bomber with speed, power, maneuverability and size that so impressed the military, that even though the bomber crashed on a later test flight, it ordered thirteen. Until 1939, Boeing, AFL unionized since July 1, 1936, built the B-17 Flying Fortress at a loss because non-union California competitors like Douglas, Martin and Lockheed paid lower wages, forcing aircraft prices down.[28] In 1939, a block of military orders, first from Britain and then from the United States, began massive production resulting in over 12,000 B-17s before the war ended. Toward the end of the war, Boeing also built 3,970 larger B-29 Superfortresses. Although most B-17s and B-29s were built in Seattle and Renton, almost half of the B-29s were built at Boeing's Wichita factory.

In 1941, Boeing, mostly with government funds, built an enormous new plant in Renton at the southern tip of Lake Washington. It adjoined long-established Pacific Car and Foundry (PACCAR), whose high-grade steel complemented airplane construction.[29] PACCAR subcontracted to build wingspans for Boeing's bombers and also produced 926 M-4 Sherman tanks. After the war PACCAR purchased the highly successful Kenworth and Peterbilt truck-building firms.

By July 1941, Boeing had 10,000 employees, by September, 20,000, in December, 30,000.[30] Even though Washington's population had increased

10 percent during the 1930s and unemployment had remained high, Boeing soon needed to recruit workers from far and wide. In 1941, a full page ad in the neighboring Kent newspaper announced, "Your Government has stepped up Boeing production schedules calling for more Flying Fortresses. . . More women as well as men, are needed now to do this vital work. . . Special service direct to Boeing Renton plant from Kent . . . minimum monthly wages $185 at the end of the 12th week."[31] With beginning pay of 62.5 cents an hour Boeing had an annual turnover rate of well over 100 percent in 1942, primarily because area shipyards started at ninety cents an hour. With a chance to earn more in a month than many cleared annually during the Depression, migrants from the Midwest could make the transition to the West Coast much more comfortably than most of their 1930s counterparts. Huge numbers pursued this unprecedented opportunity for economic betterment.

One Boeing B-17 required the amount of aluminum needed for fifty thousand aluminum stew pans and an aluminum shortage temporarily held up Boeing production.[32] New aluminum plants at Tacoma, Spokane, Vancouver, Longview and Troutdale, Oregon, lured to the Pacific Northwest by the promise of low cost electricity from the Bonneville power grid, soon met the need.[33] In 1940, The Aluminum Company of America (ALCOA) produced the first commercial aluminum west of the Mississippi River at its new 300 acre, $3 million Vancouver facility. By 1944, 5800 were employed and the Pacific Northwest was producing 36 percent of the nation's aluminum.[34] At that point ALCOA's Vancouver plant used more electricity than the entire city of Portland.[35]

When William Boeing died in 1956 aboard his yacht, *Taconite*, the *Seattle Times* devoted its Sunday editorial page to him. The *Times* said, "It is safe to say that no living man has made the name of the city more widely known in the far corners of the earth than the original builder of the Boeing aircraft. . ."[36] Boeing moved to Washington in 1903 to pursue family timber interests. His German immigrant father made a fortune in Michigan timber and held a major interest in Minnesota's rich Mesabi Iron Range, but died when William was only eight. Young Boeing attended an exclusive private school in Switzerland, then majored in engineering at Yale where he dropped out after two years. Reportedly at odds with his stepfather, the twenty-two year old left Minnesota to manage family timber interests at Grays Harbor (Hoquiam). After a successful six years he moved to Seattle where he bought a small shipyard.[37]

Tall, aloof and still single, described by one writer as "the playboy of the American West," Boeing became a prominent Seattle socialite.[38] He became infatuated with airplanes, learning to fly at the Glen Martin School in

California. Convinced he could build a better plane and aware that he commanded an outstanding supply of light, tough spruce, then the preferred wood for airplane manufacturing, Boeing formed a small corporation and built planes out of his shipyard. The complex skills involved in shipbuilding easily transferred to airplane manufacture. A demanding perfectionist Boeing ordered "leave no stone unturned" in the pursuit of a quality product. In 1917, Boeing sold fifty seaplane trainers to the navy, but that order was cut in half when the war ended. To make ends meet during the postwar slump the company also produced high quality furniture but Boeing still had to dip into his considerable private funds to keep the business going.[39]

In 1925, Boeing formed the Boeing Air Transport Company. It became a leader in airmail delivery and air passenger service in the late 1920s and early 1930s. In 1933, the reform minded federal government cancelled all air mail contracts with Boeing, charging fraud, collusion, and conspiracy. Boeing's passenger service, United Airlines, also was ordered broken up as a monopoly. Outraged by what he deemed unfair government interference, Boeing sold all of his stock (at a handsome profit) and left to pursue other business interests although he continued to serve as a Boeing Corporation consultant. At Aldarra, his nearby five-hundred-acre farm, Boeing became one of the leading thoroughbred horse breeders in the country.[40]

Power from the BPA directly benefited construction magnate Henry Kaiser's huge ship building enterprises in Portland and Richmond, California. Both facilities profited from ALCOA's aluminum and Portland was a direct beneficiary of the BPA's abundant, low cost power. Kaiser foresaw that light metals had a tremendous future for use in airplanes, autos, ships and countless other venues. A plentiful supply of electricity was essential for aluminum production and Kaiser knew where it was available. Ultimately, he used loans from the Reconstruction Finance Corporation to build and operate five new aluminum plants in the Pacific Northwest, breaking the ALCOA monopoly.

Other than their German backgrounds and phenomenal business success, Kaiser and Boeing had little in common. Stocky and affable Kaiser grew up in modest circumstances on a small farm near Utica, New York. He quit school at age thirteen becoming a photographer at Lake Placid during the summer and in Florida during the winter. Kaiser moved to Spokane in 1907 to fulfill his future father-in-law's demand that he had to achieve greater financial success before marriage. A gregarious, naturally gifted salesman and a driven organizational genius, Kaiser used his success in the hardware business and association with a local paving contractor to start his own road paving company in 1914. Kaiser soon developed a reputation for being fast and good in another booming industry based on the internal combustion engine. He gained national recognition as the point man for the consortiums that built Boulder, Bonneville and Grand Coulee dams. His consortium was outbid for the original Grand Coulee low dam but entered a partnership with the winner to finish the later approved high dam portion. When he lost the construction contract for Shasta dam, Kaiser successfully bid to supply the cement, forming what would become Kaiser Permanente.[41]

Temporarily partnering with long established Todd Shipyards, Kaiser started a shipyard in Portland in 1940 although he admitted he didn't know anything about shipbuilding. In 1940, Todd Shipyards had received a $100 million contract from the British to build freighters. Already committed to a number of other projects, Todd executives invited Kaiser to help fill the British contract. Kaiser learned the business very quickly, refining shipbuilding to an exact science. He eschewed the traditional practice of building from the keel up, and used assembly line methods. Kaiser's ships were built in separate sections and welded together in a few days. Soon the United States began a massive defense build up and Kaiser-Todd won more lucrative contracts. By May 1941, he launched the first of 2710 United States Liberty ships, earning him the nickname, "Sir Launchalot." In 1942, to supply steel for his shipyards Kaiser completed one of the largest steel mills in the world at Fontana near Los Angeles. *Time* began referring to the irrepressible builder as the "big, bald miracle man from the West Coast."

Kaiser and Todd soon agreed to go their own ways for corporate simplification to speed production. In sharp contrast to the 1930s, Kaiser recruiters scoured the country for capable workers, offering free transportation to the West Coast, high wages, subsidized-housing and other benefits. Kaiser, known as a fair employer, had established a prepaid health plan for his workers in 1938. He also built "Miracle City" at Vanport to help house the more than 72,000 migrants who swarmed into the Portland area.[42] When the war ended the shipyards closed, but most of the migrants stayed, finding employment in other businesses and industries during the postwar economic boom. Fueled by the boom in housing and other construction, the rapidly expanding timber industry absorbed many. Unfortunately, the record 1948 Columbia River Flood destroyed Vanport.[43]

Additional to the private industrial boom, the war created immense growth in Pacific Northwest military installations. By drawing a crush of military personnel to the area, bases also created a need for thousands of civilian employees. Now known as the Puget Sound Naval Shipyard, Navy Yard Puget Sound at Bremerton had been a West-Coast leader in military shipbuilding and repair since 1901. In the 1930s, Bremerton maintained a steady employment level of skilled workers earning good wages, benefiting from the quiet build up in naval strength.[44] Because of the extensive damage at Pearl Harbor it became the main repair yard for the Pacific Fleet during World War II, employing thousands of civilians.[45]

Fort Vancouver, across the Columbia River from Portland, originally was the regional headquarters for the British Hudson Bay Company. Fort Vancouver served as the Army's principal base in the Pacific Northwest since the United States takeover in 1846. Many young officers stationed at Fort Vancouver later became renowned. Among them were generals Grant, McClellan, Sheridan, Pope and Pickett of Civil War fame. Indian fighters Howard, Miles, Gibbon, and Harney also spent time there. More strategically located Fort Lewis overshadowed it by the 1930s, and it was on the verge of being closed. But Fort Vancouver persevered until after World War II when it became the regional headquarters for the CCC.

Brigadier General George C. Marshall served as commanding officer from 1936–1938. Marshall became Army Chief of Staff during the war, then Secretary of State and the only professional soldier to win the Nobel peace prize. A conservative Democrat who opposed most the New Deal work relief projects, Marshall, nevertheless, was devoted to CCC work. His dedication to the CCC no doubt was spurred by the Army's role in supervision and providing many local camps. CCC work made a significant contribution toward maintaining Army bases and an effective Regular Army Officer corps enduring the bare bones Depression defense budgets. In addition to Regular Army Officers more than 30,000 Army Reserve Officers served at the 2,700 CCC camps. Although CCC participants retained civilian status, the military implications of a semi-military environment providing valuable training for possible future soldiers were inescapable. Marshall had established successful camps in Georgia and Florida before taking over at Fort Vancouver. Although much of his time was spent leading the CCC, Marshall also commanded the nation's largest military exercise to that point at Fort Lewis in 1937 involving 7,500 soldiers.[46] The City of Vancouver later honored Marshall by naming an elementary school, a recreation center and park, and a well-funded lecture series for him.

Fort Lewis, now a premier military site on the West Coast, owed its existence to the foresight of the citizens of Pierce County, led by Tacoma, "The City of Destiny." In 1917, they voted to bond themselves for $2 million to purchase seventy thousand acres for donation to the federal government as a military base. Camp Lewis became the first military installation created from an outright gift of lands by citizens. After war was declared, ten thousand men built 1,757 buildings, established streets, roads and railroad spurs that made it the leading military post on the West Coast. After the World War I boom government neglect of the camp prompted a Tacoma civic group to demand the land back, prodding Congress to pass a ten-year building plan in 1926. In 1939, Peter Kiewitt Construction of Omaha won a $7.5 million contract to build 760 barracks and related facilities. With war pending that contract was doubled immediately. During the period 1939–1941 the fort's population grew from 5,000 to 30,000 troops.

Fort Lewis hosted as many as 50,000 troops at once by 1943. The author remembers restaurants in Olympia crowded with young soldiers on Saturday leave and a 1941 family trip to visit with a cousin taking basic training. There were masses of young men in uniform and a long line of saddled horses tied to a hitching rail. Fortunately, not many horses were needed in combat. The Army used the state-owned Black Hills for maneuvers and military vehicles and personnel streamed by our elementary school. Our stump ranch, three miles west, almost immediately adjoined the training area. Once a concealed sentry stepped out from the brush and stopped my sister and me from walking down a private road.

In 1930, Pierce County purchased a thousand acres adjoining Fort Lewis for an expensive new airport that by 1933 was losing $40,000 a year. The Army agreed to take over the field in 1934. WPA workers cleared room for a much larger facility at the bargain basement cost of $61,000. In 1938, it was named McCord Field in honor of Colonel William McCord who had perished in a 1937 crash. By 1943, McCord was the largest bomber-training base in the United States.[47]

Seattle, always in competition with Tacoma, zealously pursued economic expansion including military bases and contracts, often invoking "The Seattle Spirit." In 1898, the Seattle Chamber of Commerce donated 703 acres to found Fort Lawton in its Magnolia district. Restricted by its urban setting and small area, Fort Lawton stayed active until 1970.

Winning the construction contract for the *USS Nebraska* in 1901 greatly helped transform Seattle into a major industrial city and epitomized "The Seattle Spirit." Moran Brothers Shipyard submitted the low bid of $3.5 million, but the navy rejected it as $300,000 too high. Project leader Robert Moran, mayor of Seattle during the catastrophic 1899 fire, offered to absorb $200 thousand if the city could contribute $100 thousand. More than Five hundred citizens donated the needed amount. Construction of the only battleship built in Seattle took three years and drew an estimated one thousand families to Seattle.[48] In 1916, Moran Brothers merged into the Todd Pacific Shipyards Corporation that made a major contribution in both World Wars.

After World War I, King County Commissioners purchased several hundred acres at Sand Point for a proposed naval air station on Lake Washington's northern end. In 1922, the government accepted the 268–acre site that was expanded to 413 acres in 1926. King County had spent $500,000 acquiring and developing the property and New Deal work programs dramatically improved the base in the 1930s.[49] The Sand Point Naval Air Station peaked at 8000 military and civilian personnel during World War II but was closed by 1970.

After the war and continuing to the present, a substantial number of military personnel, impressed with the appealing physical environment, the informal social structure and the abundant economic opportunity, chose to remain in the area, either for retirement or civilian employment. According to a 2005 Veteran's Day estimate 600,000 veterans, about one of ten residents, were living in Washington.

World War II provided a catalyst for enormous economic growth in the Pacific Northwest. Historian Gerald Nash's thesis that the war transformed the West from a sparsely populated underdeveloped region with a colonial dependence upon the East into an area of innovation and self-sufficiency is accepted widely. During the war the Far West received about $27 billion in federal government defense funds, an estimated one-eighth of the national total, mainly for manufacture of ships and aircraft. Much of money went to California but Washington and Oregon both benefited enormously.[50]

The evolutionary quality of the transformation to increased economic independence with emphasis on value added manufacturing rather than extractive industry should not be overlooked, though. Washington and Oregon already had established a substantial infrastructure of resources, facilities and personnel able to accommodate the World War II surge. Washington, especially, had provided aggressive leadership in timber products, airplane manufacture and shipbuilding during the pre war period. New Deal programs helped develop the enormous land and water resources of the region, as did earlier efforts by the Bureau of Reclamation and the Army Corps of engineers. The Pacific Northwest's geographical proximity to militaristic Japan also demanded increased defense expenditures.[51]

Many believed the West Coast economy would collapse at war's end because of the cutback in defense contracts and the return of job-seeking veterans. There was considerable concern that a large percentage of those who had moved to the West Coast for defense jobs would return to their home states after the war. To the surprise of many the West Coast economy continued to surge. The huge build up of liquid capital during the war and a resounding housing boom were leading factors. Dramatic population expansion provided a comparable growth in markets and a surge of small businesses helped absorb those transferring out of defense industries. Most of the workers who had moved to the West Coast for defense jobs elected to stay and readily found other occupations. Some did return to their home states but migration back was costly and non-agricultural jobs were scarce in rural areas.

Much greater emphasis on Asia, both from a geo-political and economic standpoint, combined with Cold War demands, an increasing domestic market, and aggressive, innovative industrial and business development combined to insure continuing growth in the region. By 2000, the combined population of Oregon, Washington, and Idaho exceeded ten million. Washington led with over 5,674,900 while Oregon had 3,266,800. Idaho doubled its 1950 population to 1,221,500. Boise, selected in 2005 by *Forbes* as the country's best city to start a business or a career, has swelled to 488,000 alone. In 1960, Boise had only 34,000, by the early 1990s it had 215,000. Since then, spurred by rapid growth in Micron Technology and Hewlett Packard, it has more than doubled again. All three states showed substantial growth in the Census Bureau's report on county change from 2000–2004.[52] Predicting the future is always perilous, but demographers see no end in sight for the rapid expansion of the West Coast. Western historian Walter Nugent suggests, "The coastal and border West may become the dominant region of North America, facing an East Asia whose economies at last match its huge population."[53]

Dust Bowl migrants, having achieved a comfortable lifestyle for the most part, quietly melded into their communities, pleased with their relocation and prosperity. Those who experienced severe 1930s hardship preferred to forget those difficult times. But, even though they bought new cars and new homes and extolled the virtues of American capitalism they remain scarred by their Depression experience. Most reflected a Depression-bred caution about change or risk in employment or business ventures. Several observers suggest (accurately by this writer's experience) victims of the Depression never throw anything away and know the value of a dollar. As held true for those remaining on the Great Plains, large numbers returned to political conservatism. They turned their backs on the New Deal Democrats who had helped them enormously in the 1930s and whose foresight had helped insure the economic growth that created an affluent society.[54]

Journalists and historians have shown a disappointing tendency to overlook the Northern Great Plains record drought as well. All college level introductory history texts reviewed by this author confine the Dust Bowl to the Southwest. Regional historians, most of who reflect upper-middle class backgrounds, moreover, favor cultural interpretations over economic and geographic explanations. To many, the Dust Bowl was more a result of what people did to nature rather than what nature did to people. The 1930s migration frequently is portrayed as a part of a redistribution of population that had been taking place over a long period of time because of human greed and government malfeasance. An almost sovereign way to make former and present Great Plains farmers bristle with indignation is to suggest their avarice caused the Dust Bowl. They insist they did the best they could under highly unusual conditions and point to today's generally healthy and improving Great Plains environment.[55]

By the 1970s, a young group of western historians emerged, reflecting the prevailing hostile attitude toward established dogma. They promoted a "new" western history that rejected the famous Turner thesis that emphasized geographical and economic factors and portrayed the conquest of the West as an historic achievement that shaped American democracy. Led by Donald Worster, William Cronon, Richard White, and Patricia Nelson Limerick, the new western history championed the viewpoint of those on the margin with emphasis on cultural factors. Indians, women, other minorities and the environment were portrayed as victims of western expansion and unfettered capitalism. Regarding the Dust Bowl crisis, Worster maintained farmers were lured to marginal land by the government, where by plowing it they created an ecological catastrophe. Worster said, ". . . the most incredible fact of the dirty thirties was the tenacity of bourgeois optimism and its imperiousness to all warnings."[56] Farmers in the Dust Bowl were punished for poor farming practices and lack of care of a fragile environment according to Worster. That the Great Plains suffered the worst drought in recorded history in the 1930s was not given significance.[57] White also opined Dust Bowl migrants were victims of the capitalist system.[58]

William Riebsame, an expert on drought and resource management, recently analyzed 189 contemporary articles about the Dust Bowl. Of the eighty-seven articles that discussed causes of the Dust Bowl, two-thirds blamed human factors such as marginal lands, poor farming practices and bank failures. Only 30 percent cited weather, climate, or some other non-human force. Riebsame lamented that the Dust Bowl symbol was not now wholly appropriate and it might actually hinder long-term adaptation to the Plains environment.[59]

Although the Great Plains have experienced several droughts since the 1930s, nothing that catastrophic has occurred since. One can travel from El Paso, Texas, to Edmonton, Canada, moreover, and find only limited evidence of permanent erosion caused in the 1930s. Remarkably, an estimated 90 percent of land plowed in the Dust Bowl was in crops in 1950, including 60 percent of land abandoned in the 1930s. Terracing, contour plowing and new crop mixes contributed to this phenomenal recovery.[60] Other significant strategies improved the environment as well. Planting over 200 million trees really did make a difference. Critics said, "If God couldn't grow trees on the plains, the New Deal certainly can't!" It did and they improved the environment by holding the soil, serving as windbreaks and slowing evaporation. Also, the inter-related systems of countless ponds and reservoirs created by the New Deal in the 1930s have helped with flood control and water storage plus adding more moisture in the air during hot weather.[61]

In addition to funding conservation measures, New Deal programs produced an impressive array of the current infrastructure and established an ongoing system of subsidies for agriculture. The project list includes roads, bridges, airports, parks, public-buildings, play fields, sewage systems and much more. New Deal improvements stand out especially on the Great Plains, because they have not been dwarfed by the rapid expansion common to many other regions. Agricultural subsidies include price supports, payments to limit production, favorable irrigation rates, federally funded research and more. Although Great Plain's residents have shown more gratitude for New Deal economic help, they remain overwhelmingly Republican.

Improved infrastructure and agricultural conditions, however, have not stopped the steady outflow of rural Northern Great Plains farm residents who have to "get big or get out." Some experts question whether the area from the 98th meridian to the eastern slope of the Rockies could support a stable population without government subsidy.[62] The average size of a South Dakota farm expanded from 438 acres in 1930 to 674 in 1950 and since has increased substantially. Many displaced farmers migrated to the nearest urban areas such as Billings, Rapid City, Minot, and Scottsbluff. Others retired to Arizona or Arkansas, but most continued to move to the West Coast leaving counties throughout the Great Plains dotted with abandoned farmsteads and decaying small towns.[63] Northwestern North Dakota has suffered the most depletion in recent years, so much so that *U. S. News and World Report* chose to feature Divide and Burke Counties in a feature article, "Broken Heartland," in its May 7, 2001, edition.[64]

Burke and Divide have declined from a combined population of 19,634 in 1930 to 5525 in 2000, the most precipitous percentage decline in the nation. Columbus, Noonan, Ambrose, and Larson, once vital small towns virtually have been abandoned and the death rate of the aging population far exceeds the birthrate. Columbus had nearly seven hundred people in the 1950s. On Wednesday and Saturday nights stores stayed open until midnight. So many people flocked into town that families had to arrive before seven in order to get a parking place near the main part of town. Now, with a population of only 151, there are no stores of consequence in Columbus. Neighboring Larson dwindled to seventeen. Myron Watterud, a retired farmer and former Larson businessman, said, "If the leaders of this town saw what happened, they would turn over in their graves."[65] Nearby Crosby gained national publicity in 2004 by offering free land to settlers. In exchange, improvement of the property was required. No one accepted the offer.[66] Many western North Dakotans elected to move to Minot, Dickinson, or Williston the leading urban centers in the area. All three have reflected a steady growth since World War II, attracting rural population and nudged by region's enormous energy resources that have provided thousands of well paying jobs.

All states in the Missouri River Basin have benefited from the Pick-Sloan Flood Control Act of 1944. It led to construction of over fifty new dams and lakes intended for conservation, hydroelectric generation and control and use of water resources in the entire Missouri River Basin. Major Missouri River dams complementing New Deal Fort Peck, Montana, include Garrison in North Dakota, and Oahe, Big Bend, Fort Randal, and Gavins Point, all in South Dakota. All generate substantial hydroelectricity and provide flood control, irrigation, navigation recreation and other benefits. The total installed annual hydroelectric capacity of all dams in the system is estimated at about 2.5 million kilowatts. Ambitious plans for irrigation, however, have not been realized because of cost considerations and difficult soil conditions. Only about ten percent of the planned irrigation acreage receives water, but that still totals around three million acres. The theory that huge, inexpensive supplies of electrical power will attract industry has not proven true for the area, primarily because industry prefers locations closer to large markets.

Besides hydroelectricity, Montana, Wyoming and North Dakota have impressive oil and coal resources. In 2004, North Dakota was the nation's ninth largest oil producing state and also its ninth largest coal producer. Early in the twentieth century geologists were convinced North Dakota contained significant oil resources. Between 1910 and 1951, sixty-four dry wells were drilled with little success. On April 4, 1951, an Amerada Oil test well gushed at the Clarence Iverson farm near Tioga which promptly declared itself "The Oil Capital of North Dakota." Oil representatives from around the country rushed to procure mineral rights on the vast Williston Basin, estimated at 300,000 square miles in area. Formerly the bottom of a prehistoric sea, it lies in North Dakota, Montana and Canada. By May 20,1951, 30 million of the 44.8 million acres in North Dakota were under lease for as little as ten cents to as much as $235 an acre. Mineral rights sold for $100 to $700 an acre in known oil fields. Outside the oil fields most mineral rights brought less than $30 an acre. By the end of 1960 the oil industry had invested an estimated $650 million in North Dakota.[67] When the Iverson well flowed, future president George H. W. Bush immediately flew to Minot from Amerada headquarters at Midland, Texas, to procure oil leases.[68]

Hundreds of wells came in and refineries were built at Williston, Dickinson and Mandan. An oil boom commenced but declined in the late 1960s and early 1970s because of low oil prices and high transportation costs. Higher prices increased production in the late 1970s and early 1980s with production peaking at 52 million barrels in 1984. The boom proved not nearly as dramatic as predicted as lower prices for oil eased production and exploration after the mid 1980s resurgence. Presently the only operating oil refinery in North Dakota is at Mandan, but the abundance of natural gas supports nine Western North Dakota natural gas processing plants. Oil production has leveled to over 30 million barrels a year, but that makes a substantial contribution to North Dakota's economy and tax revenue. High oil and natural gas prices propelled the states petroleum tax revenue to $95,800,000 in 2004. The newly perfected horizontal well drilling process shows great promise for Williston Basin oil because geologists suggest much more oil awaits discovery there. The first horizontal well in North Dakota came in production on August 1, 2005, in Bottineau County.[69]

Ironically, and with considerable justice, nature favored Williams, McKenzie, Mountrail, Billings, Bottineau and Burke Counties. These counties, so adversely affected by the 1930s drought, became the centers of North Dakota oil and natural gas production. In 1959, one of the best oil wells in Burke County came in on Jake and Elsie Dewing's farm. It has been producing ever since and has provided substantial, although not huge, income for the numerous Dewing descendants. One oil well has equaled or surpassed the total net income generated by farming a thousand acres over sixty years. Sadly, the former Dewing family home and other buildings, no longer needed by the large operator who bought the acreage, now are leveled.

That western North Dakota contained enormous reserves of lignite coal was known since the Lewis and Clark expedition. Land promoters touted lignite's abundance to encourage settlers who were reluctant to move to a country with little wood for fuel. A soft brownish-black coal containing more carbon than peat and 25–35 percent water, lignite only was marketed locally for heating homes and other buildings. During the Depression it sold for less that two dollars a ton and was so abundant many farmers mined their own coal. The first significant lignite power plant was completed at Stanton in 1966, although lignite had fueled electric power plants since 1919.

Inexpensive, almost inexhaustible, easily strip-mined lignite emerged as the most economical fuel for electrical generation. Unlike Wyoming's low-sulfur coal that is shipped to urban centers by rail, lignite feeds on-site generators using power lines to transmit the electricity. The Freedom Mine at Beulah, eighty miles northwest of Bismarck, produces about half of the state's annual approximately forty million tons of lignite. At Beulah more than thirteen percent of total mined lignite is used to generate synthetic natural gas. North Dakota now has twelve lignite fueled power plants generating electricity for an estimated two million homes in its region. Careful monitoring and large investment allows all plants to meet government air-quality standards. State tax revenues from coal amount to $60 million a year.[70] The average annual wage of $68,163 for coal miners in North Dakota led the state and power plant employees earned an average of $67,164. Both figures were well over twice the $28,287 average and bolsted state income tax revues significantly. The two energy industries employ 4000 with an estimated generation of 18,000 indirect jobs.[71] The 2005 National Energy Bill should further enhance the state's strong energy position. It proposes $750 million for a North Dakota coal-liquid-fuel plant, plus tax incentives for creation of new natural gas infrastructure.

Rural areas in western Nebraska and South Dakota suffered similar if not quite as severe as North Dakota rural population declines. By the 1990s, South Dakota's West River country had only one third of the farms that existed in the 1930s and their average size had more than quadrupled.[72] But western South Dakota has balanced the loss in agricultural population with tourism, Ellsworth Air Base, lumbering, gambling and retirees. Mount Rushmore now hosts three million visitors a year. Legalization of gambling at historic Deadwood helped offset the closure of the important Lead-Deadwood Homestake gold mine. Black Hills lumber production is anchored by the Pope and Talbot sawmill at Spearfish that has the capacity to produce 120 million board feet of Ponderosa Pine lumber per year. The ambiance of the Black Hills and no state income tax also has attracted a number of retirees, including many "equity exiles" from California. Shannon County with over six percent growth in the past four years is dominated by the Pine Ridge Indian Reservation, the home of about thirty thousand Oglala Sioux who largely depend upon federal grants earned from long-standing treaty agreements.[73]

In May 2005, the Pentagon designated Ellsworth Air Base for closure, creating a storm of protest from South Dakota and especially the Rapid City area. If Ellsworth were shut down the economic consequences of losing South Dakota's second leading employer, which provides 5,500 jobs and a $278 million impact, would be wrenching. On August 26, 2005, the Defense Base Realignment and Closure Commission, a panel appointed by President Bush charged with evaluating the Pentagon recommendations, voted to retain Ellsworth. North Dakota's significant Minot Air Base was not on the Pentagon list.

Western Nebraska's small towns and rural areas also declined in population, but the area's agriculture, especially the southwestern part, enjoyed more stability due to extensive irrigation in the Platte River Valley and substantial growth in towns situated along Interstate 80. More diversification of the meat packing industry also promoted the economies of several towns—especially Lexington. Western Nebraska also profited by a surge of railroad expansion generated by the great demand for low sulfur Wyoming coal. Those counties almost totally dependent upon grazing and dry land crops, however, declined rapidly. Sioux County, in the northwest, for example, declined from 4667 in 1930 to l549 in 2000. Sioux County continues to dwindle as do all similar Western Nebraska counties.[74]

In 1987, Rutgers land use planner Frank Popper and his wife geographer Deborah Eptstein Popper suggested that quantitative data showed the exodus from the rural Great Plains had reached a crisis situation that required drastic change. "The Great Plains from Dust to Dust," an article they co-published in *Planning,* suggested the government buy vast tracts for a "Buffalo Commons" that would return the land to buffalo and create national parks to attract tourists.[75] Their piece received so much publicity from the popular press that the Poppers became instant celebrities.

Great-Plains farmers and ranchers who saw their way of life threatened by eastern Ivory Tower academics reacted with predictable hostility. They pointed out, even though the Poppers' demographic data was accurate, their solutions lacked validity. Buffalo had been promoted as an alternative to cattle for a long time. But they had never gained widespread acceptance because they were harder to handle, less efficient meat producers, and ate as much grass as cattle. Critics also argued that grain production, which had not declined on the Great Plains, made it the nation's breadbasket and was far too crucial to be terminated. Later, the Poppers modified their Buffalo Commons theory, but maintained the demography of the area promised continuing decline in rural areas creating a need for increased government intervention.

Those who were young adults in the 1930s became part of journalist Tom Brokaw's "Greatest Generation." They survived the Great Depression, fought World War II and built a prosperous, stable society after it. Many grew up in the 1920s in relative stability, making the 1930s merely an unfortunate glitch in lives that achieved prosperity in the long run. Dust Bowl migrants to the Pacific Northwest were grateful for an environment that provided economic success after a difficult start. The hard lessons of difficult times instilled a determination to work and succeed and a fiscal and social conservatism that complemented that goal.[76]

Migrant children born in the 1930s may have suffered more "wounds that do not bleed" than their parents. Their lives were yet unshaped and they were forced to compete in a more urban society under extremely adverse circumstances. Many endured an environment of social, cultural and economic deprivation. They were cut off from associating with middle class children, felt to be inferiors, and were forced to absorb an atmosphere of defeatism. It took more than a little fortitude to compete, but, perhaps in part motivated by the discomfort of their situation, most managed to overcome their difficult start.

NOTES

1. Pacific Northwest Regional Planning Commission. *Migration and the Development of Economic Opportunity in the Pacific Northwest. A Report Prepared in*

cooperation with the Pacific Northwest Land Advisory Committee. (Portland: Pacific Northwest Regional Planning Commission, 1939) 17,132.

2. Leo A. Borah. "North Dakota Comes into Its Own," *National Geographic* (September 1951): 283–322.

3. Herbert Schell, *History of South Dakota* (Lincoln: University of Nebraska Press, 1975), 302–3.

4. Walter Nugent, *Into the West: The Story of Its People* (New York: Knopf, 1999), *298–300.*

5. Herber Resner, *Power in the State of Washington: A Survey of Power, Irrigation and* [*sic*] (Seattle: Works Progress Administration, 1937), 42.

6. R. Gregory Nokes, "Hard Times in the 1930s," in *The Oregon Story,* ed. Vivian C. Atterbury (Portland Binfords and Mort, 1959), 59–69.

7. Paul C. Pitzer, *Grand Coulee: Harnessing a Dream* (Pullman: Washington State University Press, 1994), 216–18.

8. Paul C. Pitzer, "Visions, Plans, and Realities: A History of the Columbia Basin Project" (master's thesis, University of Oregon, 1990), 357–58; Robert E. Ficken, *Rufus Woods: The Columbia River, and the Building of Modern Washington* (Pullman: Washington State University Press, 1995), 149–50.

9. James E. Brooks, "Settlement Problems Related to Farm Size in the Columbia Basin Project, Washington" (PhD dissertation, University of Washington, 1957).

10. Donald Swain, "The Bureau of Reclamation and the New Deal, 1933–1940." *The Pacific Northwest Quarterly* 61 (July 1970): 137–46, 138.

11. *Life,* November 23, 1936; Frederick L. Quivak, "New Deal Oasis on the High Plains," *Montana* (Winter 2004), 69–74.

12. Pitzer, "Visions," 42–43.

13. Ibid., 72–73.

14. Gus Norwood, et al, *Columbia River Power for the People: A History of Policies of the Bonneville Power Administration* (Portland: U. S. Government Printing Office, 1981), 41.

15. William Dietrich, *Northwest Passage: The Great Columbia River* (Seattle: University of Washington Press, 1996), 304.

16. Swain, "The Bureau of Reclamation," 138.

17. Pacific Northwest Regional Planning Commission, *Migration,* 294.

18. Don C. Reading, "New Deal Activity and the State, 1933–1939," *Journal of Economic History* 33 (1973): 794–95.

19. T. H. Watkins, *Righteous Pilgrim: The Life and Times of Harold L. Ickes, 1874–1952* (New York: Henry Holt, 1990): 294.

20. Resner, *Power*, 33.

21. Pitzer, *Grand Coulee*, 212.

22. Robert A. Carriker, "Ten Dollars a Song: Woody Guthrie Sells His Talent to the BPA," *Columbia* 16 (Spring 2001): 32.

23. James N. Gregory, *The American Exodus: The Dust Bowl Migration and Okie Culture in California* (New York: Oxford University Press, 1989), 229–30.

24. "American Song During the Great Depression," http:///www.newworldrecords .org/linenotes/80270.pdf. (accessed August 12, 2005)

25. Michael Majdic and Denise Matthews, *Roll on Columbia: Woody Guthrie and the Bonneville Power Administration,* Video Documentary (University of Oregon, 2001); Joe Klein, *Woody Guthrie: A Life* (New York: Knopf, 1980), 189–98.

26. Charles McKinly, *Uncle Sam in the Pacific Northwest* (Berkeley: University of California Press, 1952), 15–17.

27. *Year by Year: 75 Years of Boeing History, 1816–1991* (Seattle: Taken from *Boeing News* in Boeing History Archives, 1991), 35.

28. Jacob Vander Meulen, "West Coast Labor and the Military Aircraft Industry, 1935–1941," *Pacific Northwest Quarterly* (Spring 1997): 87–88.

29. Alex Groner. *PACCAR, the Pursuit of Quality* (Bellevue, WA: Documentary Book Publishers Company, 1981), 94.

30. Roger Sale, *Seattle: Past to Present: An Interpretation of the History of the Foremost City in the Pacific Northwest* (Seattle: University of Washington Press, 1976), 180–82.

31. Florence K. Lentz, *Kent: Valley of Opportunity* (Chatsworth, CA: Windsor Publications, 1990), 66.

32. W. L. White "Out of the Doghouse" *Saturday Evening Post* (November 15, 1941), 14–15.

33. Terry M. Sells, *Wings of Power: Boeing and the Politics of Growth in the Northwest* (Seattle: University of Washington Press, 2001); David M. Buerge, *Renton: Where the Water Took Wing* (Northridge, CA: Windsor Publications, 1989).

34. *Seattle Times*, September 30, 1956.

35. E. Kimbark MacColl, *The Growth of a City: Power and Politics in Portland, Oregon, 1915–1950* (Portland: The Georgian Press, 1979), 558.

36. *Seattle Times,* September 30, 1956.

37. Harold Mansfield, *Vision: A Saga of the Sky* (New York: Duell, Sloan and Pearce, 1956), 8–9; M. J. Hardy, *Boeing* (New York: Beaufort Books, 1982), 6.

38. After his home was raided by prohibition agents Boeing became a leader of the Association Against Prohibition.

39. Norman H. Clark, *Washington: A Bicentennial History* (New York: W. W. Norton, 1976), 174–75; The Museum of Flight at Boeing Field in Seattle has an excellent history of the Boeing company complemented with outstanding exhibits.

40. *Year by Year*, 32.

41. Mark S. Foster, *Henry J. Kaiser: Builder in the Modern American West* (Austin: University of Texas Press, 1989); Gerald Nash, *The American West Transformed: The Impact of the Second World War* (Bloomington: Indiana University Press, 1985), 28–29.

42. Dorothy O. Johansen, *Empire of the Columbia* (New York: Harper & Row, 1966), Tables 607–30; Frederick Simpich, "Wartime in the Pacific Northwest," *National Geographic,* (October 1942): 421–64.

43. MacColl, *Growth of a City,* 572–74.

44. Harold Ickes, *The Autobiography of a Curmudgeon* (Chicago: Quadrangle Books, 1969), Chapter Thirteen, "We Gird for War," 279–98.

45. Louise Reh and Helen Lou Ross, *NIPSIC to Nimitz: A Centennial History of Puget Sound Naval Shipyard* (Bremerton, WA: Federally Employed Women, Incor-

porated, 1991). The Bremerton Naval Museum is also excellent—visited December 2001.

46. Forest C. Pogue, *George C. Marshall: Education of a General-1880–1939* (New York: The Viking Press, 1963), 300–16.

47. Murray Morgan, *South on the Sound: An Illustrated History of Tacoma and Pierce County* (Woodland Hills, CA: Windsor Publications, 1984), 293–94.

48. Stuart Eskenazi, "Ship Made Splash a Century Ago," *Seattle Times* (2 October 2004), 1. Christened in 1907 the *Nebraska* already was obsolete. It never fired a shot in battle and was sold for scrap in 1923.

49. Harold Ickes, *The Autobiography*, 293–94.

50. Gerald Nash, *The American West Transformed,* 17 and appendices, 217–24.

51. Paul Rhode, "The Nash Thesis Revisited: An Economic Historian's View," *Pacific Historical Review* 63 (August 1994): 363–92. Rhode emphasizes California.

52. *USA Today,* "Population change by county," *USA Today* (15 April 2005), 7A.

53. Nugent, *Into the West*, 379.

54. William R. Lindley, *Hard Times and Good Times in Oregon: Recollections of the 1930s* (Manhattan, KA: Sunflower Press, 1995), 3; Gordon Dodds *The American Northwest: A History of Oregon and Washington* (Arlington Heights, ILL, 1986), 353; Author's observation; Not all drought victims deserted the Democrats, see Mark Clapp and Rolland Dewing. *A Pioneer's Dream Come True: The Mirage Flats Irrigation Project* (Chadron, NE: B &B Printing, 1990), 13.

55. Author conversations with many Dust Bowl farmers.

56. Donald Worster, *Dust Bowl: The Southern Plains in the 1930s* (New York: Oxford, 1979), 22–28.

57. ——, "The Dirty Thirties: A Study in Agricultural Capitalism," *Great Plains Quarterly* 6 (Spring 1986): 107–116. The entire edition is devoted to the Great Plains Dust Bowl.

58. Richard White, *It's Your Misfortune and None of My Own: A History of the American West* (Norman: University of Oklahoma Press, 1991), 483.

59. William E. Riebsame, "The Dust Bowl: Historical Image, Psychological Anchor, and Ecological Taboo," *Great Plains Quarterly* 6 (Spring 1986): 127–36.

60. Leslie Hewes, "The Great Plains One Hundred Years after Major John Wesley Powell," in *Images of the Plains: The Role of Human Nature in Settlement,"* ed. W. Blouet and Merlin P. Lawson (Lincoln: University of Nebraska Press, 1975), 208–12.

61. Robert Goldston, *The Great Depression* (New York: Fawcett, 1968), 199–200.

62. Carl Kraenzel, *The Great Plains in Transition* (Norman: University of Oklahoma Press, 1955), 3–4, 7.

63. Nugent, *Into the West*, 299–300, 371.

64. Jeff Glasser, "Broken Heartland." *U. S. News and World Report*, (May 7, 2001): 16–22. Datelined Larson, North Dakota.

65. Ibid., 22. Watterud is married to the author's first cousin. The last Dewing family reunion in northwest North Dakota was held in the early 1980s at Watterud's restaurant and lounge at Larson.

66. Floyd J. McKay, "N. Dakota Town Tries to Re-Invent Itself with Land Give-away," *Seattle Times*, (14 September 2005), B7.

67. Robinson, *History of North Dakota*, 458–61.

68. Stephen F. Cox, "A Life in the Oil Patch," *Montana* 50, (Autumn 2000): 32–45; author's observations and conversations with relatives.

69. "North Dakota's Oil Patch," http://WWW.ndoil.org/pdf/factswoo5.pdf. (accessed August 22, 2005)

70. "Energy Resources," http://www.bmda.org/energy.htm. (accessed August 22, 2005)

71. Ibid.

72. Nelson, *The Prairie*, 202.

73. *USA Today*, "Population," 15 April, 2005, 7A; Dewing, "Depression on South Dakota's Indian Reservations," 85–86, 96.

74. Francis Moul, "The Biggest Partner: The Federal Government and Sioux County Nebraska *Nebraska History* 80 (Winter 1999): 156.

75. Deborah Epstein Popper and Frank J. Popper, "The Great Plains: From Dust to Dust," *Planning* 53 (December 1987): 12–18; John G. Mitchell, "The Late Great Plains," *National Geographic* (May 2004): 2–29; Amanda Rees, "The Buffalo Commons: Great Plains Residents' Responses to a Radical Vision," *Great Plains Quarterly* 25 (Summer 2005): 161–72.

76. Frederick Lewis Allen, *The Big Change, 1900–1950* (New York: Bantam Books, 1964), 130–34; Caroline Bird, *The Invisible Scar* (New York: David McKay Company, 1966), 311–12; Bill Ganzel, *Dust Bowl Descent* (Lincoln: University of Nebraska Press, 1984), 124.

Bibliography

BOOKS

Abbey, Wallace W. *The Little Jewell: Soo Line Railroad and the Locomotives that Make It Go.* Pueblo: Pinon Productions, 1984.

Adams, W. Claude. *History of Papermaking in the Pacific Northwest.* Portland: Binfords and Mort, 1951.

Alexander, Charles C. *Breaking the Slump: Baseball in the Depression Era.* New York: Columbia University Press, 2002.

Alexander, William. *Film on the Left: American Documentary Film from 1931 to 1942.* Princeton, N.J.: Princeton University Press, 1981.

Allen, Frederick L. *The Big Change: America Transforms Itself 1900–1950.* New York: Bantam Books, 1965.

Allen, Michael, and Mary L. Hanneman, eds. *Frontiers of Western History: The Origins, Evolution, and Future of Western History*. Needham Heights: Simon and Schuster, 1999.

Arrington, Leonard. *History of Idaho.* Moscow, ID: University of Idaho Press and Boise: Idaho StateHistorical Society, 1994.

Attebury, Louie. J. R. Simplot: A Billionaire the Hard Way. Caldwell, ID: Caxton Press, 2000.

Atterbury, Vivian C. *The Oregon Story.* Portland: Binfords and Mort, 1959.

Avery, Mary W. *Washington: A History of the Evergreen State.* Seattle: University Of Washington Press, 1961.

Badger, Anthony J. *The New Deal: The Depression Years, 1933–1940.* New York: Hill and Wang, 1989.

Bakken, Gordon M. *Surviving the North Dakota Depression.* Pasadena: Wood and Jones, 1992.

Baldwin, Sidney. *Poverty and Politics: The Rise and Decline of the Farm Security Administration.* Chapel Hill: University of North Carolina Press, 1968.

Bauman, John F., and Thomas H. Coode. *In the Eye of the Great Depression: New Deal Reporters and the* Agony *of the American People.* DeKalb: Northern Illinois University Press, 1988.

Banks, Ann. *First Person America.* New York: Alfred A. Knopf, 1980.

Berner, Richard C. *Seattle in the 20th Century.* Seattle: Charles Press, 1991.

Bernstein, Irving. *The Lean Years: A History of the American Worker, 1920–1933.* Baltimore: Penquin Books, 1966.

Bird, Caroline. *The Invisible Scar: The Great Depression and What It Did to American Life, From Then Until Now.* 10th Printing. New York: David McKay, 1975.

Blackorby, Edward. *Prairie Populist: The Life and Times of Usher L. Burdick.* Fargo: Published jointly by the State Historical Society of North Dakota and The North Dakota Institute for Regional Studies, 2001.

———. *Prairie Rebel: The Public Life of William Lemke.* Lincoln: University of Nebraska Press, 1964.

Blair, Karen J., ed. *Women of the Pacific Northwest.* Revised Edition. Seattle: University of Washington Press, 2001.

Bloor, Ella Reeve. *We Are Many.* New York: International Publishers, 1940.

W. Blouet and Merlin P. Lawson, eds. *Images of the Plains: The Role of Human Nature in Settlement.* Lincoln: University of Nebraska Press, 1975.

Blumell, Bruce D. *The Development of Public Assistance in the State of Washington During the Great Depression.* New York: Garland, 1984.

Bremer, Richard G. *Agricultural Change in an Urban Age: The Loup Country of Nebraska, 1910–1970.* Lincoln: University of Nebraska Press, 1976.

Brier, Howard M. *Sawdust Empire: The Pacific Northwest.* New York: Knopf, 1958.

Brown, Josephine. *Public Relief, 1929–39.* New York: Holt, 1940.

Burke, Robert E., and Richard Lowitt, eds. *The New Era and the New Deal, 1920–1940.* Arlington Heights, IL: Harlan Davidson, 1981.

Burton, Robert E. *Democrats of Oregon: The Pattern of Minority Politics, 1900–1956.* Eugene: University of Oregon Press, 1970.

Cannon, Brian Q. *Remaking the Agrarian Dream: New Deal Rural Resettlement in the Mountain West.* Albuquerque: University of New Mexico Press, 1996.

Carey, Charles H. *General History of Oregon through Statehood.* Portland: Binfords and Mort, 1971.

Carlton, David L. and Peter A. Coclanis, eds. *Confronting Southern Poverty in the Great Depression: The Report on Economic Condition of the South with Related Documents.* New York: Bedford Books of St Martins Press, 1996.

Chambers, Whittaker. *Witness.* Washington, D.C.: Regenery Publishing, 1952.

Chasan, Daniel J. *Speaker of the House: The Political Career and Times of John L. O'Brien.* Seattle: University of Washington Press, 1990.

Chase, Stuart. *Rich Land, Poor Land.* New York: McGraw-Hill, 1936.

Christopher, Warren. *Chances of a Lifetime.* New York: Scribner, 2001.

Ciment, James. *Encyclopedia of the Great Depression.* Two Volumes, Armouk, NY: Sharpe Reference, 2001.

Clark, Norman H. *The Dry Years: Prohibition and Social Change in Washington.* Seattle: University of Washington Press, 1988.

———. *Milltown: The Story of Everett, Washington, from Its Earliest Beginnings on the Shores of Puget Sound to the Tragic and Infamous Event Known as the Everett Massacre.* Seattle: University of Washington Press, 1970.

———. *Washington: A Bicentennial History.* New York: W. W. Norton, 1976.

Collins, Henry H., Jr. *America's Own Refugees: Our 4,000,000 Homeless Migrants.* Princeton: Princeton University Press, 1941.

Conklin, Edwin P. *Logging on Puget Sound, as Illustrated in the Lives of Sol Simpson and Mark E. Reed.* Somerville, NJ: American Historical Society, 1935.

Conlin, Joseph R., ed. *At the Point of Production: The Local History of the IWW.* Westport CT: Greenwood Press, 1981.

Cour, Robert M. *The Plywood Age: A History of the Fir Plywood Industry's First Fifty Years.* Portland: Binfords and Mort, 1955.

Creigh, Dorothy Wyler. *Nebraska: A Bicentennial History.* New York: W. W. Norton, 1977.

Curtis, James. *Mind's Eye, Mind's Truth: FSA Photography Reconsidered.* Philadelphia: Temple University Press, 1989.

Danbom, David B. *Born in the Country: A History of Rural America.* Baltimore: Johns Hopkins University Press, 1995.

Davis, Kenneth S. *The New Deal Years, 1933–1937.* New York: Random House, 1986.

Davis, Nelley P. *Stump Ranch Pioneer.* New York: Dodd Mead, 1942.

De Pastino, Todd. *Citizen Hobo: How a Century of Homelessness Shaped America.* Chicago: University of Chicago Press, 2003.

Derleth, August W. *The Milwaukee Road: Its First Hundred Years.* New York: Creative Age Press, 1948.

Dietrich, William. *Northwest Passage: The Great Columbia River.* Seattle: University of Washington Press, 1996.

Dill, Clarence. *Where Water Falls.* Spokane: C. W. Hill, 1970.

Dodds, Gordon B. *The American Northwest: A History of Oregon and Washington.* Arlington, Heights, IL: The Forum Press, 1986.

———. *Oregon: A Bicentennial History.* New York: Norton, 1977.

Dorpat, Paul and Genevieve McCoy. *Building Washington: A History of Washington State Public Works.* Seattle: Tartu Publications, 1998.

Dubofsky, Melvin. *"Big Bill" Haywood.* Manchester: Manchester University Press, 1987.

Dudley, Kathryn M. *Debt and Dispossession: Farm Loss in America's Heartland.* Chicago: University of Chicago Press, 2000.

Dulles, Foster R. *The American Red Cross: A History.* New York: Harper, 1950.

Dyson, Lowell. *Red Harvest: The Communist Party and American Farmers.* Lincoln: University of Nebraska Press, 1982.

Edwards, G. Thomas, and Carlos A. Schwantes, eds. *Experiences in a Promised Land: Essays on Pacific Northwest History.* Seattle: University of Washington Press, 1986.

Etulain, Richard W., ed. *The American West in the Twentieth Century: A Bibliography.* Norman, OK: University of Oklahoma Press, 1994.

Felt, Margaret E. *Gyppo Logger.* Seattle: University of Washington Press, 2001.

Ficken, Robert E. *The Forested Land: A History of Lumbering in Western Washington.* Seattle: University of Washington Press, 1987.

———. *Rufus Woods: The Columbia River, and the Building of modern Washington.* Pullman: Washington State University Press, 1995.

Ficken, Robert E., and Charles P. Le Warne. *Washington: A Centennial History.* Seattle: University of Washington Press, 1988.

Feinman, Ronald L. *Twilight of Progressivism: The Western Republican Senators and the New Deal.* Baltimore: Johns Hopkins University Press, 1981.

Fite, Gilbert. *Mount Rushmore.* Norman, OK: University of Oklahoma Press, 1952.

———. *Peter Norbeck: Prairie Statesman.* Columbia, MO: University of Missouri Press, 1948.

Fleischhauer, Carl, and Beverly Brannan, eds. *Documenting America, 1935–1943.* Berkeley: University of California Press, 1988.

Foster, Mark S. *Henry J. Kaiser: Builder in the Modern American West.* Austin: University of Texas Press, 1989.

Freidel, Frank. *Franklin D. Roosevelt: The Triumph.* Boston: Little, Brown and Company, 1956.

Friedman, Ralph. *The Other Side of Oregon.* Caldwell, ID: Private Printing, 1993.

Funigrillo, Philip. *Toward a National Power Policy: The New Deal and the Electric Utility Industry, 1933–1941.* Pittsburgh: University of Pittsburgh Press, 1973.

Ganzel, Bill. *Dust Bowl Descent.* Lincoln: University of Nebraska Press, 1984.

Gastil, Raymond D. *Cultural Regions of the United States.* Seattle: University of Washington Press, 1975.

Gates, Charles M. *The First Century at the University of Washington, 186l–1961.* Seattle: University of Washington Press, 1961.

Gates, Paul. *History of Public Land Development.* Washington: U. S. Government Printing Office, 1968.

Gist, Gladys Leffler and James Marten, ed. *Chasing Rainbows: A Recollection of the Great Plains, 1921–1925.* Ames, IA: Iowa State University Press, 1993.

Goldston, Robert. *The Great Depression.* New York: Fawcett, 1968.

Goodrich, Carter, et al. *Migration and Economic Opportunity.* Philadelphia: University of Pennsylvania Press, 1936.

Grant, Michael J. *Down and Out on the Family Farm: Rural Rehabilitation in the Great Plains, 1929–1945.* Lincoln: University of Nebraska Press, 2002.

Gregory, James N. *American Exodus: The Dust Bowl Migration and Okie Culture in California.* New York: Oxford University Press, 1989.

Gunther, John. *Inside U.S.A.* New York: Harper, 1947.

Haley, Delphine. *Dorothy Stimson Bullitt: An Uncommon Life.* Seattle: Sasquatch Books, 1995.

Hamil, Harold. *Nebraska: No Place Like It!* Kansas City, MO: Lowell Press, 1985.

Hardy, M. J. *Boeing.* New York: Beaufort Books, 1982.

Hargreaves, Mary. *Dry Farming on the Great Plains: 1900–1925.* Cambridge: Harvard University Press, 1957.

———. *Dry Farming on the Great Plains: Years of Adjustment, 1920–1990.* Lexington, KY: University of Kentucky Press, 1993.

Hassebrock, Kenneth. *Rural Reminiscences: The Agony of Survival.* Ames, IA: Iowa State University Press, 1990.

Healy, Dorothy. *Dorothy Healy Remembers: A Life in the American Communist Party.* New York: Oxford University Press, 1990.

Hidy, Ralph. *Timber and Men: The Weyerhaeuser Story.* New York: Macmillan, 1963.

Hidy, Ralph, et al. *The Great Northern Railway: A History.* Boston: Harvard Business School Press, 1988.

Hill, Edwin G. *In the Shadow of the Mountain: The Spirit of the CCC.* Pullman: Washington State University Press, 1990.

Hillanbrand, Laura. *Seabiscuit: An American Legend.* New York: Ballentine Books, 2003.

Hillman, Arthur. *The Unemployed Citizens' League of Seattle.* Seattle: University of Washington Press, 1934.

Himmelberg, Robert F. *The Great Depression and the New Deal.* Westport, CT: Greenwood Press, 2001.

Hobbs, Susan A. *The Art of Thomas Wilmer Dewing: Beauty Reconfigured.* Washington: Smithsonian Press, 1996.

Holbrook, Stewart H. *The Yankee Exodus: An Account of Migration from New England.* New York: Macmillan, 1950.

Hollingworth, Harold, and William F. Holmes, eds. *Essays on the New Deal.* Austin: University of Texas Press, 1969.

Hopkins, June. *Harry Hopkins: Sudden Hero, Brash Reformer.* New York: St. Martins Press,

Horowitz, David A., ed. "*Inside the Klavern: The Secret History of a Ku Klux Klan of the 1920s* [La Grande, Oregon, weekly Ku Klux Klan minutes]. Carbondale, IL: Southern Illinois University Press, 1999.

Hudson, John C. *Plains Country Towns.* Minneapolis: University of Minnesota Press, 1985.

Hudson, Lois Phillips. *Reapers of the Dust: A Prairie Chronicle.* Boston: Little-Brown, 1964.

Hurt, R. Douglas. *The Dust Bowl: An Agricultural ands Social History.* Chicago: Nelson-Hall, 1981.

Hyde, Frederick W. *The Milwaukee Road.* Denver: Hyrail Productions, 1990.

Ickes, Harold. *The Autobiography of a Curmudgeon.* Chicago: Quadrangle Books, 1969.

——. *Back to Work: The Story of the PWA.* New York: De Capo Press 1973.

Isern, Thomas D. *Bull Threshers and Bindlestiffs: Harvesting and Threshing on the North American Plains.* Lawrence: University Press of Kansas, 1990.

Jasper, James M. *Starting Over in America.* Chicago: University of Chicago Press, 2000.

Johansen, Dorothy O. *Empire of the Columbia.* 2nd ed. New York: Harper and Row, 1966.

Johnson, Vance. *Heaven's Tableland: The Dust Bowl Story.* New York: Farrar-Straus, 1947.

Jones, Lawrence A., and David Durand. *Mortgage Lending Experience in Agriculture.* Princeton: Princeton University Press, 1954.

Kaufman, Robert G. *Henry Jackson: A Life in Politics.* Seattle: University of Washington Press, 2000.

Kelly, Robin. *Hammer and Hoe: Alabama Communists and the Great Depression.* Chapel Hill: University of North Carolina Press, 1990.

Kennedy, John F. *Profiles in Courage. New York: Harper and Row, 1961.*

Kesey, Ken. *Sometimes a Great Notion.* New York: Viking, 1964.

Klein, Joe. *Woody Guthrie: A Life.* New York: Knopf, 1980.

Klehr, Harvey. *The Heyday of American Communism: The Depression Decade.* New York: Basic Books, 1984.

Kraenzel, Carl. *The Great Plains in Transition.* Norman: University of Oklahoma Press, 1955.

Kuznets, Simon S. *Population, Redistribution and Economic Growth: United States 1870–1950.* Philadelphia: American Philosophical Society, 1964.

Kyvig, David E. *Daily Life in the United States, 1920–1940: How Americans Lived Through the "Roaring Twenties" and the Great Depression.* Chicago: Ivan R. Dee, 2004.

Kyvig, David E., and Mary Ann Blasio. *New Day/New Deal: A Bibliography of the Great Depression, 1929–1941.* New York: Greenwood Press, 1988.

Landis, Paul H. *Rural Life in Process.* New York: McGraw-Hill, 1940.

Lang, William L., ed. *The Centennial West: Essays on the Northern Tier States.* Seattle: University of Washington Press, 1991.

Lange, Dorothea, and Paul Taylor. *An American Exodus.* New Haven: Yale University Press, 1969.

Latham, Earl. *The Communist Party in Washington.* Cambridge: Harvard University Press, 1966.

Lay, Shawn. *The KKK in the West.* Urbana: University of Illinois Press, 1992.

Leuchtenburg, William E. *Franklin D. Roosevelt and the New Deal, 1932–1940.* New York: Harper & Row, 1963.

Lien. Carsten. *Olympic Battleground: The Power Politics of Timber Preservation.* Seattle: Mountaineers, 2000.

Limerick, Patricia Nelson. *The Legacy of Conquest: The Unbroken Past of the American West.*New York: Norton, 1987.

Lindley, Betty. *A New Deal for Youth: The Story of the National Youth Administration.* New York: Da Capo Press, 1972.

Lindly, William R. *Hard Times and Good Times in Oregon: Recollections of the 1930s.* Manhattan, KA: Sunflower Press, 1995.

Lookingbill, Brad D. *Dust Bowl USA: Depression America and the Ecological Imagination, 1929–1941.* Athens, OH: Ohio University Press, 2001.

Low, Ann. *Dust Bowl Diary.* Lincoln: University of Nebraska Press, 1984.

Lowitt, Richard. *George W. Norris: The Triumph of a Progressive, 1933–1944.* Urbana: University of Illinois Press, 1978.

———. *The New Deal and the West.* Bloomington: Indiana University Press, 1984.

Lowitt, Richard, and Maurine Beasly, eds. *One Third of a Nation: Lorena Hickock Reports on the Great Depression.* Urbana: University of Illinois Press, 1981.

Loy, William G. ed. *Atlas of Oregon.* 2nd ed. Eugene: University of Oregon Press, 2001.

Luebke, Frederick C., ed. *Ethnicity on the Great Plains.* Lincoln: University of Nebraska Press, 1980.

———. *Nebraska: an Illustrated History.* Lincoln: University of Nebraska Press, 1995.

MacColl, E. Kimbark. *The Growth of a City: Power and Politics in Portland, Oregon, 1915 to 1950.* Portland: The Georgian Press, 1979.

MacDonald, Betty. *The Egg and I.* Philadelphia: Lippincott, 1945.

MacDonald, J. Fred. *Don't Touch that Dial: Radio Programming in American Life, 1920–1960.* Chicago: Nelson-Hall, 1979.

Madison, James H, ed. *Heartland: Comparative Histories of the Midwestern States.* Bloomington: Indiana University Press, 1988.

Malin, James C. *The Grasslands of North America: Prolegomena to Its History.* Lawrence, KA: Private Printing, 1947.

Malone, Michael P., *C. Ben Ross and the New Deal in Idaho.* Seattle: University of WashingtonPress, 1970.

———, ed. *Historians and the American West.* Lincoln: University of Nebraska Press, 1983.

Malone, Michael P., Richard B. Roeder, and William Lang. *Montana: A History of Two Centuries.* Seattle: University of Washington Press, 1991.

Mangione, Jerre. *The Dream and the Deal: The Federal Writers Project, 1935–1943.* Syracuse: Syracuse University Press, 1996.

Mansfield, Harold. *Vision: A Saga of the Sky.* New York: Duell, Sloan and Pearce, 1956.

Matthews, Anne. *Where the Buffalo Roam: The Storm over the Revolutionary Plan to Restore America's Great Plains.* New York: Grove Weidenfeld, 1992.

McCoy, Donald. *Angry Voices: Left-of-Center Politics in the New Deal Era*: Lawrence: University of Kansas Press, 1958.

McElvaine, Robert S., ed. *Down and Out in the Great Depression: Letters from the Forgotten Man.* Chapell Hill: University of North Carolina Press, 1983.

McGovern, James R. *And a Time for Hope: Americans in the Great Depression.* Westport, CT: Praeger, 2000.

McGregor, Alexander C. *Counting Sheep: From Open Range to the Agribusiness on the Columbia Plateau.* Seattle: University of Washington Press, 1982.

McKay, Floyd J. *An Editor for Oregon: Charles A. Sprague and the Politics of Change.* Corvallis: Oregon State University Press, 1998.

McKinly, Charles. *Uncle Sam in the Pacific Northwest.* Berkeley: University of California Press, 1952.

McLagan, Elizabeth. *A Peculiar Paradise: A History of Blacks in Oregon, 1788–1940.* Portland: Georgian Press, 1980

McWilliams, Carey. *Ill Fares the Land: Migrants and Migratory Labor in the United States.* New York: Barnes and Noble, 1941.

Miles, Charles, and O. B. Sparling, eds. *Building a State: Washington 1889–1939.* Tacoma: Washington State Historical Society, 1940.

Miller, Donald L. *The New American Radicalism: Alfred M. Bingham and Non-Marxian Insurgency in the New Deal Era.* Port Washington, NY: Kennikat Press, 1979.

Milton, John R. *South Dakota: A History.* New York: W. W. Norton, 1977.

Morgan, Murray C. *The Mill on the Boot: The Story of the St. Paul and Tacoma Lumber Company.* Seattle: University of Washington Press, 1982.

———. *South on the Sound: An Illustrated History of Tacoma and Pierce County.* Woodland Hills, CA: Windsor Publishers, 1984.

Morgan, Neil. *Westward Tilt.* New York: Random House, 1963.

Mullins, William H. *The Depression and the Urban West Coast, 1929–1933: Los Angeles, San Francisco, Seattle, and Portland.* Bloomington: Indiana University Press, 1991.

Murrell, Gary. *Iron Pants: Oregon's anti New Deal Governor, Charles Henry Martin.* Pullman: Washington State University Press, 2000.

Murphy, Bruce A. *Wild Bill: The Legend and Life of William O. Douglas.* New York: Random House, 2003.

Nash, Gerald D. *The American West Transformed: The Impact of the Second World War.* Bloomington: Indiana University Press, 1985.

Nash, Gerald D., and Richard W, Etulain, eds. *The Twentieth-Century West: Historical Interpretations.* Albuquerque: University of New Mexico Press, 1989.

Neal, Steve. *McNary of Oregon: A Political Biography.* Portland: Western Imprints, 1985.

Nelson, Paula M. *After the West Was Won: Homesteaders and Townbuilders in Western South Dakota, 1900–1917.* Iowa City: University of Iowa Press, 1986.

———. *The Prairie Winnows Its Own: The West River Country of South Dakota in the Years of The Great Depression.* Iowa City: University of Iowa Press, 1996.

Neth, Mary. *Preserving the Family Farm: Women, Community, and the Foundations of Agribusiness in the Midwest, 1900–1940.* Baltimore: The Johns Hopkins University Press, 1995.

Neuberger, Richard. *Our Promised Land.* New York: Macmillan, 1938.

———. *They Never Go Back to Pocatello: The Selected Essays of Richard Neuberger.* Edited by Steve Neal, Portland: Oregon Historical Society Press, 1988.

Nichols, David, ed. *Ernie's America: The Best of Ernie Pyle's 1930's Travel Dispatches.* New York: Random House, 1989.

Norris, Kathleen. *Dakota: A Spiritual Geography.* New York: Houghton Mifflin, 1993.

Nugent, Walter. *Into the West: The Story of Its People.* New York: Knopf, 1999.

O'Donnell, Terrance. *That Balance So Rare: The Story of Oregon.* Portland: Oregon Historical Society Press, 1988.

Oihus, Colleen A. *A History of Coal Mining in North Dakota, 1873–1982.* Grand Forks, ND: North Dakota Geological Survey, 1983.

Olson, James C. *History of Nebraska.* Lincoln: University of Nebraska Press, 1974.

Ottoson, Howard W., et al. *Land and People in the Northern Plains Transition Area.* Lincoln: University of Nebraska Press, 1966.

Peelers, David. *Hope Among Us Yet: Social Criticism and Social Solace in Depression America.* Athens: University of Georgia Press, 1987.

Peirce, Neal R. *The Great Plains States of America: People, Politics, and Power in the Nine Great Plains States.* New York: W. W. Norton, 1973.

———. *The Pacific States of America: People, Politics, and Power in the Five Pacific Basin States.* New York: W. W. Norton, 1972.

Perloff, Harvey, et al. *Regions, Resources and Economic Growth.* Baltimore: Johns Hopkins University Press, 1960.

Persico, Joseph E. *Edward R. Murrow: An American Original.* New York: McGraw-Hill, 1984.

Peterson, Emil R. *A Century of Coos and Curry: A History of Southwest Oregon.* Portland: Binfords and Mort, 1952.

Peterson, F. Ross. *Idaho: A Bicentennial History.* New York: Norton, 1976.

Peterson, Keith C. and Mary Reed. *Discovering Washington: A Guide to State and Local History.* Pullman: Washington State University Press, 1989.

Phillips, Cabell. *From the Crash to the Blitz, 1929–1939.* New York: Macmillan, 1969.

Pierce, Walter M. *Oregon Cattleman/Governor, Congressman: Memoirs And Times of Walter M. Pierce.* Edited and expanded by Arthur H. Bone. Portland: Oregon Historical Society, 1981.

Pierson, Frank, and Stanley K. Sheinbaum. *A Nation Lost and Found: 1936 America Remembered by Ordinary and Extraorinary People.* Los Angeles: Tallfellow Press, 2002.

Pisani, Donald J. *Water and American Government: The Reclamation Bureau, National Water Policy, and the West, 1902–1935.* Berkeley: University of California Press, 2002.

Pitzer, Paul C. *Building the Skagit: A Century of Upper Skagit Valley History, 1870–1970.* Portland: Galley Press, 1978.

———. *Grand Coulee: Harnessing a Dream.* Pullman: Washington State University Press, 1994.

Pogue, Forrest C. *George C. Marshall: Education of a General, 1880–1939.* New York: Viking Press, 1963.

Pollard, Lancaster. *A History of Washington.* Four Volumes, New York: American Historical Society, 1937.

———. *Oregon and the Pacific Northwest.* (Portland: Binfords and Mort, 1946).

Pomeroy, Earl. *The Pacific Slope.* New York: Knopf, 1965.

Pressly, Thomas, and William Scofield. *Farm Real Estate Values in the United States by Counties, 1850–1959.* Seattle: University of Washington Press, 1965.

Pyle, Ernie. *Home Country.* New York: Macmillan, 1947.

Raaen, Aagot. *Grass of the Earth: Immigrant Life in the Dakota Country.* New York: Arno Press, 1979.

Reeves, George. *A Man from South Dakota.* New York: Dutton, 1950.

Ribuffo, Leo. *The Old Christian Right: The Protestant Far Right from the Great Depression To the Cold War.* Philadelphia: Temple University Press, 1983.

Riegel, Robert E., and Robert G. Athearn. *AmericaMoves West.* 4th ed. New York: Holt, Rinehart, and Winston, 1964.

Riley, Glenda. *Building and Breaking Families in the American West.* Albuquerque: University of New Mexico press, 1996.

Robbins, William G., ed. *The Great Northwest: The Search for a Regional Identity.* Corvallis: Oregon State University Press, 2001.

———. *Hard Times in Paradise: Coos Bay Oregon, 1850–1986.* Seattle: University of Washington Press, 1988.

——. *Landscapes of Promise: The Oregon Story, 1840–1940.* Seattle: University of Washington Press, 1997.

Roberts, Phil. A Penny for the Governor, a Dollar for Uncle Sam: Income Taxation in Washington. Seattle: University of Washington Press, 2002.

Robinson, Elwyn B. *History of North Dakota.* Lincoln: University of Nebraska Press, 1966.

Robinson, Frank B. *The Strange Autobiography of Frank B. Robinson.* Moscow, ID: Psychiana Incorporated, 1941. Arrington, Volume II, 70.

Rodman, Paul W. *The Far West and the Great Plains in Transition, 1859–1900.* New York: Harper & Row, 1988.

Saalfelt, Lawrence J. *Forces of Prejudice in Oregon, 1920–25.* Portland: Archdiocean Historical Commission, 1984.

Sale, Roger. *Seattle: Past to Present: An Interpretation of the History of the Foremost City in the Pacific Northwest.* Seattle: University of Washington Press, 1976.

Scates, Shelby. *Senator Warren Magnuson and the Shaping of Twentieth Century America.* Seattle: University of Washington Press, 1997.

Schell, Herbert S. *History of South Dakota.* Lincoln: University of Nebraska Press, 1975.

Schlebecker, John T. *Cattle Raising on the Great Plains, 1900–1961*. Lincoln: University of Nebraska Press. 1963.

Schmid, Calvin F. *Social Trends in Seattle.* Seattle: University of Washington Press, 1944.

Schlesinger, Arthur M. *The Coming of the New Deal.* Second Edition. Boston: Houghton Mifflin, 1958.

——. *The Politics of Upheaval.* Boston: Houghton Mifflin, 1960.

Schoenberg, Wilfred P., S.J. *A History of the Catholic Church in the Pacific Northwest.* Washington, D.C.: Pastoral Press, 1987.

Schuyler, Michael W. *The Dread of Plenty: Agricultural Relief Activities of the Federal Government in the Middle West, 1933–1939.* Manhattan, KS: Sunflower Press, 1989.

Schwantes, Carlos. *Going Places: Transportation Redefines the Twentieth Century West.*Bloomington: Indiana University Press, 2003.

——. *Hard Traveling: A Portrait of Work Life in the New Northwest.* Lincoln: University of Nebraska Press, 1994.

——. *In Mountain Shadows: A History of Idaho.* Lincoln: University of Nebraska Press, 1991.

——. *The Pacific Northwest: An Interpretive History.* Lincoln: University of Nebraska Press, 1996.

Schwieder, Dorothy Hubbard. *Growing up with the Town: Family & Community on the Great Plains.* Iowa City: University of Iowa Press, 2002.

Seldes, Gilbert. *The Years of the Locust.* Boston: Little, Brown, and Company, 1933.

Sell, Terry M. *Wings of Power: Boeing and the Politics of Growth in the Northwest.* Seattle: University of Washington Press, 20001.

Severeid, Eric. *Not So Wild a Dream.* New York: Anthenum, 1976.

Shaff, Howard, and Audrey K. Shaff. *Six Wars at a Time: The Life and Times of Gutzon Borglum, Sculptor of Mount Rushmore.* Sioux Falls, SD: Center for Western Studies, 1985.

Sherman, William C. *Prairie Mosaic: An Ethnic Atlas of Rural North Dakota.* Fargo: North Dakota Institute for Regional Studies, 1983.

Singleton, Jeff. *The American Dole: Unemployment Relief and Welfare State in the Great Depression.* Westport, CT: Greenwood, 2000.

Smith, J. Russell. *North America.* New York: Harcourt, Brace and Company, 1947.

Snyder, Robert. *Pare Lorentz and the Documentary Film.* Norman: University of Oklahoma Press, 1968.

Starr, Kevin. *Endangered Dreams: The Great Depression in California.* New York: Oxford University Press, 1996.

Sternsher, Bernard, ed. *Hitting Home: The Great Depression in Town and Country.* Chicago: Ivan R. Dee, 1989.

———. *New Day New Deal: A Bibliography of the Great American Depression, 1929–1941.*New York: Greenwood, 1988.

Stein, Walter. *California and Dust Bowl Migration.* Westport, CT: Greenwood, 1972.

Steinbeck, John. *The Grapes of Wrath.* New York: The Viking Press. 1972.

Steward, Edgar. *Washington: Northwest Frontier.* Four Volumes. New York: Lewis Historical Publishing Company, 1957.

Stock, Catherine M. *Main Street in Crisis: The Great Depression and the Old Middle Class on the Northern Great Plains.* Chapel Hill: University of North Carolina Press, 1992.

———. *Rural Radicals: Righteous Rage in the American Grain.* Ithaca: Cornell University Press, 1996.

Strom, Claire. *Profiting from the Great Plains: The Great Northern Railway and Corporate Development of the American West.* Seattle: University of Washington Press, 2003.

Tanenhaus, Sam. *Whittaker Chambers.* New York: Random House, 1997.

Terkel, Studs. *My American Century.* New York: W. W. Norton, 1997.

Tweton, D. Jerome. *The New Deal at the Grass Roots: Programs for the People in Otter Tail County, Minnesota.* St. Paul: Minnesota Historical Society Press, 1988.

Tweton, D. Jerome, and Daniel F, Rylance. *The Years of Despair: North Dakota in The Depression.* Grand Forks: University of North Dakota Press, 1973.

Tyler, Robert L. *Rebels of the Woods: The I.W.W. in the Pacific Northwest.* Eugene: University Of Oregon Press, 1967.

Utley, Robert, ed. *The Story of the West.* New York: D K Publishing, 2003.

Vachon, John. *John Vachon's America: Photographs and Letters from the Depression to World War II.* Berkeley: University of California Press, 2003.

Wallaston, Percy. *Homesteading: A Montana Family Album.* New York: The Lyons Press, 1997.

Walter, Edward. *The Rise and Fall of Leftist Radicalism in America.* Westport, CT: Praeger,1992.

Warren, James R. *Seattle: 150 Years of Progress.* Carslbad, CA: Heritage Media Group, 2001.

Watkins, Marilyn P. *Rural Democracy: Family Farmers and Politics in Western Washington, 1890–1925.* Ithaca: Cornell University Press, 1995.

Watkins, T. H. *The Hungry Years.* New York: Holt, 1999.

———. *Righteous Pilgrim: The Life and Times of Harol L. Ickes, 1874–1952.* New York: Henry Holt, 1990.

Watson, Emmett. *Digressions of a Native Son.* Seattle: Pacific Institute, 1982.

———. *Once Upon a Time in Seattle.* Seattle: Lesser Seattle Publishing, 1999.

Webb, Walter P. *The Great Plains.* New York: Houghton-Mifflin, 1936.

Wells, Merle, and Arthur Hart. *Idaho: The Gem of the Mountains.* Northridge, CA: Windsor Publications, 1985.

White, Richard. *"It's Your Misfortune and None of My Own": A History of the American West.* Norman: University of Oklahoma Press, 1991.

———. *Land Use, Environment and Social Change: The Shaping of Island County, Washington.* Seattle: University of Washington Press, 1980.

White, Richard, and John M. Findlay. *Power and Place in the North American West.* Seattle: Center for the Study of the Pacific Northwest in association with the University of Washington Press, 1999

White, Sid, and S. E. Salberg, eds. *Peoples of Washington: Perspectives on Cultural Diversity.* Pullman: Washington State University Press, 1989.

Wickens, James F. *Colorado in the Great Depression.* New York: Garland, 1979.

Wilkins, Robert P., and Amy Wynona Wilkins. *North Dakota Centennial History.* New York: W. W. Norton, 1977.

Winslow, Susan. *Brother Can You Spare a Dime? America from the Wall Street Crash to Pearl Harbor.* New York: Paddington Press, 1976.

Wollner, Craig. *Electrifying Eden: Portland General Electric 1889–1995.* Portland: Oregon Historical Society Press, 1990.

Woofter, T. J., and Ellen Winston. *Seven Lean Years.* Chapel Hill: University of North Carolina Press, 1939.

Worster, Donald. *Dust Bowl: The Southern Plains in the 1930s.* New York: Oxford, 1979.

Wunder, John R., Frances W. Kaye, and Vernon Carstensen, eds. *Americans View Their Dust Bowl Experience.* Niwot, CO: University of Colorado Press, 1999.

Wyatt, David, ed. *New Essays on the Grapes of Wrath.* New York: Cambridge University Press, 1990.

Young, Carrie. *Nothing to Do But Stay.* New York: Delta, 1993.

Young, William H., and Nancy K. Young. *The 1930s.* Westport, CT: Greenwood Press, 2002.

DISSERTATIONS, THESES, AND UNPUBLISHED PAPERS

Acena, Albert A. "The Washington Commonwealth Federation: Reform Politics and Popular Front." Dissertation, University of Washington, 1975.

Brooks, James E. "Settlement Problems Related to Farm Size in the Columbia Basin Project." Dissertation, University of Washington, 1957.

Carras, Mary. "Everett, Washington: A Demographic and Economic Analysis: 1954." Thesis, University of Washington, 1954.

Chaskel, Ruth. "The Administration of the Works Progress Administration in the State of Washington." Thesis, University of Washington, 1942.

Clark, Donald H. "An Analysis of Forest Utilization as a Factor in Colonizing the Pacific Northwest and in Subsequent Population Transitions." Thesis, University of Washington, 1952.

Clevinger, Woodrow R. "The Western Washington Cascades: A Study of Migration And Mountain Settlement." Thesis, University of Washington, 1955.

Crowder, David L. "Moses Alexander, Idaho's Jewish Governor, 1914–1918." Dissertation, University of Utah, 1972.

Fisch, Richard E. "A History of the Democratic Party in the State of Washington, 1854–1956." Dissertation, University of Oregon, 1975.

Green, Michael K. "A History of the Public Rural Electrification Movement in Washington to 1942." Thesis, University of Idaho, 1967.

Grey, Michael R. "Disease and the New Deal: The Farm Security Administration Migrant Health Programs, 1935–1945." Thesis, University of Washington, 1989.

Gunns, Albert. "Roland Hartley and the Politics of Washington State." Thesis, University of Washington, 1963.

Herman, Theodore. "The Manufacture of Aluminum Products in the State of Washington as of June 1950." Thesis, University of Washington, 1951.

Hoppes, Karen E. "William Dudley Pelley and the Silvershirt Legion: A Case Study of the Legion in Washington State, 1933–1942." Dissertation, City University of New York, 1992.

Hughs, Eloise A. "The Great Depression: An Analysis of Selected High School Texbooks for United States History, 1939–1974." Dissertation, University of Colorado, 1975.

Hummasti, Paul G. "Finnish Radicals in Astoria, Oregon, 1904–1940: A Study in Immigrant Socialism." Dissertation, University of Oregon, 1975.

Irish, Kerry E. "Eternal Vengeance: A History of the Centralia Massacre." Thesis, University of Washington, 1989.

Jordan, Myron. "The Kilowatt Wars: James D. Ross, Public Power and the Public Relations Contest for the Hearts and Minds of Pacific Northwesterners." Dissertation, University of Washington, 1991.

Krause, Fayette E. "Democratic Party Politics in the State of Washington During the New Deal: 1932–1940." Dissertation. University of Washington, 1971.

Kreiss, James. "A County by County Analysis of Voting Trends in the State of Washington from 1920 to 1962." Thesis, University of Washington, 1964.

McGinley, Mace. "The Effects of the Great Depression on Grant County, Nebraska." Graduate Research Paper, Chadron State College, 1994.

McLain, Annie. "Unmasking the Oregon Klansman: The Ku Klux Klan in Astoria 1920–1925." Thesis, Pacific University, 2003.

Mullins, William H. "San Francisco and Seattle During the Hoover Years of the Depression." Dissertation, University of Washington, 1975.

Murphy, Campbell G. "Farmers on Cutover Timber Lands in Western Washington State." Thesis, University of Washington, 1943.

Roy, Donald F. "A Study of a Community of Homeless Men in Seattle." Thesis, University of Washington, 1935.

Scott, George W. "Arthur B. Langlie: Republican Governor in a Democratic Age." Dissertation, University of Washington, 1971.

Van de Vere, Emmett K. "History of Irrigation in Washington." Thesis, University of Washington, 1949.

Wrigley, Robert L. "The Occupational Structure of Pocatello, Idaho." Thesis, University of Chicago, 1942.

Younce, Frederick. "Public Land Disposal in Washington." Dissertation, University of Washington, 1969.

GOVERNMENT DOCUMENTS

Ash, Berta, and A. R. Mangus. *Farmers on Relief and Rehabilitation.* Washington: United States Government Printing Office, 1937.

Bell, Roscoe E. *A Survey of the Current Migration of Settlers from the Drought Areas into Idaho, Oregon, and Washington.* Portland: Resettlement Administration, 1936.

Blanchard, John. *Caravans to the Northwest.* Portland: Northwest Regional Council, 1940.

———. *Pacific Northwest Problems and Materials; an Introduction.* Portland: Northwest Regional Council, 1940.

Breithaupt, L. R., and C. S. Hoffman. *Preliminary Information Concerning Immigration Into Rural Districts in Oregon, January 1933 to June 1936.* Corvallis, OR: Oregon Agricultural Experiment Station Circular of Information Number 157, August 1936.

Bultmann, Phyllis W. *The Great Depression and Its Fifty Year Shadow: Proceedings of a Conference Held at Western Washington University, November 1981* Bellingham, WA: Western Washington University, 1981.

Cronin, Francis, and Edward Beers. *Areas of Intense Drought Distress, 1930–1936.* WPA Research Bulletin, Series 5. Number 1. Washington, DC: United States Government Printing Office, 1937.

Dahlberg, et al. *Investigation of Concentration of Economic Power.* Monograph 25 "Recovery Plans." Washington, DC: United States Government Printing Office, 1940.

Erickson, Eugene C. *Selected Population Characteristics in Washington: 1950–1960.* Bulletin 661. Pullman, WA: Washington State University, 1965.

Ernst, Charles F. *Migrants: Our Potential New Settlers.* Olympia: State of Washington Department of Social Services, 1939.

Felt, Margaret E. *Capitol Forest . . . the Forest that Came Back.* Olympia: Washington State Department of Natural Resources, 1975.

Grays Harbor Regional Planning Commission. *The History of Aberdeen, 1775–1982.* Aberdeen, WA: Grays Harbor Regional Planning Commission, 1982.

Great Plains Committee. *The Future of the Great Plains.* House Document 144, 75th Congress.Washington, DC: United States Government Printing Office, 1937.

Hay, Donald. *Estimated Movement to and from Farms in North Dakota During 1936–37.* Fargo, ND: North Dakota State Agricultural Experiment Station, 1938.

Heiseig, Carl P. *New Farms on New Land.* Washington, DC: United States Department of Agriculture, 1941.

———. *Settlement Experience and Opportunities on the Cutover Lands of Western Washington.* Pullman, WA: Washington State College, 1941.

Heiseig, Carl P., and Marion Clauson. *Migration and Settlement on the Pacific Coast.* Washington. DC: United States Department of Agriculture, 1941.

History of Public Assistance in the State of Washington. Olympia: Department of Public Assistance, Research and Statistics Unit, 1967.

Hopkins, William S. *Seasonal Unemployment in the State of Washington.* Seattle: University of Washington Publications in Social Science, Volume 8, Number 5, December 1936.

Kerr, William J. *Oregon's Problem in Marketing Agricultural and Industrial Products.* Salem, OR: Oregon State Board of Higher Education, 1938.

Kifer, R.S., and H. L. Stewart. *Farming Hazards in the Drought Area.* Washington, DC: United States Government Printing Office, 1938.

Landis, Paul H. *After Three Years: A Restudy of the Social and Economic Adjustment of a Group of Drought Migrants.* Series in Rural Population, Number 7, Bulletin Number 407. Pullman, WA: Washington State College, 1941.

———. *Fifty Years of Population Growth in Washington.* Bulletin Number 419. Pullman. WA: Washington Agricultural Experiment Station, September 1942.

———. *Rural Emergency Relief in Washington State.* Pullman, WA: Washington State College. July 1936.

———. *Rural Immigrants to Washington State.* Pullman, WA: Washington Agricultural Experiment Station, July 1936.

Landis, Paul H., and C. Reuss. *Interstate Movement of Washington Farm Labor Households During 1937.* Pullman, WA: Washington State College Department of Sociology, Mimeo, 1937.

Landis, Paul H., and Melvin Brooks. *Farm Labor in the Yakima Valley, Washington.* Bulletin Number 343. Pullman, WA: Washington State College Agricultural Experiment Station, 1936.

Le Mieux, Rachel A. *A Discussion and History of Taxes in Washington.* Olympia: State Department of Revenue, 1989.

Mangus, Arthur R. *Changing Aspects of Rural Relief.* Washington, DC: United States Government Printing Office, 1938.

Martin, Clarence. *Washington on the Threshold of Prosperity.* Olympia: State of Washington, 1936.

Maxwell, James E. *Preliminary Analysis of Population Data in Pacific Northwest States.* Portland: Pacific Northwest Regional Planning Commission, 1939.

Meir, Ben (Director). *North Dakota Blue Book.* Bismarck: State of North Dakota, 1981.

Melvin, Bruce L. and Edna N. Smith. *Rural Youth: Their Situation and Prospects.* Washington, DC: WPA Division of Social Research, United States Government Printing Office, 1938.

Norwood, Gus, et al. *Columbia River Power for the People: A History of Policies of the Bonneville Power Administration.* Portland: United States Department of Energy, 1981.

Ordos, Jan. *History of Medical Care for the Poor in Washington, 1833–1988.* Olympia: Washington State Department of Health and Services, 1988.

Oregon State Planning Board. *Oregon Looks Ahead.* Salem, OR: State Printing Department, 1938.

Oregon State Planning Board. *Study of Migration Into Oregon, 1933–39.* Salem, OR: State Printing Department, 1939.

Pacific Northwest Regional Planning Commission. *Migration and the Development of Economic Opportunity in the Pacific Northwest. A Report Prepared in Cooperation with the Pacific Northwest Land Advisory Committee.* Portland: Pacific Northwest Regional Planning Commission, 1939.

Resettlement Administration. *Suggestions to Prospective Settlers in Idaho, Washington and Oregon.* Portland: Resettlement Administration, 1936.

Resner, Herbert A. *Power in the State of Washington: A Survey of Power, Irrigation and* Seattle: Works Progress Administration, 1937.

Rettie, James C. *Taxation of Industrial Corporations in Washington and Oregon.* Portland: Northwest Regional Planning Commission Natural Resources Board, Bonneville Power Administration, 1941.

Reuss, Carl F. *Characteristics of Part-Time Farmers in Washington.* Rural Sociology Series in Population, Number 5, Bulletin 380. Pullman, WA: Washington State College, 1939.

Sanderson, Dwight. *Research Memorandum on Rural Life in the Depression.* New York: Social Science Research Council, 1937.

Schmid, Calvin F., and Stanton E. Schmid. *Growth of Cities and Towns: State of Washington.* Olympia: Washington State Planning and Community Affairs Agency, 1969.

Seasonal Employment and Unemployment Compensation in Oregon, Report to the Committee on Social Security. New York: Social Science Research Council, September 15, 1936.

Sherman, William C. *Prairie Mosaic: An Ethnic Atlas of Rural North Dakota.* Fargo: North Dakota Institute for Regional Studies, 1983.

Sidell, James. *Pick for your Supper: A Study of Child Labor Among Migrants on the Pacific Coast.* New York: National Child Labor Committee, 1939.

South Dakota Emergency Relief Administration. *Survey of Indian Reservations,* 1935, National Archives, Washington, DC. (microfilm ed., Frederick, MD: University Publications of America, 1986).

The State of Washington: A Review of the State's Natural Resources and Their Development and Its Commercial, Industrial, Agricultural and Official Life. Seattle: Davis Publishing Company, 1936.

Stone, Peter A. *Economic Problems of the Lumber and Timber Products Industry.* Washington, DC: Office of National Recovery Administration, 1936.

Taeuber, Conrad, and Carl Taylor. *The People of the Drought States.* Washington, DC: WPA Research Bulletin, Series 5, Number 2, 1937.

Tolan, John H. (Chairman). *House Select Committee to Investigate the Interstate Migration of Destitute Citizens.* Hearings on House Resolution 63 and House Resolution 491, 76th Congress, July 29–December 11, 1940, 10 volumes. Washington DC: United States Government Printing Office, 1941.

Troxel, Willard and Paul O'Day. *Migration Into the States of the Pacific Northwest, 1930–1938.* Portland: Farm Security Administration, May 1940.

United States. Public Works Administration. *America Builds: The Record of the PWA.* Washington: United States Government Printing Office, 1939.

United States. Bureau of the Census. *Censuses of Population, 1890–1990.* Publisher and Dates vary; usually published by Government Printing Office, Washington, DC.

———. *Historical Abstracts of the United States, 1789–1945: a supplement.* Washington, DC: United State Government Printing Office, 1946.

———. *Population-Internal Migration, 1935–1940.* Washington, DC: United States Government Printing Office, 1940.

United States Department of Agriculture. Bureau of Agricultural Economics. *Cash Receipts from Farming by States and Commodities, Calendar Years 1924–44.* Washington, DC: United States Government Printing Office, January 1946.

United States Bureau of Labor Statistics. *Handbook of Labor Statistics.* Bulletin Number 694. Washington, DC: United States Government Printing Office, 1941.

United States Congress. House. *The Future of the Great Plains.* Report of the Great Plains Committee. 75th Congress; 1st session, House Document 114. Washington, DC: United States Government Printing Office, 1936.

United States Department of Agriculture, Bureau of Agricultural Economics. *Cash Receipts from Farming by States and Commodities, Calendar Years 1924–44.* Washington, DC: United States Government Printing Office, 1946.

United States Federal Emergency Relief Administration, North Dakota. *Relief in Review in North Dakota Through December 15, 1935.* Bismarck: The FERA, 1935.

United States Forest Service. *Forest Land Ownership in Oregon and Washington.* Portland: United States Forest Service, 1934.

United States Temporary National Economic Committee. *Investigation of Concentration of Economic Power.* Washington, DC: United States Government Printing Office, 1941.

Wakefield, Richard, and Paul Landis. *The Drought Farmer Adjusts to the West.* Washington State Agricultural Extension Bulletin 378. Pullman, WA: 1939.

Washington State Emergency Relief Administration. *WERA Report to Governor Clarence D. Martin and the Legislature, January 1933 to December, 1934.* Olympia: Emergency Relief Commission, 1935.

Washington State Historical Society. *Building a State: Washington 1889–1939.* Tacoma: Washington State Historical Society, 1940.

Washington State Planning Council. *The Cascade Low Level Tunnel: An Inquiry as to the Economic Feasibility of Building a Tunnel Through the Cascade Range in Washington For Rail and Vehicular Traffic as Proposed by the Late Brigadier General Hiram Chittenden.* Olympia: State Planning Commission, 1936.

———. *The Elma Survey.* Olympia: State Planning Commission, 1941.

——. *Employment and Payrolls, Basic Industries of Washington, 1920–1944.* Olympia: State Planning Commission, 1945.

——. *A Survey of the Common School System of Washington with Suggested First Steps Toward Its Progressive Development and Improvement.* Olympia: State Planning Commission, 1938.

Webb, John, and Malcom Brown. *Migrant Families.* WPA Research Monograph 18. Washington, DC: United States Government Printing Office.

Whiting, Theodore. *WPA Final Statistical Report of the Federal Emergency Relief Administration.* Washington, DC: United States Government Printing Office, 1942.

Will, George F. *Tree Ring Study in North Dakota [From 1406–1940].* Bulletin Number 338. Fargo: North Dakota State Agricultural College, 1946.

Wilson, E., H. C. Hoffsommer, and A. H. Benton. *Rural Changes in Western North Dakota."* Bulletin Number 214. Fargo: North Dakota Agricultural College, 1946.

Wilson, Sinclair A. *Facts Bearing Upon Instability of Forest Land Ownership in Western Washington.* Portland: United States Forest Service, 1934.

WPA Writer's Program. *Idaho: A Guide in Word and Pictures.* 2nd ed. New York: Oxford University Press, 1950.

——. *Nebraska: A Guide to the Cornhusker State.* New York: Viking Press, 1939.

——. *The New Washington: A Guide to the Evergreen State.* 2nd ed. Portland: Binfords and Mott, 1950.

——. *North Dakota: A Guide to the Northern Prairie State.* 2nd ed. New York: Oxford University Press, 1950.

——. *Oregon: End of the Trail.* Portland: Binfords and Mott, 1940.

——. *South Dakota: A Guide to the State.* 2nd ed. revised by M. Leslie Reese. New York: Hastings House, 1952.

LOCAL PUBLICATIONS

Aldwell, Thomas J. *Conquering the Last Frontier* [Port Angeles, WA]. Seattle: Artcraft Engraving and Electrotype Company, 1950.

Aznoff. Dan. *Renton: The First 100 Years, 1901–2001.* Kent, WA: King County Journal Newspapers, 2001.

Barrett, Helen, Anne Carlson and Margaret Wills. *Skagit County Grows Up, 1917–1941.* Mount Vernon, WA: Skagit County Historical Society, 1983.

Berwyn, Thomas B. *Shelton: The First Century Plus Ten.* Shelton, WA: Mason County Historical Society, 1996.

Burerge, David M. *Renton: Where the Water Took Wing.* Chatsworth, CA: Windsor Publication, 1989.

Burke County Committee. *Pioneers and Progress.* Volume II. Rugby, ND: Burke County Historical Society, 1989.

Clapp, Mark, and Rolland Dewing. *A Pioneer's Dream Come True: The Mirage Flats Irrigation Project.* Chadron, NE: B&B Printing, 1990.

Clark, Don. *What Depression? How America's Kids Beat the Blahs of the 1930s.* Victoria, Canada: Trafford Publishing, 2003

Clymer, Shawn. "Longacres to Hollywood Park: the Horse Racing Family of Jack Leonard." *Renton Historical Society Quarterly*, 30 (May 1999).

Crow, Dan, and Stephen Davis. *The Seattle Rainiers.* Documentary-75 Minutes. Seattle: PerpetualMotion Pictures, 1999.

Dafoe, Bernadine. *History of Maytown, Washington.* Olympia: South Thurston County Historical Society, 1985.

Dalebout, Joyce, and Mary Dalebout Dewing. *Dalebouts, 1631–2000.* Private Printing: Olympia, WA, 2000.

Dalebout, Maatje. *Memoirs.* Private Scrap Book, 1912–1967.

Dewing, Adam R. *The Descendents of Andrew Dewing, 1638–2002.* Green Lake, WI: Private Printing, 2002.

Dewing Benjamin Franklin. *Descendants of Andrew Dewing of Dedham, Massachusetts.* Boston: Private Printing, 1904.

Dewing, Mary. *Lloyd and Mary Dewing's Family Cookbook and History.* Private Printing: Olympia, WA, 1993.

Dewing, Rolland, ed. *Chadron* [NE] *Centennial History.* Freeman, SD: Pine Hill Press, 1985.

Divide County Committee. *Stories and Histories of Divide County* [ND]. Private Printing, Undated, (around 1970).

Dryden, Cecil. *Light for an Empire: The Story of Eastern Washington State College.* Spokane: C. W. Hill Publishing Company, 1965.

Dwelley, Art. *Tenino, The First Hundred Years: A Brief History and Historic Photos of Tenino's Past.* Tenino, WA: The Tenino Centennial Commission, 1971.

Eikworth, Lorance W. *Eighty-Eight Years on Coos Bay: From March 21, 2005–March 21, 1993.* Coos Bay, OR: Private Printing, 1993.

Engel, Pearl, and Jeannette Hlavin. *History of Tacoma Eastern Area.* Eatonville: Private Printing, 1954.

Ferguson, Les. *Smellin' Like a Skunk.* Hot Springs, SD: Private Printing, Undated, about 2001.

Fleury, Alfred J. *Memoirs: Mercer Island, Washington, 1930–1975.* 120 typewritten pages available at Mercer Island Public Library. Obtained from Barbara Pozner, Renton Public Librarian.

French, Giles. *The Golden Land: A History of Sherman County Oregon.* Portland: Oregon Historical Society, 1958.

Friedman, Ralph. *The Other Side of Oregon.* Caldwell, ID: Private Printing, 1993.

Gellatly, Judy. *Mercer Island Heritage.* Mercer Island, WA: Mercer Island Historical Society, 1989.

Groner, Alex. *PACCAR, The Pursuit of Quality.* Bellevue. WA: Documentary Book Publishing Company, 1981.

History Committee. *Spawn of Coal Dust: A History of Roslyn, 1886–1955.* Revised Edition 1979. Roslyn, WA: Private Printing, 1979.

Howell, Alice. "*B. O.* Hostetler, District Judge." From *Buffalo Tales*, Volume 6, Number 7. Buffalo County, Nebraska, Historical Society, July/August 1983.

Lamb, Frank H. *Fifty Years in Hoquiam: Memoirs of Frank H. Lamb.* Hoquiam, WA: Private Printing, 1948.

Lemmerman, Kathe L. *Columbus/Noonan Study: The Impact of Coal Development and Decline on Two North Dakota Communities.* Minot, ND: Minot State College, 1974.

Lentz, Florence K. *Kent: Valley of Opportunity.* Chatsworth, CA: Windsor Publications, 1990.

Majdic, Michael, and Denise Matthews. *Roll On Columbia: Woody Guthrie and the Bonneville Power Administration.* Video-56 Minutes. Eugene: University of Oregon Knight Library Media Services, 2000.

Marshall, Con. *Continuing to Thrive after 75 Years—The Story of Chadron State College.*Chadron, NE: Chadron State Foundation, 1986.

Martin, Grace Brandt. *An Oregon Schoolm'am, Book Two: The Depression Years.* Brownsville, OR: Calapooia Publishing, 1987.

McCallum, John D. and Lorrain Wilcox Ross. *Port Angeles, U.S.A.* Seattle: Wood and Reber, 1961.

Mohler, Samuel R. *The First 75 Years: A History of Central Washington College.* Ellensburg, WA: Central Washington State College, 1967.

Newell, Gordon. *Rogues, Buffoons and Statesmen: The Inside Story of Washington's Capital City and the Hilarious History of 120 Years of State Politics.* Seattle: Superior Publications, 1975.

Reh, Louise and Helen Lou Ross. *NIPSIC to Nimitz: A Centennial History of Puget Sound Naval Shipyard.* Bremerton, WA: Federally Employed Women, Incorporated, 1991.

Rutledge, Dale. *Littlerock Community: United Methodist Church, Early History.* Littlerock, WA: Privately Printed, 1989.

Sadis, Stephen. *The Miracle Strip: A Story of Longacres Race Track.* Video-80 Minutes. Seattle: Perpetual Motion Pictures, 1992.

Shepherd, Allen. Letter to Author. July19, 2004.

Shidele, John C. *Coal Towns in the Cascades: A Centennial History of Roslyn and Cle Elum, Washington.* Spokane: Melior Publications, 1996.

Stevenson, Shanna B. *Lacey, Olympia and Tumwater.* Norfolk, VA: The Downing Company, 1985.

Thorfinnson, S. M. *Sargent County History.* Sargent County, ND: Sargent County Commissioners (Publishers), Undated- Post World War II.

Vab Arsdal, Ted. *Vancouver on the Columbia.* Northridge, CA: Windsor Publications, 1986.

Van Syckle, Edwin. *The Tried to Cut It All: Grays Harbor—the Turbulent Years of Greed and Greatness.* Aberdeen, WA: Friends of the Public Library, 1980.

Waddington, Gary. *The Seattle Rainiers, 1938–1942.* Seattle: Writers Publication Services, 1987.

Year by Year: 75 Years of Boeing History, 1816–1991. Seattle: Taken from *Boeing News* in Boeing History Archives, 1991.

NEWSPAPERS

Aberdeen [WA] *Daily World*
Burke County Tribune, Bowbells, ND
Chadron [NE] *Record*
Chicago Tribune
Cle Elum [WA] *Miner-Echo*
Daily Olympian
Dickinson Press
Divide County Journal, Crosby, ND
Ellensburg Record
Grand Island Independent
Hutchinson [MN] *Leader*
Loup City [NE] *Times*
Modesto Bee
New York Times
Noonan [ND] *Miner*
Northwood [ND] *Gleaner*
Peninsula [WA] *Daily News*
Portland Oregonian
Rapid City Journal
Renton Chronicle
Salem [OR] *Statesman*
Seattle Post Intelligencer
Seattle Times
Tacoma News Tribune
USA Today
Williston Herald

PERIODICALS

Alexander, Thomas, and Jessi L. Embry. "Toward a Twentieth Century Synthesis: The Historiography of Utah and Idaho." *Pacific Historical Review* 50, November 1981, 475–98.

Allen, Howard, and Erik W. Asistin. "From the Populist Era to the New Deal: A Study of Partisan Realignment in Washington State, 1889–1950." *Social Science History* 3, Winter 1979, 115–43.

Anderegg, Michael. "The Fiction Film as Artifact: History, Image, and Meaning in 'Northern Lights.'" *North Dakota History* 57, Summer 1990, 14–23.

Anderson, Elizabeth. "Depression Legacy: Nebraska's Post Office Art." *Nebraska History* 71, Spring 1990, 123–33.

Anhalt, Walter S., and Glen H. Smith. "He Saved the Farm? Governor Langer and the Mortgage Moratoria." *North Dakota Quarterly* 44, Autumn 1976, 5–17.

Ankli, Robert E. "Farm Income on the Great Plains and Canadian Prairies, 1920–1940." *Agricultural History* 51, January 1977, 92–103.

Arrington, Leonard J. "Idaho in the Great Depression." *Idaho Yesterdays* 13, Summer 1969, 2–8.

——. "The New Deal in the West: A Preliminary Statistical Inquiry." *Pacific Historical Review* 38, August 1969, 311–16.

——. "Western Agriculture and the New Deal." *Agricultural History* 49, 1970, 337–51.

Austin, Judith. "The CCC in Idaho." *Idaho Yesterdays* 27, Fall 1983, 13–18.

Avery, Inda. "Some South Dakota Opinions About the New Deal." *South Dakota History* 7, Summer 1977, 309–24.

Barber, Charles M. "A Diamond in the Rough: William Langer Re-examined." *North Dakota History* 64, Fall 1998, 2–18.

Barrett, Glen. "Reclamation's New Deal for Heavy Construction: M-K in the Great Depression." *Idaho Yesterdays* 22, Fall 1978, 21–27.

Beasley, Maurine H. "Lorena Hickock to Harry Hopkins, 1933: A Woman Reporter Views Prairie Hard Times." *Montana* 32, Spring 1982, 58–66.

Beddow, James B. "Depression and New Deal: Letters from the Plains." *Kansas Historical Quarterly* 43, Summer 1977, 140–53.

——. "Midwestern Editorial Responses to the New Deal, 1932–1940." *South Dakota History* 4, 1977.

Beecroft, Eric, and Seymin Janow. "Toward a National Policy for Migration." *Social Forces*, May 1938, 475–92.

Bengston, Bennie. "Radio Comes to the Farm." *North Dakota Horizons* 20, Winter 1990, 25.

Bern, Enid. "Memoirs of a Prairie Schoolteacher." *North Dakota History* 42, Summer 1975, 5–18.

Bigelow, William, and Norman Diamond. "Agitate, Educate, Organize: Portland 1934." *Oregon Historical Quarterly* 89, Spring 1988.

Billington, Monroe, and Cal Clark. "Clergy Opinion and the New Deal: The State of Washington as a Test Case." *Pacific Northwest Quarterly* 81, July 1990, 96–100.

Borah, Leo A. "Washington the Evergreen State: The Amazing Commonwealth of the Pacific Northwest which Has Emerged from the Wilderness in a Span of Fifty Years. *National Geographic,* February 1933, 131–96.

——."North Dakota Comes Into Its Own." *National Geographic*, September 1951, 283–322.

Bourke-White, Margaret. "The Drought." *Fortune* X, October 1934, 76–83.

——. "Dust Bowl." *Life*. June 21, 1937.

——. "Dust Changes America." *The Nation*, May 22, 1935, 597–98.

Braeman, John. "The Dust Bowl: An Introduction." *Great Plains Quarterly* 6, Spring 1986, 67–68.

Brauer, Ralph A. "When the Lights Went Out: Hollywood, the Depression and the Thirties." *Journal of Popular Film and Television* 8, Winter 1981, 18–29.

Bremer, William W. "Along the American Way: The New Deal's Work Relief Programs for the Unemployed." *Journal of American History* 62, December 1975, 636–52.

Bromberg, Erick. "A Bibliography of Theses and Dissertations Concerning the Pacific Northwest and Alaska." *Oregon Historical Quarterly* 5, March 1958, 27–85.

Brown, Sheldon. "The Depression and World War II as Seen through Country Music." *Social Education* 49, October 1985, 588–95.

Brunner, Edmund. "Internal Migration in the United States, 1935–40." *Rural Sociology* 13, March 1948, 9–22.

Buskind, Samantha. "The 'True' Story *Life* Magazine, Horace Bristol, and John Steinbeck's *TheGrapes of Wrath.*" *Steinbeck Studies*, 15, Winter 2004, 40–74.

Carlson, Paul H., and Steve Porter. "South Dakota Congressmen and the Hundred Days of the New Deal." *South Dakota History* 8, Fall 1978, 327–33.

Carriker, Robert A. "Ten Dollars a Song: Woody Guthrie Sells His Talent to the Bonneville Power Administration. *Columbia* 16, Spring 2001, 32–36.

Carstensen, Vernon. "The Good Old Days or the Bad Old Days?: History and Related Muses in the Northwest in the 1930s." *Pacific Northwest Quarterly* 68, July 1977,105–11.

Choate, Jean. "Dust, Drought, and Depression: South Dakota in the 1930s." *Journal of the West.* 31, October 1992, 33–44.

Clark, Malcom, Jr. "The Bigot Disclosed: 90 Years of Nativism." *Oregon Historical Quarterly* 75, June 1974, 109–83.

Clark, Rufus G. "The Political Suicide of Senator Fred T. Dubois of Idaho." *Pacific Northwest Quarterly* 60, October 1969, 193–98.

Clawson, Marion, McEntire, David and Heisy, Carl P. "Stump Ranching." *Land Policy Review* III, May-June 1940, 32–38.

Coulter, Calvin. "Victory of National Irrigation in the Yakima Valley." *Pacific Northwest Quarterly* 42, April 1951, 99–122.

Cox, Stephen F. "A Life in the Oil Patch." *Montana* 50. Autumn 2000, 32–45.

Danbom, David B. "The Future of Agriculture in North Dakota." *North Dakota History* 56, Winter 1989, 31–37.

Davenport, Walter. "Land Where Our Children Die." *Colliers*, September 18, 1937, 73–77.

DeJong, Gerald. "The Coming of the Dutch to the Dakotas." *South Dakota History* 5, Winter 1974, 20–51.

Dembo. Jonathan. "The Pacific Northwest Lumber Industry during the Great Depression."*Journal of the West* 24, October 1985, 51–62.

Dewing, Rolland L. "Depression on South Dakota's Indian Reservations: The SDERA Survey of 1935." *South Dakota History* 21, Spring 1991, 84–96.

———."The Great Depression: A Dust Bowl Migrant's Memoir of Coming to the Pacific Northwest." *Columbia* 10. Spring 1996, 29–32.

———. "Introduction: Environment Versus Culture on the Prairies." *Kansas History: A Journal of the Central Plains* 3. Autumn 1989, 148.

Dodd, James W. "Resolutions, Programs, and Policies of the North Dakota Farmer's Holiday Association." *North Dakota History* 28, April-July 1961, 107–17.

Drache, Hiram M. "Thomas B. Campbell-The Plower of the Plains." *Agricultural History* 51, January 1977, 78–91.

Dwelley, Arthur. "Wooden Money: The Depression-era Scrip from Tenino." *Columbia,* Spring 1997, 41–44.

Erickson, Erling A. "A North Dakota Farm Auction in the Great Depression." *North Dakota Quarterly* 39, Winter 1971, 37–49.

Fite, Gilbert. "The Pioneer Farmer: A View Over Three Centuries." *Agricultural History* 50. January 1976, 275–89.

"Fortune Quarterly Survey." *Fortune,* October 1937, 108–9.

Freidel, Frank. "FDR in the Northwest: Informal Glimpses." *Pacific Northwest Quarterly* 76, October 1985, 122–31.

Frykman, George A. "Thoughts Toward a Philosophy of Northwest History." *Idaho Yesterdays* Fall 1964, 26–32.

Gastil, Raymond D. "The Pacific Northwest as a Cultural Region." *Pacific Northwest Quarterly* 64, October 1973, 147–56.

Glaser, David. "Migration in Idaho's History." *Idaho Yesterdays* 11, Fall 1967, 22–31.

Glasser, Jeff. "Broken Heartland." *U.S. News*, May 7, 2001, 16–21.

Green, Michael K. "Hard Times in the Promised Land: The Depression and the New Deal In Washington State." *Pacific Northwest Forum* 2, Spring/Fall 1989. Entire Issue.

Gregory, James M. "The Great Depression." *National Geographic* in "Eyewitness to the 20th Century." 1998, 122–31.

Griffith, Thomas. "The Pacific Northwest." *Atlantic Monthly* 237, April 1976, 47–93.

Gropper, William. "The Dust Bowl." *Nation* 145, August 21, 1937, 194.

Harbaugh, William H. "Twentieth Century Tenancy and Soil Conservation: Some Comparisons and Questions." *Agricultural history* 66. 1992, 95–119.

Hazen, W. B. "The Great Middle Region of the United States and Its Limited Space of Arable Land." *North American Review*, January 1975, 11–13.

Hedges, James B. "The Colonization Work of the Northern Pacific Railroad." *Mississippi Valley Historical Review* 13, December 1926, 311–42.

Heisig, Carl P. "The Migrants II: New Farms on Newly Irrigated Land." *Land Policy Review,* November-December 1939, 10–16.

Henderson, Caroline. "Letters from the Dust Bowl." *Atlantic* 157, May 1936, 540–51.

Hendrickson, Kenneth E., Jr. "The CCC in South Dakota." *South Dakota History* 11, Winter 1980, 1–20.

———."Relief for Youth: The Civilian Conservation Corps and the National Youth Administration in North Dakota." *North Dakota History* 48, Fall 1981, 17–27.

———. "The NYA in South Dakota." *South Dakota History* 9, Spring 1979, 130–51.

Hewes, Leslie. "Wheat Failure in Western Nebraska, 1931–1954." *Annals of the Association of American Geographers* 48, December 1958, 375–97.

Hoffman, Charles. "Drought and Depression Migration into Oregon, 1930 to 1936." *Monthly Labor Review* 46, January 1938, 27–35.

Holsinger, Paul. "The Oregon School Bill Controversy, 1922–1925." *Pacific Historical Review* 37, August 1968, 327–41.

Hope, Clifford. "Kansas in the 1930s." *Kansas Historical Quarterly* 36, Spring 1970, 2–3.

Horowitz, David A. "The Klansman as Outsider: Ethnocultural Solidarity and Antielitism In the 1920s." *Pacific Northwest Quarterly* 80, January 1989, 12–20.

———. "Social Morality and Personal Revitalization: Oregon's Ku Klux Klan in the 1920s." *Oregon Historical Quarterly* 90, Winter 1989, 365–84.

Hudson, John C. "Who was the 'Forest Man?' Sources of Migration to the Plains." *Great Plains Quarterly* 6, Spring 1986, 69–83.

Hugh-Jones, E. M. "A Little Nest of Fascists." *The New Republic*, May 30, 1934.

Idaho Yesterdays 30, Spring-Summer 1986. Entire special issue is devoted to Idaho Water history.

Iseminger, Gordon L. "The McIntosh County German-Russians: The First Fifty Years." *North Dakota History* 51, Summer 1984, 4–23.

Isern, Thomas D. "The Folklore of Farming on the Northern Great Plains." *North Dakota History* 56, Fall 1989, 30–36.

Johansen, Dorothy O. "A Working Hypothesis for the Study of Migrations." *Pacific Historical Review* 36, February 1967, 1–13.

Jorgenson, Lloyd. "Agricultural Expansion into Semiarid Lands of the West North Central States during the First World War." *Agricultural History* 23, January 1949, 30–40.

Journal of the West 41, Special Issue "Depression Politics in the West." Fall 2002.

Kesselman, Steven. "The Frontier Thesis and the Great Depression." *Journal of the History of the History of Ideas* 29, April-June 1968, 253–68.

Klauser, Alfred. "It Can't Rain Here." *Nation*, August 8, 1936, 152.

Kress, Philip. "North Dakota Weather: An Analytic Summary of Conditions Over the Last Century." *North Dakota History* 34, Summer 1967, 258–71.

La Lande, Jeff. "The Jackson County Rebellion: Social Turmoil and Political Insurgence In Southern Oregon During the Great Depression." *Oregon Historical Quarterly* 95, Winter 1994–95, 406–71.

Lambert, C. Roger. "The Drought Cattle Purchase, 1934–1935: Problems and Complaints." *Agricultural History,* April 1971, 85–93.

Lane, Neil. "The Dust Farmer Goes West." *Land Policy Review* 1, May-June 1938, 21–25.

Larson, T. A. "The New Deal in Wyoming." *Pacific Historical Review* 38, August 1969, 249–73.

Latta, Maurice C. "The Economic Effects of Drought and Depression upon Custer County, 1929–1942.*Nebraska History* 33, December 1952, 220–36.

Leighton, G. R. "Seattle, Washington: The Edge of the Last Frontier." *Harpers,* Part I, February 1939, 306–28. Part II, March 1939, 422–40.

Lovin, Hugh T. "The CIO and that 'Damnable Bickering' in the Pacific Northwest, 1937–1971." *Pacific Historian* 23, Spring 1979, 66–79.

———. "Thomas R. Amlie's Crusade and the Dissonant Farmers—A New Deal Windfall." *North Dakota Quarterly* 49, Winter 1981, 91–105.

Lucht, Gary. "Scobey's Touring Pros: Wheat, Baseball, and Illicit Booze." *Montana* 20, Summer 1970, 88–93.

Luebke, Frederick. "Ethnic Group Settlement on the Great Plains." *Western Historical Quarterly* 8, October 1977, 405–30.

McCarthy, Mary. "Circus Politics in Washington State." *The Nation* 17, October 17, 1936.

McClintock, Thomas. "Seth Lewelling, Williams S. U'Ren and the Birth of the Oregon Progressive Movement." *Oregon Historical Quarterly* 68, June 1967, 197–220.

McDean, Harry C. "Dust Bowl Historiography." *Great Plains Quarterly* 6, Spring 1986, 117–26.

———. "Federal Farm Policy and the Dust Bowl: The Half Right Solution." *North Dakota History* 47, Summer 1980, 21–31.

———. "Social Scientists and Farm Poverty on the Northern Great Plains, 1933–1940." *Great Plains Quarterly* 3, Winter 1983, 17–29.

McEntire, David. "Migrants and Resettlement in the Pacific Coast States." *Land Policy Review* 1, July-August 1938, 1–7.

McEntire, David, and Marion Clawson. "Migration and Resettlement in the Pacific Northwest, 1932–1940." *Social Science* 16, April 1941, 102–15.

MacMillan, Robert T. "Farm Families in the Dust Bowl." *Land Policy Review*, September–October 1938, 14–17.

Malone, Michael P. "The New Deal in Idaho." *Pacific Historical Review* 38, August 1969, 293–310.

Martin, James. "Continuity and Change in the Twentieth Century Farm: the Gists of South Dakota, 1921–1971." *Great Plains Quarterly* 11, 1991, 37–52

Mathews, Allan. "Agrarian Radicals: The United Farmers League of South Dakota." *South Dakota History* 3, Fall 1973, 408–21.

Mencken, H. L. "The Dole for Bogus Farmers." *American Mercury* 39, December 1936, 404.

Miller, John E. "Restrained Respectable Radicals: The South Dakota Farm Holiday." *Agricultural History* 59, July 1985, 429–47.

Mitchell, John G. "The Late Great Plains." *National Geographic,* May 2004, 2–29.

Mortinson, Henry R. "Comes the Revolution. . . .!: A Personal Memoir." *North Dakota History* 36, Winter 1969, 40–109.

Moul, Francis. "The Biggest Partner: The Federal Government and Sioux County Nebraska." *Nebraska History* 80, Winter 1999, 150–65.

Mullins, William. "I'll Wreck the Town If It Will Give Employment: Portland in the Hoover Years of the Depression." *Pacific Northwest Quarterly* 79, July 1988, 109–18.

Munro, J. A. "Grasshopper Outbreaks in North Dakota, 1808–1948." *North Dakota History* 16, July 1949, 143–64.

Murray, Keith A. "Issues and Personalities of Pacific Northwest Politics, 1889–1950." *Pacific Northwest Quarterly* 41, July 1950, 213–33.

Murrill, Gary. "Democrats Disintegrate: No New Deal for Governor Charles Martin." *Columbia: The Magazine of Northwest History,* Fall 2003, 5–12.

Nash, Gerald D. "Point of View: One Hundred Years of Western History." *Journal of the West* 32, January 1993, 3–4+.

Nelson, Paula M. "Everything I want is Here!: The Dakota Farmer's Rural Ideal, 1884–1934." *South Dakota History* 22 Summer 1992, 105–35.

Newsweek. "It Was a Wunnerful Life: Heartland Hero Lawrence Welk: 1903–1992." June 1, 1992, 76.

Neuberger, Richard L. "Refugees from the Dust Bowl." *Current History* 50, April 1939, 32–35.

Nicandri, David L. "Washington, the State: A Bibliography." *Pacific Northwest Quarterly* 74, July 1983, 114–15.

North Dakota History, Fall 1977, Entire issue devoted to interviews of individuals who Experienced the Great Depression in North Dakota.

O'Callaghan, Jerry A. "Senator John H. Mitchell and the Oregon Land Frauds, 1905." *Pacific Historical Review* 21, August 1952, 255–61,

Olin, Spencer, C., Jr. "Toward a Synthesis of the Political and Social History of the American West." *Pacific Historical Review* 55 November 1986, 599–611.

Oliphant, J. Orin. "Some Neglected Aspects of the History of the Pacific Northwest." *Pacific Northwest Quarterly* 61, January 1970, 1–9+.

O'Rourke, Paul A. "South Dakota Politics During the New Deal Years." *South Dakota History* 1, Summer 1971, 231–71.

Osterberg, June. "Threshing Time." *North Dakota Horizons* 16, Fall 1986, 25–27.

"Out of the Dust." *Christian Century*, May 22, 1935, 691–92.

"Parched Plains: Experts Survey Drought Ravages as Government Speeds Relief Moves."*Literary Digest* 122, August 29, 1936, 7–8.

Parfit, Michael. "The Dust Bowl." *Smithsonian* 20, June 1989, 44–56+.

Patterson, James T. "The New Deal and the States." *American Historical Review.* October 1967, 70–84.

Pitzer, Paul C. "The Atmosphere Tasted Like Turnips: The Pacific Northwest Dust Storm of 1931." *Pacific Northwest Quarterly* 79, April 1988, 50–55.

"Plow That Broke the Plains Comment." *Time,* May 25, 1936, 47–48.

Popper, Deborah E., and Frank J. Popper. "The Great Plains: From Dust to Dust." *Planning* 53, December 1978, 12–18+.

Pratt, William C. "Radicals, Farmers, and Historians: Some Recent Scholarship about Agrarian Radicalism in the Upper-Midwest." *North Dakota History* 52, Fall 1985, 12–25.

———. "Rethinking the Farm Revolt of the 1930s." *Great Plains Quarterly* 8, Summer 1988, 131–44.

———. "Rural Radicalism on the Northern Plains, 1912–1950." *Montana* 42, Winter 1992, 42–55.

Quivak, Fredric L. "New Deal Oasis on the High Plains." *Montana*, Winter 2004, 69–74.

Reading, Don. "The New Deal Activity and the States, 1933 to 1939." *Journal of Economic History* 33, 1973, 792–810.

Rees, Amanda. "The Buffalo Commons: Great Plains Residents' Responses to a Radical Vision." *Great Plains Quarterly* 25, Summer 2005, 161–72.

Remele, Larry. "The North Dakota Farm Strike of 1932." *North Dakota History* 41, Fall 1974, 5–18.

Rhode, Paul. "The Nash Thesis Revisited: An Economic Historian's View." *Pacific Historical Review* 63, August 1994, 363–92.

Richards, Kent D. "In Search of the Pacific Northwest: The History of Oregon and Washington." *Pacific Historical Review* 50, November 1981, 415–43.

Richardson, Elmo R. "Western Politics and New Deal Policies: A Study of T. S. Walters of Idaho." *Pacific Northwest Quarterly* 54, January 1963, 9–18.

Ridgley, Ronald. "The Railroads and Rural Development in the Dakotas." *North Dakota History* 36, Spring 1969, 163–87.

Riebsame, William E. "The Dust Bowl: Historical Image, Psychological Anchor, and Ecological Taboo." *Great Plains Quarterly* 6, Spring 1986, 127–36.

Robbins, William G. "The Social Context of Forestry: The Pacific Northwest in the Twentieth Century." *Western Historical Quarterly* 16, October 1985, 413–27.

Roberts, Roy. "Population Changes in the Great Plains." *Rural Sociology* 7, March 1942, 40–48.

"Roosevelt and the Drought." *Nation* 143, July 18, 1936, 61–62.

Rowley, William D. "The Loup City Riot of 1934: Main Street vs. the 'Far-Out' Left." *Nebraska History* 47, September 1966, 295–327.

Saloutos, Theodore. "The Immigrant in Pacific Coast Agriculture, 1880–1940." *Agricultural History* 49, January 1975, 182–201.

———. "The New Deal and Farm Policy in the Great Plains." *Agricultural History* 43, July 1969, 345–55.

Schmidt, Louis B. "The Agricultural Revolution in the Prairies and Great Plains of the United States." *Agricultural History* 8, October 1934, 169–95.

Schneider, Mary J. "North Dakota Society in the Second Century." *North Dakota History* 56, Winter 1989, 39–47.

Schulten, Susan. "How to See Colorado: The Federal Writer's Project, American Regionalism, and the 'Old New Western History.' " *The Western Historical Quarterly* 36, Spring 2005, 49–70.

Schuyler, Michael W. "The Ku Klux Klan in Nebraska, 1920–1930." *Nebraska History* 66, Fall 1985, 234–56.

Schwantes, Carlos A, "The Case of the Missing Century, or Where Did the American West Go after 1900?" *Pacific Historical Review* 70, February 2001, 1–20.

———. "Farmer-Labor Insurgency in Washington State: William Bouck, the Grange, and the Western Progressive Farmers." *Pacific Northwest Quarterly* 76, January 1985, 2–11.

———. "Uncle Sam's Response to the Great Depression." *Columbia,* Spring 1997, 14–19.

Schwieder, Dorothy. "South Dakota Farm Women and the Great Depression." *Journal of the West* 24, October 1985, 6–18.

Schwieder, Dorothy, and Deborah Fink. "Plains Women: Rural Life in the 1930s." *Great Plains Quarterly* 8, Spring 1988, 79–88.

Sellers, James. "Nebraska-One Hundred Years," *Nebraska History* 34, December 1953, 257–65.

Shinn, Paul L. "Eugene in the Depression, 1929–1935." *Oregon Historical Quarterly* 86, Spring 1985, 341–69.

Shover, John L. "The Communist Party and the Midwest Farm Crisis of 1933." *Journal of American History* 51, September 1964, 248–66.

——. "Depression Letters from American Farmers." *Agricultural History* 36, July 1962, 163–68.

——. "Drought, Dust, and Good Times." *Kansas Quarterly* 12, 1980, 17–22.

——. "The Penny Auction Rebellion." *The American West* 2, Fall 1965, 64–72.

Sims, Robert C. "James P. Pope, Senator from Idaho: Borah's New Deal Senator Colleague." *Idaho Yesterdays* 15, Fall 1971, 9–15.

Simmons, Jerold. "Dawson County Responds to the New Deal, 1933–1940." *Nebraska History* 62, Spring 1981, 47–72.

Simpich, Frederick. "Wartime in the Pacific Northwest." *National Geographic*, October 1942, 421–64.

Smith, Henry N. "Rain Follows the Plow: The Notion of Increased Rainfall for the Great Plains." *Huntington Library Quarterly* 10, February 1947, 169–93.

Smith, J. Patrick. "North Dakota's Prairie Communities: The Journey From Twilight to a Dawn." *North Dakota History* 56, Winter 1989, 49–56.

South Dakota History. "The Enduring Frontier: The Impact of Weather on South Dakota History." Spring-Summer 1985, 26–65.

Stewart, M.S. "Nebraska Fights for Survival: Irrigation and Power Development Projects." *Nation* 144, April 3, 1937, 375–77.

Stough, Mary L. "Centralia's Union Mural." *Columbia* 13, Fall 1989, 24–26

Stout, W. "They Can Take It." *Saturday Evening Post*, October 27, 1934, 10–11+.

Summer, David S. "In Memoriam: David Eugene Strandness, Jr. M.D. (1928–2002)." *Annals ofVascular Surgery* 16–2, 2002, 139–40.

Swain, Donald. "The Bureau of Reclamation and the New Deal, 1933–1940." *Pacific Northwest Quarterly* 61, July 1970, 137–46.

Swanson, Mervin R. "The Civil Works Administration in Idaho." *Idaho Yesterdays* 32, Winter 1989, 2–10.

——. "Hope Restored: The New Deal in Pocatello." *Idaho Yesterdays* 23, Summer 1979, 53–57.

Taber, Ronald W. "Vardis Fisher and the 'Idaho Guide': Preserving the Culture for the New Deal." *Pacific Northwest Quarterly* 59, April 1968, 68–76.

——. "Writers on Relief: The Making of the Washington Guide, 1935–1941." *Pacific Northwest Quarterly* 61, October 1970, 185–92.

Taeuber, Conrad and Hoffman, Charles. "Recent Migration from the Drought Area." *Land Policy Circular*, September 1937, 16–20.

Taylor, Frank J. "Promised Land." *Reader's Digest*, February 1940, 29–32.

Toy, Eckard V. Jr. "Silver Shirts in the Northwest: Politics, Prophecies and Personalities in the 1930s." *Pacific Northwest Quarterly* 80, October 1989, 139–46.

Troxell, William, and O'Day, W. Paul. "The Migration to the Pacific Northwest, 1930–1938." *Land Policy Review,* January-February 1940, 32–43.

Tweton, D. Jerome. "The Politics of Chaos: North Dakota in the 1930s." *Journal of the West*, Fall 2002, 30–35.

——. " 'Taking Pictures of the History of Today': The Federal Government Photographs North Dakota." *North Dakota History* 57, Fall 1990, 2–13.

Tyler, Robert. "Violence at Centralia." *Pacific Northwest Quarterly* 45. October 1954, 116–24.

Van West, Carroll. " 'The Best Kind of Building': The New Deal Landscape of the Northern Plains, 1933–42." *Great Plains Quarterly*, Spring 1994, 129–41.

Vander Meulen, Jacob. "West Coast Labor and the Military Aircraft Industry, 1935–1941." *Pacific Northwest Quarterly*, Spring 1997, 82–92.

Vindex, Charles. "Radical Rule in Montana." *Montana* 18, Winter 1968, 2–18.

Vyzralek, Frank E. "The Commons: The Life Cycles of the Great Plains Has Inspired Good and Bad Ideas Over the Decades." *North Dakota Horizons*. Winter 1991, 49.

Wagner, Jonathon F. "Nazi Propaganda Among North Dakota's Germans, 1934–1941." *North Dakota History* 54, Winter 1987, 15–24.

Weakly, Harold E. "History of Drought in Nebraska." *Journal of Soil and Water Conservation* 17, June 1962, 272.

——. "Tree Ring Record of Precipitation in Western Nebraska." *Journal of Forestry* 41, November 1943, 816–19.

Welch, Robert. "The Loser Who Won: The Story of the Legendary Gil Dobie." *Columbia* 1, Fall 1987, 38–45.

Wertheim, Arthur F. "Relieving Social Tensions: Radio Comedy and the Great Depression." *Journal of Popular Culture* 10 (3), 1976, 501–19.

"West in Black Crisis of Drought." *Literary Digest*, July 18, 1936, 122–23+.

White, Gilbert F. "The Future of the Great Plains Re-Visited." *Great Plains* Quarterly 6, Spring 1986, 84–93.

White, Richard. "Poor Men on Poor Lands: The Back to the Land Movement of the Early Twentieth Century." *Pacific Historical Review*, February 1980.

White, W. L. "Out of the Doghouse." [Boeing] *Saturday Evening Post*, November 15, 1941, 14–15.

Wickens, James F. "The New Deal in Colorado." *Pacific Historical Review* 38, August 1969, 275–91.

Williams, Maynard O. "The Columbia Turns on the Power." *National Geographic*. June 1941, 749–92.

Wolff, Gerald W., and Cash, Joseph H. "South Dakotans Remember the Great Depression." *South Dakota History* 19, Summer 1989, 224–58.

Worster, Ronald W. "Grass to Dust: The Great Plains in the 1930s." *Environmental Review* 3, 1977, 2–13.

——."The Dirty Thirties: A Study in Agricultural Capitalism." *Great Plains Quarterly* 6, Spring 1986, 107–16.

Zahavi, Gerald. " 'Who's Going to Dance with Somebody Who Calls You a Mainstreeter?': Communism, Culture and Community in Sheridan County, Montana, 1918–1934." *Great Plains Quarterly* 16, Fall 1996, 251–86.

Index

Aberdeen Daily World, 137
Aberdeen, WA, 150, 161
Aberdeen, SD, 50, 60, 83
Agnes, Fran, 178
Agnew Land Clearing Service, 66
Agricultural Adjustment Act (AAA), 40, 127
alder, 164
Alliance, NE
Alsberg, Henry, 48
aluminum, 191
Aluminum Company of America (ALCOA), 191
apples, 166
Arbor Day, 45
Army Corps of Engineers, 138, 177–79
Asia, 196–97

Bagshaw, Enoch, 79
Baker, George, 101
baseball, 132, 144, 170–71
Beach Advance, 137
Beck, Dave, 90, 170
Bellingham, WA, 88–89
Berner, Richard, 86, 138
Berry, Tom, 41
berry picking, 168
Bessey Nursery, 45
blackberry, 165–66
black blizzard, 134
Black Hills, SD, 202
Black Hills, WA, 161
Black River, 168
black wheat rust, 136
Bloom, Sam, 24, 26, 31
Bloor, Ella Reeves, 30–33, 189
Boeing Aircraft Company, 190–92
Boeing Air Transport Company, 192
Boeing, William, 58, 78, 191–92
Boetigger, John, 59
Boise, ID, 197
Bonneville Dam, 102, 185–89
Bonneville Power Administration (BPA), 102, 185–89
Borah, William, 115–16, 118–19
Bordeaux Logging Company, 61
Bothell, WA, 179
Bottineau County, ND, 49
Bouck, William, 77
Bourke-White, Margaret, 187
Bowbells, ND, 30
Bowbells Tribune, 134
Braught, Frank and Marie, 141
Bremerton Naval Shipyard, 58, 193
Bryan, Charles, 43, 50
Bullitt, Dorothy Stimpson, 90

Burdick, Usher, 26
Bureau of Reclamation (USBR), 116–17, 186–87
Burke County, ND, 142, 199, 201
Burlington Northern, 10
Bushfield, Harlan, 42, 53

Caldwell, Erskine, 172
California, 22, 41, 96, 106 172
Campbell, Hardy Webster, 11
Canada, 32
canning, 166, 172
Capitol Forest, 161
Carcometal, 58
Carey Act, 115
cascara, 164
Centralia, WA, 75–76
Chadron Normal, 24–25
Chehalis River, 161
Chicago Northwestern Railroad, 10
Chicago Tribune, 26–27
Christmas, 171
Christopher, Warren, 29
Civil Works Administration (CWA), 130–31
Civilian Conservation Corps (CCC), 40, 81, 86, 119–20, 103–4,194
Clark, Norman, 72
Clausen, John, 174
Cle Elum, WA, 84, 88
Colorado, 84
Columbia River, 185
Columbia River Basin Project, 187
Columbus, ND, 30, 145, 179, 199
Columbus Reporter, 29
Communism, 29–36, 50, 73, 80
Compulsory School Law, 99–100
Congdon Orchards Battle, 84
Cooke, Jay, 7
Cooke, Morris L., 138
Crater Lake National Park, 103–104
Crites, Wally, 24
Crosby, ND, 24
cutover land, 60–64, 109, 172–3

Dalebout, Cornelia, 144
Dalebout, Karel, 144–46, 168, 171–74
Dalebout, Maajte, 148
Dalebout, Nicholas, 146–48, 174
Davis, Nelley, 148–49
De Jong, Dirk, 104
Democratic Party, 40–41
Dewing, Charles, C., 142
Dewing, Elsie (Bowyer), 143, 201
Dewing, Eugene, 146
Dewing, Jacob (Jake), 142–43, 201
Dewing, Lloyd, 142–47, 151, 172–73
Dewing, Mary (Dalebout), 144–47, 172–73
Dewing, William, 142
Dickinson, ND, 49, 136
Dickinson Press, 138
Dishman, WA, 147
Divide County, ND, 136, 138, 199
Doby, Gil, 80
Dodds, Gordon, 65
Dokies, 128
Donation Land Claim Act of 1850, 62
Donelson, Royal, 179
Douglas fir, 59, 97
Douglas, William O., 90–91,
Drought, 22–23, 63, 132–40
Dubois, Fred, 115–16
Duffey, Walter, 91
dust, 22–23
Dust Bowl migration, 62–66, 108–9, 128–30, 145–52, 160–63, 174–81, 192–98

Earl, Dorothy, 23
education, 175–76
Ellis, George, 178–79
Ellsworth Air Base, 202
Elma Survey, 161–63
Elma, WA, 160–63
Ernst, Charles, 84
Evans, Vernon, 140–41
Everest, Wesley, 76
Everett, WA, 126–129

Fargo, 51
Fargo Forum, 51
Farley, James, 73
Farm Credit Administration (FCA), 40
Farm Security Administration (FSA), 53, 66, 128
Federal Emergency Relief Administration (FERA) 131
Federal One Program, 46–48
Feist, Lillian Husa, 34–35
Ferguson, Les, 25
Fisher, Charles H., 88–89
Fisher, Vardis, 120–21
flax, 144
Flaxton, ND, 32
Fleeing a Dust Storm, 51
Fleury, Alfred, 179
Fort Lawton, 194
Fort Lewis, 194–95
Fort Peck, 187
Fortune, 57
Fort Vancouver, 194
Frazier, Lynn J., 14
Freedom Mine, 201
Future of the Great Plains, 150–56

Gafkjen, Selmer, 23
German-Russian, 9
Gipson, Lawrence Henry, 121
Gloom Chasers, 132
Gottstein, Joe, 86–87
Grand Coulee Dam, 85, 185–89
Grange, 76–77
Grantham, Milton, 17
grasshoppers, 23, 25
Grapes of Wrath, 60, 64
Graveyard of the Pacific, 97
Grays Harbor County, WA, 161
Great Northern Railroad, 8
Great Plains, 87–89
Great Plains Drought Area Study, 138
Guthrie, Woody, 189
Gunther, John, 13

Hanson, Ole, 75
Hanson, Manley, 147
Hartley, Roland Hill, 77–81
Hayes, T. E., 140
Haywood, Bill, 73–74
Hickock, Lorena, 48–50
Hill, James J., 8, 16, 97
Himalaya blackberry, 166
Hipple, John, 131
Hollywood, WA, 172
Homestake Gold Mine, 41
Homestead Act, 6–7
Hoover, Herbert, 125
Hoovervilles, 80
Hopkins, Harry, 41
Hoquiam, WA, 191
horses, 143
Hostetler, Bruno, 33
Howe, Oscar, 47
huckleberry, 165
Hudson, Lois Phillips, 177–78
Husa, Ivar and Sophia, 34, 179
Husa, Lennie, 34, 82, 149, 178

Idaho, 114–26, 147–9, 166, 197
Idaho: A Guide in Word and Pictures, 88–89
Industrial Workers of the World (IWW), 74–76, 83–84

Jackson, Henry, 90
Jackson, Keith, 171
Japan, 67–68
Johnson, Edward, 133
Johnson, Marie (Braught), 144
Johnston, Chet, 144
Johnston, Les, 144

Kadoka, SD, 133–34, 137
Kaiser, Henry, 192–93
Ketchum, ID, 123
Keup, George, 27
King County, WA, 74–76, 80–81, 87–90
Kitsap County, WA, 163

Knudsen, Morris, 123–24
Kubli, Kasper K., 100–101
Ku Klux Klan, 98–101

Lake McConaughy Reservoir, 44
Lamar, Howard, 22√
Langer, William, 26, 42–43
Langlie, Arthur, 89, 174
Larsen, John, 17
Larson, ND, 17, 199
Lassen, Leo, 171
lawlessness, 28
Lemke, William, 14–15, 43
Lewelling brothers, 98
Lewis County, WA, 160
Lignite, 201–202
Life, 51, 187
Lincoln, NE, 32, 50
Littlerock, WA, 167–68
Livestock Purchase Program, 24
Longacres, 86
Lorentz, Pare, 50–53
Louis, Joe, 170
Loup City, NE, 32–33
Lux, Eugene, 28, 33
Lux, Harry, 28, 33

Magnuson, Warren, 83, 90
Mahoney, Leo, 29, 145
Malin, James, 52
marriage, 280–81
Marshall, George C., 194
Martin, Charles, 102–6
Martin, Clarence, 81–89
McCord Field, 194
McDonald, Betty, 167
McGregor, Alexander, 68
McGregor Land and Livestock Company, 68
McNary, Charles, 99, 102
medical and dental problems, 175
Mencken, H. L., 148–50
Meier, Julius, 101–2
Mercer Island, WA, 179
Merriam, Frank, 105
Meyers, Victor, 82–83
Miller, Frank, 24–25
Miller, John H., 169
Miller, L. C., 29, 31–32
Millersylvania State Park, 169
Mima Mounds, 168
Minnesota, 13, 49, 83, 89,90
Minot, ND, 10
Moline, Ed, 172
Montana, 11–12, 15–16, 34–35, 117
Moran Brothers Shipyard, 195
Moran, Robert, 195
Mormons, 114–16
Morrison, Harry, 123
Morrison-Knudsen, 123–24
Morton, Sterling J., 45
Moscow, ID, 122
Mount Rushmore, 41–42
Muller v. Oregon, 98
Mundt, Karl, 53
Mutton, 146

Nash, Gerald, 196
National Youth Administration (NYA), 131–32
Nebraska, 9–10, 17, 23–28, 32–33, 43, 108, 202
Nebraska National Forest, 45
Nelson, Paula, 37
New Deal, 68–89
Newlands Act, 116–17
Nonpartisan League, 13–14, 76–77
Noonan Miner, 30,135
Noonan, 144–46
Norbeck, Peter, 41–42
Norgard, Virlyn, 23
Norris, George, 53–54
North Dakota, 8–17, 22–32, 42–43, 49, 131–46, 200–2.
North Dakota Farm Holiday Association, 26
Northern Lights, 14
North Platte River Valley, 44

Norwegians, 8–9
Northwood Gleanor, 134
Nugent, Walter, 128

Oklahoma, 129
Olcott, Ben, 99
Olympia, WA, 131–35
Oregon, 96–113,
Oregon Commonwealth Federation, 105
Oregon Criminal Syndicalism Law, 105
Oregon grape, 164
Oregon Looks Ahead, 108
Oregon State Planning Board, 107–8
Oregon System, 97–93
Owyhee Dam, 117

Pacific Coast League, 170–71
Pacific Car and Foundry (PACCAR), 58, 190
Pacific Northwest, 94–118, 128–30, 145, 159–60, 185
Pacific Northwest Planning Commission, 59–60, 151
penny auctions, 27–28
Pick-Sloan Flood Control Act, 199
Pierce County, WA, 195
Pierce, Walter, 99–101
Pigott, William, 58
Pine Ridge Indian Reservation, 202
pinochle, 169
Plentywood, MT, 34
Plow That Broke the Plains, 86–88
plywood, 58–59, 67
Pocatello, 120
Pope, James P., 119
Popper, Frank and Deborah Epstein, 202–3
Populists, 11, 97–99
Port Angeles, WA, 178–79
Portland Beavers, 170–71
Powell, John Wesley, 10
Pratt, William, 34
Priest River, ID, 147–148
Producers News, 34–35
Psychiana, 121–22
public power, 53–54, 101–2, 189
Public Works Administration (PWA), 40
Puget Sound, 160
pulp, 58–59
Pyle, Ernie, 23, 137

radio, 144, 169–70
Rapid City, SD, 25
Red Cross, 25–26
recreation, 169–71
Redfield, SD, 131–32
Red River Valley, 10
Renton, WA, 86
Resettlement Administration, 50, 53, 64, 162
Riebsame, William, 198
Rhonemus, Ida, 186
Rigby, ID, 120
Robinson, Doane, 42
Robinson, Elwyn, 132
Robinson, Frank Bruce, 122–23
Rochester, WA, 149, 178
Roll on Columbia, 189
Roosevelt, Franklin, 40–41, 59–60, 131, 139
Roslyn, WA, 84, 88
Ross, Ben, 118, 121–22
Rothstein, Arthur, 50–51, 140–41
Roundtree, Orville, 83

Salal, 164
Salem Statesman, 106
salmon, 166,169
Sande, Earl, 117–18
Sand Point Naval Air Station, 195
Scandinavians, 74, 76
Schlesinger, Arthur, 35
Seattle, 74–76, 80–81, 195
Seattle Post Intelligencer, 59, 87
Seattle Rainiers, 170–71
Sefrit, Frank, 89
settlement laws, 130
Severeid, Eric, 29

Shannon County, SD, 202
Shelterbelts, 45–46, 198
Shepherd, Allen, 142
Shepherd, Harold and LaDeen, 141–42
Sick, Emil, 86, 170
Simplot, J. R., 124
Sinclair, Upton, 105
Sioux County, NE, 202
Skaare, Palmer, 23,31
Socialist Party, 13
soil conservation districts, 46, 61
Soo Line, 10
South Dakota, 12–13, 25–27, 41–42, 133–39, 202
Soviet Union, 29–30
Soviet of Washington, 73
Spokane, 147
Sprague, Charles, 105
Spruce Army, 175
Stompro, Odin, 146
Strandness, Donald Jr., 177
strawberries, 168
strip farming, 22
Stryker, Roy, 50, 53
stump ranch, 148–49, 172–73
Stump Ranch Pioneer, 148–49
Sun Valley, 123
suicides, 27
Suzzalo, Henry, 79–80
Swanson, Mervin, 120
sword fern, 165

Tacoma, 194
Taylor, Charles, 34–35
Taylor, Fred J., 159
taxes, 69–70, 135–40
Tenino, WA, 80
Test Oath, 115
Teton County pea picking rebellion, 121
The Egg and I, 167
The Plow That Broke the Plains, 51–53
thistles, 24–25
three corners area, 143
Three Faces West, 106
Thurston County, 160
Timber Claim Act, 62
timber industry, 66–67, 74–77, 80, 101
Timberline Lodge, 104
Timber Culture Act, 45
Tioga, ND, 200
Todd Shipyards, 193
Tolan, John, 65, 180
Tolan Report, 180
Townley, A. C., 13–14
Tugwell, Rexford, 50

Unemployed Citizens League (UCL), 80–81
unicameral, 53–54
University of Washington, 79–80, 85
U'Ren, William, 97
U. S. News and World Report, 199
USS Nebraska, 195

Vancouver, WA, 191
Vanport, OR, 193

Waddell Creek, 146, 167–69
Wallgren, Monrad, 90
Walters, T. A., 119–20
Ware, Harold. 30–31
Washington, DC, 31
Washington, 73–95, 160–64, 167–74, 187–89
Watterud, Myron, 199
Wayne, John,106
Webster. Daniel, 57
Welk, Lawrence, 9
Westdorp, John,143
western hemlock, 58
western red cedar,162
Weyerhaeuser, George, 78
wheat, 8, 11–12, 27, 52, 67
White, Richard, 176, 198
Whiskey Gap, 143
White Spot of the Nation, 44
Willamette Valley, 160
Willamette Valley federal flood control project, 109–110

Williams, F. L., 186
Willis, Aggie (Andreason), 178
Williston, ND, 25–26
Williston Basin oil boom, 200–201
Williston Herald, 26
Works Progress Administration (WPA), 40, 81, 86, 119–20, 103–14, 194
World War I, 12
World War II, 180–81
Worster, Donald, 198
Wyoming, 32, 44

Yakima Valley, 83–84
Yankees, 9–10

Zioncheck, Marion, 83